Goddesses, Mages,
and Wise Women

Goddesses, Mages, and Wise Women

The Female Pastoral Guide
in Sixteenth- and Seventeenth-Century
English Drama

Sharon Rose Yang

Selinsgrove: Susquehanna University Press

Associated University Presses
2010 Eastpark Boulevard
Cranbury, NJ 08512

Library of Congress Cataloging-in-Publication Data

Yang, Sharon R.
   Goddesses, mages, and wise women: the female pastoral guide in sixteenth and seventeenth century English drama / Sharon Rose Yang.
    p. cm.
Includes bibliographical references and index.
ISBN 978-57591-156-4 (alk. paper)
1. Pastoral drama, English–History and criticism.   2. English drama–16th century–History and criticism.   3. English drama–17th century–History and criticism.   4. Women in literature.   I. Title.
  PR635.P3Y34 2011
  822',3096522–dc22
  2010040676

Contents

Acknowledgments

The history of this book is almost as far reaching as the guide's, or at least it seems that way to me. She has a grandmother in my master's thesis study of Rosalind as a stage manager in *As You Like It* and a mother in the introduction of my dissertation study of guides in Victorian novels. Many people have helped me along the road of taking the guide from thesis to book. So, here I will give credit where it is due. If I have left anyone out, please know that in my heart I have treasured your help.

Dr. Ginger Vaughan of Clark University patiently challenged me to create, to think out, research, and write a thesis of which I could be proud. My dissertation committee at the University of Connecticut (Drs. Thomas Recchio, Jean Marsden, Richard Peterson) similarly pushed me to create a dissertation that could become a springboard for further research.

I also owe a great deal of thanks to Dr. Elizabeth Hart of the University of Connecticut and Dr. Carole Levin of the University of Nebraska who saw promise in my early manuscript and pushed me to dig deeper and create a more thoughtful, richer work.

Additionally, several of my colleagues at Worcester State College provided me with invaluable input. Dr. Ruth Haber endured various rewrites and gave me incisive suggestions for corrections and clarifications. Amy West was a master copy editor, noting form and content. Both encouraged me by enjoying my sense of humor in my writing. Pamela McKay from our Library gave me helpful research advice. Others, such as Dr. Mary-Lynn Saul, Dr. Patricia Marshall, Dr. Kathy Healey, Dr. Judy Jeon-Chapman, and Rini Kilcoyne patiently listened to me as I bounced my ideas for revision off them and shared their own research interests to strengthen my writing project. And I say thanks to the students who encouraged me when I was working and applauded me when my book was accepted. Colleagues in the Central New England Undergraduate Shakespeare Conference also helped me by listening to my ideas and cheering me on: Dr. Helen Whall, Dr. Lisa Gim, and Dr. Michelle Ephraim.

I also have only wonderful things to say about the editorial people with whom I worked, especially Rachana Sachdev at Susquehanna University Press and Julien Yoseloff at Associated University Presses. I also received helpful direction from Sarah Bailey and Joshua Allen, who were especially patient and helpful with all my questions and concerns. In addition

Mindy Rosenkrantz and Patrick Dunn at Taylor and Francis permissions were lightning fast at answering my questions.

Finally, I want to thank my family. My parents Grace and Leo Healy developed in me a love of learning, and my brother Leo, when not making wisecracks at my expense, has always been one of my biggest boosters. Of course Natasha and Rosalind Yang have provided the kind of supervisory effort that only cats can. Most important of all, I want to thank my husband De-Ping Yang. A hard-working physics professor, he still found time to take all outside burdens off my shoulders, to encourage me when my spirits were low, and to take pride in and enjoy my work. Life is so much better when you have a partner like him.

Goddesses, Mages, and Wise Women

Introduction

I

OVER THE CENTURIES, WRITERS' VIEWS ON THE AIMS, focus, and audience of the pastoral genre have changed, often contradictorily. In the Renaissance, Philip Sidney and George Puttenham agreed that under "rude speeches" a poet might "insinuate and glaunce at greater matters" in order to establish "morall discipline" and the "amendment of mans [*sic*] behaviour." Within fifteen years, John Fletcher, in his introduction to *The Faithful Shepherdess*, was criticizing his audience's taste in the pastoral as being too lowly and playful to examine "greater matters."[1]

In the eighteenth century, Samuel Johnson's views on the pastoral negated Sidney and Puttenham's claim of the moral value inherent in the genre's simplicity. Instead, Johnson condemned the pastoral precisely because of its humble and uncivilized subjects and style, writing that "pastoral [is] easy, vulgar, and therefore disgusting." Even worse in Johnson's eyes, the genre's mixing lowly shepherds with "sacred" "Christian" symbolism was not merely "unskillful" but "indecent" and "approach[ing] impiety." Although Alexander Pope, writing earlier, was not so condemnatory, he did not consider the genre a vehicle for weighty social or philosophical commentary but only light entertainment.[2]

With the advent of the nineteenth century and the Romantics' emphasis on ultimate truth found in untainted nature rather than in corrupt civilization, appreciation of the pastoral's virtues staged a comeback, though with a twist. William Wordsworth may have agreed with Sidney and Puttenham that a purer, truer reality could be portrayed in rustic scenes.[3] However, Wordsworth also felt that the pastoral tradition of Sidney, Shakespeare, and Spenser failed because they created an artificially festive green world lacking the beauty found in even the harsher aspects of the rural reality.[4] Even with a notable contingent of Victorian writers asserting that realism required facing a nature "red in tooth and claw," the pastoral was still seen as an important genre by writers of the era such as Elizabeth Gaskell, Thomas Hardy, William Morris, and George Eliot. In fact, Eliot wrote in "The Natural History of German Life" that the genre's moral importance did not lie in celebrating rural purity. She believed that "[t]o make men moral, something more is requisite than to turn them out to grass." The pastoral's value, instead, derived from expanding the minds of the upper

11

classes so that that they would see rustics as humans, not quaint amuse-
ments, and help them to help themselves.[5] Paradoxically, in the same era,
the pastoral could also be looked at as a pleasant refuge from pressing
social and scientific issues; witness such disparate writers as John Ruskin,
Sarah Stickney Ellis, Coventry Patmore, and Walter Pater portraying the
comforting bliss of the domestic sphere in pastoral metaphor or Geoffrey
Horne's applauding Mary Mitford's easeful pastorals.[6]

More recently, twentieth-century critics have also held varying, sometimes conflicting, views on the nature of pastoral. William Empson asserts
that the essential element of pastoral rested in containing complex social
relations within the framework of simple individuals and settings. On this
ground, he extends the boundaries of the genre beyond such traditional
writers as Shakespeare, Marvell, and Milton to the ironies and empowerment of the marginalized in *The Beggars' Opera* and *Alice in Wonderland*.
Others see the defining principle of the pastoral as recapturing a golden
age: Hallet Smith sees Renaissance pastoral representing the golden age
created by Elizabeth's ideal reign; Thomas MacFarland's psychoanalytic
approach turns on the human longing for childhood's era of play; and Richard Cody observes an underlying drive for a Platonic ideal. For François
Laroque and C. L. Barber, pastoral drama is shaped by the transference of
the pre-Christian and Christian festivals celebrating sacred connections
between humans and nature to dramatic forms in an increasingly secular
Renaissance society transforming the spectacle of ritual into the spectacle
of the stage. Thomas Rosenmeyer, on the other hand, limits this genre only
to traits found in Virgil's and Theocritus's pastorals. Most recently, Paul
Alpers asserts that the defining characteristic of pastoral depends more
on the relations of characters amongst themselves and with their audiences than on plot and setting, privileging emotional support over political commentary: "Pastoral convenings are characteristically occasions for
songs and colloquies that express and thereby seek to redress separation,
absence, or loss."[7] In some ways, Alpers's perception of the pastoralist's
poetic shepherds seems to circle back to George Eliot's views on the role of
the pastoral writer, to bring humans closer by emphasizing shared humanity without indulging in false sentimentality: "Pastoral poetry represents
these plights and these pleasures as shared and accepted, but it avoids
naiveté and sentimentality because its usages retain an awareness of their
conditions—the limitations that are seen to define, in the literal sense, any
life, and their intensification in situations of separation and loss that can
and must be dealt with, but are not to be denied or overcome."[8]

Still, although views of pastoral's aim and focus seem constantly shifting to reflect the philosophical values of the eras that produce these views,
the writers on the genre have managed to concur on a list of conventions
that draws on some combination of the following traits. The pastoral is a

rustic green world that is much less complicated and more "natural" than the urban or court world.[9] The pastoral's inhabitants (foresters, herdsmen and women, nymphs and satyrs, sojourners, disguised or exiled royalty, hermits, refugees, gods, or priests) tend to reflect green world simplicity: they are courteous, charitable, lacking envy, unencumbered by driving ambition, honest, humble, straightforward, close to the natural world and its inherent divinity, often unsophisticated. Nature and often the Divine (pagan, Christian, or a melding of both) are usually empathetic to the pastoral dwellers. Love, repose, and art are most often the main concerns in this world. The poet's or singer's artistry in recreating nature, celebrating divinity, and expressing sorrow in love wins the admiration and empathy of elements of Nature, gods, fellow natives, and visitors to the pastoral realm. Frequently, this green-world artist seems to represent the artist creating the pastoral, illustrating the broadening of human understanding of self, humanity, nature, and divinity through poetic creation, much in the vein lauded by Sidney and Puttenham, Wordsworth, Eliot, and Alpers. Pastoralists and the scholars studying their works have repeatedly observed that through combinations of all these traits, the pastoral has come to serve as a corrective to the faults of the everyday world, whether Elizabethan court ambition and hypocrisy, deism and corrupt eighteenth-century conservatism, natural selection and capitalism, or twentieth- and twenty-first-century angst.

There are several ways that the pastoral world might be used by its creator for social commentary. Pastoralists might hold their green world up as an ideal corrective to the workaday world, as in Spenser's *Colin Clouts Come Home Againe*, Wordsworth's *Prelude* and poetic rural celebrations, or Morris's *News from Nowhere*. Writers of pastoral might show how the taint of everyday world corruption threatens the ideal that the pastoral embodies: Virgil's *Eclogue* 1, Drayton's Nimphall 10 in *Muses Elizium*, Gaskell's *Cousin Phillis*, Jewett's "The White Heron." On the other hand, in the case of many Victorian and twentieth-century authors, a pastoral writer might even question the ideal that the pastoral represents: Eliot's *The Mill on the Floss*, Hardy's *Tess of the d'Urbervilles*, Woolf's *Between the Acts*.

Whatever the case, pastoral inhabitants or visitors (characters or audience) are supposed to emerge from their sojourn in pastoral environs enlightened about their place in the world. As Sidney has it, "sometimes, under the pretty tales of wolves and sheep, [a pastoralist] can include the whole considerations of wrong doing and patience."[10] No less determined to use the genre for teaching his readers, Wordsworth sees himself using pastoral to open our minds and hearts to humanity through sharing his experiences with the simple yet grand heroism of the true shepherd and the beauty and sublimity of Nature: "the unluxuriant produce of a life

/ Intent on little but substantial needs, / Yet rich in beauty, beauty that was felt."[11] Amongst Victorian novelists, Eliot and Hardy show the limits of nature and society. In the twentieth century, critics see the pastoral leading to attainment and comprehension of a Platonic ideal of good, Christianized from Good to God (Robert Cody); bringing together of high and low, simple and complex (William Empson); providing the "festive release" of having pastoral drama stand in for pagan and Christian festivals of rebirth and renewal (C. L. Barber); returning to a world of play important in Freudian mental development and stability (Thomas MacFarland); or having an artist offer comfort by speaking an audience's suffering to acknowledge and empathize with its pain over love, life, and death (Paul Alpers).

Especially pertinent to this book's discussion are Sarah Way Sherman's observations in *Sarah Orne Jewett: An American Persephone* on the Demeter/Persephone mythos informing pastorals of nineteenth-century women writers. Sherman touches on a trend that other scholars have sorely neglected: a female inhabitant of the pastoral sphere, sometimes herself divine, who not only embodies its virtues of harmony amongst humans, nature, and the sacred but helps impart those values to citizens of and visitors to the pastoral realm. Sherman writes that "[f]rom Margaret Fuller to T. W. Higginson to Charlotte Perkins Gilman, Americans searched for the Goddess" who would answer the spiritual and intellectual lament in nineteenth-century America over the loss of the feminine aspect of Godhead in Protestant Christianity. "Whether she was to be revived from deathlike sleep, reborn in modern form, or rediscovered in our green places wasn't clear. Only one thing was: she was needed" to serve the same needs of the rejected Catholic tradition of combining the purity of virginity with fecund rebirth and growth associated with the Virgin Mary.[12] The most often cited embodiment of such a figure would have been Demeter and Persephone embodying the Mother/Virgin—Life/Death/Rebirth cycle.[13] Sherman's main thrust is that Sarah Orne Jewett was powerfully influenced by her foremothers in fiction, as well as by both masculine and feminine intellectuals, to draw on the plot of holy goddesses creating renewal and guiding humanity to a happier and holier harmony with nature, one another, and the divine in each. Further, like Vera Norwood in her study of the fiction of Susan Cooper and female naturalist and garden essayists of the nineteenth and early twentieth centuries,[14] Sherman explores contemporary associations of the cultivation of the garden with the spiritual cultivation of family in the domestic sphere. Sherman, in particular, notes that this domestic/garden sphere for which the divine woman was responsible was often depicted in terms of the pastoral as ideal, true nature.[15]

As insightful as her studies on Sarah Orne Jewett and American pastoral are, Sherman does not recognize the fact that the concept of a spiritually uplifting, illuminating female guide inhabiting the pastoral sphere far predates writings of nineteenth-century American intellectuals. Boccaccio's *Ameto* and *Diana's Hunt* merged Venus with the Virgin long before Henry Adams did. Lady Mary Wroth's pastoral *Love's Victory* paired Venus with the chaste Silvesta to restore family and romantic harmony in the early seventeenth century. Felicia of Montemayor's *Diana* and Yonge's English translation, as well as Clorin of Fletcher's *The Faithful Shepherdess*, were able to heal and enlighten because they walked with the Divine and knew Nature and human nature long before Sarah Orne Jewett's Almira Todd in *The Country of the Pointed Firs*. Over three hundred years earlier, British Protestants were fulfilling their need for a Marian combination of virgin purity with fecundity in the Elizas, Cynthias, Dianas, and Bellybones embodying the Virgin Queen presiding over a golden age of England represented in pastoral metaphor. If anything, the nineteenth-century essayists and novelists that Sarah Way Sherman discusses are not so much contributing to the creation of a new pastoral convention as adapting a much older one to the needs and tastes of their own culture.

In truth, a distinct female pastoral guide can be found as early as Boccaccio, but the figure seems to come into prominence in the English sixteenth- and seventeenth-century pastoral, especially in drama. Strangely enough, as much as scholars seem to agree on some combination of common pastoral traits, none have called attention to the existence, let alone importance, of this female figure. Even sixteenth- and seventeenth-century writers on the pastoral do not cite this figure as a convention. Yet a study of pastoral poetry, prose, and drama reveals her significant presence time and again. Why does she seem to come into prominence with the Renaissance? This is a question that can only be answered by studying the cultural contexts that drew this figure into prominence. However, before understanding how this figure came to be and how she functions within the pastoral genre, it is necessary to define her more clearly.

The Renaissance female pastoral guide, in the form of goddess, mage, and/or wise woman, uses magic, witty game playing, advice, and penance or tests of virtue to guide the other characters to a better understanding of themselves and their relationship to society. She possesses a bond with the sacred harmony of nature that enables her to recognize the corruptions of society and to use her insight to guide others toward pastoral values. Her link to the pastoral also authorizes her to be a figure of misrule and overturn others' damaging misconceptions. The pastoral's removal of profane world barriers separating humans from nature and the supernatural also removes barriers between humans. In consequence, the guide can have a powerful empathy with others. This empathy provides her with an understanding of how best to reach her charges.

The neglect of this figure by writers on the pastoral from the Renaissance onward is especially unfortunate because she becomes an important means for accomplishing the various goals that critics have discussed as shaping the pastoral. She is Alpers's "herdsm[a]n or . . . equivalent" who brings together characters, earlier pastoralists, and readers to celebrate "common pleasures" or to offer solace for their "common plights" by showing how the latter "must be dealt with" if "not . . . denied or overcome." She is the "Lady of Misrule" of the festive green world who creates the reconciliation, release, and community that Barber and Laroque discuss.[16] The wisdom of her humor, game playing, trials, and her medicine and magic effect the "amendment of mens [*sic*] behaviour," develop "morall discipline" or "insinuate and glaunce at greater matters." Still, though this guide may be powerful, she is not necessarily a symbol of women's independence in a patriarchal Renaissance society. The sources of and the qualifications on her powers often reflect early modern anxieties about women's dangerous verbal and sexual inconstancy, conflicted feelings about Elizabeth's restoration of English glory with her ruling absolutely while an unmarried woman, and the lack of control in life generating fears about witchcraft and the supernatural.

Readings of *As You Like It, Endymion, The Faithful Shepherdess*, and *The Sad Shepherd* first alerted me to the presence of a female pastoral guide. To determine if the presence of this figure in these four plays was part of a wider trend, I turned to numerous critical texts. As a starting point, W. W. Greg's *Pastoral Poetry and Pastoral Drama* proved invaluable. Although over a hundred years old, Greg's book provides, arguably, the most thorough enumeration and description of British pastoral of all genres. I also discovered pertinent pastoral works in Hallett Smith's *Elizabethan Poetry*, Frank Kermode's *English Pastoral Poetry: From Beginnings to Marvell*, Harry Levin's *The Myth of the Golden Age in the Renaissance*, Helen Cooper's *Pastoral: Medieval into Renaissance*, Paul Alpers's *What Is Pastoral?* and Annabel Patterson's *Pastoral and Ideology*, to name a few.

Appearing in poetry, prose, and drama, the female pastoral guide is presented in essentially the same way in all of them. To avoid redundancy, I selected one literary form to exemplify her significance. Since this study seeks to explore her influence on the culture in which she exists, the best genre on which to focus is the one that would reach the most people in the sixteenth and seventeenth centuries. Poetry and prose by men and women were frequently circulated among various aristocratic intellectual coteries or written for particular noble patrons. For example, Sidney's *Old Arcadia* was written for and circulated in his sister the Countess of Pembroke's circle. Edmund Spenser was involved in private poetic interchanges with Sir Walter Raleigh and Gabriel Harvey, while coterie exchanges were the norm in the sixteenth and seventeenth centuries for John Donne, Samuel Daniel, Lady Mary Sidney Herbert, John Davies, Barnabe Googe, Thomas Traherne, the Earl of Rochester, Anne Killigrew, and Katherine Philips.[17] Though these and other works of pastoral prose and poetry became increasingly available in print throughout the sixteenth and seventeenth centuries, their audience was limited to those who could read—an extremely low percentage of the English population. Even with circles of women working diligently at their properly domestic sewing or needlework while one of them read, the extensiveness of such an audience was severely curtailed by the fact that female literacy was somewhere around a paltry ten percent.[18]

Drama, however, was far more accessible to all levels of society than literature in book or manuscript form. As a visual and spoken form, plays could reach women and economic groups handicapped by limited literacy and thereby prove more accessible to a larger audience.[19] In consequence, private and royal stagings brought the female pastoral guide before the eyes and ears of the aristocratic classes in productions of, for example, *Endymion*, *A Midsummer Night's Dream*, *As You Like It*, *Comus*, and *The Shepherds' Paradise*, while Lady Mary Wroth's *Love's Victory* would have entertained her circle as a closet drama. On the public stage, the guide exerted her magic before working-class, merchant, and aristocratic viewers alike in plays such as *All's Well That Ends Well* and *The Faithful Shepherdess,* as well as in some plays, such as *As You Like It*, *A Midsummer Night's Dream*, and *Endymion,* that were selected for private performances. Even guild productions drew on the female guide in creating pastoral drama, as seen in *Rhodon and Iris*. Thus, drama, cutting across social and gender boundaries, seems the wisest literary form to examine for understanding the guide's importance in the era of her flourishing, the late sixteenth century almost into the mid-seventeenth. Consequently, although the guide's presence in other genres will be touched on in this book, focusing on her appearance in drama will provide the broadest source for understanding how she reflected contemporary cultural concerns, especially in terms of gender relations.[20] Recognizing the female pastoral guide's value to early modern studies of women requires looking at her in the context of how these studies have developed.

II

The underlying movement for over thirty years of study on early modern woman is away from the polar extremes of Jacob Burkhardt's claim that during the Renaissance women "stood on a footing of perfect equality with men" socially and intellectually[21] and Virginia Woolf's mythos of Judith Shakespeare exemplifying women beaten, mocked, and legislated into subjugation and suicidal despair.[22] Instead, scholarly research has centered on delving into the nuanced complexity of early modern gender relations that lies between. In the first case, Burkhardt's claim of ideal gender parity has been disproved by studies of how the patriarchal culture's determination to contain what it perceived as woman's verbal, emotional, mental, and sexual wantonness was constantly reiterated in sermons, pamphlets, conduct manuals, education treatises, and medical texts, as well as in literary forms such as plays, romances, and poetry. In fact, even texts that sought to counter outright misogynist views of women as not merely inferior, but dangerous, still tended to applaud virtues such as obedience and modesty (sexual and verbal) that contain and channel the development of women's intellectual abilities into service of ministers, husbands, fathers, and God within the domestic sphere.[23] Though Thomas More, Juan de Vives, and Richard Mulcaster might have written in favor of women's education, they did so to channel that education into serving not competing with masculine authority. Early modern women did internalize this perspective. Witness Margaret Roper's refusing to publish her translation of Eusebius's "ecclesiastical history" when she realized that Bishop Christopherson was working on the same project.[24]

However, all this is not to confirm Woolf's claim of women's complete suppression. As Margaret Ezell warns, Woolf and, later, many anthologists of women's writings in the 1970s based their decisions of what constitutes literature on considerations anachronistic to early modern women writers: professional publication in genres privileged by the "literary hierarchies found in the male canon: poetry, drama, fiction, and belles lettres."[25] However, through the 1980s onwards, especially in Elaine Beilin's *Redeeming Eve* (1987), Pamela Benson's *The Invention of the Renaissance Woman* (1992), and Ezell's own *Writing Women's Literary History* (1993), scholars have opened up the literary canon to include other genres in which early modern women demonstrated their intellectual and creative powers[26] (letters and diaries, translations, mothers' guides to children, religious meditations, and even needlework samplers),[27] while also exploring the artistic and philosophical influence exerted by women as patrons like the Countess of Bedford, the Duchess of Cumberland, and Lady Mary Herbert.

Critics such as Mary Ellen Lamb, Sasha Roberts, and Helen Hackett have discussed how women's ability to buy and read books established them as consumers of poetry, romances, and devotional works whom male writers sought to attract to earn their bread or to instruct, though not always without ambivalent feelings about serving a gender that tradition declared should serve them.[28] Especially relevant to this book's study of the female pastoral guide in drama, Phyllis Rackin, Richard Levin, and Jean Howard also note that women were consumers of stage performances, public and private. So, as Phyllis Rackin writes: "There were women in the audience as well as men—perhaps, in the view of some theatre historians, more women than men—and the prologues and epilogues to many plays explicitly mark the players' awareness that they needed to please those female playgoers."[29]

Continuing the study within a relevant cultural context of early-modern writing women and writing about women, Tina Krontiris's *Oppositional Voices* (1992) explores negotiations with class and gender issues by women writers and translators of various backgrounds such as Isabella Whitney, Aemilia Lanyer, Lady Mary Herbert, Lady Mary Wroth, and Elizabeth Carey (Lady Falkland) in writing and getting the opportunity to share their works with audiences, private and public. Lorna Hutson's *Feminism and Renaissance Studies* (1999) is a collection of essays that addresses how early modern women writers and artists were affected by contemporary medical, religious, aesthetic, and social beliefs. Clare Brant and Diane Purkiss's *Women, Texts, & Histories 1575–1760* (1992) covers similar territory. *Women's Writing in English, Early Modern England* (2005), by Patricia Demers, is a detailed, extensive critical survey and analysis of the varied genres of work women of all classes created. Hurley and Goldblatt's *Women Editing/Editing Women* (2009) is an anthology of critical essays by luminaries of early-modern women studies such as Betty Travitsky, Anne Lake Prescott, Josephine Roberts, Leah Marcus, Gary Waller, and Wendy Wall that looks into the politics and philosophies informing anthologizing, canonizing, and editing early-modern women writers over the past decades.

Further, starting with anthologists and editors such as Betty Travitsky (*The Paradise of Women*, 1981) and Angeline Goreau (*The Whole Duty of a Woman*, 1985), and continuing with Anne Ott; Suzanne Trill, Kate Chedgzoy, and Melanie Osborne; Marian Wynne-Davies and S. P. Cerasano; and Jane Stevenson and Peter Davidson, much early-modern women's poetry, drama, prose romances, and other literary forms that had been suppressed after writing or publication or nudged out of circulation have been recovered and published. In addition, electronic editions of early modern women's writing have abounded through the Perdita Project, the Brown project, Renascence Editions, and the Illuminarium.[30] Still, even while moving beyond Burkhardt's and Woolf's faulty visions to search for the lost or hidden voices of early modern woman, as well as her society's definitions, goals, and limits of her agency, scholars have also struggled with avoiding falling into traps of their own cultural biases.

Scholars had to heed Margaret Ezell's warning to resist searching for early-modern "good feminists": interpreting and judging the writings of these women and men by the light of nineteenth- through twenty-first-century views of what constitutes women's equality and freedom in sexuality, work, political and social action, and self-expression.[31] For example, Betty Travitsky directs readers not to get overenthusiastic about "a small number of Renaissance Englishwomen [who] wrote 'feminist' tracts." Travitsky points out that these women were not striking a blow for women's independence from faulty patriarchal oppression, but "protest[ing] the writing or behavior of particular men." Equally important, she adds that these women writers "did not suggest that women not continue to be submissive to men, their heads." Helen Hackett further cautions that although there were early modern women benefiting from educations enabling them to read philosophy, romance, and poetry, or in some cases translate or write such literature, they were most likely too culturally conditioned to applaud fictional Amazons and "unruly women" whose sexual, verbal, and active independence might appear more attuned to twentieth-century acculturation.[32]

Finally, those studying early-modern women have also warned against a tendency to perceive these women's writings as reflecting a teleological evolution of growing confidence and economic and intellectual independence[33]—for example, seeing the Renaissance as a flowering of opportunities for women as a result of an English female monarch setting off a steady progress toward a modern liberation for women. In truth, there were tremendous social and religious conflicts in England over a woman upsetting God's established gender hierarchy. Although education of women began to trickle down from the aristocracy to the lower classes during the sixteenth and seventeenth centuries, there were also repeated backlashes based on strong beliefs in the dangerous, even unnatural, immodesty of women putting themselves before the public in print as well as on women's inability to resist corruption through immoral or trashy reading. Although midwives might have begun to gain some respect for their knowledge, even legitimizing their authority through printing manuals, the growing institutionalization of medicine by doctors was marginalizing them for their lack of formal education (unavailable to women) and society's associating them with superstition and folk cures.[34]

However, this caution against hunting for Renaissance proto-feminists who sparked a steady improvement of woman's condition is not to assert the opposite extreme, that the era's men and women were completely strait-jacketed into gender roles that they accepted unquestioningly. Instead, Helen Hackett is most accurate when she observes that women would more likely "negotiate" a role within patriarchal strictures that would allow them to "embody female strength," even "defiance." Some negotiations stretched the conventions containing female behavior with surprising elasticity. For example, female or male writers might applaud "female" virtues such as "constancy and endurance" and chastity, but in doing so redefine them from proscriptive controls on women to assertions of female choice and resistance, as in the heroic virgins of Margaret Tyler's translation of *The Mirrour of Princely Deedes and Knighthood* and Sir Philip Sidney's *Arcadia*. Or, as with Lady Mary Wroth's *Urania* and *Love's Victory* and Montemayor's *Diana* (original and English translation), spiritual and sexual purity might be reinterpreted as fidelity to one love, as opposed to forgoing extramarital sexual experience entirely. Tyler's translation becomes a significant example of another form of negotiation within the social system for women: under cover of preserving their modesty by claiming faithfully to translate men's works these women could express themselves in writing—at times with more creativity and artistry, as well as with somewhat different perspectives, than the male-authored originals.[35]

Some women also wrote original poetry, romance, drama, or argumentative prose for their coteries (aristocrats like Mary Herbert, Mary Wroth, and Elizabeth Carey) or as professional writers (working women or gentlewomen like Isabella Whitney, Aemilia Lanyer, and Rachel Speght) by modestly asserting their intentions not to challenge men's intellectual superiority but all the while using deft reason and biblical or classical evidence to expose the illogic and hypocrisy in patriarchal assertions of female inferiority.

An additional important way scholars have striven not to reduce their study of early-modern women to a hunt for heroic subversives, cruel oppressors, and weak collaborators is to consider that treatment of women is frequently less important in and of itself than as a way to control class struggles for power. Valerie Wayne's collection *The Matter of Difference* and Dympna Callaghan, Lorraine Helms, and Jyotsna Singh's *The Weyward Sisters* are feminist cultural materialist studies that illuminate the influence of socioeconomic issues on the practice of gender conventions. Furthermore, scholars have cautioned against too quickly assuming the intent of a work based on the gender of the name signed to it,[36] especially looking into how early modern male writers "ventriloquized" a female voice for ends that may have nothing to do with women's own views or may even be used to reassert the need for masculine control. Diane Purkiss warns that the famous pamphlet war of the early seventeenth century instigated by Joseph Swetnam might have been less an actual gender debate than a chance for the writers involved to make money, lament the dearth of opportunities for university men, or show off their own rhetorical ability. In fact, Purkiss posits, through the writings evidencing a knowledge of university life not easily accessible to women, that some of Swetnam's attackers signing female noms des plumes were likely men. Purkiss explains that by adopting female pseudonyms, these men could complain about the unsatisfactory economic situation left to university wits or even criticize female immodestly under the cover of female garrulity.[37]

Elizabeth Harvey raises a related point concerning work both earlier and later than this pamphlet war when she explores how a male writer's adopting the persona of a female narrator enabled him to use the conception of female verbal wantonness and disruptiveness to deflect opprobrium from himself when expressing criticism of a society that would not brook outright challenges to political and religious authority.[38]

All these approaches to literary scholarship have yielded a better understanding of early modern women's limitations and opportunities by not just expanding traditional definitions of what constitutes literature but also by striving to eschew modern definitions of femininity, feminism, equality, or intellectual moral value to focus on the cultural context of these women's lives. Studying the female pastoral guide becomes important because in her varied characterizations she also reflects the complicated nuances of early modern gender relations. The guide could be the woman whose power as healer, spiritual guide, and intellectual are effective when channeled into traditional domestic roles, her voice directed or inspired by a masculine authority (father, husband, a god): Coelia in Book One of the *Faerie Queene*, Marian of *The Sad Shepherd*, Clorin of *The Faithful Shepherdess*. She could just as well be the educated, gifted, creative, clever woman who heals and guides by working within the system like the Duchess of Cumberland in "The Description of Cooke-ham." Or she might, instead "work the system"; like Shakespeare's Rosalind and Helena, she may seem to conform to traditional conventions but question their validity by showing her charges that women's eloquence and independence do not denote the threatening wantonness and wordiness of immodesty. She could also be a straightforward challenge to patriarchal ascendancy, like Wroth's Silvesta in *Love's Victory*. Like these three, the guide might be the virgin whose celibacy is an assertion of power over her body, or she might be the woman whose sexual purity must be measured by fidelity and purity of spirit. Or she might be a trickier figure, like Lyly's Cynthia, the virginal and spiritual goddess of the moon who is not omniscient or above flattery and testiness: an uneasy portrait of a Virgin Queen whom Lyly needs to honor and flatter for advancement, but who leaves him uncomfortable with how she will use her power over him.

The female pastoral guide might find herself ventriloquized by male authors to assert her sexual purity and obedience, calming masculine anxiety over female agency with her words and by serving as a model for a female audience, like Fletcher's Clorin. Or a male might calm anxieties in a more complicated way: allowing her to ventriloquize the discourse of masculine authority over women to give her a cover for mocking masculine anxieties and illustrating a woman's ability to deploy wisdom, wit, and vivacity helpfully to all, like a Helena or a Rosalind.

Especially pertinent to this study of the female pastoral guide on the stage, she might prove an adept way for a playwright to please the female constituents of the audience. While Richard Levin cautions against exaggerating playwrights' concerns with pleasing women, he does conclude that "during the Renaissance women were generally regarded as a significant component of the theatre audience, and that their interests and feelings seem to have been taken into account by at least some of the playwrights of the period."[39] Levin's survey of sixteenth- and seventeenth-century plays yields a noticeable number of addresses to the audience that request the favor of its female members (or imply the favor of both women and men); praise women's wisdom, taste, and feeling; and come down favorably on the side of women in the battle of the sexes. He also notes that in the context of these addresses, the dialogue and action portraying women favorably in plays also suggest an eye to "the gender-concern or even gender-loyalty of women spectators."[40] Significantly, two of the playwrights whom Levin cites constitute a major portion of this book's study, Fletcher (*The Faithful Shepherdess*) and Shakespeare (*A Midsummer Night's Dream, As You Like It, and All's Well That Ends Well*). In fact, Levin points out that Fletcher's reputation for satisfying the women in his audience by characterizing them pleasingly is recounted in a prologue created for the 1638 production of *The Woman-Hater*.[41] In this context, studying the female pastoral guide's depictions on the stage provides a useful means of exploring the various ways playwrights responded to the "gender-concerns" and "gender-loyalty" of women to teach, influence, and please their female audiences.

But in order to analyze systematically the role of the female pastoral guide in sixteenth- and seventeenth-century literature, a theoretical framework is necessary. One such concept active in early modern scholarship in the past ten years that is especially useful is Mikhail Bakhtin's carnival. In his work, Bakhtin describes a spirit of upending, destabilizing, icon-smashing "world inside out" that he calls carnival as a vital component of human social relations. Inherent in Saturnalian festivals of the ancient world, holiday feasts and festivals of the Middle Ages, and enlivening literature of the Renaissance, the spirit of carnival or the "comic" "liberates" humans and the societies in which they exist by dethroning through mockery in word and deed the rule of "seriousness" or "dogmas" that holds politics, philosophy, art, and human relations in a "static," repressive, unchanging hierarchy of power.[42] As Bakhtin puts it: "The principle of laughter and the carnival spirit . . . destroys this limited seriousness and all pretense of an extratemporal meaning and unconditional value of necessity. It frees human consciousness, thought, and imagination for new potentialities."[43]

In the comic or carnival world, then, traditional dyads of power are neutralized. Undone are conventional ascendancies such as nobility over peasants, sages over fools, men over women, religious over secular, spirit and mind over body, life over death, so that the vertical relations of these pairs become horizontal.[44] The emphasis of order disordered is often represented by the elevation of all that is on the lower "strat[a]": the holiday King, a lower-class or uneducated individual who changes places with the ruler of the everyday hierarchy, while the traditional ruler becomes the mocked and abused fool; or the juxtaposition of the sacred or intellectual with a celebration of the lower body—belly, buttocks, and genitals (literally on the bottom, and figuratively so for representing the animal nature of humanity); or the lesser gender, the woman on top.[45] However, the "lower stratum" (including body, class, gender), does not merely create a new mode of suppression but blends all in what Bakhtin calls the original meaning of "grotesque," a mergence of animal, plant, human, and divine, sacredly blurring away separating categories of being.[46] Serious and comic blend together in a vitalizing, mutually enlivening balance: "seriousness and laughter . . . coexist and reflect each other, and are indeed whole aspects, not separate serious and comic images" to create an "ambivalence" in which

> laughter does not deny seriousness but purifies and completes it. Laughter purifies from dogmatism, from the intolerant and the petrified; it liberates from fanaticism and pedantry, from fear and intimidation, from didacticism, näiveté and illusion, from the single meaning, the single level, from sentimentality. Laughter does not permit seriousness to atrophy and to be torn away from the one being, forever incomplete. It restores this ambivalent wholeness.[47]

So, for example, the lower stratum of the body holds life and death in a never ending cycle: the belly takes in food, the urination and defecation of that dead matter fertilizes the ground to create more life to be consumed, etc. Moreover, that cycle is perpetuated by an integration of the body organs, for those that eliminate the "dead" matter that will bring life to the earth exist next to those of procreation.[48] Similarly, Bakhtin observes on the clay figure of the laughing pregnant hag from the ancient world that her simultaneous age and fecundity indicate that death and life coexist in an unending cycle; her laughter reveals that the ambivalence of her blending the states rather than privileging one over the other lends hope to existence's cycles of renewal.[49] In this vein of fluid identity and power, those who shatter dogmatisms' suffocating holds on the human spirit must not merely be new despots replacing the old but self-mockers as well. Carnival's "abusers" or wise fools flout all authority, including their own. And this mocker can be either female or male. Bakhtin, in fact, sees the female as a powerful embodiment of the delightful revivifying iconoclasm of carnival. In the realm of carnival, when woman is presented as "a wayward, sensual, concupiscent character of falsehood, materialism, and baseness," this characterization should not be read as a listing of "abstract moral traits of a human being," but as "perform[ing] the functions of debasement and at the same time of renewal of life. Womanhood is shown in contrast to the limitations of her partner (husband, lover, or suitor); she is a foil to his avarice, jealousy, stupidity, hypocrisy, bigotry, sterile senility, false heroism, and abstract idealism. . . . She represents in person the undoing of pretentiousness, of all that is finished, completed, and exhausted."[50]

So, the waywardness of tongue and body, the duplicity, sharpness, emotionalism, and lasciviousness that many in early modern society feared as the traits of actual women, Bakhtin saw in festivals and literature as symbolic correctives to repressive dogma about privileging the male, the rational, the spiritual, the aristocratic.

This "woman on top," as more recent critics have termed her, has been of strong interest for addressing the literary and actual eruption of unruliness of women and men toward sixteenth- and seventeenth-century strictures on gender and class. This is not surprising in light of Bakhtin's assertions that the spirit of carnival "flowers" in the sixteenth-century Renaissance literature of Rabelais, Shakespeare, Cervantes, and others before becoming more and more sanitized moving through the seventeenth and into the eighteenth centuries.[51] The role of woman in the carnivalesque and literature's gradually rendering her less iconoclastic is especially pertinent to the female pastoral guide of this book. The female pastoral guide will also use festival abuse of word and action to "liberate" or "purify" her charges from "dogmatic" beliefs that cut them off from living, smother their souls, stifle their hearts. She will often also be willing to mock herself, as well, to create a pastoral reconciliation of humans with themselves, each other, and the divine. Nevertheless, she is a good deal more "respectable" than Bakhtin's eternal woman, who is an abuser "lift[ing] her skirts and show[ing] the parts through which everything passes . . . and from which everything issues forth."[52] As the ribald spirit of carnival is tamed by demands of decorum and satire, the female pastoral guide of the late sixteenth- and early seventeenth-century English stage does not exhibit the complete sexual freedom or fieriness of carnival's eternal woman. Nevertheless, the female pastoral guide will still attempt to counter, with varying degrees of openness and nonconformity, the fear, disapproval, and underestimation of women underlying her culture's hierarchical split of the genders in favor of masculine ascendancy.

Critics of early-modern literature and history have disagreed over carnivalesque's power to shake up society. Against Bakhtin's claims about its efficacy in Renaissance literature, writers in the school of cultural materialism tend to believe that the comic spirit of the woman on top is often exploited less to challenge the social order's views on women than actually to strengthen traditional hierarchy. For example, Jyotsna Singh argues that the presentation of prostitutes in Shakespeare's plays does not put these women "on top," but tends to confirm cultural standards by showing their sexual and economic independence as the degraded opposite of the ideal submissive wife, with both kinds of women portrayed as objects of man's desire not as desiring beings. Mary Russo questions the effectiveness of actual women behaving as women on top and even whether men who precipitated riots dressed as women, Lady Skimmingtons, were not merely confirming negative views of the social disruptiveness of froward women. Peter Stallybrass points out that in *Sir Thomas More* the women who rise up to threaten "foreign artisans" in England are not an example of the lower gender stratum demonstrating its parity with the higher. Instead, the women move out of their usual place only to assert more firmly gender and nationalism traditions, protecting their husbands and their country from economic infringement. After this issue is resolved, when women and apprentices begin to challenge the ruling elite of the country, they must be dispersed. Stallybrass argues that even if carnival is not an organ of an all-powerful social order, it is certainly not as freeing as Bakhtin implies, rather serving as an individual "safety valve" for localized issues. Singh's observations on Mistress Quickly in *2 Henry IV* aptly sum up most of the cultural materialist perspective on carnival's social role in literature. Although Quickly's "carnivalesque malapropisms mock at the linguistic order buttressing the world of kingly hierarchy," "she is also a source of the laughter, a butt of jokes that have little subversive impact because they leave the *categories of social representation* largely untouched."[53]

Still, Natalie Zemon Davis enumerates instances where women spoke or acted out and were heard by clergy, politicians, and writers, where writers and artists themselves created positive women on top.[54] Significantly, the female pastoral guide's stage incarnations reflect a similar diversity of views. In a wonderfully Bakhtinian sense, the guide does not elevate one perspective above the other but reflects the fact that conflicting conceptions of the woman on top existed in early-modern history and literature. In Cynthia and Clorin, what Singh calls "the categories of social representation" will remain "largely untouched"; however, with Venus, Silvesta, Rosalind, and Helena we will find characters who desire as well as are objects of desire—and their creators will address and attempt to alleviate the tensions created by their violation of traditional expectations. That none of these guides exhibits the complete freedom of action, words, or sexuality of Bakhtin's eternal female lies in the difference between his using woman as a symbol for psycho/social impulses and the playwrights' creation of characters who represented the possibilities for actual women's agency and influence within their culture.

This book is set up with the initial two chapters laying out the foundations for the guide These two chapters discuss not only the immediate source texts for the guide as goddess (chapter 1) or the wise woman/mage (chapter 2), but how this development is driven by the cultural influences of patriarchal concerns about the feminine Other, centering on women's sexuality, voice, and intelligence. Chapter 1 traces the evolution of the goddess guide from late antiquity pastorals, examining her roots in a conflict between ancient goddess beliefs and patriarchal social organization that extends into the Christianization of these goddesses, then explores the attempt to bridge this rift in the forms of the supernatural female guides of Boccaccio's *Ameto*. Chapter 2, in covering the guide as mage and wise woman, will explore a more contemporary influence. This chapter will look at how this form of the guide is shaped in response to medieval and Renaissance concerns about witchcraft, which also came to reflect similar fears about the feminine Other. The main foundation texts studied in this chapter will be Sannazaro's *Arcadia* and Montemayor's *Diana*.

Chapters 3 through 7 will center on how selected plays reveal the varied views on gender relations in the sixteenth and seventeenth centuries through their depictions of the female pastoral guide. Chapter 3 will examine how, in response to concerns about the "unnatural" situation of a female prince, versions of the goddess guide in *Loves Metamorphosis, Endymion, A Midsummer Night's Dream*, and *Love's Victory* express world views ranging from affirming contentions of the necessity of patriarchal control of feminine agency to challenging that belief. This chapter will also explore how Lyly ventriloquizes a female voice in Cynthia to affirm the validity of patriarchal control.

Chapter 4 will provide a foundation for discussion of the guide as mage or wise woman by surveying contemporary views of women as scholars and healers. Carnival's concepts of realigning hierarchy to put high and low strata on the same level proves particularly helpful here. For these female pastoral guides turn their worlds upside down in two important ways. They wield medical and intellectual knowledge and skills of both their own level of the hierarchy (domestic, folk) and of that of the males (learned, Paracelsian). At the same time, they underscore their hierarchical inversion by exhibiting the reason and morality attributed to men to cure others, especially men, of the flaws attributed to women. Chapter 5 will explore how in this vein *The Faithful Shepherdess* asserts the need for patriarchal guidance, ventriloquizing woman's voice in a much less harsh version than in Lyly's play, while also chiding men for neglecting their responsibilities toward women. Chapters 6 and 7 will delve into the more iconoclastic approaches of *All's Well That Ends Well* and *As You Like It*, where *women* ventriloquize men's voices through comic abuse and disguise as they use their wit and medical scholarship to heal the souls of their charges. Chapter 8 will sum up the reasons that the guide fades from drama moving into the eighteenth century.

1

The Early Guide as "the Light in the Sky"

I

THERE IS A CONSENSUS THAT THE ENGLISH RENAISSANCE pastoral was shaped most strongly by the continental works *Ameto* (Boccaccio), *Arcadia* (Sannazaro), and *Diana* (Montemayor). Critics[1] have credited these three as major sources for the English pastoral's adopting the conventions of nymphs and shepherds interacting; celebrations of song and feasting at sacred nature festivals; allusions to classical mythology; dwelling on "love with all its pains and raptures";[2] and exploring how characters' adventures in love can be read as an allegory for spiritual and moral development, a trait that will underlie much of Spenser's, Sidney's, Lyly's, Shakespeare's, Fletcher's, Wroth's, and so many others' pastoral writings.[3] The female pastoral guide as goddess, mage, or wise woman appears as an important figure, or figures, in all three pastorals as well: in *Ameto,* Venus and her nymphs act as goddess and mage guides; in *Arcadia,* Pales and the Nymph of Arcadia play the same roles, respectively; in *Diana*, Felicia is a mage and Felismena a wise woman.

However, to understand the female pastoral guide of the sixteenth and seventeenth centuries, one must realize that *Ameto, Arcadia,* and *Diana* do not hold the English pastoral guide's initial incarnations, merely her more immediate ancestors. She owes her beginnings to works of literature reaching back to late antiquity, some of which are ancestors of *Ameto, Arcadia,* and *Diana.* To understand the artistic, social, and psychological needs the guide serves in early-modern English pastoral, it is necessary to go back to her earliest pastoral roots in the works of Theocritus, Virgil, and Longus, as well as in the genre of romance. In these writings, powerful female figures associated with both the natural and the supernatural strive to take control of disharmonious situations, prefiguring the guides' struggles in drama of early modern England. However, the spilt between reason or spirit and body that came to predominate Western thought more in early-modern culture than in the romance and pastoral of eastern Mediterranean late antiquity complicates how the guide may use her wit, compassion, and pluck to restore herself and her world to harmony. Furthermore, the medieval and Renaissance depiction of this split between spirit and body into a battle of God against Satan and his human minions, witches, provides a more contemporary problematizing of any depiction

29

of a woman exercising power, especially magical. For witches had come to incarnate the worst fears of "froward women" that the patriarchal culture drew on to justify its social and legal constraint of women. This first chapter will start with the oldest roots of the female pastoral guide in ancient-world pastoral, examine the shift in world views that underlie both her goal of healing the wounded psyche and an uneasiness with giving her the power to do so, and close with the most influential foundation text for the guide as goddess, Boccaccio's *Ameto*. Chapter 2 will explore the further development of the goddess by studying how medieval and Renaissance concerns about witchcraft shaped the other form of the guide, mage or wise woman.

The female pastoral guide's earliest inceptions in Longus's *Daphnis and Chloe* and Theocritus's and Virgil's pastorals provide the easiest starting point for understanding her mythic history. Though not the earliest of pastorals, Longus's *Daphnis and Chloe* will be discussed first because it holds the least problematic of the Renaissance female pastoral guide's ancient ancestresses. Written circa late second or early third century A.D., this prose work, "[h]aving survived to the sixteenth century in various manuscripts, . . . was published in a French translation nearly forty years before its Greek text was first printed" by Raffaello Colombani in 1598.[4] An English version was published by Angel Day in 1587, rewriting the work's Dionysian feast into an annual celebration of Elizabeth I's reign. The work's popularity continued with George Thornley publishing another translation in 1657.[5] Many critics concur that specific narrative traits peculiar to this text were highly influential on Renaissance pastoral: hidden regal identities for the pastoral lovers; matching the seasons' development with the maturing love of the main characters; the artist's explication of love; and the pastoral world's vulnerability to outside brutal invaders.[6]

Another narrative strategy that the work includes, but has gone mainly unremarked, is the guidance provided at key moments of crisis by wise supernatural females.[7] In *Daphnis and Chloe*, the Nymphs of a sacred cave act as pastoral guides to Daphnis and the other characters, making predictions, giving advice, and drawing down the support of Pan to re-establish harmony in the pastoral world. The Nymphs shelter the abandoned baby Chloe in their cave, where she is nursed by an ewe. They also appear in dreams to the stepparents of Daphnis and Chloe, cryptically revealing the royal heritage of both, and inspiring these stepparents to plan special futures for the children.[8] When invading Methymneans kidnap Chloe and ravage the green world, the Nymphs answer Daphnis's challenge to set things right by promising him in a mystical dream that they will call on Pan to free Chloe and the stolen livestock, as well as to punish and drive off the marauders.[9] Later, fearing that pride and greed will prompt Chloe's stepfather, Dryas, to refuse his request for her in marriage, Daphnis calls on the Nymphs for help. They appear in a dream to instruct him where he can find the money to satisfy Chloe's father, as well as how to make a convincing offer with that treasure.[10]

These Nymphs are supernatural guides who seem even to incarnate the pastoral topos, for Longus's descriptions of them evoke the voluptuousness of the pastoral's nature. Lesbos is overwhelmed and overrun by "[h]illsides covered with vines, and pastures full of flocks" and "wood[s] containing a bramble-thicket, some wandering ivy, and some soft grass." The Nymphs are portrayed as equally lush, free, and appealing: "Their feet were bare, their arms were naked to the shoulder, and their hair hung down loose over their necks. They had girdles round their waists and smiles on their faces; and their attitude was suggestive of dancing."[11] Imbuing a cave and fountain with their spirits and serving the pastoral world's god Pan, the Nymphs are merged with nature. Aligned to the divine in nature, they appear mystically in dreams, commune with a god, receive worship from pastoral citizens, and possess omniscience. As go-betweens for Daphnis with Pan, they serve as conduits between the human and the divine. Providing timely advice and suggestions, helping to restore order destroyed by savage invaders, and bringing together lovers and parents and children with their advice, the Nymphs prove adept at guiding humans to harmonious relations with one another. In fact, Longus presents the Nymphs' power to move humans toward harmony with one another, Nature, and the Divine as being firmly connected to Love. The Nymphs guide Daphnis with visions that help him keep Chloe as his own lover. Not only is the first vision they grant to Dryas of Love's pledging the two young lovers together but they also work with Pan to maintain that love. In addition, the Nymphs' facilitating the reunion of lost parents and children, masters (biological parents) and peasants (adoptive parents), and enemies with friends comes to fruition in the consummation of Daphnis and Chloe's love in marriage. Finally, Longus constantly links the Nymphs, Pan, and Love, usually with Love as the directive force or final authority.[12]

As will be discussed in greater detail later, the Nymphs of Boccaccio's *Diana's Hunt* and *Ameto*, of Sannazaro's *Arcadia*, of Montemayor's *Diana* (and in Younge's translation), and of Drayton's *Muses' Elisium* all carry on this tradition: female incarnations of pastoral harmony guiding humans toward inner harmony, usually in conjunction with teaching how to love. However, a notable difference between this classical and those Renaissance pastorals seems to be that in *Daphnis and Chloe*, love's ultimate communion stresses the sexual as much as the emotional or spiritual. Longus's emphasis on sexuality is further underscored by another "guiding" female in *Daphnis and Chloe*, Lyceanion, who teaches Daphnis how to carry his passion beyond kisses and embraces to the consummation that will make humans as fecund as a landscape rich in lambs, kids, grains, flowers, and the lush "grapes and figs and pomegranates" of Lesbos.[13] Significantly, though, Lyceanion's schooling in sex incorporates pastoral social harmony. She does not merely teach physical movements but impresses on Daphnis how to give his partner, as well as himself, the most pleasure: "[m]aking love doesn't just mean kissing and embracing and doing what the rams and he-goats do. It means a form of intercourse quite different from theirs and far sweeter—for the pleasure lasts longer."[14] As Margaret Doody observes, "The lesson in sex makes a man of Daphnis—not in giving him new power [over a woman], and the new pleasure of potency, but in giving him responsibility"[15] to express his love empathetically, with a restraint demonstrating his compassion for his beloved. This knowledge enables Daphnis to satisfy his and his lover's sexual needs as well as his society's requirements for continuation through procreation in marriage.[16]

Satisfying sexual desires is a concern of a powerful female figure in the pastoral world of two even earlier works, Theocritus's *Idyll* 2 and Virgil's *Eclogue* 8. However, these poems present the dark flip side of Longus's Nymphs and Lyceanion. In both of these texts, Virgil emulating Theocritus's work, a woman rages about her lost love while using witchcraft to recapture his devotion. This analysis will center on Virgil's version since Latin writings were often more accessible than Greek in western Europe during most of the Middle Ages and into the Renaissance.[17] In *Eclogue* 8, the woman, Alphesiboeus, is trying to re-establish harmony through love by recapturing her lost lover, but her exercise of powers is all darkness, fury, horror, and chaos. She calls on "songs" of Circe (lines 69–107)[18] to make her charms work (in Theocritus it is Hecate). Using herbs sacred to the dark sorceress Circe and imbued with magical powers by spells, the scorned woman merges nature and the supernatural to work her ends in love (lines 64–107), but those ends include vengeance and the inflicting of suffering on her rejecting paramour (85–100). Her words are fraught with fury, hatred, and obsession. In this eclogue, nature, supernatural, mind, and emotions roam freely but not like lush vines, exuberant kids and lambs, or sexually delighting lovers. Instead, the female of this poem incarnates the unfettering of all human fears about the divine, nature, other humans, and one's self. Alphesiboeus uses "herbs and . . . poisons" to "assail" her lover (lines 95–104). She likens her craft to that of Moeris, who turned himself into a wolf and "call[ed] spirits from the depth of the grave, and charm[ed] sown corn away to other fields" (lines 95–99). She wishes to destroy reason so that the Daphnis in this poem will "melt with love" for her (line 81).

Both the dark and the light female figures of pastoral power emerge in the Renaissance female pastoral guide, rewritten to reflect a Christian culture's views on God, nature, humanity, and love and sexuality. In the pre-Christian texts, sexuality could be not just an attribute of divinity but the force through which the Divine rewards, punishes, or communicates with humanity.[19] However, in the Christian revision of the pastoral, human love frequently becomes more of a symbol of the intensity and transcendence of divine love. Rather than running unfettered like Cupid in Philetas's garden,[20] love must be refined, trained to balance reason, emotion, and faith.

This point is eloquently expressed in that popular Renaissance guidebook of spiritual, social, and political deportment, *The Courtier*, written by Castiglione in 1528 and translated into English by Thomas Hoby in 1561. Although this text is not a pastoral, it connects to the genre in outlining the ultimate spiritual end of courtly love, a concept that shapes the literary and philosophical environment of medieval and early-modern pastoral writers. Using the "bridle of reason"[21] on passion creates an individual whose strength lies in his "meekenesse, courtesie, and prowesse."[22] Failure "to shonn throughlye all filthinesse of commune love, and so entre into the holye way of love with the guide of reason" leads to the uncontrolled chaos of lust, violence, despair, and destructiveness, where "the soule . . . seeth her selfe drowned in the earthly prison."[23] Thus, rejecting or ignoring the "bridle of reason" creates dissociation from God, nature, society, and the self, as Virgil's Alphesiboeus does in her violent attempt to make Daphnis "melt with love for" her in *Eclogue* 8. By embracing a love that transforms the sensual through reason, one moves from appreciating an individual woman's beauty up the "stayers . . . to true love"[24] to appreciating the beauty of creation in humans, artistry, and nature as the "footsteppes of God." This elevation of courtly/spiritual love over the earthly/sensual variety depicts beauty's inspiration of love as leading to a transcendent union with Good or God. This enlightened courtier now approaches the angels in perceiving and understanding.[25] As Hoby lays it out in his translation of Castiglione:

> In conclusion this comelye and holye beawtie is a wonderous setting out of everie thinge. And it may be said that Good and beawtifull be after a sort one selfe thinge, especiallie in the bodies of men: of the beawtie wherof the nighest cause (I suppose) is the beawtie of the soule: the which as a partner of the right and heavenlye beawtie, maketh sightlye and beawtifull what ever she toucheth, and most of all, if the bodye, where she dwelleth, be not of so vile a matter, that she can not imprint in it her propertye. Therfore Beawtie is the true monument and spoile of the victorye of the soule, whan she with heavenlye influence beareth rule over materiall and grosse nature, and with her light overcommeth the darkeness of the bodye.[26]

God both creates and is true beauty, a beauty that is inherent in humans and the universe as both are his "footsteppes." The glory of that beauty draws all souls, but it is reason that refines love's passionate devotion to a woman into something purer. Thus, the importance of passion is not denied, but its end is redirected from both the sensual and earthly toward Christian otherworldliness. As will be discussed in more depth later, the woman initially inspiring devotion is not so much a "hands on," as it were, instructor in love but the object of the lover's admiration, not valuable in herself but as an initial step on the "stayers" of love leading to God.[27]

Critics attribute courtly love's treatment of love, women, and the divine to medieval and Renaissance passion for Neoplatonism. Frank Kermode writes: "During the Renaissance this well-established [courtly love] convention is strengthened by Neo-platonic teaching, which systematizes the relationship between spiritual and physical love and beauty, as Spenser does in his Hymns; and, further to enrich it, there was always in men's minds the *Song of Solomon*."[28] RoseAnna Mueller concurs: "Beginning in the 15th century, Neoplatonism became widespread after Marsilio Ficino's commentaries on Plato's *Symposium*. The philosophy, according to Báez, was an attempt to exclude all that is ugly and to take delight in all that was free from imperfection (x). Neoplatonism helped distinguish Renaissance pastoral from Greek pastoral, with its references to carnal love and details that reveal a working knowledge of rural life."[29]

In this context, rather than behaving like *Daphnis and Chloe*'s sensual Nymphs or Lyceanion, the Renaissance pastoral guide is a more a combination of Danté's Virgil and Beatrice symbolizing, respectively, human reason and faith opening the human mind to a divine love that transcends, though does not necessarily disparage, earthly love.[30]

In varying degrees, the Renaissance female pastoral guides will find the fierceness of their carnival impulses tamed by this concept. Some may treat the ideal vision of courtly love as what Bakhtin defines as a "serious" dogma that must be comically abused to aid those they guide. Under the Christianizing influence of courtly love that developed in the Middle Ages and onward into the Renaissance, the female pastoral guide enacts her role by taking on one or more of three forms. The first form is a goddess or other divine supernatural figure who presides over the green world and incarnates pastoral values of community and harmony amongst nature, humanity, and divinity, as well as within the individual. Good examples are the Dianas, Cynthias, and Elizas whose purity, discipline, merciful justice, and defense of their realms against invaders or native corruptors of pastoral order celebrate Elizabeth I's reign. In Lyly's *Love's Metamorphosis*, the goddess Ceres rules the green world, punishing Erisicthon's pride and greed and warning her nymphs against pride and cruelty to lovers. Sabrina of Milton's *Comus* frees the virginal Lady from Comus's immobilizing spell. In *Love's Victory*, Lady Mary Wroth's Venus teaches fidelity, unselfishness, and spirituality in love to help her charges attain pastoral harmony. The beauty, wisdom, comfort, and sometimes literal guidance of supernatural nymphs, as in Sannazaro's *Arcadia* and Boccaccio's *Diana's Hunt* and *Ameto*, is another variation on the guide as goddess.

The other incarnation of the guide is the learned woman, who may take two related forms. First is a priestess or mage whose understanding of and communion with pastoral values puts her in touch with the divine in the pastoral world so that she can use her psychological insight as well as her training in magic to heal the psychic and physical wounds of both pastoral natives and visitors. In *Diana* (1559), Felicia draws on all these qualities to help despairing and abused lovers. Other versions of the mage continue to appear in the seventeenth-century English pastoral of various genres: Protea of *Loves Metamorphosis* (1588/89); Clorin, a priestess of Pan in *The Faithful Shepherdess* (w.1608/09); Lamia in *Hymen's Triumph* (w.1614); Urania in *The Queen's Arcadia* (1605); Mellisea in *Urania* (1621); and Claudia, Queen of Corinth, in *Love Crowns the End* (w.1632).

The other form of learned woman guide is a variation on the mage. She is a wise woman who may not have magical powers or be guided by a god or goddess but has sufficient knowledge of the medicinal uses of herbs or of the human heart (including her own) to draw on nature to rule wisely or to help others. In "The Description of Cooke-ham" (1609/10), Aemila Lanyer's Duchess of Cumberland serves as a Christian version of this sacred wise woman, reading biblical truths and communing with Old and New Testament heroes in the natural surroundings of trees and park at Cooke-ham, where she instructs two young women in the wisdom, charity, and beatitude that she has imbibed. Other wise women would include Elizabeth I's participation in *The Lady of May* (1578), the wise nymphs of Drayton's *Muses Elizium* (1630), Maid Marian in *The Sad Shepherd* (1640), Rosalind in *As You Like It* (1600), Silvesta of *Love's Victory* (1620), Clematis in *Rhodon and Iris* (1631), Pamphillia and Urania in *Urania* (1621), and Bellessa and Sabina in *The Shepherd's Paradise* (1632/33).

Ultimately, all versions of the guide restore the human soul. They revive fellowship, compassion, and empathy amongst fellow humans. They open their charges' eyes to love and appreciation of the transcendent beauty in valuing the spiritual as well as the physical, balancing reason and emotion (often through opening themselves to love of God). Achieving these goals, the female pastoral guide returns to her charges a sense of security that they can be part of both the natural and the spiritual worlds. Usually, the guide seeks to purge from individuals the cynicism, selfishness, solipsism, pride, cruelty, or ungoverned passion that disrupts their harmony with other people, nature, and the Divine, or even within themselves. In this way she is a variation on carnival's comic abuser who "purifies [others] from dogmatism, from the intolerant and the petrified . . . liberates from fanaticism and pedantry, from fear and intimidation, from didacticism, näiveté and illusion, . . . [and] restores . . . ambivalent wholeness."[31]

So how can the sensual spirit of carnival square with the Christian insistence of purifying the spiritual from the sensual? The earliest of the pastoral romances featuring the guide is Boccaccio's *Ameto*, in which Venus enacts the role of guide as a goddess. Boccaccio's Venus does indeed embody a startlingly carnivalesque "ambivalent" blend of her traditional attributes as the goddess of love and sensuality with the Virgin Mary's purity to inspire the title character. To understand how Boccaccio pulls this off, it is necessary to look back at the Great Goddess tradition, of which Venus and Christianity's Virgin Mary are a part, to see why the Christian "Queen of Heaven" evolved as she did. And it is also necessary to recognize how the genre of romance, from which *Ameto* and later pastorals with female guides emerged, initially came from writers and audiences still attuned to the power and efficacy of the Great Goddess in the midst of Iron Age patriarchal theology.

II

Scholars such as Anne Baring with Jules Cashford, Marina Warner, Barbette Stanley Spaeth, R. E. Witt, Robert Graves, Erich Neumann, and Joseph Campbell have pointed out that the development of Marian doctrine often reflected Christianity's intersection with the ancient-world religions it strove to supplant. In fact, a tendency that all these mythical systems share, from the worship of Inanna/Ishtar down through Christianity, is particularly germane to the formation and cultural work of the female pastoral guide. That tendency is a tradition of incarnating the mystery of good and evil, control and chaos, fecundity and death in a female divinity.

Still, looking into the history of the ancient Great Goddess is not to subscribe to Neumann's and Jung's (and to some extent Campbell's) theory of a matriarchal society predominating human society in the dim mists of antiquity.[32] Instead, this embodiment of the dark/light in female supernatural force often reinforces the power of patriarchy, especially from the mid-Bronze Age onward.[33] In this mode of thought, the Self through whose perspective experience is shaped and interpreted is Male, while the Other, the outsider to the social order, that can be chaotic, frightening, and destructive is connected to the Female. The Other's virtues, such as fertility, passion, and knowledge of the natural and supernatural, are undercut by being paired with their opposite traits, such as death, chaos, and hoarding knowledge. Further, re-emphasizing the pattern of the Male Self's not only propitiating but seducing or conquering the divine Female

Other in order to gain control of her power, these mythical systems tend to raise the aspect of female power mainly to assert patriarchal right to that power. A brief survey of representative myths will clarify these points. More importantly, such a survey reveals how specific traits concerning these female divinities and the ways in which cultures project anxieties onto women via their myths are directly pertinent to the characterization and treatment of the female pastoral guide from Boccaccio's Venus and her nymphs down to the seventeenth-century English form.

One of the most ancient of goddesses is Inanna/Ishtar, worshipped by the Sumerians as far back as "the fifth millennium B.C.E."[34] Called "Lady of the Largest Heart," Inanna contains within herself both light and dark, order and chaos, life and death. Barbara De Shong Meador points out that Inanna's combining these traits made her unique in her culture as "the only Mesopotamian deity whose character so prominently included contradictions. The characteristic reflected a central Mesopotamian perspective, one that Assyriologist Rivkah Harris depicts as, 'the existence of antitheses and contradictions, the delicate balancing of order and disorder,' 'a deity who incorporated fundamental and irreducible paradoxes.'"[35]

Thus, Inanna is the goddess of both love/fertility/life and war. She descends into the realm of death and returns to life, but she chooses as replacement in the dark realm, "the house of dust," the lover (Tamuz) who betrayed her in her absence.[36] She offers Gilgamesh divine love but punishes both him and humanity for his rejection by sending fiercely destructive elements of nature, a supernatural bull that creates earthquakes that kill humans by the thousands.[37] Inanna is "a goddess of play," who "approaches sexual arousal with abandon, with revelry, [and] with delight."[38] At the same time, she is also described in the poetry of her devout priestess Enheduanna as "a lioness 'prowling the roads / [who] shows her fangs / gnashes her teeth.'" Enheduanna warns, "Woe the city under [Inanna's] frown," for in war "she mauls/slashes the cows and bulls"; "[s]he is a 'pit trap for the headstrong.'"[39] De Shong Meador points out that Innana's integration, even reconciling, of the glorious and the horrific extremes of human experience within herself brought her "immense popularity in antiquity." Thus, exposure to the supernatural energy and knowledge of Innana's Being painfully and pleasurably sanctifies; but unlike a Christian Virgin or a Renaissance courtier's inspirational lady, she transforms without separating body from spirit. Contact with Inanna's "raw libidinous vitality" makes her "the whetstone against which the devotee hones her course toward spiritual maturation,"[40] a combination that carnival's melding of ambiguities in the comic grotesque also evokes.

Even possessing such great power, Inanna still does not stand as proof of ancient matriarchy, for Mesopotamian culture's political and religious human authority was patriarchal.[41] Rather, Inanna could also stand for

Other as a repository for patriarchy's desire to appease or to partake of the knowledge of life forces it cannot control. In these ways, Inanna establishes the foundation for the pastoral guide as a female figure whose sexuality, independence, and knowledge can be desired or feared.

A similarly influential antecedent of the guide is Isis, who originated in Egyptian mythology and continued to be worshipped across the ancient world into the early era of Christianity.[42] As consort to Osiris, the god of agriculture and judgment in the underworld, she is associated with sexuality, fertility, and rebirth. Isis's iconography also denotes fertility, the crescent moon and the wings representing the wind that brings moisture and life.[43] Her giving birth to Osiris's divine child Horus, her recovery of Osiris's body, her participation in the resurrections of Horus and Osiris, and her sanctification of the child of the King and Queen of Byblus further bespeak her connection with earthly fruitfulness and heavenly eternal life.

The beneficence that Isis brings through providing agricultural plenty extended to other aspects of life for the individual and for society as a whole. Indicating that she is a goddess whose generative powers provide insight and stability to humanity, Isis sought to purify the child of Byblos, and her divine child defeated Set, a divinity representing natural and supernatural destruction. *The Golden Ass,* by Apuleius in the second century CE, depicts Isis using her powers as "the natural mother of all life" to save humanity in times of trouble so that we can spiritually blossom. In response to the narrator's plea for salvation from his suffering, Isis appears to comfort him with, "Behold, I am come to you in your calamity. I am come with solace and aid. Away then with tears. Cease to moan. Send sorrow packing. Soon through my providence shall the sun of your salvation arise."[44]

Part of Isis's role as comforter was to be a teacher who shares her supernatural knowledge with humanity for positive ends, initially joining with Osiris to educate humanity about agriculture and the rites of mummification.[45] Based on such stories, Isis was frequently read as instructing doctors and healers to preserve humanity.[46] Particularly relevant, R. E. Witt's description of Isis as "the great sorceress" of "wisdom immeasurable," as "the lady who saved" because "skillful as healer and discoverer of the mysteries of birth, life, and death" anticipates the Renaissance pastoral guide's role as a magical spiritual and physical healer. Still, Isis's characterization "as not bound by the normal law of sex" and resolute against "any prudery about sex"[47] would prove more problematic for Christian writers.

Isis, like Inanna, possessed a dark, deceptive, uncontrollable aspect as well as a shining, enlightening, protective one. She may, as R. E. Witt writes, have gained the magic of "great god Re [Ra],"[48] but she did so by hurting, deceiving, and extorting him. After arranging for him to be bitten by a serpent that she surreptitiously placed in his path, Isis offered to cure Ra of his suffering, but only if he promised to give up the magic of his name to her.[49] In terms of carnival's cosmic vision, she could be interpreted as the comic trickster, undermining the aged head of hierarchy to free his power not just for her personal benefit but for the life force of rebirth that she represents. On the other hand, in the eyes of traditional masculine power, the guardians of "seriousness" and "dogma" that carnival exorcises, Isis would represent the female force deceptively and ruthlessly poisoning, disrupting the natural order, to gain a power over the male to which patriarchy would deem her unentitled.

Even when Isis shares her divinity with humans, the result can be terrifying and even deadly to those who reject the spirit of enlightenment and revival that she embodies. When the Queen of Byblos sees her child being cured in Isis's divine fire, she can only perceive her child being burned in a fire of logs. So she screams and "rescues" her child from what her conventional understanding can only interpret as flames of death.[50] Later, Isis seeks to honor the King and Queen of Byblos by taking one of their children with her when she carries off Osiris in his coffin. Unfortunately, the limitations of human understanding, based on what Bakhtin calls "single meaning," "the single level" of perception, "didacticism and naïvieté," render the goddess's unveiled visage too awful for the boy to see and live.[51]

Other pre-Christian fertility goddesses can be said to resonate Isis's embodying both the dark and the light aspects of the cycle of birth, life, death, and rebirth. In a passage from *The Golden Ass,* Isis, herself, asserts that she is the original of all fertility goddesses, including the Venus who will preside over Boccaccio's *Ameto,* claiming that her "single godhead is venerated all over the earth under manifold forms, varying rites, and changing names." She justifies this assertion by detailing her myriad incarnations in mythologies spanning the then-known ancient world: "The Phrygians that are the oldest human stock call me Pessinuntia, Mother of the Gods. The aboriginal races of Attica call me Cecropian Minerva. The Cyprians in their island-home call me Paphian Venus. . . . The Eleusinians call me the ancient goddess Ceres. Some call me Juno."[52]

Two of the alternative guises Isis claims for herself above are pertinent to the study of the female pastoral guide. Venus's link to Adonis repeats the Isis/Osiris/Horus' Goddess and dying/reborn consort mythos. But perhaps most closely paralleling Isis's mythology is the story of Ceres and Proserpina, which descends from Demeter and Persephone. The Demeter/Ceres myth continues the presence of light/dark, life/death in the goddess but with some notable variations.[53] The Egyptian, Greek, and Roman myths all deal with the goddess's search for a loved one unfairly lost to death. However, in the Greco-Roman version the goddess is a mother searching for a daughter kidnapped and raped by Hades/Pluto, the deity presiding over the world of the dead. In all the legends, also, the searching goddess visits a human kingdom and there attempts to purify a human royal child, only to be forestalled by his mother's fears. She also teaches sacred mysteries to humans. In the Greek and Roman tales, however, she disguises herself as an old woman and does not take a child away with her. Instead, the goddess teaches the people of the kingdom her sacred mysteries. In another significant difference from the Isis myth, Demeter/Ceres punishes the earth and its human inhabitants for her loss by depriving both of fertility until her child is returned to her.[54]

Thus, it can be said that like Isis, Demeter, as a goddess of fecundity, is the loyal mother as well as caretaker and teacher of humanity. She is also, however, a fierce figure: rising in fury at the Eleusinian queen's ignorant protest over the purification of her son; destroying the earth's fertility and consequently harming humanity when her love for her daughter is thwarted; and appearing to humans as a crone, symbolizing death or sterility, rather than a sexually mature female like Isis or Inanna. This myth creates some variations that will descend to the guide. Rather than incarnating all aspects of life in the seasons of womanhood, the goddess is split into multiple forms. Persephone is the virgin, while Demeter is sexual maturity as the mother and death as the crone. Other mythos will continue this splitting: for example Athene/Diana represents the virgin/youth, Venus/Aphrodite sexual maturity, and Hecate the crone/death. Chapter 2's study of the relationship of the guide with contemporary views of the witch will delve into how and why this split is particularly important to medieval and Renaissance writers.

These split forms in the Demeter/Ceres mythology also reflect a greater assertion of control by patriarchal authority. Baring and Cashford do point out that worship of Demeter seems to have originated in Crete and moved to Greece "sometime in the fifteenth century" BCE, with her embodying the tremendous power of the Great Goddess over life, death, and resurrection; fertility and sterility; and knowledge and ignorance.[55] However, this mythos begins to diverge from that of Isis or Inanna in significant ways, especially in terms of her wielding power through her sexuality. For example, as noted above, Demeter/Ceres does not incorporate all aspects of the life cycle in herself, but only those of sexual maturity and death. Further, the virgin, woman unpracticed in sexual power, is given greater emphasis in this myth as the most valuable pawn in the struggle for ascendancy between the maternal force (Demeter/Ceres) and patriarchal figures: Hades/Pluto, who seizes her, and Zeus/Jupiter, who first ignores the goddess's grief and anger, then ultimately forces a negotiation between her and her daughter's ravisher. The myth also asserts the necessity of patriarchal control by showing the female force as unable to wield power without irrationality, resulting in chaos. When Demeter/Ceres tries to force the hands of Pluto and Zeus by reducing the earth to famine, she is portrayed as the vindictive, insensitive destroyer of natural harmony and human life innocent of causing her pain. Interestingly, when this divine mother does involve herself with humans, it is in the guise of the crone, harbinger of death and waste, thereby symbolic of how her anger with the other gods will make humanity unjustly suffer.

This remolding of the mythology, in the case of Ceres and earlier, seems to reflect a cultural shift to contain and control female agency by two mutually reinforcing methods. First, one of the ways invading herdsman and warrior cultures consolidated their conquest over the agrarian goddess worshippers was to establish cultural hegemony by degrading and even demonizing the goddesses around whom the subjugated societies were centered. Second, as these colonizing groups' stongly patrilineal organization used women as commodities to maintain or expand family and national power and property, the goddess's (and her culture's women's) independent sexuality would effectively destabilize masculine control of paternity. By downgrading, even blotting out, female power in the realm of the Divine, a patrilineal society could neutralize a model for female agency that it perceived as threatening its authority[56] Lacan's view of how the Law of the Father is based in marriage and inheritance concerns, through patronymy, the Father's name establishing identity within the purview of all that is masculine, traces some of its ancestry to here. More apropos to early-modern studies, feminist cultural materialists study the sixteenth- and seventeenth-century descendents of this cultural pattern, exploring how women are items of not just economic but emotional or sexual exchange: objects of desire but not desiring objects.[57]

Thus, Margaret Doody, in her work on the influence of Great Goddess worship on the development of the novel in late antiquity, relates that cults of Isis and the Great Goddess of Asia created tremendous anxiety for the patriarchal rulers of Rome for threatening to contaminate Roman culture and confuse bloodlines with alien beliefs that seemed to foster women's sexual freedom.[58] Barbette Stanley Spaeth describes an appropriation and refocusing of the Ceres/Proserpina mythos in Middle Republic Rome to protect against this threat to order: "The cult of Ceres and Proserpina," she asserts, was propagated to "reinforc[e] the status quo and retur[n] Roman women to their proper role in society, as defined by the male ruling class" as obedient daughters and wives who would reproduce sufficient quantities of legitimate Roman citizens.[59] So, although Baring and Cashford contend that Ceres, as a Great Mother Goddess, was an important part of Roman culture at the time,[60] the goddess had been co-opted by the reigning masculine hierarchy to confirm female obedience to its social dictates.

Another important mythos to the guide, emerging while the cults of Isis and Ceres were still influential, is that of the Virgin Mary. Jaroslav Pelikan insists that there exists sufficient biblical evidence and early Church exegesis to refute such links as the similarities between " 'the mother goddesses' of Graeco-Roman paganism" and the Christian Theotokus (Mother of God).[61] However, the fact remains that startlingly similar goddess myths not only predate but coexist with that of Mary in proximate cultural and geographic contexts. Such evidence severely undercuts the likelihood that the development of Marian mythology was a culturally isolated event. Most obviously, iconography, places of worship, and symbolism link Mary with pagan ancestors and contemporary counterparts. Plastic and pictorial images of the Virgin are often modeled on those of earlier pagan goddesses. For example many images of Mary holding the Christ child match those of Inanna holding Dumuzi, Ishtar with Tamuz, Isis with Horus, and Demeter with Triptolemus.[62] Similarly, the image of Mary holding her dying son strikingly resembles artwork or poetry depicting various Great Goddesses as they lament or hold their sons and/or consorts who have made a sacrificial death and will be reborn.[63] Even some shrines and images originally created to venerate various forms of the Great Goddess were converted for the worship of the Christian Mary. In a particularly noteworthy case, Marina Warner reports that "at Enna . . . , where Persephone was swallowed into the underworld, the cathedral used to display a Greek statue of Demeter and her daughter on the altar" in front of Christian worshippers.[64]

There is evidence of Mary's absorbing the iconography of other goddesses such as Inanna/Ishtar's, Hera's, Isis's, and Demeter and Perspehone's association with fertility in the form of the pomegranate.[65] Similarly, Erich Neumann points out that "Isis, Demeter, or later the Madonna" can all be connected through their association with the rose.[66] The girdle of fertility connected with Hera, Aphrodite, and Diana of Ephesus (an incarnation of Diana that evokes fertility rather than virginity) strongly parallels the Virgin's girdle, depicted in images and folktales across medieval Europe as having the power to cure infertile married couples. Anne Baring and Jules Cashford write that images of Mary holding the Christ child and the tree of life, surrounded by sheaves of wheat, or sleeping "on a bed of corn covered by a quilt embroidered with the heads of sheep" draw on similar images of Inanna/Ishtar, Isis, Ceres, and Cybele as nature goddesses promising life-saving bountiful harvests.[67]

Christianity's Mary carries on and modifies traditions of pagan goddesses in her own mythic tales. For instance, the myth of Demeter and Persephone, which precedes the Christian myth but continues during Christianity's development, resembles that of Jesus and Mary in some notable ways. Although Demeter is a goddess, not a mortal, and the child she loses is a daughter, her child's return from death restores life in the form of spring's bounty to humanity. Mary's child redeems humans from sin and so brings them the possibility of eternal life after death. Further, although part of Demeter's response to her loss is destructive, unlike Mary's, her expression of grief has another side—that of a teaching, helping, and inspiring mother. In this, she is much like the Virgin Mary when she is portrayed as the Mater Dolorosa, whose patient suffering teaches Christians a path to salvation and whose intercession with God may ease their hardships in earthly existence. The myth of Demeter as mother of a resurrected child and comforter of humanity associates her with another goddess whose links to Christianity's Mary, both antecedent and contemporary, is also striking: Isis.

In fact, Isis even more strongly anticipates much of the Marian mythos. At first glance, her conception of the divine child Horus by her husband/brother Osiris may seem to diverge radically from Mary's being impregnated by the unrelated, ethereal Holy Spirit. However, the similarities between Mary and Isis as mothers of divine children are much stronger than the differences. R. E. Witt undercuts the difference in the paternity of their children by pointing out that early in the Christian mythos, "in palaeochristian thinking[,] Mary was Christ's 'sister, mother, consort.'"[68] The resemblance between Isis and Mary is even more apparent in their facilitating a masculine deity's spiritual salvation of humanity. Isis's husband/brother and child are both killed by evil but both are resurrected to help destroy evil. Her brother/husband Osiris becomes the god of the underworld who saves the good and punishes the wicked. Like Christ, then, he has harrowed hell and sits in judgment of all souls. Their son Horus is also like Christ who negates Satan's hold on humanity. He vanquishes Set, the perpetrator of evil and creator of disorder for humans and gods, redeeming the world from a reign of chaos. Marina Warner sums up the parallel nicely: "Like Isis, who snatched Osiris' dismembered body from the powers of evil by reanimating his corpse and conceiving his child, Mary through the virgin birth had defeated the death of sin."[69]

Many of the roles Christians assigned to the Virgin Mary are analogous to those given to Isis as a version of the Great Goddess. Isis is seen as a loving intercessor with the highest god for the good of humanity because she empathizes with human pain, having lost husband and son and having wandered in search of them. Further, not only in her stay at Byblos, paralleling Demeter's in Eleusis, but in her general duties as a goddess, she gives comfort to humanity. Goddess of the grains, she helps feed all; goddess of health and medicine, she helps heal all; goddess known for her cleverness and wisdom, she helps educate the devoted. Daughter of Geb, wife of Osiris, and mother of Horus, she can use her influence on these gods to ease the plight of humanity. Both Isis and Mary are also protectresses of shipwrecked sailors.[70]

Mary also shares many epithets with Isis indicating their roles as loving mothers to humanity, preservers of peace, and beloved of God: "Queen of Peace," "Mistress of Heaven" or of "the World," *Inventrix, Justitia,* "The Maiden," "Throne of the King," and "God's bride." Additionally, the lunar imagery, star imagery, blue clothing, and physical descriptions of Mary and her associations with fertility, conquest of death and evil, spiritual purity, loving protection of humanity, and wisdom not only powerfully parallel but can be linked to descriptions of Isis.[71]

Through Mary, Christianity effectively tamed the divine in the Great Goddess, particularly in redefining her role as mother to the divine child. Most obviously, Christian tradition weakens the Great Goddess by turning her into a human. An even more interesting twist is to exalt her by *isolating* her from her sexuality. Anne Baring and Jules Cashford explain that the ancient world's conception of the Great Goddess's incarnation of virginity "had nothing to do with sexual 'purity' in the sense it has been given to it in our culture. The goddess is a virgin because she carries within herself her own fertilizing power; and life pours into manifestation from the 'sea' of her womb in a never-ending stream." In fact because she was both earthy/sensual and spiritual/otherworldly, she incorporated all aspects of creation within herself, and that very unity enabled her spiritually and physically to renew creation.[72] However, as Betty De Shong Meador writes: "The separation of the spirit from matter that took place in antiquity [shapes] Yahweh's split and Greek-influenced Christianity's additions to the separation of good and evil[,] provid[ing] divine sanction for the dark/light opposition mentality that pervades our [contemporary] psychology. Dominant monotheistic religions effectively taught generations that evil is outside ourselves, with Satan over there, in others."[73] So, earlier, positive understandings of the Great Goddess were lost as a deifying of spirit and reason (associated with patriarchal gods) and a concurrent demonizing as Other of body and passion (associated with the Great Goddess tradition) inherited from Hebrew, Greek, and Roman belief shaped the crystallizing Christian dogma of late antiquity onward. Scholars have additionally observed that early Christianity developed this perspective from other sources, a combination of classical and scriptural "evidence." Subscription to Plato's and Aristotle's views of women as inferior creatures was buttressed with the biblical creation myth portraying Eve's essence as secondary to man and tertiary to God, with her susceptibility to the serpent/Satan signaling her fallen, earthly state.[74]

Thus, although Mary shares with many of her predecessors epitaphs and roles as a fertility goddess, even a virginal fertility goddess, she does not come close to holding the totality of life that they do because Christian thinkers redefined the sacredness of fertility to square with their views of female chastity and submission.[75] The Virgin Mary is idealized for not experiencing, let alone enjoying, her sexuality, as well as for placidly accepting impregnation. Unlike the Great Goddess, she no longer chooses her divine consort. In fact, she has been rendered so "untainted" by sexuality that, unlike goddesses and mortals of other mythologies, she does not even experience sexual congress with the Divine. Her impregnation is entirely spiritual with no aspect of the sensual or physical. According to the Angel Gabriel, "The Holy Spirit shall come upon thee and the power of the Most High shall overshadow thee."[76] The obedience of Mary's submissive response to the prospect of fecundity without sexuality further emphasizes that Christianity requires the female to forgo her independence in order to link with the Divine: "Behold the handmaid of the Lord; be it unto me according to thy word."[77] The female "divinity" no longer controls passion, life, and death but is a human woman whose connection to divine power is to serve as its passive, humble receptacle. She does not generate passion and life like Inanna and Isis, nor does she regenerate life like Isis, Inanna, and Demeter/Ceres. The supernatural enters into her, uses her, and exits her at birth.

Both Baring and Cashford and Marina Warner explain that by the eleventh century CE the idea of Mary as a type of purity, silence, and obedience for women had become established. Across Europe, these character traits informed not only religious but secular texts, such as *Le Ménagier de Paris* (1392–94) and *Livre du Chevalier de la Tour Landry* (1372), inculcating the necessity for "obedience" and "long-suffering compliance" in women under the model of the Virgin's divine example.[78] Even Christine de Pisan's *City of Ladies*, which celebrates the virtue, reason, and integrity of educated woman, has the Virgin as its queen, thus "dignifying humility, benignity, patience, piety, and chastity."[79] Later, in the early sixteenth century, Juan Vives's tremendously popular conduct book for women *The Instruction of a Christian Woman*, translated by Richard Hyrde circa 1529,[80] taught women to emulate Mary's silent obedience to masculine authority, be it God's or humans': acceding to the divine announcement that she would bear God's child by "fynish[ing] the matter with fewe wordes"; "gatherynge and kepynge in her remembraunce all [the] sayenges" of angels, shepherds, wise men witnessing her newborn divine child rather than chatting them up about where they came from; presenting her son at the temple and silently accepting the prophesies of Symeon rather than asking about "whan, howe, and where hit shulde have ben"; and enduring the crucifixion of her son without complaint—"she was clene dumme." The Virgin Mary does not act; she bears her suffering silently and humbly eschews trying to question, even understand, patriarchal authority in human or supernatural form. In this, Vives instructs his readers, she is a role model to all women: "All maydes, and all women folowe you her: for she was but of fewe wordes: but wonderous wise."[81] In sum, as Elaine Beilin puts it, "[the] image of the virtuous woman is a domesticated version of the Virgin: remaining at home to keep the household goods, a good woman was pious, humble, constant, and patient, as well as obedient, chaste, and silent."[82]

Thus, during the Middle Ages and the Renaissance the impulse to inversion and change that the goddess shares with carnival's eternal woman is tamed and contained by reconfiguring her as the Virgin Mary, reflecting the culture's desire to keep the Other, embodied by divine and human woman, non-threatening and under control.[83] Yet, as Baring and Cashford observe, this drive from the middle of the Bronze Age onward to privilege reason/spirit over passion/nature, of male over female through demonizing or disempowering the Great Goddess, never truly achieves its goal but only creates a psychic alienation. The worship of Canaanite goddesses constantly resurfaces to be attacked by the monotheistic devotees of a resolute Hebrew God; rites of Demeter and Isis keep defying suppression by Roman emperors; in the characterization of Eve, the Great Goddesses' connections with the natural world and fertility must be portrayed as blasphemous and destructive; and in Christianity the mother of the dying and risen god may no longer be his consort, experience sexuality, or even be a goddess.[84] This attempt to control the terrifying Other through a separation and exaltation of the spirit over body, divine over mortal, conscious over unconscious, male over female does not satisfy a culture's spiritual needs but creates a psychic "wound that continually challenges us to understand our relation to nature, and to heal the separation in ourselves between our 'human' and our 'animal' natures."[85] Bakhtin's observations on medieval "seriousness" and carnival's comic perspective tie in here, for he points out that one way that the hierarchies of religion and state imposed strict control on human behavior was to exploit the release of resentment against that control within the time and social constraints of limited holidays as a kind of safety valve that would permit long term social stability. According to critics and historians such as Joystna Syngh, Diane Purkiss, and Peter Stallybrass, this use of carnival to divert and control the frustrations of those lowest in the power hierarchy, by virtue of gender or class, remained an effective technique to divert frustrations with the status quo from taking active form throughout the early-modern era.[86]

Still, the Great Goddess never completely loses her power for some worshippers. As noted earlier, Baring and Cashford point out that in the form of worshipping Cybele, Ceres, and Tellus Mater the goddess had adherents in Roman culture well into the rise of the Christianity that would eventually demonize and supplant it.[87] Margaret Doody not only concurs with them but does so to explain how the continued influence on writers and readers by Egyptian and Eastern Mediterranean Isis worship or the Eluesinian and Dionysian mystery cults shaped the development of the romance or earliest novels.[88] Her exploration of how plot, character, and narrative demonstrate that the classical romance, rather than work of the eighteenth century, is truly the first incarnation of the novel is fascinating. However, what is vital to understanding the female pastoral guide is Doody's examination of the incarnations of the Great Goddess in writings such as *Chaireas and Kallirrhoé, Kleitophon and Leukippé, The Golden Ass, Paul and Thekla, Apollonious of Tyre, Aithiopkia,*—in addition to the already discussed *Daphnis and Chloé.* This is not to say all these romances are pastorals, nor that all pastorals where the guide appears are romances. What matters to this study is that these early romances hold two important prototypes for the female pastoral guide.

Doody maintains that in these early romances the depiction of a goddess and her power speaks to a longing for the past where healing goddesses presided. Artemis in *Kleitophon and Leukippé,* Isis in *The Golden Ass* and *Aithiopkia,* Aphrodite in *Chaireas and Kallirrhoé,* or the Nymphs in *Daphnis and Chloé* are wise, powerful, and compassionate female divinities unfettered by patriarchy who bring comfort and knowledge that reconciles life and death, sexuality and purity. In fact, these goddesses usually step in to defeat oppressive fathers and kings by restoring rightful rule, uniting lovers, and comforting the despondent.[89] The mortal heroines of these texts serve the same goal. The romances give readers plucky heroines who use their wits, courage, and independence to escape the cruel or perverse threats of patriarchs (kings and fathers) to their lives, their virginity, their loved ones, and even to society. Frequently, the young women disguise themselves so that they can go off on adventures to set their worlds right and to be with their true loves; they are adept at either unraveling riddles that lead them to truth or at devising a series of riddles that trick those who threaten them into just punishment or those they love into self-discovery that reforms them.[90] A heroine might even arm herself like Artemis with bow and arrow to slay her enemies (*Aithiopkia*). In fact, these young women are usually much brighter, more determined, and more courageous than their easily discouraged or distracted lovers.[91]

Interestingly, their sexuality is far from a dangerous trait that must be kept under masculine control. Doody observes that in *Chaireas and Kallirrhoé* and *Aithiopkia* purity is defined as demonstrating fidelity to the beloved the heroine has chosen rather than as being sexually uncontaminated.[92] In *Paul and Thekla* and *Apollonious of Tyre,* virginity becomes an example of female empowerment. The young woman chooses virginity as a way of removing herself from patriarchal commodification. Her virginity is no longer to be sold by her father to the highest bidder so that her husband might preserve his property within his family through inheritance. The heroine has the power to decide on whom to bestow her body and her soul, whether to a Christian God (*Paul and Thekla*) or the man of her choice (*Chaireas and Kallirrhoé, Kleitophon and Leukippé, Apollonious of Tyre, Aithiopika*).[93] In all these cases, these romances' creation of female figures, divine or human, who combine reason with passion, sexuality with spirituality, and the earthly with the heavenly is an artistic means to heal the psychic wound inflicted by elevating the masculine and heavenly through alienating and demonizing all that is female and earthly. These romances might even be seen as re-establishing a healthy comic ambivalence.

The female characters of early romance display traits that strikingly foreshadow the female pastoral guide of late medieval and Renaissance texts. These independent heroines setting off in disguise on adventure and even martial exploits prefigure the Felismenas and Rosalinds who put on a "swashing and martial outside" to leave the protection and the troubles of court to venture into pastoral green worlds. The ability of these characters to outwit their adversaries and create or puzzle out riddles to restore harmony to their lives in romances of late antiquity lays the groundwork for a Lia, Felicia, Helena, Rosalind, Marian, or a Clorin to use wit, game-playing, and psychological insight to work similar ends. In Renaissance drama, like the heroines of classical romance, the female pastoral guide will refute the patriarchal demonizing of her sexuality. And the Venuses, Cynthias, and other pastoral goddesses of medieval and Renaissance pastorals draw on late antiquity romances' female deities, acting as powerful divine figures restoring a balance between body and spirit, earth and heaven. Still, not all versions of the guide, mortal or divine, are the same. If the female pastoral guide is an attempt to assuage an anxiety with the Self defined as masculine and the Other as feminine, to create a comic overturning of oppressive, "exhausted" dogmas in patriarchal culture, then the decided variations on this pastoral figure reveal a plethora of views on how this can be done.

III

It is not hard to discern a direct link from the romances of late antiquity to *Ameto, Arcadia,* and *Diana,* the immediate foundation texts for the English versions of the guide. Helen Hackett and Margaret Doody assert not just the survival but the continued popularity of several of the romances, discussed in the previous section, during the Middle Ages and into the seventeenth century, both in Greek and in translations: *Kleitophon and Leukippé, The Golden Ass, Apollonious of Tyre, Aithiopika*—in addition to the already discussed *Daphnis and Chloé.*[94] Margaret Doody observes the influence of *Paul and Thekla* in medieval female saints' martyrdom stories that echo Thekla's fierce independence and faith in the face of horrific torture.[95] Although Hackett focuses on romances in the Renaissance, both she and Doody establish that medieval and Renaissance romances drew on surviving works or surviving *descriptions* of these works from late antiquity for such conventions as lovers in flight from persecuting parents or rulers, shipwrecks, hidden royal identities, adventures in foreign locals, threats to women's bodies, strong-willed virgins, and supernatural intervention.[96]

In this cultural and artistic context, the presence of two versions of the female pastoral guide appearing in Boccaccio's *Ameto* is not at all surprising. Boccaccio, himself, had a strong interest in Greek language and literature, "singlehandedly establish[ing] Greek studies in the Florentine academy" and "invit[ing] a Greek scholar to come to Florence," whom he persuaded to translate the *Iliad* and the *Odyssey* into Latin. Boccaccio's *Filocolo* strongly echoes *Apollonius of Tyre* with the shipwrecks and heroine's guardians selling her into slavery while faking her death, as well as exhibiting similarities to the plot and characters of *Kleitophon and Leukippé* and *Aithiopika*.[97] Victoria Kirkham and Anthony Cassell see the plot of his *Diana's Hunt* inheriting from *The Golden Ass* the concept of a soul purged of its "lower faculties" through the transformative divine love of "Ceres-Proserpine-Venus-Artemis . . . Isis, 'Nature, Universal mother'."[98] In *Ameto,* a more well-known and influential text than *Diana's Hunt*, Boccaccio most effectively draws on the Greek romance's characterization of mortal and divine women to create two forms of the female pastoral guide. In this medieval romance, the independent, wise heroine becomes Lia and her band of nymphs, while the goddess who heals is Venus. Where Boccaccio seems to diverge from traditional Western Christian thought on woman and the Great Goddess is that his guides succeed because they lead the shepherd Ameto to spiritual heights by refining rather than demonizing sensual, earthly joys. Or it might be said that in a form of carnival spirit they merge seemingly contrasting impulses of the soul and the body.

Ameto begins with a two-chapter frame of an unnamed narrator, implied to be a persona for Boccaccio in the concluding dedication.[99] The action of the piece commences with the third chapter, where Ameto, a rude, "vagabond," lively "youth" skilled in hunting is returning from a pleasant day of indulging in this pastime, "laden" "with very plentiful results." Ameto has great pride in his abilities, so he is "exceedingly pleased with himself" when on this day he also finds a bevy of indescribably beautiful nymphs also resting from hunting.[100] As immature, uncouth, and proud as Ameto is, Boccaccio still credits the young man with the potential to recognize his unworthiness in the face of the nymphs' glory. For after seeing the nymphs in their sacred beauty, he "withdr[aws] timidly, and f[alls] on his knees stupefied, not knowing what he should say."[101]

Here, Boccaccio brings in Ovid's tale of the great hunter Actaeon, turned into a stag and torn to shreds by his own hunting dogs as Diana's punishment for viewing her naked. Scholars have interpreted this myth to describe the terrible ineffableness of pure divinity to earthly human comprehension,[102] recalling the fate of the child driven to death or insanity by the unmasked glory of Isis. Baring and Cashford go so far as to point out that the myth's modifying similar images and narrative where the male consort to the goddess is torn asunder in order to fertilize the earth and be reborn as life-giving plants is a clear example of a patriarchal demonizing of the Goddess's vivifying power and sexuality as vindictive, destructive, and irrational.[103]

Indeed, the behavior of the actors in the myth, as retold from the ancient world into Boccaccio's time, seem to portray the dangers of allowing the principle of masculine rationality to be overwhelmed by the demonic female. Actaeon is considered a great hunter,[104] so that his control over the prey he stalks and kills, as well as over his hounds, demonstrates his power over the bestial, the earthly. He is the rational man enjoying power when he controls the bestial aspects outside himself (prey) or within (the dogs he owns). However, when Acteaon tries to spy on, to experience, the feminine Other, he is overwhelmed and loses his power. Artemis/Diana is no longer a giver of life and rebirth through her sexuality, but a destroyer, vicious in her vengeance when unconstrained. Congress with the sensuality, the dark and forbidden knowledge that the feminine embodies, turns Acteaon into the beast he sought to capture; leaves him to be devoured by the beasts within that his separation from the feminine had put under his control. The implication, then, is that there can be no integration of masculine and feminine principles. The lady of the beasts and the wild things, as Artemis and other incarnations of the Great Goddess have been called,[105] will overwhelm and destroy all rationality and order. One may not be able to deny the power and allure of the Goddess's representation of thousands of years of human desire to combine the earthly and the heavenly, the rational, mystical, and passionate; but one can claim that her allure and power is purely demonic. So that only by never looking where one should not, thereby suppressing or avoiding any emanation of her, will one avert chaos.

This interpretation of Actaeon's destruction by Diana undergirded masculine projections of woman as embodying the threatening, uncontrolled Other through the millennia. There is Aristotle's definition of woman as an amorphous being whose sexuality and mentality need outside control to keep her influence from overwhelming the social order with her chaos. There is the early Christian Patriarchs' depiction of Eve condemning Adam and all humanity to suffering and disorder because her weak intellect rendered her easily swayed by Satan into using her sexual and verbal allure to seduce Adam away from the rational and moral guidance of the masculine deity. There is Saint Paul's assertion that women's speaking or teaching religion is not merely foolish but blasphemous, requiring strong husbands to silence and guide them. As already discussed, there is also the

Christian teaching that sacredness in women is exemplified by the modesty in sexuality, action, and words of the Virgin Mary. This interpretation predominated in the patriarchal structure of Boccaccio's medieval Europe and beyond.

Surprisingly, Boccaccio does not adopt this mainstream approach to the myth of Actaeon and Artemis/Diana. In his revision of the myth, which substitutes Ameto and the nymphs of Venus for Acteaon and Diana, Boccaccio is not interested in showing how humanity's earthly desires degrade us. Instead, his female incarnations of divinity treat their "Actaeon" with clemency and reason. The nymphs' dogs scent Ameto and corner him, but the nymphs call off their animals and welcome the young man into their circle.[106] Significantly, it is the female forms of divinity who take control of the dogs to save Ameto. Significantly, it will also be these female forms of divinity who will enable Ameto to escape an animalistic preoccupation with purely earthly values, but not by alienating the sensual from the spiritual. As agents of Venus, lesser incarnations of her divinity, these nymphs will gradually prepare Ameto for communion with her through the course of the romance by teaching him that the sensual and spiritual can intertwine to uplift the soul. Boccaccio's depiction of the nymphs in the tales they tell Ameto will reveal that separating the earthly from the spiritual does not always give omnipotence to the latter while eliminating the former.

Still, Boccaccio's pastoral romance is not just a return to worshipping the Great Goddesses but an attempt within the context of a Christian culture to recreate an ancient fusion, to heal the wound of psyche and soul, "the separation of the spirit from matter that took place in antiquity,"[107] discussed by De Shong Meador, Campbell, and Baring and Cashford. In this equalizing and blending of spirit and body can also be perceived a carnivalesque attempt at creating revelation and vitality by embracing ambivalence without too violently overthrowing traditional order. So, although Ameto "recall[s] Acteon [*sic*]" and "f[eels] his head for horns,"[108] the transformation he will eventually undergo is spiritual, not physical, strengthening and elevating, not destructive.

Of Venus's nymphs in this romance, their leader Lia stands out as Ameto's guide. She is the first nymph to attract Ameto's devotion; and, although the other nymphs provide stories to teach him, she mediates his interaction with them to facilitate the gradual evolution of his soul so that he may eventually face the divinity of Venus, whom she leads him to. Of significance to the female pastoral guide, Lia possesses specific traits, inherited from the heroines of classical romance, on which future guides will rely to direct their charges toward inner and social harmony. These earlier heroines' redefinition of purity to empower rather than enchain women is reflected in Lia's ability to assuage fears about women's uncontrolled sexuality. The ability of ancient romance's heroines to use wit and initiative to create or unravel riddles that ultimately lead to truth and justice become her ability to teach and heal through play and/or trial, based on a deep understanding of human nature. These early romance heroines' link to divine protectresses such as Isis, Venus, Artemis, or even Thekla's Christian God is reflected in Lia's connection to Christian faith and in Venus's sanctification of her work.

Later versions of the guide will adapt these traits to reflect their creators' different views on how to address anxieties about the feminine Other, but Boccaccio's Lia still provides a decided, essential link between the heroines of the romances of late antiquity and the sixteenth- and seventeenth-century female pastoral guides. There is, however, a notable difference between Lia and the heroines of early romances: her predecessors were not guides. Perhaps with the exception of Lycanaeon and the nymphs of *Daphnis and Chloe*, the earlier heroines faced adventures and untangled or offered protective riddles as co-mates with their lovers on their journeys, albeit as sometimes shrewder co-mates. However, Lia sets a precedent by taking charge from the start, living to heal the spiritual inadequacies of Ameto; this is the essential point that sets her as the foremother of six-teenth- and seventeenth-century female pastoral guides.

Lia embodies the first trait of the guide, redefining purity as reconcilia-tion of the physical and the spiritual, and that trait informs her other traits. Ameto starts out drawn mainly to Lia's physical beauty, yet this early superficial attraction paves the way for divine inspiration. Lia's "eyes . . . had the power to drag [Ameto] from [his] shadows," raising his soul from darkness toward light; and he, consequently, begins to change his life to direct his abilities to please her.[109] Lia, herself, explains that the power of her love to inspire and enlighten emerges from her ability to fuse pas-sion and pleasure with the spiritual: "Whoever deems to open the eyes of his heart to my countenance and bind me with love through his virtue, to him I will offer that delight which is most cherished by lovers, when desire is strong and burning. Nor will he ever know bitterness because of me, if he will seek my beauty with wisdom, as it has already been sought by those whom I brought to their deserts."[110] Here, Lia portrays herself as a guide to "wisdom" that is not mutually exclusive of "delight"; she inspires spiritual sanctity by requiring lovers to prove their "virtue" and "deserts" through encouraging not suppressing passion, "desire that is strong and burning."[111]

Similarly, when Lia explains that her love is neither the self-centered, laziness of her brother, Narcissus, nor the besotted obsession of his unre-quited admirer, Echo, she still does not separate the earthly from the spiritual: "To flee from idleness I visit the sylvan gods, and I rush with my chorus to places that were unknown to him [Narcissus]; indeed, that which was hard and harsh in him—love and the art of pleasing others—is dear to me and more welcome than anything else." She is saying that her love's altruistic involvement with others does not merely exist on a spiritual plane. Instead, the "love and the art of pleasing others" occur in union with the physical joy of "rush[ing] . . . to places that were unknown" and "flee[ing]" to the natural abode of "sylvan gods."[112] In carnival mode, Lia reorganizes the hierarchy of spirit over body into a horizontal plane where both interconnect with and enrich each other.

The conclusion of Lia's self-portrait even suggests how her reconciliation of the earthly and the spiritual will inform future female pastoral guides' interactions with their charges: "My art, along with subtle understanding, gave me the name Lia; and I rule this place, more worthy than any other of my beauty, bright with that fire in which all Mount Cytherea burns; and it is that fire that moves me to make feast with play and to serve the loving goddess."[113] Lia's "art" and "subtle understanding" are the groundwork for the guide's ability to draw on a deep insight into human and divine nature in order to know how to direct her life and to instruct and inspire others to follow her lead. Setting a precedent for even priestess or mage guides, Lia is inspirited by the Divine, "bright with that fire in which all Mount Cytherea burns." Nevertheless, that "fire" does not burn away her pleasure in earthly delights but sanctifies them, "mov[ing her] to make feast with play and to serve the loving goddess."

Still, Lia is not the verbally, sexually fierce and socially disruptive symbolic woman as carnivalesque abuser described by Bakhtin. This representative of Venus sets the pattern for future female pastoral guides as a gentler, if not always gentle, adaptation of the female comic abuser. For one thing, though Lia exhibits an unconventionally happy freedom from masculine control of her wit and body, she is not presented as entirely at odds with Christian tradition. Judith Serafini-Sauli notes that this nymph can also be said to personify "Christian Faith." Citing that the nymph's name means "river," Serafini-Sauli explains that Lia "is born of a river (Cephissus) symbolizing baptism, and unlike her brother, Narcissus, she knows how to love and to bring her lovers, among them Ameto, to eternal joy."[114] Appropriately, it is Lia, who "plunges [Ameto] in a 'clear font'" after he has renounced a self-centered worldview that blinds him to the connections between earthly love and divine love.[115] Emphasizing this connection is her song at the conclusion of her instructive tale and at Ameto's acceptance into her community of Venus's faithful devotees. Not only does this song include the main articles of Christian faith asserted in the Apostle's Creed, but its expression of those articles of faith at Ameto's baptism emulates the recitation of the Creed after a Christian baptism.[116] In Lia, physical beauty and pleasure, then, are not portrayed as separate from spiritual joy and transcendence.

To teach Ameto, Lia sets a precedent for later pastoral guides such as Felicia, Rosalind, and Helena in wielding a firm but still gentle, almost decorous, version of carnival's enlightening abuse in the forms of mockery, thrashings, and humiliations. She allows Ameto to bask in the beauty of the nymphs, share in their hunts, and listen to their songs, all the while emphasizing the importance of service and fidelity in a lover.[117] Then she parts from him during the winter months, leaving him to pine and "rightfully curse" their separation, so that he develops fortitude and faith for never doubting that she will return to him in the spring.[118] Their reunion in the spring increases both the difficulty of his trials and the pleasure of his rewards for passing them. Lia brings Ameto together with seven other nymphs during a noontime respite from the heat during a sacred pastoral celebration. Here, she proposes that each nymph recount her autobiography, not merely to while away time, but because "we do not pass the clear day idly."[119] Delight and instruction, sentence and solas combine. In her plan is to teach Ameto to understand more about the true nature of divine love,[120] Lia organizes the nymphs' tales so that each conveys a virtue that builds upon the others to teach Ameto the inner harmony necessary to approach divinity.[121] Significantly, the lessons Ameto learns come not from Christian patriarchs but from nymphs, each of whom is associated both with a goddess and a Christian virtue: Mopsa, Wisdom/Pallas; Emilia, Justice/Diana; Adiona, Temperance/Pomona; Acrimonia, Fortitude/Bellona; Agape, Charity/Venus; and Fiametta, Hope/Ariadne.[122]

Anthony Cassell and Victoria Kirkham write that in each autobiography the allegorical nymph accepts a lover representing "the contrary vice she conquers" in herself.[123] However, a deeper understanding of the relationships between the nymphs and their lovers is necessary to elucidate how their choices become, instead of adultery, an example of ancient romance's interpretation of purity as not lack of sexual knowledge, or even of experience, but of treating that knowledge or experience as sacred. In carnival vein, the force of life in sexuality is to be cherished, delighted in—although in this romance, one may not delight too much. First, in *Ameto* each woman's vow of chastity, or earthly marriage, actually stands for a wedding to earthly or material values, ironically undercutting the belief that alienating the earthly from the spiritual will create superior, pristine, transcendent beings. Fiametta's marriage is founded on serving her husband's and her parents' expectations.[124] Mopsa's and Emilia's marriages are based on their parents' desire for children to carry on their names and power. Agape's and Acrimonia's are both based on their parents' desire for money and position. Distinguishing her from Agape, Acrimonia's "fidelity" is not so much to her husband as to her pride, callousness, and love of power over others. On the other hand, Agape's old, impotent husband's disgusting, punishing infliction of sex on her portrays this marriage as based on a preoccupation with sex for its own sake.[125] These marriages represent the prospect that separating the earthly and the spiritual may result in humans choosing the earthly over the heavenly. In other words, the marriages symbolize that rather than purifying, oppressive dogmas may push humans to escape to equally repressive dogmas based on the very traits the original sought to eradicate. Instead of producing the expected spiritual transcendence, this split creates obsessions with solely material values of money, power, social standing, pride, and sex.

In a dizzying reversal, turning the world upside down, when marriage represents commitment to the earthly alone, adultery becomes sacred rather than sinful. The nymphs' lovers actually draw them into an altruistic devotion to divine love. For example, Acrimonia becomes less proud and egocentric through her devotion to a youth she has previously scorned; Agape is freed from a degrading sexual love, completely divorced from the spiritual; and Mopsa learns to replace pride and egocentric independence with humility and devotion to others.[126] Perhaps most important, the conclusion of each nymph's biography focuses on a lovely carnivalesque ambivalence: merging the earthly pleasures of love with the spiritual delight of mutual service in mutual giving.

Agape's tale, mentioned above, is a particularly interesting example of how a nymph is translated to spiritual transcendence through extramarital love in *Ameto* and so merits deeper discussion. This nymph is married to an old man obsessed with sex. The inanity and unnaturalness of the old husband with the young bride is a staple of medieval literature.[127] However, in the greater context of *Ameto*, Agape's story can also be interpreted as a critique of abstracting the spiritual aspect from sex. The impotent old man can be interpreted as an incarnation of the selfish, brutish "fruitlessness" of preoccupation with only the physical aspects of love. Or even what Bakhtin calls the life force that has become "finished, completed, and exhausted."[128] Creating a family cannot truly be part of the old man's scheme because his "old ploughshare," "eroded by age" cannot penetrate his wife, let alone impregnate her. Further, his selfish torturing of his wife, "without any consolation for [her]," in "distasteful leaps and unseemly acts" shows that self-gratification is his only consideration. Such love ultimately leaves one lover frustrated and the other degraded.[129]

To save herself, Agape prays to Venus for a lover to "compensat[e] with delight" her "ill-spent nights," even lusting a little after Cupid,[130] but what Venus gives her is not merely a lover but a chance to experience and understand sex as sacred, spiritually uplifting. As Venus explains: "We give [Apiros] to you as sole and unique servant; he has no defect other than that of our fires, which have just been ignited within him for you; and you must secure that they are nourished, so that they will chase from his heart the coldness that makes him resemble Aglauros and make him similar to our great Jove."[131] Warmed by the fires of Agape/Charity, the young man will be inspired to achieve greatness through good. Conversely, choosing this young man over the husband, when one considers their allegorical significance, is not actually choosing adultery over fidelity. Instead, in "refus[ing] the cold embraces of [her] aged husband," Agape/Charity rejects the coldness, sterility, depravity of selfish sexuality. By, instead, "enjoying those of the youth in whom I had brought back a bright red color,"[132] Charity is redirected to an object of fruitful, joyous giving. Here is a gentle, but still passionate and vitalizing, version of carnival's woman whose "sacred" symbolic cuckolding is a form of comic abuse that destroys "stupidity" and "sterile senility" and undermines "all that is finished, completed, and exhausted"[133] in order to heal and regenerate individuals.

Similarly, in all these symbolic tales of the nymphs and their lovers, their unions are not equated with a corrupt, fallen world but instead illustrate the soul's liberation and evolution toward the transcendent joy of reconciling earthly and spiritual love. The romance also definitely shows this spiritual evolution coming to Ameto as he first meets and follows Lia, then gradually changes his understanding as he listens to each successive nymph's story. As the first nymphs begin their stories, Ameto focuses on the physical beauties of each speaker, sometimes almost to the point of missing the moral of her hymn at her story's close.[134] Initially, his reaction to the stories is to lament enviously that he could not enjoy the physical and emotional pleasures of each nymph, since he proudly considers himself the equal of her selected lover.[135] However, his attitude gradually starts to change, incorporating the wisdom, sense of justice, temperance, and fortitude of the nymphs that enable them to harmonize the spiritual and the physical. After the teachings of the previous six nymphs, Ameto now is "rather remote from his former thoughts" and has so "varied his reflections"[136] that he is ready for the final tale of Fiametta, Hope.

Fiametta's story does not engender hope of only sexual fulfillment or of only spiritual joy, but a carnivalesque chimeric fusion of the two. Looking at Lia, considering the lessons she had instructed the nymphs/ Virtues to teach him, Ameto "feel[s] . . . rich in her grace, with his mind fixed upon her." Now, after being readied for complete translation by these tales, Ameto approaches Lia with "pious words" and "humble prayers that she speak [to him] as the others had done,"[137] that she teach him with her story. Her tale ends with her pronouncing Ameto "uncouth" but with noble potential "carr[ying] him with [her] light from spiritual blindness to a knowledge of worthy matters, . . . mak[ing] him willing to pursue these." Lia asserts her success with the words, "He no longer seems rough and coarse if one considers well; instead, he appears able, gentle, and disposed to lofty goals."[138] Ameto proves her assessment correct with his ability to recognize and embrace the divine as well as physical aspect of love embodied in Venus.[139]

Lia, then, guides Ameto from a fallen-world split of heavenly and earthly, male and female to the rapturous harmony of divine love. At the conclusion of the nymphs' tales, Ameto rather than feeling his devotion torn amongst them and Lia,[140] sees his love of their beauties increasing his adoration and understanding of Lia/Christian Faith.[141] Only when he has been guided to embrace Christian Faith because he perceives the true nature of its beauty and delight can he attain the sacred transcendence of Divine Christian love, embodied unexpectedly enough in Venus. Then again, as the illuminated and uplifted Ameto points out, only "fools" or the unperceptive mistake "disordered lust" for Venus.[142]

These nymphs' methods for guiding their lovers and Lia's for guiding Ameto set an important precedent for future guides. In this paradigm, the relationship between the guide and her charges stresses that although she is powerful and attractive, she does not force change on others but inspires them to make the choice to accept her guidance. Adapting Lia's tactics, the guide of later pastorals works with methods strongly rooted in carnival. Using methods both pleasing and trying as Lia did, the guide draws on carnival abuse to cure them with laughter. And by, like Lia, not merely instructing her charges but using trials and rewards to inspire them to think for themselves, the guide gives them the power to break through the dogmatisms that blind and suffocate them. As later chapters will show, though, a writer might co-opt carnival methods to impose decidedly uncarnivalesque views.

IV

Lia and her allegorical nymphs are not the only guides with sacred powers in *Ameto*. The most important guide of all and the most powerful divinity is Venus, a character whom critics have dubbed a symbol for "divine love" or "God's grace and love."[143] Cassell and Kirkham point out that in *Ameto*, Boccaccio rewrites the roguish, promiscuous Venus of classical and medieval literature, especially Ovid's *Metamorphoses*,[144] but their assessment of her implies that she does not so much reconcile the sensual with the spiritual as give reason a tight rein over passion. Furthermore, these two critics, in addition to Judith Serafini-Sauli, perceive Boccaccio's re-characterization of Venus in *Ameto* and in *Diana's Hunt* as colored by Dante's portrait of Mary as not only an intercessor for humankind with God but an incarnation of God's divine love.[145]

The similarities between the Virgin Mary and Venus are especially important, for they will reverberate through adaptations of various pre-Christian goddesses in later pastorals as well as in a British Reformation adaptation of the Virgin Mary in Elizabeth I. Venus, herself, had a tradition of being viewed as an intercessor since the third century BCE.[146] So it is not surprising that Boccaccio would draw on this role to link her with the Virgin Mary. Yet this is not exactly the characterization he emphasizes. This distinction reveals a carnivalesque revision of Marian divinity into a form of the woman on top embodying the grotesque's undoing of boundaries and hierarchy. Still, *Ameto*'s Venus possesses some important distinctions from the Christian holy virgin mother whom Danté calls the "Rose in which the Word became incarnate."[147] For unlike the Christian Mary, the sacredness of Boccaccio's Venus does not reside in her unadulterated spirituality. Although Boccaccio's Venus also dispenses divine compassion and grace to humans, she is far more than a conduit between pre-eminent masculine divinity and humanity. Instead, without completely excluding Christian influence, she recreates what Baring and Cashford describe as the ancient goddesses' "sacred marriage"[148] of oppositions by fusing masculine and feminine deity within herself. In other words, she is a striking embodiment of carnival's beautiful, unifying grotesque, a fusion of opposites underlying her power.

Where Danté must look beyond the Virgin to be "subsumed in" the "dazzling splendor" of the Divine "Ray," God, Boccaccio has Ameto proclaim that he has found Danté's "Light Supreme"[149] in Venus, herself, "Oh sacred deity, sole light likewise of the heavens and the earth, if you bend to any prayer, gaze within me, and by your holy and ineffable triform name, come and grant your valuable aid; and may the eternal hand confirm the grace I ask. Here is my soul . . . which up to this day, whose memory will never fail me, has been ignited by a fire that is gracious and pleasing above all things . . . consumed by seven flames [Christian virtues]. [T]hey spur me with the most fervent desire to dissolve myself and to dwell with you."[150] In this passage, Venus incorporates within herself Christian symbolism of the patriarchal God, for the reference to a "triform name" evokes the Holy Trinity of Father, Son, and Holy Spirit. She wields the "seven flames" of Christian virtues to "consume" Ameto.

In another passage, Venus even more emphatically proclaims that she contains all aspects of Christian deity within herself; unlike Mary she does not merely serve as a link to God:

> I am the light of the sky, one and triune, the beginning and ending of all things; pray, what was ever equal to me or ever will be? And so true and gracious a light am I, that he who follows me will never go erring in a sad or shadowy place, but in happiness he will follow me to the angelic rays in

eternal blessings, which are reserved for him from the time I created them. For those who speak of me, keeping their mind on the heavenly good with a sincere heart, and scorning the world and modern matters—which have power to draw pure souls into error—I am always with them, enflaming them ever more with my ardor. Therefore for you, Oh gracious chorus, may there always be peace, and may you dwell free of care; do not be frightened by my sonorous arrival or the bright light in these dark places.[151]

Venus's self-description is rich with biblical allusions to the Christian God in all His three forms. She is "one and triune," reflecting the concept of the Holy Trinity as a whole. Other references in this passage reveal her fusion with the individual members of the Trinity. "[T]he bright light in these dark places" strongly echoes John's description of the mergence of God the Father and the Son in "In him was life, and the life was the light of men. And the light shines in the darkness; and the darkness grasped it not." "[T]he beginning and ending of all things" similarly recalls John's description of the eternal nature of existence inherent to God the Father and the Son,[152] as does Venus's reference to universal creation. The promise of guidance in "sad or shadowy place" harkens back to the 23rd Psalm. "For those who speak of me. . . . I am always with them" recalls the promise of Jesus Christ's "[f]or where two or three are gathered together for my sake, there am I in the midst of them."[153] Finally, the ecstatic inspiration of the Holy Spirit is reflected in "enflaming them with my ardor." Thus, where Mary is a bridge to God, Venus is the Divine Love, Ultimate Good.

This is an intriguing variation on carnival's version of the world turned upside down by the woman now on top. Patriarchal divinity and priests do not control and direct her. She shapes Ameto and her other charges. They learn because female divinity is in control. In addition, Venus's subsuming the Holy Trinity within herself makes her a powerful incarnation of carnival's life-giving grotesque. Female not only merges with male but contains all three aspects of male divinity in unity within herself to enlighten, uplift, and vitalize her dedicated followers.

Indeed, in *Ameto* that very embracing of the ambivalence of mind and body, spirit and passion makes Venus's influence on her followers so sacred. In Boccaccio's romance, individuals actually find their spiritual salvation in being passionately set afire by Venus. As touched on earlier, Emilia feels Venus "[enter] with her flames," while Diana still accepts her as an acolyte of chastity and justice. Acrimonia feels herself "light up with licking flames from my feet to the top of my head . . . , [that] gathered in my spirit, where they reassured me, together with the comforting goddess."[154] Ameto is so inflamed with love of his sacred goddess that he cries out: "These flames [of Christian Virtue] do not suck my blood and do not diminish the power of my soul . . . , they spur me with most fervent desire to dissolve myself and to dwell with you. And therefore I beg that you make the loves that I have taken up indivisible and long-lived, without any offense from Fortune or the heavens, and that they may show their loveliness in me, just as today they have happily showed it to capture me."[155] The Ameto speaking here is not overwhelmed by lust, has not lost his senses to the Venus of legend who leads humanity away from reason and peace, though he does use the language of sexual ecstasy, "to dissolve myself and to dwell with you." On the other hand, although Ameto speaks of spiritual uplifting, "these flames [of Christian Virtue] do not suck my blood and do not diminish the power of my soul," it only comes in conjunction with venerating the physical beauties of the nymphs/Virtues: "I beg that you make the loves that I have taken up indivisible and long-lived. . . . and that they may show their loveliness in me, just as today they have happily showed it to capture me." Passionate language reveals a fusion of emotion and spirit inspiring and uplifting the speaker.

Particularly important, the way Venus saves and requires worship reflects a reconciling of the earthly and the spiritual. She is more tender than carnival usually requires or her society would expect of a woman with power, is merciful rather than vengeful. When a proud youth uses his talents self-destructively, Venus does not condemn him but blesses him with the virtue of Justice (Emilia) to teach him to use his talents to help himself and others. When unconditional love or Charity (Agape) is degraded by lustful, possessive sexuality, she answers the nymph's plea for fulfilling salvation by bringing a lover who will enable the girl to give of herself productively, unselfishly. When a youth is scorned by Acrimonia (Fortitude), he pleads with Venus either to make the nymph love him or at least teach her pity by making her love someone as unrequitedly and humiliatingly as he had loved Acrimonia. Then, rather than humiliating Acrimonia by saddling her with a degrading lover, Venus charges the nymph to improve the swain and give this young man help he did not realize he needed.[156] In all these cases, Venus is a guide and spiritual healer who has created the opportunity for moral and emotional happiness through physical love in communion with the spiritual. Thus, her reconciliation of the psychic split transforms harshness, cruelty, pride, frustration, or weakness into Justice, Fortitude, and Charity, achieving the social and psychic rebirth promised by carnival's turning the world upside.

By directing the heroines of ancient romances' sacredness, wit, independence, and insight into choosing to make well humans wounded in heart and soul, Boccaccio's *Ameto* creates a variation of an older tradition that will grow and flourish in the form of the female pastoral guide, as either a wise woman/mage or a goddess. Like Lia, the mortal guides will strive to use pleasure and trial to move their charges to a deeper understanding of themselves and their place in their societies. Also like her, they will use a deep insight into human nature to judge how best to inspire. And equally important, they will leave the ultimate choice of accepting or rejecting their lessons, their medicines (psychological and physical) to those charges. Similarly, the divine guides will follow Venus in possessing great power over the supernatural, natural, and human to enlighten and heal charges, who must choose for themselves whether to accept their blessings. And, as with Ameto, the nature of illness or misery in the later guides' charges frequently centers on gender relations, on some level harking back to the problems radiating out of projecting onto women anxieties about a patriarchal society's inability to truly order the world on a natural, social, or personal level. However, although later pastorals may portray a female guide who challenges the fear of women's verbal and sexual modesty, few veer quite so far away from traditional views as Boccaccio does with Venus and the nymphs.

Even when later pastoral plays deal in secular love, this love must accommodate the Renaissance value of balancing reason and feeling. The mage's magic should not completely subvert Christian or political order, and though wit may criticize, generally, wit ought not exert itself with the complete passion and freedom that Bakhtin claims carnival grants to women's voices and bodies. The next two foundation texts, *Arcadia* and *Diana* carry this development into themes that will be the concerns of the Renaissance pastoral dramas. These texts transfer uplifting power to secular love, either in personal or political terms, even when they take supernatural form. Especially important, in shifting the focus from the goddess figure toward a learned, but human, guide, both texts reflect a tendency in the contemporary social order to try to make less threatening the power that patriarchal societies associate with the sexual, outspoken, unbounded woman. To understand how these texts do so, it is necessary to examine how medieval and Renaissance cultures dealt with the frightening, disruptive side of the Great Goddess. With the exaltation of obedience, tenderness, piety, humility, and silence in the Virgin Mary and Ceres, the negative aspect does not disappear but is displaced by society onto the female in the form of the witch.

2

Mages and Sages Versus the Witch

I

AS NOTED IN THE PREVIOUS CHAPTER, BETTY DE SHONG Meador asserts that Western cultures developed a "dark/light oppositional mentality" that split "good and evil[,]" "with Satan over there, in others."[1] One of the most threatening of the "others" was its female supernatural incarnation. In other words, veneration of the Virgin Mary as divine, gentle, loving mother did not erase the "dark" half of the female Other. Instead, the "dark" female Other came to manifest itself in beliefs in the witch as a supernatural root cause of misfortune in medieval and Renaissance life under the direction of the greatest of Others, Satan. Though Bakhtin describes the enlivening chaos of carnival as providing hope and release to those lowest in the hierarchies of power, medieval and Renaissance people also had very real fear of actual chaos in health, personal relations, politics, nature, and economics. Projecting their fears onto a supernatural figure that they could fight and try to control provided them with some psychic security. So, to some extent the lower as well as higher strata of society could well view carnival's disruption as a force to be feared and contained in the form of the supernatural, especially the witch.

These beliefs exert a powerful influence on the development of the female guide in Renaissance pastoral. To see how the witch came to be read as the dark female Other and how this role shaped the formation of the female pastoral guide, this chapter will first study medieval and Renaissance thought on the power of the supernatural over daily life, then explore how such fears of the witch's supernatural disruptive powers converged with similar anxieties over the uncontrolled female Other, especially in terms of garrulity and sexuality. After this background is established, the chapter will delve into how the female pastoral guides' wielding magic wisely and lovingly to heal breaches of social order is a literary attempt to assuage or even contradict fears of female agency symbolized by the witch's dangerous, demonic exercise of power.

In general, recent studies have found that sixteenth- and seventeenth-century beliefs concerning the supernatural reflect attempts both to understand and to conquer contemporary anxieties. Keith Thomas explains that early-modern humanity lived in "an intensely insecure environment" of debilitating and incurable injury or illness, unexpected death, crop and livestock failure, calamitous weather, devastating fires, and chaotic political, religious, and social shifts in power.[2] Individuals armed themselves against powerlessness and despair with the belief that both good and evil supernatural forces shaped weather, fire, and personal and political fate, thus answering the "need to explain misfortune as more than the result of chance or incompetence."[3] If, at St. Osyth in 1582, butter should not turn, yeast should not rise, cows should give blood, children's hands should rotate palm inward, or "hogs [should] skip and leap about the yard in a strange sort" there was a cause—and once a cause was identified it could be counteracted.[4]

Whether in the form of Christian dogma, astrology, prophecy, or conjuring, mortal attempts to understand or even to wield supernatural powers were a way for medieval and early-modern humans to protect themselves psychologically by giving meaning and order to an uncertain world, as well as a feeling that they could take control of it.[5] Thus, supernatural forces could be called upon for protection against Satan, other witches, or even human enemies. Several instances illustrate this belief particularly well. One could call on village cunning men and women to reverse the curses on children, crops, livestock, and oneself.[6] Carlo Ginzburg relates that the benandanti of Friuli, Italy, described themselves as battling the evil witches in Night Battles to save the crops of their lands.[7] Lay people and clergy would work in conjunction to protect crops from supernaturally driven threats: ringing church bells to drive off hail and thunder storms,[8] blessing houses with holy water "to drive away the evil spirits in the air,"[9] or blessing the fields during specific holidays of the agricultural calendar.[10] Individuals might also attempt to wield magic. Diane Purkiss writes that women who believed their spinning, churning, brewing, or dairy production had been bewitched might attempt to reverse the curse through practicing sympathetic magic, for example purifying the products of their housewifery with red hot metal objects.[11]

Such belief that humans could wield supernatural power was not limited to only the peasantry. Elite, learned Neoplatonists such as Marcilio Ficino, Pico della Mirandola, Cornelius Agrippa, Roger Bacon, and John Dee, ranging across the centuries and across Europe, sought to manipulate the spirits directing this world, peer into the future, shift the form of matter, and understand and define the universe through the study of alchemy, astrology, and necromancy. Most of these individuals did not see themselves as working with dark powers contrary to God's laws. As John Mebane puts it, they believed just the opposite, that they "should strive to imitate God and to become co-workers with Him. . . . To realize [their] divine potential [they] must, like God, exercise [their] powers in creative acts through which [they] reproduce in the external world the perfection [they] have come to see within [their] own minds."[12] These mages developed their powers by purifying their earthly flaws with a regimen of self-discipline, such as "a rigorous course of prayer, fasting and devotional preparation" to enable themselves to approach divine perfection and consequently divine knowledge. As Keith Thomas clarifies, their desire was not at all to aggrandize themselves, to set themselves above God: "For many, this was no mechanical manipulation of set formulae, but a humble supplication that God should extend to them the privilege of a unique view of his mysteries. 'The art of magic,' wrote Sir Walter Raleigh, 'is the art of worshipping God.'"[13] These mages believed that perfecting human intellectual and spiritual powers by better understanding creation and how to control it allowed them to honor God by fully developing humanity's divinely granted capability to become like God.

Though Sir Walter Raleigh may have claimed that the mage approached God in "humble supplication," Catholic and Protestant Churches alike saw such pursuits as too closely paralleling Satan's hubristic ambition for power and Adam and Eve's transgressive desire for power and knowledge. Consequently, the churches worried over and fought against what they perceived in the mage's philosophy as a dangerous erosion of their authority and as a delusive egotism that would leave the aspiring mage prey to Satan.[14] Giordano Bruno was condemned by Catholic divine Jean Bodin and Anglican divine William Perkins[15] and executed. Pico della Mirandola and Marsilio Ficino each had his own run-in with the Church Inquisitions.[16] Jean Bodin even "explicitly accuse[d] Giovanni Pico [della Mirandola] and Cornelius Agrippa of witchcraft."[17] John Dee found himself ostracized from James I's court, and Walter Raleigh became the center of uneasy controversies concerning his occult interests.[18] The murderous plots of Dr. Lambe gave ammunition to the religious who saw Neoplatonism as a self-deluding lapse into Satan's power.[19]

Individuals of all levels of class or education found hope of protecting themselves from a chaotic universe by drawing on the supernatural to predict when catastrophes might occur. From the poorer classes up through the educated elite, people turned to horoscopes to predict the general or immediate future.[20] Belief in astrology's power to predict was so strong that casting the Queen's horoscope, including the time of her death, was considered seditious. The statute AD 1580–1.23 Elizabeth c.2 set the penalty for doing so as "death and [forfeit] . . . without any benefit of clergy or sanctuary."[21] Predictions drawn from the interpretations of biblical passages, seers of various religious sects, and arcane proverbs were also perceived as a way of predicting political or religious vagaries.[22] This belief in supernatural powers directing humanity and its environment gave people a picture of the world as ordered, if not always hospitable, and so subject to control.

The supernatural also helped humans to explain the shifts in the religious and social/political environment. Peter Elmer's observation that Puritans and Royalists "sought to depict the conflict as a struggle . . . between the forces of good and evil, order and disorder, God and the devil"[23] can be applied to some extent to the major religious struggles of both the sixteenth and seventeenth centuries. As Keith Thomas and Barbara Rosen[24] both point out, each of the major sects vying for power in these centuries laid charges of witchcraft and association with Satan at the doors of its rivals. Protestants, Anglican or Puritan, associated the Roman Catholic Church with political, social, and moral disorder firmly linked to Satan, the supreme purveyor of chaos, directly opposed to the perfection of God's natural order. The Printer's Preface to *The Examination of John Walsh* (1566) vividly conveys this view of the Roman Catholic Church as loosing Satanic moral degeneration, even national chaos, on the world: "thou mayest see the fruits of Papists and Papistry, and their ill exercises of their idle lives, which hath been no small hurt to all commonweals. For hereby not only the simple people have been falsely seduced and superstitiously led, but all estates have been sore grieved and troubled by these their practices of sorcery and witchcraft."[25] Further, Anglicans and Puritans both linked the Roman Church's use of ritual and Latin incantations with pagan rituals and incantations.

The English Protestants had additional reason to see the Church of Rome as in league with the Prince of Chaos: fear of Catholic plots (real and imagined) to overthrow English church and state. Protestants could point to such cases as the Jesuit-backed stratagems of Thomas Campion against Elizabeth as well as the Gunpowder Plot against James and Parliament. One 1595 pamphlet detailed the death through bewitchment and/or poisoning of Ferdinando Stanley, Lord Strange, for turning down a plan broached by a Jesuit to "rebel, seize the crown from Elizabeth, and rule as a Catholic king."[26] To Protestant eyes, then, "[t]he Roman Church was," as Gareth Roberts has it, "seductive, glamorous, magical, bestially transforming, poisonous, enfeebling, effeminating."[27]

In the sixteenth and seventeenth centuries, Puritans condemned Anglicans as linked to Satan for similar reasons, especially moral corruption and retention of rituals.[28] On the other hand, Anglicans saw in the Puritans' fasting and conversion experiences a form of demonic possession that mirrored the social disruption their rejection of Anglican religious and political authority threatened.[29] Similarly, Puritans, once in power, attacked Quakers as the new rebels, portraying their meetings in terms of witches' sabbats and their conversions in terms of possessions.[30] Thus, the challenge to one's faith by other religions' claims to divine truth might be turned back on itself by condemning those faiths as Satanic. At the same time, one's own faith could be given greater authority by pronouncing it a divinely sanctioned bastion against social and moral chaos.

The intermingling of both high and low culture shaping sixteenth- and seventeenth-century views on witchcraft reveals the pervasiveness of the fear of it. On the one hand, witchcraft trials could reflect issues most relevant to the elite ruling society: the 1591 trial of the witches accused of plotting the storm to drown the then Scottish King James VI and his bride; the repeated linking of plots against Elizabeth with acts of witchcraft,[31] the connecting of the corruptions of Stuart court with Dr. Lambe and Anne Bodenham,[32] and the trial of Frances Howard and her cunning-woman confederate Anne Turner for the poisoning of Howard's husband and the murder of Overbury.[33] Moving down from national to local politics, Malcolm Gaskill points out that witchcraft accusations, prosecutions, acquittals, and convictions often reflected the shifts of religious and political power within village communities.[34] As high-profile as some cases were, the majority of trials, let alone craze of prosecutions in England (East Anglia, Kent, Chelmsford, St. Osryth) and on the Continent (Ausburg, Friuli), were not provoked by threats to king and State but by issues relevant to the life of peasants and the middle class: failure at housewifery (brewing, dairy work, spinning, cooking); failure at farming and keeping livestock; injury or illness, especially if it left a family without support; illness or death of children; or a threat to an individual's life.

Often witchcraft trials depended on cooperation between classes. As Robin Briggs writes: "A very high proportion of known European witchcraft trials were clearly instigated from below, although this was only possible with the aid of a legal machinery established by the elites, and some degree of interaction between local law enforcers and the general population was commonplace."[35] Especially indicative of how these classes reflexively shaped each other's beliefs are recent scholars' warnings about too sharply differentiating the educated elite's emphasis on diabolical pacts from the lower classes' emphasizing *maleficium* as the source of witchcraft's danger. For example, Jim Sharpe asserts that testimony from the East Anglian witch trials of 1645–47 indicates that "the notion of a polarity between a 'learned', 'continental', and 'demonological' set of beliefs held by the elite and a popular concern with witchcraft which centred on *maleficium* is a gross oversimplification."[36] Sharpe points out that although a major prosecutor like Matthew Hopkins would push for admissions of pacts with Satan, sabbat meetings, and the suckling and commanding of diabolical familiars, all usually associated with educated and Continental traditions, these acts also had analogues in folk traditions. As a result, the trials portray "a jumble of popular and 'educated' beliefs which were mobilised into an agitated interaction by the conditions of a mass witch hunt."[37] However, Diane Purkiss notes that the interaction of high culture prosecutors and low culture accuseds produces more than "a jumble of popular and 'educated' beliefs." Rather, she sees this combination as a carefully worked out synthesis of both perspectives: "Early modern people knew that confession was not a single act, but a series of negotiations between the accuser and the accused, which would gradually result in increasing agreement on the parameters of 'the truth' and eventually would issue in a statement or series of statements as part of the trial evidence. . . . Often the confession retained material unassimilable by the categories of the learned, traces of the agency of witch rather than questioner."[38]

Examples from England and the Continent bear out Purkiss's insight. In the pamphlet, *The Examination of John Walsh* (1566), the examinee exhibits the spirited give and take with his prosecutor that Purkiss describes. He initially refused the insistence of "Master Thomas William (commissary to the reverend father in God William, Bishop of Exeter)" that he must have Satanic familiars, instead asserting that he relies on the more homely British tradition of working with "fairies" that he can only call up "between the hours of 12 and one at noon, or at midnight." Eventually, he was forced to agree he has a familiar but only acknowledged it in forms that, while admitting the Satanic (man with cloven feet), are predominately homely (culver, dog). Even after his confession, he kept insisting that his main aids are the fairies and that "he never did any such hurt [to man, woman, or child] in body or goods."[39] During the Friuli witch trials of benandanti, the Inquisitor Marchetto "yelled at the benandante [*sic*] that 'he considered him to be a real witch, and in no way a benandante [*sic*]; that this term had no meaning, and therefore he had to be a witch'." The accused shepherd "burst" into tears and gave his accuser the story he wanted to hear. However, returning home, the accused revealed his resistance to the identity imposed from above. He told his master that he had been so "outraged" by the denial of his beliefs that he had not revealed "even half of what *he* [emphasis added] knew" to be the truth about his supernatural identity.[40] So, even while deferring publicly, in court, to scholarly theory on witchcraft, these accuseds still maintained either traces of their beliefs in an official forum or reasserted traditional beliefs once free of that setting. Consequently, there is an uneasy but definite co-existence of scholarly and folk belief in social discourse about witchcraft, and this convergence will also shape the portrayal of the female pastoral guide.

The interaction of folk and elite culture in shaping sixteenth- and seventeenth-century views on witchcraft circulates through printed as well as oral discourse. Diane Purkiss points out that although masques and plays were created for the elite, they still drew on popular cultural perceptions of the power of the cunning woman to control nature (elements, fertility, herbs for medicine or poison) and humanity (health, perceptions of reality, love). Popular plays that she discusses such as *The Witch of Edmunton, Macbeth,* and *The Witch* re-circulate the popular traditions to the general public.[41] Sermons and church teachings could bring to the middle and peasant classes ideas derived from elite sources, which listeners might internalize in the context of their own folk beliefs.[42] Robin

Briggs explains that "widespread practice of reading out material from trials at the time of executions" "reinforced" intermingling of "popular and learned notions of witchcraft" in the recorded negotiations between prosecutors and those giving testimony.[43] Further, the intermingling of popular and elite positions on witchcraft in trials was disseminated to a general public of readers and listeners through the highly in-demand tracts, pamphlets, and ballads on notorious witch trials such as those at Chelmsford, Windsor, St. Osyth, East Anglia, and those of Anne Bodenham and of Frances Howard and Anne Turner.[44]

Keith Thomas raises the important question of why witchcraft trials flared so much more frequently in the sixteenth and seventeenth centuries than in previous eras when humans were equally plagued with "the hazards of an intensely insecure environment." Thomas posits that the main "features" "colouring" the "sixteenth- and seventeenth-century environment" were feelings of social guilt peculiar to these centuries.[45] As he explains it, a shift from the manorial social structural of the Middle Ages to one stressing self-reliance and capitalism left the peasantry even more vulnerable in hard times. Although economic, health, or personal disaster certainly plagued earlier eras, protection by a lord granting land to work and live on provided relative security in times of war, crop failure, ill health, or old age. With the more profitable enclosure practices displacing individuals from their only source of livelihood, with landlords indifferent to the welfare of the nonproductive tenants, or with the loss of a lord as safety net for independent farmers in times of trouble, the weak were thrown onto the community at large—their only support in difficult times being their equally vulnerable village neighbors. Thomas raises the point that in an era where most villagers were living at subsistence level, the burden of helping others was frequently too much, forcing them to turn away the old or needy.[46] The double bind of the situation was that the very precariousness of a peasant's security prevented him/her from helping neighbors or doing so more than grudgingly. The more fortunate peasant, aware of how vulnerable his superior situation was, then, saw the needy as painful reminders of how close he/she was to sliding into a similarly parlous situation, or as Thomas writes: "Everyone else had reason to think that today's charity to a neighbour might become tomorrow's charity to oneself."[47] Guilt over being unable to do for others as they would want done for themselves, coupled with their needy neighbors' reminding them of their own vulnerability, could lead more fortunate villagers to displace their anxiety into hostility toward their suffering neighbors. Either in anticipation of their neighbors' justified resentment or in an attempt to feel less guilty when some misfortune seemed a punishment for denying requests for aid, individuals might soothe themselves by charging neighbors with maleficium.[48]

Thomas's successors stress that his emphasis on the guilt factor sparking witchcraft trials needs to be modified in light of other social and political influences. In *Witches and Neighbors*, Robin Briggs concludes that trial transcripts reveal that the guilts and resentments underlying accusations of witchcraft do not merely reflect tensions between neighbors but reveal the stresses within family units: husbands and wives, children and parents.[49] Even more important, Purkiss, Briggs, Roper, and Hester conclude that Thomas's failure to connect gender conflicts with the guilt and anxiety-inspiring charges of maleficium misses a vital component. To be fair, Thomas does not entirely ignore the predominance of women as accuseds. He does, however, only see their majority evidencing that they were poorer than men, without considering that the social and legal restrictions put on women as workers and owners of property because they are women reduce them more frequently than men to poverty.[50] More recent analyses of British and Continental patterns of witch persecutions reveal that the anxieties prompting witch accusations, the very nature of most accusations of maleficium, and connections between women's social roles and their roles as accusers and accuseds all reflect the powerful influence of tense gender relations in their times.

Many more recent critics provide valuable insights into how gender relations shaped witchcraft perceptions and persecutions during the era under study. Revising Thomas's views on the importance of guilt underlying witchcraft perceptions, Briggs, Purkiss, and Roper conclude that much of this guilt was tied into the roles assigned to women by contemporary society. Briggs points out that transcripts of witch trials reveal projection onto the accused witches the guilt of the patriarchal authorities conducting the trials, as well as women's uneasiness about not being able to live up to the definitions of womanhood set by that authority.[51] Focusing on several sixteenth- and seventeenth-century trials, Diane Purkiss similarly observes that most accusations centered on the witch's destructiveness as a type of unnatural anti-mother: her power to destroy children, cut off the milk supply in humans and animals, and to suckle unnatural familiars on blood from oddly, even "foully," placed teats.[52] She concludes that the repeated focus on these forms of destruction indicates that society's anxieties do not stem from guilt over not supporting dependent adults but from patriarchal fears concerning women's failure to fulfill the expected role of nurturing mother.[53]

Purkiss furthers Briggs's conclusions by noting that the guilt is also shaped by women's own fears that they cannot fulfill the role society has assigned them. Most obviously, charges of attacks of witchcraft by bereaved mothers enable women to displace their guilt onto an unnatural "anti-mother" when they cannot protect their children in an environment of high infant and child mortality.[54] Thus, Richard Saunders's wife blames

Mother Staunton's resentment over "denied yeast" as the identifiable and combatable cause for her child suddenly "to [have] take[n] vehemently sick" and for its "cradle to [have] rock[ed]" several times on its own.[55] This explains the charges brought against Jean Pelisson, Barbelline Antoine, and Marye Sotterel by mothers trying to "defen[d] their children" against "a witch's resentment."[56] In such cases, Purkiss argues that women's accusations of witchcraft spring not only from concern over the physical danger to their children but from fear of what their failure to protect says about their fulfilling the role assigned them as women by society. As she explains it, "[t]he socialisation of children is the mother's responsibility, and the lapsing of bewitched children into the presocial signifies the failure of her power over them and their outright rejection of that power . . ."[57] In this light, Mrs. Throckmorton's daughters' uncontrollable writhings, moanings, blurtings, and violent rejection of prayer and household duties[58] is not a sign of her inability to control her own children and mold them as society requires. Instead, she can redirect the blame by claiming that the evil Agnes Samuel has perverted the natural order.

Diana Purkiss observes that women's domestic duties in general also shaped the sixteenth and seventeenth centuries' underlying fears of witches. Significantly, a major danger of maleficium, equal in importance to the anti-mother, was its portrayal as a dangerous invasion of the home and an attack on the work done there. Woman's place in the social order was to help maintain civilized order against the chaos of raw nature through her assigned duties of "cooking, churning, spinning, skimming, washing and spinning." However, "[w]hen this process is disrupted by witchcraft, the authority and identity of the housewife are put in question; she can no longer predict or control the process of transformation required." Since the woman's dairy and poultry were a vital buffer protecting her family from starvation and utter poverty, her failure in this area was grave.[59] However, by shifting blame onto witches, "good" women could relieve themselves of a tremendous burden. If a witch inflicted misfortune on a woman's family, no one could accuse that woman of causing her family's suffering because she failed to meet the social standards giving her value. Society could also use the witch as a convenient scapegoat. Instead of responding to these failures by questioning whether expectations for women were realistic, it could direct blame onto witches maliciously trying to disrupt "natural" order.[60]

Thus, the social order powerfully inscribes a specific and limited identity as self-sacrificing, all-nurturing, and protective mother or housewife on women by equating inability to live up to this definition with the negative extreme of being destructive, even Satanic. This inscription might not always be blatantly misogynistic, for, as Lyndal Roper writes of seventeenth-century German and Basque prosecutions, "It was because the state took the fears and accusations of suffering mothers seriously that cases could be prosecuted."[61] However, the frequency of condemning any woman stepping outside the parameters of woman's social role as a witch indicates the relevance of gender conventions to sixteenth- and seventeenth-century anxieties about this phenomenon.

The studies of later scholars further undercut another of Thomas's claims that there is little actual gender bias in witchcraft accusations: women accuse women more than men do; therefore, the persecutions cannot be defined as a misogynist plot.[62] These scholars suggest that Thomas's argument needs to be refocused, that the gender bias stems from a subtler source. A bias is apparent in that witchcraft is frequently defined in terms that coincide with women's work, or women's failure to fulfill their socially assigned work.[63] A particularly important factor in suspecting a woman of witchcraft would be if she violated the standard economic or work parameters usually set for women. Marianne Hester writes of accusations against women: "There appears to be a link between male-female relations, economic change and witchcraft accusation." Hester elaborates that the characterization of witches as old, widowed, or otherwise husbandless, independent women also applied to the only kind of woman who could independently own or run a business in an Elizabethan and Jacobean society.[64] Making her case more specifically in terms of the craft of brewing, Hester points out that during the sixteenth and seventeenth centuries, alongside growing government and craft regulation to exclude women, the female brewer was predominantly portrayed as either similar to, or actually, a witch: dishonest, a poisoner, old and unnaturally oversexed, ugly, slovenly, or even leagued with Satan.[65] Hester concludes that linking financially independent women with the blasphemous figure of the witch was an effective way of marking such women as dangerously unnatural in order to "maintain the status quo" in the "male-female conflict around resources and livelihoods."[66] Even if only indirectly, then, tensions concerning gender relations in early modern society were an important force in the definition and prosecution of the witch.

Concerns about housewifery would most likely pervade the peasant and middle classes, while anxieties over motherhood would affect all levels of society. However, studies of witchcraft persecutions also reveal broader-based anxieties over gender relations shaping perceptions of the essential threat of witchery. Anne Baring and Jules Cashford describe this anxiety over witches as a medieval and early-modern evolution of demonizing the unbounded sexuality and agency of earlier goddesses.[67] Similarly, what many scholars have found to be a major component underlying sixteenth- and seventeenth-century witchcraft beliefs and persecutions is the characterization of woman as an amorphous, chaotic, uncontrollable Other who threatens the divinely inspired order of reason, discipline, and morality that patriarchal society defines as its province. Patricia Parker sums up contemporary views of women: "faulty, imperfect, and secondary, a lapsus or falling off from the more perfect male, . . . both baser matter and adulterating mixture, a frail or 'weaker vessel,' . . . a creature whose status is also figured by sexual parts that are secret, occult, or hidden from the eye."[68]

As touched on in chapter 1, classical authorities on whom medieval and Renaissance thinkers depended clearly defined women in these terms. Aristotle, "the standard authority on natural scientific 'fact' throughout the seventeenth century" and earlier, asserted along with his equally influential disciple Galen[69] that "woman is less fully developed than man. Because of lack of heat in generation, her sexual organs have remained internal, she is incomplete, colder and moister in dominant humours, and unable to 'concoct' perfect semen from blood[,]" the seed from which she grew never completely blooming. Her cold, moist, unstable, diffuse state, in opposition to man's heat and firmness, even rendered her unable to generate or shape the human life she receives from man, serving only as a passive container for the seed that man's physiology enables him to give stable shape and to deposit in her.[70]

Equally important, Aristotle held that the female's "unbalanced," "leak[y]," "mess[y]," "runn[y]"[71] physical state was reflected in the dangerously undisciplined and vicious attributes of her psyche:

> In all genera in which the distinction of male and female is found, Nature makes a similar differentiation in the mental characteristics of the sexes. This differentiation is the most obvious in the case of human kind. . . . The female is less spirited than the male, . . . [*sic*] softer in disposition, more mischievous, less simple, more impulsive, and more attentive to the nurture of the young. . . . Woman is more compassionate than man, more easily moved to tears, at the same time more jealous, more querulous, more apt to scold and strike. She is, furthermore, more prone to despondency and less hopeful than the man, more void of shame and self-respect, more false of speech, more deceptive, and of more retentive of memory. She is also more wakeful, more shrinking, more difficult to rouse to action, and requires a smaller quantity of nutriment.[72]

Even if women are "more compassionate" and "attentive to nurture the young," these few virtues might be dismissed as examples of her uncontrolled emotions and are overwhelmingly swamped by the array of traits rendering her untrustworthy or vicious in thought, word, and action: "mischievous," "impulsive," "jealous," "querulous," "scold[ing]," "desponden[t]," shameless, and duplicitous. In the context of her predominantly vicious and small-minded characteristics, women's being "more retentive of memory" seems less a virtue than a vindictive tendency to hold a grudge.

Contemporary medical opinion tended to support classical medical theory about women. Paracelsus, an influential early modern physician whose theories competed with those of Aristotle's and Galen's in some areas, agreed with their assessment of woman's essential nature, writing: "Women have more imagination and restlessness and are more easily conquered by the very strength of their nature [than are men]."[73] There was also a general concurrence in medical thought that women's unstable, malleable physical state rendered them prone to mental illnesses that did not affect the more stable male. For example, the influence of the moon could trigger green sickness in young virgins, or a woman might find uncontrollable urges for sex causing her womb to dislodge itself and meander about her innards, the infamous "wandering womb" syndrome. Even as more seventeenth-century scientists and doctors came to accept Gabriele Fallopio and others' rejection of the belief that women's bodies were "an imperfect and incomplete version" of the male, they still held that though the woman's body might be perfect in and of itself, that perfection was still inferior to male physiology, greatly affecting her mental and moral condition.[74]

This view underlies texts defining women's place in early modern society. As noted in the prior chapter, one of the most influential such books in sixteenth- and seventeenth-century England on training women for their duties as daughters, wives, and mothers was Richard Hyrde's translation of Juan Vives's Latin *The Instruction of a Christen Woman. Instruction* warns that a young woman must be constantly occupied by wise elders with useful, pious tasks to discipline her into sanctity because "the mynde of a woman is unstable, and abydeth nat longe in one place, it falleth from the good unto the bad without any labour. And Syrus the poet semeth nat all without a cause to have sayd, a woman that thynketh alone thinketh evyll."[75] Especially germane to the discussion of women and witchcraft, Kramer and Sprenger in their *Malleus Maleficarum* (1487) specifically observe that woman's inherent mental, spiritual, and physical instability explains how easily she is tempted by Satan into practicing witchcraft. On a physical level, woman "is more carnal than man, as is clear from her many carnal abominations."[76] In tune with contemporary medical thought, Sprenger and Kramer claim that women's mental and spiritual characteristics match the physical: "they [women] are more credulous [than men]; and since the chief aim of the devil is to corrupt faith, therefore he rather attacks them. See *Ecclesiasticus* xix: He that is quick to believe is light-minded, and shall be diminished. . . . women are naturally more impressionable, and more ready to receive the influence of a disembodied spirit; and when they use this quality well they are very good, but when they use it ill they are very evil."[77]

And the *Malleus*'s authors definitely think that women are more inclined to use "this quality . . . ill" more often than "well." Although they cite some rare women of the Bible and antiquity as steadfast, they insist "perfidy is more often found in women than in men" because women "are feebler both in mind and body, [so] it is not surprising that they should come more under the spell of witchcraft."[78]

Diane Purkiss suggests that during the Renaissance accusations of witchcraft against women continued to express similar anxiety over the supposed disruptive, undisciplined nature of the female mind and body necessitating a patriarchal imposition of form and order. Witchcraft attacks involved not only an invasion of home boundaries (attacking children and household duties, polluting mother's milk) but a rejection of roles assigned women when the witch attacks the very "ideas about where boundaries [for women's social role] should be."[79] In two ways the witch becomes a scapegoat enabling the social order to explain away any problems with the domestic and maternal roles it imposes on women. First, women who would attack such roles as inaccurate can be portrayed as dangerously at odds with a safe ordering of chaotic nature. They are rejecting an opportunity to curb their innate flaws; and, worse, they are promulgating the disruptive effects of those flaws on society. Second, women who fail to maintain that order, themselves, can be read, not as indicating the concept's inaccuracy, but demonstrating women's susceptibility to vicious, Satanic outside force.

This patriarchal anxiety over women's inherent boundlessness is most powerfully expressed in fears of female sexuality. Marianne Hester even more specifically describes how the early modern patriarchal system displaced onto female sexuality its anxiety over the discrepancy between its belief in divine order and the reality of an uncertain world:

> societies that are male dominated rely on constructions of "the female" which present women as both different and inferior to men; and sexualisation or eroticisation, of "the female'" in a variety of ways over time, is particularly important in constructing, and thereby maintaining, this difference. Where the early modern witch hunts are concerned we have much evidence of this sexualising process, where it was particularly female sexuality that was perceived to make women different from men. Male sexuality was not discussed in a similarly negative manner. [Keith] Thomas also provided evidence of this for England from Robert Burton who wrote "of women's unnatural, unsatiable lust." Women were considered sexually insatiable and prone therefore to sinful and deviant behaviour, by contrast to the "norm" which was construed as heterosexual, procreative sex under male control.[80]

In other words, by displacing their fears about sexuality onto an Other, woman, and then constricting that gender's sexual expression within the bounds of "procreative sex under male control," the males claiming control of social order could salve their anxieties by seeing themselves as constraining the destabilizing effects of sexuality on the individual and society.

Roberts and Hester[81] observe that the witch's unrestrained sexuality serves as a symbol onto which society can displace anxieties about women and the effects of the boundlessness associated with them. The discourses of high and low culture repeatedly reveal how these anxieties about the power of woman's sexuality are crystallized in the witch as renegade womanhood. Marianne Hester points out that "[m]arriage, as the site of a heterosexual, procreative sexuality under the control of men, was—as expressed in many sermons, pamphlets and other literature at the time— deemed the only appropriate place for any sexual activity to take place."[82] In contrast, the witch, in her wanton encounters with the supernatural, is a symbol of the nighmarishness of female sexuality unrestrained by Lacan's "primordial Law," in "the *name of the Father*" that "regulat[es] marriage ties, superimposes the reign of culture over the reign of nature," and maintains order over chaos.[83]

As noted earlier, Sprenger and Kramer in *The Malleus Maleficarum* characterized women as liable to be tempted into witchcraft because they are "more carnal than a man" and prone to "carnal abominations."[84] Consequently, outside the boundaries set by society, woman's sexuality leads not only to her own immorality but to the suffering of others. Pamphlets frequently refer to prosecuted witches as "lewd" sexual temptresses of innocent men or the mothers of numerous illegitimate offspring.[85] Even worse, women unrestrained by the patriarchal boundaries of marriage may slip into such perverse couplings as Ann Usher's with "2 things like butterflies in her secret p[ar]tes."[86]

Demonstrating with especial clarity how both folk traditions and the beliefs of elite witchcraft prosecutors were preoccupied with associating the witch's sexuality with Satan is the 1566 pamphlet on the Chelmsford Witches. Here, Elizabeth Francis does not have sex with Satan but uses her bond with him to strike more directly and threateningly at men by having sex with them. Satan (in the form of her familiar cat) promises her the wealth of Andrew Byles if she allows him to sleep with her. When Byles refuses to marry her, Satan answers Francis's desire to punish the man by giving her the ability to kill him with a touch. Later, Satan helps her to snare Byles through "fornication." When marriage and motherhood bring her "much unquietness," she uses Satan to kill her child and lame her husband. Thus, the witch embodies the sexually unbound woman at her worst, freeing herself of the constrictions of marriage and motherhood through murder and maiming.[87]

The witch's sexuality seems to embody anxieties about the social roles assigned women. The failure of social limitations on female behavior is not portrayed as an inadequacy or inaccuracy of the system but as the renegade's perversion of reason, morality, decency, and order. Her seeming independence from patriarchal control deprives her of humanity when she conjoins with animals lower in the chain of being or with Satan and his minions, perversions of God's divine order. Either way, her "sinful and deviant"[88] sexuality turns her away from the all-knowing, all-ordering God, and his patriarchal representatives on earth (king, clergy, husband, father).

Another motif that conveys the society's ingrained uneasiness with sexuality in women other than "procreative" and "under the control of men"[89] is the tendency of low as well as high culture to portray witches as insatiable old women who have not reasonably abandoned their sexuality now that they are beyond its proper use: reproduction with their husbands. In court trials, people of both genders and all ages[90] were frequently urged to confess to sexual encounters with Satan or his imps. However, these confessions and the comments made on them in various forms of discourse reveal a particularly strong disquiet at the sexuality of old women. Lyndal Roper's observations on the women charged in the late 1660s Augsburg trials indicate that such considerations of age and female sexuality made the accused particularly vulnerable to the suspicions of their communities: "old, infertile and unhusbanded as the lying-in maid was, she represented a double threat to the mother, standing both for the mother's own future and sometimes representing a sexual threat as well."[91] Because they could no longer fill the conventional identity of wife and mother, these women were viewed as outside the pale; because they may have exceeded the sexual limitations imposed to maintain order, their age and past sexual history are construed as evidence that they will unreasonably continue to break rules, bewitching children and mothers physically and husbands sexually. Again, Hester's account of the disparagement of female brewers comes to mind,[92] where seventeenth-century popular culture portrayed them as perverse not only for poisoning their customers with bad ale and cheating them in business but also for being sexually active old women. Thus, both the witch and the female brewer are sexually predatory females and invaders of the masculine sphere of commerce; both seem nightmarish corrupters of social expectations for an upright old woman.

The witch of classical writings, especially in the form of Circe, stands in Elizabethan and Jacobean culture as a symbol redolent of the boundlessness of the female as a threat to rational, patriarchal civilized order. Tracing a direct line from St. Augustine well into the sixteenth century, Gareth Roberts writes, "A Circean offer of perilous pleasures is one of the ways in which witchcraft and magic were seen by treatise writers. The devil seduced witches, witches seduced men, witchcraft itself was a seduction to and of mankind." Equally dangerous, whether in terms of having actual power or of perpetrating convincing illusions, Circe was feared for transforming men into animals that luxuriated in beasts' mindless, irresponsible pleasures.[93] Thus, she was seen as a symbol of the witch's tremendous power to lure men from civilization's rationality, responsibility, and morality. Similarly, Diane Purkiss contends that in the Renaissance Circe represented the threat of female sexuality independent of patriarchal order: "Circe's transformation of men into beasts is proof of femininity's power to render categories and identities unstable; Circe like the Witch of Edmonton crosses clearly marked lines between human and the animal."[94] Essentially, then, Circe was perceived as the witch embodying female sexuality seducing men away from the masculine virtues of reason, responsibility, and control to wallow in an effeminizing, even animalizing pleasure. Roberts details how this perception is found in the learned writings of Erasmus; Arthur Golding; and Samuel Harsnet; as well as in Spenser's Acrasia, Duessa, and Mutabilitie; and in Shakespeare's *Comedy of Errors.*[95]

Medea also served as a popular Renaissance incarnation of the cultural anxieties represented by the witch. According to Diane Purkiss, the Thessaly that the Romans associated with "the various Medeas of antiquity" was home of witches as a "marginal[ized]" area symbolizing Otherness, and became a popular setting for the doings of disruptive witches in the sixteenth- and seventeenth-century dramas *Parsalia* and *Masque of the Queens.*[96] Medea herself was an important symbol of the female threat destabilizing European, masculine hegemony. Her otherness resides not merely in her national origin beyond the bounds of Greek or English civilization but in her rejection of the subordinate female roles of mother and wife, coupled with her exercise of forbidden power over men through her magic. Purkiss notes the influence of Medea on Shakespeare's creation of Sycorax and Marston's Erictho to demonstrate the ways this figure stands against patriarchal power. Even more interesting is her observation that Prospero's speech rejecting his powers strongly echoes Medea's speech affirming her own in Ovid's *Metamorphoses.* Thus Prospero's "words and claims are not simply an undoing of laboriously established differences between himself and Sycorax" but a determined effort to free himself of the seduction of "living outside the law, occupying a position from which it is possible to escape its workings—or control them."[97]

A third mythological figure commonly connected with witches in both medieval and Renaissance everyday life and in literature is Diana. For example, while trying to debunk the misguided superstitions of "certeine wicked women following sathans provocations" that they were actually powerful witches, Reginald Scot, in his *Discoverie of Witches* (1584), cites these women as having the delusion that "*Diana*, the goddesse of the *Pagans*" enables them to fly abroad with her, controlling "certeine beasts" and exercise the unlimited power to "doo whatsoever those fairies or ladies command, &c."[98] Carlo Ginzburg raises the interesting point that though the benandanti were an "off-shoot" of Diana worship, they saw themselves as fighting her to protect the crops under God's auspices.[99] Although warning against falling into accepting Margaret Murray's literal interpretation of accuseds' descriptions of Diana-cult sabbats that were made under pressure of inquisitions, Robin Briggs notes that medieval and Renaissance writers across Europe would connect Diana with witchcraft and fertility through her pagan worship.[100] According to Elizabeth Hart these writers were familiar enough with classical texts and commentaries to differentiate the Diana of Ovid from the Diana of Ephesus, a goddess of fertility and magic connected with the even more ancient Cybele.[101]

All three of these figures of the witch in Renaissance literature will prove germane to the study of the female pastoral guide. For example, Circe is the mother and teacher of Comus, who draws on both nature and nurture to corrupt the souls of humans, turning them into beasts in Milton's *Comus*.[102] In Sannazaro's *Arcadia*, Medea is teamed with Circe as the witches whose "herbs of magic" are used by an old cunning woman known for being able to pervert the natural order.[103] In a more humorous vein, a man trying to pass himself off as a learned sorcerer in *Rhodon and Iris* invokes Medea's speech celebrating her powers in the *Metamorphoses*.[104] He may be scamming a gull, but he does so at the behest of the play's female witch in order to create disharmony among the lovers. In the same play, a witch takes pride in causing ill by using Circe's drugs, which she claims are as deceptive and manipulative as "Ulysses [*sic*] wits."[105]

How various playwrights use the conflicts and contrasts between the female pastoral guides and Circean or Medean figures will be treated in greater depth later in this and subsequent chapters. Finally, Diana's or Artemis's traits are constantly evoked in various forms of the female pastoral guide: adeptness with the bow and arrow or spear, being a lady of the beasts attuned to nature and the supernatural, disquietingly bringing together the traits of two different traditions of Diana, fertility and chastity, that Elizabeth Hart discusses. The guide will use her alliance with Diana in ways that render her less fearsome and more of a healing goddess, though not necessarily by subjugating her to masculine control. Future guides will keep alive the variation of the Acteaon story of Ameto, where fury becomes compassion and clemency, though never complete subjugation.

II

Sexuality was not the only way the witch embodied the dangers of the unruly woman. In the 1615 assault on women *The Arraignment of Lewd, Idel, Froward, and Unconstant Women*, Joseph Swetnam reveals a contemporary fear of women's speech unconstrained by patriarchal authority: "but a woman's chief strength is in her tongue. The serpent hath not so much venom in his tail, as she hath in her tongue; and as the serpent never leaveth hissing and stinging, and seeking to do mischief, even so, some women are never well, except they be casting out venom with their tongues, to the hurt of their husbands, or of their neighbours." Without masculine constraint, a woman's voice is not just unpleasant ("hissing") but destructive, "stinging" and poisoning the "husbands" and "neighbours" comprising her society.[106]

The *Malleus Maleficarum,* a text cited throughout the early-modern era, specifically claims that women's sexual and verbal unruliness are the basis for their being more vulnerable than men to seduction into witchcraft. On the one hand, women "are more carnal than men" and drawn to "carnal abominations." On the other, women's innate loquacity prompts them into exercising a "backbiting tongue" for the pleasure of wreaking havoc, "disquiet[ing] many," "driv[ing] them from nation to nation," and "pull[ing] down and overthrow[ing] the houses of great men" simply by "rashly or spitefully interfer[ing] between two contending parties." Women's essential nastiness and lack of self-discipline mutually fuels their addiction to wielding witchcraft and speech for working evil and infecting others with their own corruption.[107] The *Malleus* and Swetnam's work, then, evidence that what was seen as women's verbal unruliness created as much masculine anxiety as female sexuality did, with the former text directly associating these flaws with women's predilection to witchcraft.

Not surprisingly, Marianne Hester suggests that during "the period of the witch-hunts" patriarchal fears of female unruliness were embodied in attitudes toward female "scolding" as much as toward female sexuality.[108] These fears provoked harsh suppression. Lynda Boose contends that early-modern society saw the witch's wanton speech and sexuality as linked indications of the need to contain these innately female flaws through law: "As the forms of punishment and the assumptions about what officially constituted 'crime' became progressively polarized by gender, there emerged a corresponding significant increase in instances of crime defined as exclusively female: 'scolding,' 'witchcraft,' and 'whoring.' "[109]

Attitudes toward women charged with witchcraft clarify why controlling speech became a powerful legal weapon for forestalling female challenges to patriarchal authority. Marianne Hester observes that where "physical violence" might be man's way of asserting himself in the village community, "verbal violence as represented by cursing" would be the means most women used.[110] Silencing the curses of witches, much like silencing the scold, kept unruly women in line, especially if they were poor, old, or new members of a community without any family protection. These parallels with witchcraft would especially heighten the negative perception of the outspoken woman. Illustrating this point perfectly is Agnes Samuel, suspected of witchcraft by a wealthier family and pursued by the learned men of the family in the 1593 case at Warboys. Not surprisingly, when Samuel spoke out roundly in her defense, "the scholars" who tried to interrogate her, decried her for being "very loud in her answers and impatient, not suffering any to speak but herself." Significantly, she is warned to "keep the woman's virtue and be more silent."[111]

As was noted in the previous chapter, the foundation for medieval and Renaissance views of women's inherent inability to use speech wisely without masculine guidance is both classical and biblical. For example, in *Instruction of a Christen Woman*, Juan Luis Vives cites classical authority when declaring that "Aristotel in his boke of beastis sheweth" that "Nature her selfe cryeth and commaundeth, that the woman shalbe subjecte and obedyent to the man."[112] Otherwise, woman's wayward wit and will would lead her to gossip, falsehood, shrewishness, and lewdness[113] because "[w]omans thoughts are swyfte, and for the most parte unstable, walkying and wandrynge out from home, and soone wyl slyde, by the reason of hit owne slypernes, [Vives] wot nat howe far."[114] The more profound and immediate justification for the necessity of bridling the woman's voice to preserve order was predicated on biblical and patristic writings. As touched on in the prior chapter, within the first 500 years of the Christian church St. Jerome, Tertullian, Augustine, and Aquinas established a view of women as disruptive of God's natural harmony through both their sexuality and their use of speech.[115] The patriarchs derived these beliefs, as did other divines down through the Renaissance, from specific biblical texts—or as James Turner clarifies, specific interpretations of these texts.[116] Two sources within the Christian Bible that exerted great influence on the perception of women were the story of Eve's creation from Adam's rib and the writings of Saint Paul.

The first instance is the interpretation of the Old Testament story of creation and the fall holding that man's controlling woman is both natural and necessary. Early Christian through Renaissance culture tended to portray Eve as Adam's inferior, privileging exegeses of the creation where Eve, drawn from Adam's side, is only indirectly connected to God through man. More degrading still, Eve's weak female mind and morality enabled Satan to tempt her with the forbidden fruit through which she led Adam, and hence all humanity, into sin. By doing so, "she doomed the rest of womankind to moral deficiency and moral inferiority. It was woman who caused Adam to fall; it was woman who was responsible for subsequent evil in the world and for the human predicament. Moral theology asserted that the treachery of Eve was passed down to all her female descendants, and hence woman could only be viewed as deceptive, unreliable, seductive."[117] Because "Eve's words to Adam were untrustworthy and perfidious"[118] to the extent of condemning all humanity, a woman's tongue, uncontrolled, could be perceived as a devastating threat to order, even to salvation. This view glares out of Vives's warning that descent from the original woman Eve, whose gullibility, weak reasoning powers, and lack of discretion led to humankind's fall, renders all women not only fundamentally unfit for teaching but a grave menace should they gain that opportunity to shape minds and morals:

> I gyve no licence to woman to be a teacher, not to have authorite of the man but to be in silence. For Adam was the fyrst mayde, and after Eve, and Adam was nat betrayed, the woman was betrayed in to the breche of the commandement. Therfore bicause a woman is a fraile thynge, and of weake discretion, and that maye lightlye be disceyved; whiche thyng our fyrst mother Eve sheweth, whom the devyll caught with a lyght argument. Therefore a woman shulde nat teache, leste when she hath taken a false opinion and beleve of any thyng, she spred hit into the herars by the autorite of maistershyp, and lightly bringe other into the same errour, for lerners commenly do after the teacher with good wyll."[119]

Just above this passage in his text, Vives explains that these ideas recapitulate Paul's assertion that women are required to be obedient to men in 1 Timothy 2:11–14.[120]

James Turner looks to 2 Timothy, as well as a similar injunction from 1 Timothy, as amongst the most powerful influences on defining woman's character in Christian theology. However, Turner insightfully adds that "as the Pauline epistles came to represent the definitive key to Genesis, his suprematist [*sic*] prescriptions were enshrined at the heart of Christian doctrine and repeated in every marriage-service, while his self-qualifications went largely unheard." The predominating voices in Christian theology reinforced this prescription for woman's speech to be controlled by patriarchy with Paul's statements that woman was created to serve and glorify man, not the reverse (1 Corinthians 1:11–9) and that the husband is as God to the wife, her wiser protector (Ephesians 5:22, 24–25).[121]

Thus, one hundred years after Juan Luis Vives's citing of Paul, William Whately continued the tradition of using this passage to justify masculine control of woman's voice in his *Bride-Bush* (1619): "*Paul* commands the woman to *learne in silence*. The worde is *in quietnesse*: wherein he not alone inioynes a publicke, but euen a general silence to hold in the house."[122] Similarly, William Gouge's 1622 *Domestical Duties* explains that women should heed "that exhortation of the Apostle unto [them], that they *learn in silence with all subjection* (1 Tim 2:11)." Gouge goes even further, specifically extending Paul's initial reference to behavior inside a house of worship to all areas of a woman's existence: "which though it be principally meant of learning in the Church, yet it excludeth not her learning at home of her husband: for in the next words he addeth, *I suffer not a women to usurp authority over the man, but to be in silence*."[123] Thus, women's silence becomes an outward manifestation of their obedience to the natural law of their husbands' control in matters domestic and religious.

Even as late as 1673, in *The Ladies Calling*, Richard Allestree cites the apostle's injunctions *"to keep silence in the church"* and to *"let women learn in silence"* as antidotes to the "great indecency of loquacity in women." Allestree even goes so far as to chastise "if some women of our age think they have outgone that novice state the Apostle supposes, and want no teaching, I must crave leave to believe, they want the very first principle which should set them to learn, i.e. the knowledge of their own ignorance."[124]

To sum up, the witch was associated with anxieties over a female threat to masculine social hegemony, whether in terms of her attempt to assert economic independence, her sexuality, or her outspokenness. In the patriarchal framework of sixteenth- and seventeenth-century society, the witch personifies as female the inexplicable and uncertain reality challenging a world view that insists on a cosmos rationally and morally ordered according to classical and biblical standards.[125] Studying the female pastoral guide in this context reveals that her bond to the sacred rather than the demonic, as well as the positive use to which she puts the knowledge and power resulting from that bond, shows her to be an important device for addressing these concerns through literature.

To general audiences who were so firmly inculcated with the terrible destructiveness of woman's sexuality and garrulity, especially through their fear of the witch, carnival's eternal female's ferocious sexuality and sharp verbal abuse would not have seemed quite so liberating, much less purifying, as Bakhtin depicts her. Though the spirit of carnival may have "flowered" in the literature of the 1600s, as Bakhtin claims, a too disruptive female would not have sat well with the audiences of diverse intellectual and class backgrounds attending the theatre. The female pastoral guides, on the whole, do not completely reject carnival's comic vision of woman as wise, helpful, though defiant, comic abuser, but they do modify her challenge to conventional gender restraints in her iconoclastic words and actions to address fears of any female's complete freedom in these areas. Sometimes the guide will be portrayed somewhat in the tradition of the feisty virgins of ancient world romances: chaste but still knowing and in control of her chastity, witty yet not harshly so. Or she may even be co-opted to speak the dogmas constraining women that carnival would be expected to upend. Ironically, one special woman may be put on top to keep all others safely (for themselves and men) on the bottom of the gender hierarchy.

III

Two early Renaissance pastoral works, Sannazaro's *Arcadia* (1504) and Montemayor's *Diana* (1559), address the witch's embodiment of contemporary anxieties about uncertainty, supernatural threats, and female sexuality and outspokenness. Both texts do so by creating a variation on the divine and mortal female pastoral guides of Boccaccio's *Ameto*. These later pastorals provide guides who remove the threat of hostility, boundlessness, irrationality, ungodliness, and barbarity that the witch embodies. Still, Sannazaro's and Montemayor's texts tackle the issue in different ways, enriching the matrix from which later pastoralists will create a guide reflecting their own cultural, social, and artistic milieu. In *Arcadia*, the Nymph of Arcadia and a goddess are tamed of any threatening supernatural female boundlessness, for their powers are mediated by masculine control. In *Diana*, the guides may seem less threatening because they are mortal women rather than the overwhelmingly powerful goddess figures of *Ameto*. Surprisingly, although, these human women are both far more independent of male control than Sannazaro's supernatural guides, they are still not portrayed as purveyors of social disorder.

The earlier text, Sannazaro's *Arcadia*, will be considered first. The Nymph of Arcadia, Massilia, and Pales are female pastoral guides who recall Boccaccio's Lia, nymphs, and Venus. Nevertheless, Sannazaro's guides differ from Boccaccio's in some important, if sometimes subtle, ways that address the witch's incarnation of tensions concerning the inadequacy of patriarchal society to explain and order the world. However, this study of Sannazaro's pastoral will not start by considering his recharacterization of the female pastoral guide. For the most straightforward way Sannazaro does comment on the conflict between patriarchal order and female chaos is through his juxtaposition of a "well-known old wise woman," portrayed in the tradition of the threatening witch, versus Enareto, described as a wise man and "holy shepherd."[126] The discussion will conclude with both a comparison of how the other female guides undercut the witch figure's ability to threaten boundaries and a consideration of how their doing so defines their difference from the guidance paradigms set by Lia, the nymphs, and Venus.

Portrayals of women as split into desirable and undesirable, disempowered and empowered have long been explored in cultural and literary studies. According to Bruno Bettelheim, in fairy tales mothers are frequently split into good mothers and evil stepmothers in order for the child to deal with her/his conflicting dual perceptions of mother as nurturer and protector versus punisher and denier. Gilbert and Gubar suggest that society imprints this split in the mythos of the fairy tales, religion, and literature that it creates to stigmatize the female behavior it opposes (ambition, independence, outspokenness, sexuality) and to promote the behavior it desires (compliance, nurturance, servitude, silence, chastity). Lyndal Roper links these mythic roles to witchcraft beliefs, drawing on Melanie Klein to explain that midwives and nurses were often charged as witches for seeming to be in contention with biological mothers for children's lives and well-being.[127] A similar splitting of undesirable traits onto witches can also be observed in Renaissance drama.

Diane Purkiss sees anxiety about women addressed in such works as *The Masque of the Queens* and *The Witch of Edmunton*, where the witches who direly threaten social and spiritual stability are vanquished by wise men and godly women after great struggle. In her discussion of *Endymion*, Purkiss writes that by building up the divinity Cynthia but making Dipsas, an archetypical witch, silly, inept, and ridiculous, Lyly undercuts the anxieties that the witch represents.[128] This splitting, juxtaposing the witch with a "good," nurturing, supernatural being, is not limited to *Endymion* among the pastorals but becomes a notable trend found in works of the genre: *The Faithful Shepherdess*, *Rhodon and Iris*, and *The Sad Shepherd*, for example. This pattern in Renaissance pastoral drama owes much to the contrasting depictions of the old woman and the sacred shepherd in Sannazaro's *Arcadia*. More specifically, the debt lies in the contrast Sannazaro makes between the old woman's alleged powers and the actual ones of Enareto, the Nymph of Arcadia, Pales, and Massilia.

The woman whom shepherd Clonico seeks to save him from the agony of unrequited love possesses many of traits that Sannazaro and his audience, as well as later writers and audiences, would have immediately associated with the witch at her most terrible. Her knowledge of how to use herbs and exotic ingredients to exert control is echoed across the Continent and years. She is described as being able to practice magic, "by taking the issue of mares in heat, the blood of the viper, the brain of savage bears and hairs from the tail-tip of the wolf, with other roots of herbs and most potent juices, she knew how to do many things most wondrous and incredible to relate." The shepherd describing her states that this knowledge puts the cunning woman in the same league with Circe and Medea.[129] Significantly, those most "wondrous and incredible" "things" the cunning woman does echo Medea's celebration of her terrible powers in Ovid's *Metamorphoses*:

> you have seen me still the angry oceans,
> Rouse the calm waters, drive the clouds away
> Or marshal them together, exile winds,
> Recall them; you have seen me break the fangs
> Of serpents with my charms and incantations,
> Root up rocks from the soil, root up oak-trees,
> Move forests, shake mountains, make earth rumble,
> Call ghosts from graveyards. I can make the moon
> Darken, the car of the Sun turn pale at my singing,
> The Dawn turn pale at my poisons.[130]

Similarly, Sannazaro's cunning woman can "draw . . . down from the skies the dark stars, all dripping with fresh blood," "call . . . up at midday into the world Night and the nocturnal Gods from chaos of the nether world; . . . call . . . back the souls of ancient ancestors from their deserted sepulchres[,]" and "still . . . the streams, to turn back the running waters to their sources."[131]

Like Medea, this cunning woman reverses, even perverts, the natural order of running waters, day and night, life and death. Neither Nature nor the sleeping dead can find peace in a blasphemous world where "nocturnal Gods from the chaos of the nether world" stalk freely, thanks to her. Further, Sannazaro's cunning woman even outdoes Medea in her disruptive control of the laws of God and Nature. Medea at least "still[s] angry oceans," "drive[s] clouds away," and "break[s] the fangs of serpents," but the work of Sannazaro's witch only turns the world hideously chaotic.

The *Arcadia*'s cunning woman, herself, is a blasphemy against her appropriate place in Nature. Rather than accept her human form, she is "wont to go flying through the air in the darkest night, covered with white feathers, in the shape of the nocturnal screech owl."[132] Moreover, the descriptions of her actions suggest that her obscene revising of natural order partly stems from her violating what a later witchcraft opponent called "the woman's virtue [to] be . . . silent."[133] This witch's words are the frightening, nerve-jangling "screech" of an owl, a creature associated with madness. She is guilty of "imposing laws with her words"[134] that disrupt God's natural plan, demonstrating that woman's unconstrained and self-determined speech is irrational, destructive, and blasphemous. She evokes Lacan's description of the frighteningly disruptive Other outside the Symbolic Order that organizes social relations with words that humans believe define and control reality. She is the chaos held at bay by the mutually creating Language and Law of the Father.[135] More pertinent to the relationship between carnival and the pastoral guide, this woman on top does not create a world turned upside down to free life from sterile convention but merely produces a chaos that helps no one. In this characterization, the figure's being likened to Circe and Medea[136] proves a striking example of Roberts's and Purkiss's observations that both stood as symbols for the dangers of women witches.

Truly, the old woman is a portrait of the witch as female at her most disruptive and destructive. Then, after creating this horrific threat to natural order, Sannazaro promptly undercuts it. The first response of the wise Opico to Clonico's description of the witch and his resolute plans is to turn the young man away from her to a more effective cunning person, "our own Enareto? He who (far more learned than the other shepherds) having abandoned his flocks makes his habitation in the temples of Pan our God. . . ."[137] In fact, the cunning woman is so unimportant that she does not even rate a reference from Opico here when he asserts that Enareto is the shepherd's best hope for aid. She is not even competition to a true cunning man who is "far more learned than the other shepherds." Rather, the only point of comparison worth noting is with other men, shepherds, not shepherdesses or nymphs. Not only is female power dismissed here as mere gossip or "common report," but the link between masculine power and the sacred is aggressively asserted in several ways. First, Opico points Clonico to a male (Enareto) to help him free himself from love's disruptive bondage. Second, throughout the pastoral, Enareto is constantly referred to with reverence for his power: "learned," "holy shepherd," "a man truly worthy of great reverence," and "holy priest." He is so honored he is even compared to divinity: "we may hold him in more reverence, and as if to an earthly God may render unto him due honors in our woods."[138] However, a woman claiming mystical powers over humanity and nature is either a "screech owl" or a charlatan, a contrast implying that only a man can wisely and productively wield such powers.

How Enareto wields his powers versus how the witch uses hers further emphasizes masculine superiority. In some ways, Enareto does parallel the nameless witch. He uses herbs to inspire or end love;[139] he uses magical incantations and artifacts to make people invisible or proof from weapons, to divine the future, to control thunderstorms and the seas, to direct the actions of animals, or to control the gods of the heavens and the gods of "the shadowy realms . . . of the underground," including Hecate. Enareto even has a charm to remove human fear and misunderstanding of the unknown.[140] However, unlike the witch, all his knowledge and spells do not frighten or hurt humans or disrupt Nature but bring order, security, and comfort.

A male, part of the Symbolic Order that defines and controls through language, Enareto's use of language is portrayed as legitimate while the witch's seems an unnatural usurpation. She is guilty of "screech[ing]" or "imposing laws with her words." In contrast, Enareto may have had the otherworldly experience of having his ears licked by two dragons one night when he slept, but he uses the resultant power to understand the language of animals to communicate with them, interpreting between humans and Nature. He also has set down at the Temple of Pan in writing all the god's laws for understanding Nature to help shepherds in their husbandry.[141] Enareto's use of language, a legitimate wielding of the Law of the Father, makes the world less threatening and mysterious by codifying knowledge that he reveals to humanity as he deems appropriate.

Finally, Enareto shows himself more than a cunning man. Somewhat similar to the Neoplatonists, he insists on rigorously training human nature before he will draw it into his realm of the supernatural. On several occasions he instructs the shepherds following him to purify themselves through various rites. They must wash their hands in the first stage and be baptized in the second. As Enareto warns, their way is literally and metaphorically a "most narrow and difficult" "route:"[142] to follow the path of this holy man and enjoy the aid of his mystic arts, humans must purge themselves of their darker aspects. He elevates rather than degrades his followers. This process sharply contrasts with the descriptions of witches' sabbats, where those celebrating their bond to Satan carouse, overeat, and perform bizarre feats before going off to destroy crops, homes, and lives.[143]

In Enareto, Sannazaro reasserts the patriarchy's power in the face of the feminine witch's threat. The threat of the female is undermined as fake and delusive, while the legitimacy of the male as the head of the hierarchy is affirmed. Enareto's "male" qualities of self-discipline, education, and reason help to make the world a more livable place for humanity.

Not only does the male figure undercut the threat embodied by the witch; the female guides of *Arcadia* do as well. In so crafting his female pastoral guides, Pales, Massilia, and the Nymph of Arcadia, Sannazaro makes some interesting variations on the paradigms of Boccaccio. They are, to varying degrees, women on top, but they still turn nothing in the patriarchal hierarchy upside down. As a "reverend goddess of shepherds"[144] presiding over the pastoral world, Pales could be expected to resemble Boccaccio's Venus closely: transcendent, inspiring, enflaming, actively involved in the lives of her worshippers. Pales is, indeed, transcendent, so much so that she transcends participating in any events of Sannazaro's tale.

Unlike the witch who speaks and acts out, Pales is purely an object of worship not a participant in the action. She is never seen, heard, or interacted with by the shepherds. Although called on to be a Marian intercessor with the other gods[145] and to "expunge" curses on their flocks, Pales neither replies nor clearly acts toward any of her followers. In fact, Pales might be said to be the ideal Christian woman. Particularly interesting, she does not preside over the pastoral realm alone. The text makes much of a male god, Pan, directing the pastoral world. Further, although he does not actually participate firsthand in the action of Arcadia, tales of Pan repeatedly detail his interactions with humans and gods;[146] his rules are set down in his temple for all who can approach to read; and it is to his temple, not to Pales's, that Enareto leads the shepherds when attempting to cure Clonico of love.[147] In fact, as Eugenio relates in verse, Pan is the main god who brings bounty and content, while Pales is only his assistant, "Then our Pan, in grace abounding, / with fostering Pales will increase your number / so that your mind may be well satisfied" (lines 118–20).[148] Further, Pan's exploits in love are recounted by the shepherds,[149] while Pales, whose feast seems to link her to fertility, is, ironically, never mentioned in terms of sexuality and requires the purification of those who celebrate her.[150] So, Pales becomes a supernatural female whose portrayal soothes many of the anxieties that the witch embodies: speaking out, acting out, allowing her sexuality free rein. Best of all, with all her power, she is clearly subordinate to the male. Here, the gods set up a model for human gender relations that reinforces patriarchal expectations.

Massilia proves a particularly interesting version of the guide allaying concerns with female sexuality and agency. A mother who resides in the heavens after her demise, she parallels the Virgin Mary. Her son's characterization of Massilia in song as a moral guide, intercessor, and comforter from "heaven" (line 116)[151] strikingly evokes the Virgin: "May her soul with its radiance reach down to here: / may it offer me aid and often while I am speaking / for pity may it descend to have sight of me. / And if its state be such that my language fails/ in shewing it forth, may she find excuses for me/ and teach me the way of adorning it in my verse" (lines 118–23).[152] In fact, the praises of her son Ergasto in pastoral song strongly recall the praises sung by St. Bernard or the angels and saints dancing around the Rose of Heaven in *Paradiso*. Ergasto sings of this "peregrine star" (line 87):[153]

> But you, O spirit lovely and immortal
>   beyond the rest, that hear me perhaps in heaven
>   and are pointing me out to your lovely band of peers,
> gain the grace for these thick and shady laurels
>   that they have power with their evergreen boughs
>   to cover us over, both of us buried here.
>   (lines 145–50)[154]

Yet with all these praises and pleas, Massilia is no more active than Pales. We never see her help or inspiration realized by her appearance, interactions with characters, or even disembodied speech. Like Pales, then, she is an object of devotion who does not respond in word or deed. Both she and Pales have been removed from the world of action and speech, she through death and Pales through divinity. Where Pales must defer to Pan, Massilia also defers to a male: her son. She only lives on, even exists, through the memorial of the poetry he creates and in the monument in stone that he builds. In fact, we only see her "in life," as it were, through her son's eyes. His description of her dovetails with that of the proper woman as tender, modest, encouraging, subservient: "She who erewhile was wont so sweetly to judge our contests, modestly giving cheer to the defeated and giving the victor commendation with wondrous words of praise."[155] The Massilia that Ergasto creates does not speak to assert herself or her own ideas but only to encourage or comfort the men in their endeavors. In *Arcadia*, Massilia is not allowed to manifest herself in any way, but is transformed, mediated, interpreted by her son, a man. Her complete control by a masculine figure is in complete contrast to the witch, whose defiance of words and actions wreak horrific chaos.

Also interesting, like Pales, Massilia is not allowed to be a sexual being. She is presented solely as an almost virgin mother, not as a wife or a lover to Ergasto's father, or anyone else for that matter. In this personation, Massilia is literally as well as figuratively the good mother who contrasts and undercuts the bad described by Bettelheim, Gilbert and Gubar, Roper, and Purkiss. She is like Mary, a supernatural female without Inanna's sexuality and unpredictable fury, Isis's sexuality and slyness, or the witch's perverse sexuality.

The Nymph of Arcadia is still a supernatural figure, though less formidable than Pales or Massilia. Though still a supernatural being, she is more a nature spirit than a goddess, rising out of an Arcadian river.[156] The Nymph bears some resemblance to Boccaccio's guiding Lia, leading Sannazaro's persona out of Arcadia back to Naples where he must resume his participation in the political strife, in the process taking him on a spiritual journey that teaches him both the difficulty of understanding the depths of human corruption and how to avoid falling victim to it. Also like Lia, the Nymph of Arcadia lets her charge learn at his own pace, refusing to expose him to sights or experiences, until he has developed the spirituality to understand and benefit from them.[157] However, there are some subtle but important differences between Sannazaro's guide and Lia, and these differences allay concerns about female aggressiveness.

First of all, the Nymph of Arcadia is far less sexual than Lia. Although Lia certainly does come to represent more than female sexuality alone in the course of *Ameto*, Boccaccio makes clear that his title character suffers terribly with desire for the explicitly described sexual charms of Lia: "he grew all aflame for the pleasures of this maiden."[158] In *Arcadia*, frustrated sexual desire never seems to be a major issue for the Sannazaro persona. The first description of the nymph shows her as quite attractive but does not dwell on her anatomy or the narrator's physical attraction to her.[159] Evidence that even more strongly suggests that Sannazaro's nymph is much more tightly under masculine control than was Lia is her tone in guiding her charge. Lia is much harder on Ameto than the Nymph is on Sannazaro, forcing Ameto to suffer a cold winter without her, as well as to endure other frustrations, in order to purify himself for Venus's love. On the contrary, the Arcadian Nymph is nothing but solicitous for Sannazaro. He describes her as "quietly giving [him] courage [when] she took [him] by the hand and guid[ed] [him] in most loving fashion." She protects him from seeing horrendous sights, more concerned for his feelings than with challenging him.[160] Finally, this Nymph differs from Lia in being completely at his service. Where Lia controls the timing and the contents of all meetings subsequent to her first with Ameto, the Nymph of Arcadia only appears when the Sannazaro persona is looking for someone to return him to Naples and disappears from his life once she has served her purpose of bringing him back.[161] For these reasons, the Nymph of Arcadia might, then, be considered a good mother, opposing the bad mother in the form of Clonico's witch. Beautiful, but not sexually threatening or frustrating, she exists to protect and guide without being froward; she comes on the scene only when the male wants her.

In Pales, Massilia, and the Nymph of Arcadia the female guide still aids in maintaining the social harmony characteristic of the pastoral world. She remains a figure who brings together human, natural, and divine. She even continues to be a teacher helping individuals to learn for themselves and at their own paces. However, if she is a "woman on top" it is not to liberate her charges from dogmatic seriousness but to teach women and to reassure men that patriarchal values are valid. She is not a figure who challenges the traditional order.

In Montemayor's *Diana* a different version of the guide emerges who combines the human and the supernatural. The female version of the Neoplatonic mage, she is not a goddess but a human woman who has studied and disciplined herself so that she knows nature and can act as a bridge between humanity and the divine. What she learns still affirms the patriarchal values of reason, control, learning, and logic. Her ability to wield magic, after all, comes from study and training. Nevertheless, she demonstrates that women need not always be connected with the chaotic, the irrational, the blasphemous, or the destructive. This use of the carnival does not challenge the essential values of the social order but the belief that women are incapable of living up to those values without male direction.

Actually, much of *Diana* seems to overturn the stereotype of woman as socially disruptive in word, action, thought, and sexuality. In the Temple of Diana, where Felicia and her nymphs dwell, artwork celebrates the noble princes and warriors who have saved Spain and Portugal.[162] However, there is an even more extensive array of portraits of noblewomen who have preserved social and spiritual order through their wisdom, chastity, beauty, self-control, and strength of character. These women are not portrayed as fickle because they have been manipulated by love, as weakminded and emotionally shallow women are supposed to be. Rather the poetry celebrates these women in portraits of their ability to control Love: "Love himself, [is] conquered by love" (line 78) or "Love is powerless to urge [them]" (line 92), with the woman "[a]lways the conqueror, never the conquered" (line 139). The traits repeatedly associated with the women in these portraits are not just "beauty" or "charm," but "virtue," "wisdom," "grace," and "purity."[163]

In *Diana*, the argument over who is the most unreliable in love, men or women, is certainly not resolved in favor of the masculine gender. In a debate early in the text, the shepherd Sylvano tries to force the shepherdess Selvagia to agree that women are "so fickle that one moment [they] throw down a shepherd from the zenith of his happiness to the nadir of his misery" because they "do not know what [they] hold in [their] hands. [They] trifle with love, but are not capable of understanding it, seeing how [they] come to terms with it." In other words, women are inconstant, insensitive, and mentally deficient. Selvagia, the woman, carries the day with her reasoned and thorough arguments. First, she raises the point that there are as many changeable men as there are women. Second, she asserts that circumstances beyond human control sometimes constrain us to change. Then she wraps up by pointing out that many women do have the wisdom to teach men how better to strengthen their own devotion.[164]

However, Selvagia does not rest here but deftly anticipates and silences any further arguments by pointing out that all the "crimes" of which men accuse women in the area of love are no more than men's twisted misinterpretation of woman's virtues to suit a stereotype:

> if [women] speak well of you [men], you think them dead with love; if they do not speak to you at all, you think them proud and flighty; if their shyness does not suit you, you call it hypocrisy; they have not candor but you think it excessive; if they are quiet, you say they are stupid, if they talk, you think them tedious, that no one can stand them; if they love you more than anything in the world, you believe they do it out of malice; if they forget you and withdraw from situations which may cost them their reputations, you say they are inconstant and disloyal. So that there is no such thing as a good or bad woman except for one who does not flee from what your inclination desires.[165]

In other words, no matter what choice a woman makes, to be forthright or humble, men will find a way to unjustly, foolishly condemn her. To this thorough and incisive rejoinder, Sylvano can only manage a grudging (despite the address "Fair Selvagia") concession: "If all of you had your understanding and liveliness of wit, we would never have occasion to complain of your carelessness."[166]

Another female character, Felismena uses a similar strategy to turn back the unjust criticism of the shepherd Filemón against the shepherdess Amarílida.[167] In both cases, whether the shepherd realizes it or not, Montemayor has given the laurel of victory to the woman. And in an ironic twist that undercuts beliefs about women's intellectual inferiority and dangerous use of language, eloquence based on reason is these women's weapon for that victory. Selvagia and Felismena both exhibit the woman of carnival's ability to expose the "jealousy, stupidity, hypocrisy, [and] bigotry" of men who impose limits on them, but Montemayor's characters do so with reason and intelligence rather than with "a wayward, sensual, concupiscent character of falsehood."[168]

Solidifying the preeminence of women over men, in *Diana* Montemayor creates a cast of characters that supports Selvagia's assessment over Sylvano's, turning the world of gender hierarchy upside down. True, the title character and Ysmenia seem to support Sylvano's contentions, although the text repeatedly emphasizes that Diana's forsaking true love came under pressure from her father.[169] However, what matters is that the majority of characters who demonstrate supposedly inherent female flaws are male: fickleness (Alanius, Montanus, Don Felice, Danteo); irrational jealousy (Alanius, Montanus, Filemón, Alfeo); pride (Alfeo, Filemón); and vindictiveness or cruelty (Alfeo, Alanius).

In this context, Montemayor reverses Sannazaro's characterizations of the female with magical powers as a wild, chaotic, and deceptive disrupter and the male mage as a rational, disciplined, holy restorer of law and order. In *Diana*, RoseAnna Mueller notes that the dangerous breaker of natural bounds is a man,[170] the "wizard" Alfeo, who uses his magical powers to confuse and delude. Out of jealousy, he raises two demons in the guise of two men and sends them to woo Belissa. Because he can not have Belissa, he has one man seem to kill the other and then himself, driving the grief- and guilt-stricken Belissa into exile. As would be expected of a witch, Alfeo uses his power to destroy peace of mind and separate true lovers.[171] Here, a man violates the sacred in raising demons as well as in sundering loving relations to bring much worse chaos into the world than does Sannazaro's wise woman, whose power only lives in rumor.

Most pertinent to the study of the female pastoral guide, in *Diana*, a woman, Felicia, takes over Enareto's position as wise, constructive healer with supernatural powers. Like Enareto, Felicia is noted for her wisdom and holiness. The epithet associated with her throughout the book, as many as four times on one page,[172] is "the sage Felicia." Even before readers meet Felicia, the nymph Dórida's description of her sets them up for an individual whose raison d'être is to salve the pains that irrational love inflicts on humanity: "the sage Felicia lives, whose occupation it is to cure love's passions. . . ."[173] Indisputably, this is not typical of the witch who uses her powers to torment children, allure men, or blast crops and housewifery.

Montemayor reveals that Felicia is even more impressive than Sannazaro's Enareto as she works her magic to help restore social order to the relations of lovers devastated by cruelty, infidelity, "Fortune," and folly. Where Enareto's use of purification rites somewhat resembled the practices of Neoplatonic mages, Felicia's detailed self-discipline, prudence, sophisticated learning, rationality, and compassion to work her cures define her exactly as this figure. Her first appearance brings this point home. She dresses in regal "black satin" rather than coarse shepherds' robes. This woman is not just a learned, retired shepherd but "a lady worthy of respect," displaying "stateliness and grandeur."[174] This dignity and nobility suggest that Felicia is quite a cut above common humankind.

Further, the temple with which she is associated intimates that her dignity comes from self-restraint, strength, and purity. Despite the requirement that he be purified before entering his god's temple, the god of the temple with which Enareto is associated is the randy and devilish Pan. In contrast, Felicia lives at the Temple of Diana, the huntress and goddess of chastity. Especially important, in characterizing Felicia as a sedate, rational female with sacred powers presiding over the Temple of Diana hidden in the forests, Montemayor seems to counter the perception of Diana as the threatening Lady of the Beasts. No vindictive devourer of Acteaons, Felicia is a compassionate and learned human woman promoting disciplined, moral devotion to uplifting love. Yet Montemayor's female mage is still far from a submissive subject of patriarchal control. Although the temple where Felicia presides can only be entered by those who are pure, purity is defined more in terms of being true to one's first love than one's physical state—recalling the definition of the ancient romances.[175] The guidance Felicia gives is not to excise passion, in women or men, in favor of reason but to blend both. Her methodology for transforming those she guides reflects a merging of the earthly and the heavenly, the physical and the spiritual.

Felicia, unlike Enareto of *Ameto*, does not solely rely on spells to work her ends but uses her magical powers to supplement her education of the shepherds who come to her to be cured of love's sufferings. Significantly, before she even attempts using magic, Felicia seeks to teach the shepherds through philosophical discussions. First, she teaches them about the nature of love, stressing altruism, reason, and virtue: "In cases of love I have a rule that I have found to be true, and it is that to have a generous spirit and a refined wit is a great advantage to those who love true. Since love is a virtue, and virtue always finds a place in the best places, it follows that those who are virtuous will always be more in love than those who are not."[176] With this instruction, Felicia draws them away from selfish love and emphasizes the power in the discipline of selflessness and reason, or "wit." When the shepherds express fear that, according to many, their lowly birth prevents them from possessing these virtues, she again stresses the spiritually uplifting element of love, assuring them: "It is in nothing other than in man's own virtue, to possess a lively wit, thoughts inclined toward higher things, and other virtues that he is born with."[177] Later, Sireno wants to understand how Love can disrupt reason if true Love is born of reason recognizing true, sacred beauty. In response, Felicia acknowledges the human trait of wanting to break free of the constraints of reason, as well as the fact that sometimes Love overcomes Reason for altruistic ends: devotion to God or sacrificing oneself to protect one's family, friends, or country.[178] However, she explains to her charges that when a love is true, the human lapse into irrationality will ultimately give way to a higher love: "though it be inflamed with unbridled affection, [love] is born of Reason and of true knowledge and judgment, which judges the beloved worthy of being loved for her virtues alone; and this kind of love, to my way of thinking, if I do not deceive myself, is not illicit nor dishonest, because love of this nature aims to no other end than to love the person for himself, without other interests or hope of a reward."[179] Her description of love here does not hold that physical passion is wrong but that "inflamed" and "unbridled affection" bring fulfilling higher insight when melded with selflessness, virtue, self-discipline, and wisdom.

After Felicia has instructed the shepherds and perceived their evolved understanding of "true love," she proceeds to use her magic. Again, unlike Enareto, she does not just cast spells, but uses her own powers of observation and reasoning to determine what course of treatment will work best for each individual—and sometimes she uses more psychology than magic or combines magic with psychology. For Selvagia, Sylvano, and Sireno she does use a magic potion. Nevertheless, she makes clear the reasoning behind her decision: "It would be no small bit of cruelty to place the cure of one who needs it in hands so great as Time's. In some cases, there is no remedy like it; but for great sorrows, if there were no other remedy besides it, people would waste so much time that their lives would cease before their sorrows." Thus when she gives a potion in a "crystal goblet . . . with enameled gold stem . . ." to Sireno, she says, "Forgotten shepherd [by Diana], if there was another cure for your grief besides this, I would earnestly seek it, but since you cannot have the one who once loved you without causing another's death, and that is only in God's hands, you must have another cure so you do not desire the unobtainable." Giving a different goblet to Selvagia and Sylvano to share, she says "And you, fair Selvagia, who desires the unobtainable, and disdained Sylvano, take this goblet in which you will find good cure for your sorrows and the beginning of the happiness you have forgotten." She awakens Sireno, first, with a magic book. Thanks to the potion he has imbibed, he has mercifully lost his passion for Diana, only feeling disinterested concern for her, as he would for any human being. She then awakens Sylvano and Selvagia, also with the magic book. Their unrequited loves for undeserving others are now gone, leaving their minds clear to be attracted to not just each other's physical beauty but their wit and devotion as well. Immediately, Felicia purposefully separates them, to make the lovers long for the pleasure of each other's virtues, which they now recognize and revere so that they consequently fall in love.[180] Thus, Felicia's careful observation of the troubles of her patients and logical application of the appropriate treatments for them, tempered with her compassionate desire to help others, enables her to wield her supernatural powers not just effectively but constructively.

Even more interesting is Felicia's "treatment" for Belissa and Felismena, both young women whose lovers have been lost: Belissa's through death and Felismena's through his fickleness and shame. With her supernatural grasp of knowledge beyond the normal mortal's ken, Felicia not only knows that Belissa's lover, Arselio, is not really dead but where he and Felismena's lover might be found. That is why she says, "With this medicine, I would, fair Felismena, cure your grief, as well as yours, shepherdess Belissa, if Fortune did not hold greater happiness in store for you that you yourselves can obtain."[181] However, she does not merely hand the young men over to these shepherdesses, but sets in motion plans that will help the two grow through finding the men when all are ready to be reunited.

Felicia wisely reasons that Felismena is the individual best suited to journey back into the world to find the lost lovers because she has shown the most strength, wisdom, and pluck.[182] With this choice, Felicia picks a woman whose use of spear and quiver to save Felicia's nymphs and their shepherd friends from vicious, lust-crazed wild men[183] recalls the Artemis-like martial prowess and adventurousness of *Aithiopika*'s Chariklea. In Felismena, the wise woman selects an envoy who also has demonstrated fidelity by secretly following her beloved into the court world and clever intrepidity by disguising herself as a boy to grasp the freedom denied women in the male-controlled court. Later, Felismena even is self-disciplined enough to bear her beloved's infatuation with another woman and has wit enough to outmaneuver that woman's infatuation with her masculine disguise.[184] Felismena proves Felicia's reasoning correct by not only finding her and Belissa's lovers but by wisely adjudicating the tangled loves of two other pairs of shepherds and shepherdesses.[185] It could be argued that Felicia has turned Felismena into a guide in training.

Felicia's guidance of her charges demonstrates reason, maturity, and compassion that decidedly reverse stereotypes of women, especially as perpetuated in *Arcadia*'s "wise woman." Ironically, Felicia is actually more temperate and rational than Sannazaro's "reverend shepherd." Enareto merely puts the shepherd through some rituals and casts spells without asking any questions. In contrast, Felicia, first, mentally and spiritually prepares her charges through Platonic dialogues, then decides how to use her magic by analyzing which spells will best serve the individual needs of those consulting her. All in all, Felicia's insight into human nature, coupled with her supernatural powers, render her a superlative guide, gifted at promoting the happiness and spiritual well-being of those who seek her out.

In the end, all the major players are reunited at the Temple of Diana, where Felicia presides over a wedding feast.[186] Ideal social order is restored amongst humans, whether in the sacrament of marriage or under the auspices of the holy Diana in an idyllic pastoral setting. And that order has been restored under the guidance of Felicia, who could be said to administer an intellectual version of carnival mockery to shake up misconceptions underlying an unjust order. Her mental tests and trials of discussions and her experiential tests and trials of journeys and separations, coupled with magic, lead her charges to a deeper understanding of themselves and their loved ones that will enable them to live in harmony.

Especially interesting, Felicia's guidance does not control or limit her charges but actually empowers them. It works best when they help themselves. She gives Selvagia and Sylvano a potion only to help clear away the cobwebs of lost love so they can better determine the wisest choices in love on their own. She does not merely plunk Arselio and Belissa down together, but helps Belissa develop the fortitude and faith not to despair completely in her seeming loss, and then clears up the illusion that has separated the shepherdess and her lover so that they can choose to reunite. Finally, Felicia empowers Felismena to overcome her misery by helping others and provides her with the opportunity to reunite with Don Felice, at the same time giving him the opportunity, not forcing him, to repent his betrayal of their love. As much, if not more than Boccaccio's Lia, Montemayor's Felicia spurs her charges to learn at their own pace and to learn for themselves how to uplift themselves.

Felicia could be called an anti-witch for her ability to use magic with reason and compassion rather than vengeance, lust, and selfishness—a carnivalesque overturning of the characterization of woman as demonic. The kindness with which she repeatedly offers her aid[187] undercuts anxieties about women's power by bringing her back into the realm of the Marian motherly comforter, for "there is none to whom she does not give a remedy."[188] Yet combining this compassion with the good she achieves through her learning, strength, intelligence, and eloquence and independence of masculine authority subtly undercuts the demand for the complete female submission that Mary had come to represent. In fact, of these three seminal works (*Ameto*, *Arcadia*, and *Diana*), Montemayor's leading females' carnivalesque response to the contemporary gender hierarchy is perhaps the most impressive influence on the development of the female pastoral guide in English Renaissance drama. Selvagia's witty interchanges with Sylvano is strongly echoed by Rosalind's schooling of Orlando in *As You Like It*. Felismena's judging the conflicts between proud and scornful shepherdesses and abject, obsessive shepherds bears a noticeable resemblance to Rosalind's scolding of both Phebe and Silvius. And Felicia's treatment of disquieted lovers with a deft blending of psychological insight, magic, reason, and compassion will reappear in the ministrations of Clorin in *The Faithful Shepherdess*, the mordant wit and references to instruction by a magician uncle of Rosalind in *As You Like It*, and the uneasy blending of ritual magic and well-intentioned marital legerdemain of Helena in *All's Well That Ends Well*, to name just a few examples.

All in all, the female guide of the pastoral world will come to act as an antidote to fear of the knowledge, speech, and sexuality of "unruly women" that the witch incarnates. As a goddess, she stands as a protective Mary, Pales, or Venus versus a disruptive Circe, Medea, or Hecate. As mage or wise woman, the guide demonstrates that an educated, empowered woman need not pose a threat—either because she still acts in accordance with the required virtues of obedience and humility or because her use of power does not undermine the social order. Still, literary incarnations of the guide are not always straightforward. She might battle the witch or be characterized by a modesty and an obedience that assuage fears of the feminine Other. However, the guide may also wrestle with or be tainted by such traits, either revealing an uneasiness about allowing women agency free of patriarchal direction or questioning the ability of any human to exist as such an ideal. In fact, what makes the guide's status as antidote intriguing is the range of treatments writers use to depict how she counteracts concerns about the dangers of feminine power unbounded by masculine control: from the conservative view only allowing female power when it is directed by patriarchal wisdom to the opposite extreme in which the guide's beneficial independence challenges, even disproves, contemporary beliefs about gender encoded by church, state, and custom. The next chapter will focus on the varied forms that guide as goddess takes on in English pastoral drama. However, it will be necessary first to study how she is affected by and reflects conflicting feelings about the anomaly of a woman as head of church and nation.

3

Queens and Goddesses:
Endymion, A Midsummer Night's Dream,
and *Love's Victory*

DURING THE SIXTEENTH AND SEVENTEENTH CENTURIES, the pastoral was no less an important literary genre in England than on the Continent. Edmund Spenser, Philip Sidney, Mary Herbert, Walter Raleigh, John Lyly, Michael Drayton, Samuel Daniel, William Shakespeare, Ben Jonson, John Milton, Andrew Marvell, Mary Wroth, and Robert Herrick used the pastoral to delve into and to communicate their beliefs on political and religious issues, the relationships between men and women and amongst the classes, and the importance of aesthetic principles with audiences of the general public, the court, or their intellectual and artistic coteries. Even lesser lights such as Thomas Campion, Barnabe Googe, and Sir John Davies saw the pastoral as a vehicle for celebrating the beauty of a mistress, the glory of Elizabeth I, or the pleasures of country *otium*. The female guide was not left behind in the pastoral's transition from the Continent to England. Either as goddess or learned female as mage or wise woman, she remained a powerful force in sixteenth- and seventeenth-century English pastoral, particularly on the stage. All kinds of drama featured her, from craft guild celebrations (Flora in *Rhodon and Iris*) to private university or aristocratic dramas (Chloris in *The Faery Pastorall*, Venus in *Love's Victory*, Sylvia in *The Careless Shepherd*, and Sabrina in *Comus*) to plays written for the general public of various classes (Ceres in *Loves* [sic] *Metamorphosis*, Juno in *The Maydes* [sic] *Metamorphosis*, and Titania in *A Midsummer Night's Dream*).

As an alternative to or a variation on the witch, the guide continues in English literature to enable writers and audiences to address uneasy social relations. Yet the English descendant of Sannazaro's, Boccaccio's, and Montemayor's works is not a mere copy of her continental foremother. English writers adapt the pastoral guide to express their own cultural and political experiences, sometimes to assert patriarchy's legitimacy or sometimes to challenge it. Such sixteenth- and seventeenth-century adaptations of the female pastoral guide give an overview of various strategies writers of the era used to express, contain, or respond to contemporary social anxieties. A significant adaptation of the guide in English pastoral is her mergence with the sixteenth-century deification of Elizabeth I as

98

a sacred virgin restoring England to a golden age, pastoral in a union of nature, humanity, and God. Yet though pastoral Queen Elizas, Cynthias, Dianas, and Bellphoebes may celebrate Elizabeth's restoration of golden world order, they also frequently intimate unease with the possibility of even a divine being rising above woman's natural flaws.

This tension colors many of English pastoral writers' revisions of the guide as goddess, even when they do not directly envision her as Eliza[beth], Queen of Shepherds. Some of these pastoral dramas tend to treat the goddess guide's divine powers as an anomaly in the "natural" hierarchy of male over female that must be corrected. These plays tend to draw on one or more of the following strategies to diminish the guide's powers: showing her using these powers to affirm, not challenge, masculine ascendancy; putting her under the auspices of a male divinity; or showing her inhibited by the flaws that contemporary philosophy attributed to women. On the other hand, some dramatic versions of the female pastoral guide, such as in *A Midsummer Night's Dream* and *Love's Victory*, actually overturn the concept of masculine control as a necessary bulwark against the chaotic female Other.

The several venues in which the guide appears suggests that she resonated with a variety of constituents in contemporary audiences. The four plays that will be the focus of this chapter illustrate this point. Mary Wroth's *Love's Victory* (c. 1620) was written for her aristocratic intellectual coterie. Lyly's *Endymion* was presented for the Queen at Greenwich on Candlemas, February 2, 1588, earning the playwright the honor of becoming an "Esquire of the Body." His *Loves Metamorphosis* (1598/1600) and Shakespeare's *A Midsummer Night's Dream* (*MSND*) (1595/6) were both written to be performed for the public, the former for Paul's Boys, a more elite audience, and the latter for the Globe, a much more general public— although there is speculation that *MSND* may have originally been written for an "aristocratic wedding," then adapted for more public performance.[1] Thus, the female pastoral guide as goddess pervaded the pastoral on stage, crossing class and educational barriers. She was an intellectual and entertainment nexus for writers and audiences in the general public of theaters such as the Globe, as well as of aristocratic gatherings.[2]

This chapter will be organized along the following lines. Initially, it will examine Elizabeth's assimilation of the Catholic mythos of the Virgin Mary and of the pagan mythos of the divine virgin Astraea, focusing on her society's participation in this assimilation and including its mixed reception to having a woman as a monarch in a patriarchal culture. This portion will also look into how the pastoral golden world, presided over by a wise, divine figure, was often used to support Elizabeth's power, but could also be employed to intimate challenges. Next will be a study of how John Lyly's *Endymion* serves as an important representative of the ways in which the divine guide of Boccaccio's *Ameto,* Venus, has been significantly reconfigured in terms of Elizabeth's image as divine virgin to meet a more traditionally Christian standard of spiritual purity devoid of threatening sexuality. Perhaps what makes Lyly's version of the Elizabethan goddess guide most interesting is that he radically changes the way Boccaccio's Venus addresses fears about female sensuality and independence of action and word through a variation of what Elizabeth Harvey and Diane Purkiss see as "ventriloquizing" the female voice to reassert masculine authority. Lyly's variation does not use the voice of "the unruly woman" as a shield to express criticism against the religious, political, economic or artistic order, as Harvey and Purkiss discuss, but puts in the mouth of the authoritative female guide directives designed to master unruly women and assert the preeminence of men in the gender hierarchy. Finally, this chapter will focus on how in *A Midsummer Night's Dream* and *Love's Victory* the goddess may not specifically embody Queen Elizabeth but continues to reflect tensions concerning gender conflicts, though sometimes by treating the woman's voice not as something to be enslaved but to be listened to with tolerance or even respect.

Chapter 1 addressed how the Virgin Mary answered specific emotional and spiritual needs in Western society, such as providing a divine sympathetic intermediary to soften God's wrath and supplanting sexually powerful nature goddesses with a chaste and obedient figure more acceptable to Christian patriarchy. However, in Protestant England, the Catholic view of Mary, criticized as idolatrous, would prove highly unacceptable to Anglicans and Puritans alike. The Protestant Church and State found that reinterpreting the Catholic Mary into Elizabeth as its head allowed not only the redirection of tradition to support reform but facilitated the concentration of power in the upper echelons of the religious and class hierarchy. As Louis Montrose explains, "[T]he Elizabethan government had to find ways to channel and delimit iconoclasm and to check the momentum of reform if the symbols through which its power was manifested were to remain untainted and efficacious." One effective way to do so was to supplant the Catholic "cult of the Virgin Mary" underlying pervasive "craft cycles," "medieval spirituality," and "folk culture" with "[a] virgin Queen who united church and state, brought relative peace and security to her people, and secured the triumph of the reformed religion"[3] through what Stephen Greenblatt calls "displacement and absorption." In displacement, the Catholic veneration of Mary does not entirely lose its essential sacredness, but the main force of that sacredness is "absorbed" into Elizabeth so that "the sacred may find itself serving as an adornment, a backdrop."[4] The Protestant holy days that replaced Catholic feasts serve as good examples. Celebrations of the Queen's birthday came to supplant the feast of the Virgin Mary's birth, and the Queen's Accession Day was celebrated like a holy day: as "[t]he Reformation had swept away many important Catholic feast days,. . . . [t]he rise of the Queen's Day festivities enabled these energies to be concentrated into a stream designed to glorify the monarchy and its policies."[5]

Specific traits shared with Mary permitted Elizabeth's absorption and displacement of powers associated with the Virgin. Several of her symbols aligned her with Mary. Danté's *Paradiso* had expressed the Catholic association of the unity, beauty, and purity of the rose with the Virgin Mary. Elizabeth co-opted this floral symbol into an advertisement of her bloodlines, creating national unity in her family's emblem of the Tudor rose that combined the white and the red roses of the Yorks and Lancasters, whose battle for control of England had once ripped apart the nation. Several other images that Elizabeth used, or her subjects associated with her, to symbolize her restoration of a golden age have been associated with Mary: "the Star, the Moon, the Phoenix, the Ermine, the Pearl."[6]

The purity represented by the shared symbols of the moon and the ermine is perhaps a fundamental similarity between Elizabeth and Mary, for their divine status is strongly rooted in chastity. The trait of virginity bestows on both female figures virtue above the fallen state of earthly woman, proving that they are above the inconstancy and promiscuity inherited from Mother Eve. Interestingly, much like the mother of *Arcadia*, Elizabeth's and the Virgin Mary's elevations above the sexual make them appear nonthreatening creators of spiritual fecundity. Mary's fertility comes in gestating and giving birth to the son of God, or God in human incarnation, without any form of sexual intercourse. Elizabeth creates her own version of the virginal mother by coupling her chastity with her maternal care for her subjects. Elizabeth's 1563 speech to the Commons provides a good example of what Greenblatt calls her "portraying herself as a Virgin Mother": "And so I assure you all . . . that, though after my death you may have many step-dames, yet shall you never have a more natural mother than I mean to be unto you all." Katherine Duncan-Jones notes that Philip Sidney's 1581 entertainment "Four Foster Children of Desire" also casts Elizabeth "as mother to her people," although Duncan-Jones also observes that this mother "threaten[s] to deny sustenance to her suckling courtiers."[7]

Notably, both these chaste mothers give birth to morality and redemption: Mary to Christ, savior of fallen humankind, and Elizabeth to the Protestant Reformation in England. Bishop Jewell's *Apology for the Church of England* (1560) and its *Defence* (1567), like George Foxe's *Book of Martyrs* (1554, '59, '63), sets up Elizabeth as rescuing the true Church from an Antichrist Pope. In Foxe's text, the picture inside the capital "C" beginning the name Constantine even shows Elizabeth trampling the Pope beneath her feet. Frances Yates sees this as "represent[ing] the return to the Constantinian, imperial Christianity, free from papal shackles, the kind of religion which Foxe regards as alone pure." Significantly, this image and its context also recall an image Marina Warner and Jaroslav Pelikan cite as a popular one of the Virgin: Mary, trampling Satan beneath her feet as a symbol of her giving birth to the Redeemer of humankind. This portrait of Elizabeth consolidates her power not only by absorbing one of the most impressive images from Catholicism but also by turning the symbol against that religion.[8] Suggesting that the salvation Elizabeth brings is not just national but global, John Dee's *General and rare memorials pertayning to the Perfect Arte of Navigation* (1577) commences with this same image with the initial "C" to speak in favor of British expansionism across the world's oceans.[9] Here, Dee not only applauds Elizabeth's redeeming England from the Catholic Whore of Babylon but calls for her to redeem the entire world.

One important reason that Elizabeth and Mary were viewed as giving birth to spiritual redemption is that both are perceived as intermediaries with God for humans. As the mother of Christ, as free of original sin, as God's chosen, as a humble being, Mary has the purity and humility to link with God and divine truth. Yet since she is not herself a god, she is still a part of humankind. Her humanity gives her pity for our sufferings and her connection to divinity a means to ask God to pity us. That she can rise so high while still human can inspire us to strive to emulate her sacredness.[10] Similarly, Elizabeth I was clearly flesh and blood, born of human parents. Still, imperial theory links her to divinity. Elizabeth and many of her contemporaries' view the prince as God's vicar on earth, set by God to rule over the nation. According to this line of thought, Anne Sommerset concludes, "there were no circumstances in which a withdrawal of allegiance could be legitimate. Even if a prince was evil, or governed unjustly, his people should not rise up against him, for bad rulers were accountable to God alone. . . ."[11] This outlook of maintaining the social hierarchy was sponsored and enforced by powerful supporters during Elizabeth's reign and especially in James I's.

This perspective on allegiance applied not just to political policies but to religious ones. Frances Yates relates that Bishop Jewell asserted the right of princes to direct Church matters when he stated that "[a]ll kings have come into a share of the emperor's majesty [who 'appointed the Councils' of the early church] and this gives them the religious rights of emperors in councils of the church. This legitimizes the national council under royal authority by which the Church of England was reformed."[12] Thus, the English monarch has the right and duty to direct the Church of England, while his/her subjects have the responsibility to obey these directives As head of both Church and State, then, Elizabeth possesses a link to divinity enabling her to perceive God's higher Truth and to interpret that Truth for those beneath her in the hierarchy.

An even older type than the Virgin Mary also underlies the cult of Elizabeth as divine virgin restoring the golden world, the myth of Astraea/ Virgo. This mythos of pagan divine virgin shares many similarities with the Catholic one. Like Mary, Astraea reinforces the image of Elizabeth as chaste fertility goddess in the pastoral mode. Astraea similarly recalls fecundity in images where she holds ears of corn in her hands. Foxe's and Dee's uses of the picture within their capital "C" in their texts, discussed earlier, applies here as well. In the capital "C" for "Constantine" in Foxe and for "Cum" in Dee, "the top curve of the C ends in cornucopiae."[13] Some celebratory literature explains the paradox of chaste fertility by positing that this virgin's fecundity transcends earthly sexuality to create "not the ordinary season but the eternal spring of the golden age."[14] For example, in Sir John Davies's *Hymns to Astraea*, which spell out the Queen's name with the initial letter of each line, the virginal Elizabeth/Astraea engenders a realm of pastoral lushness and tranquility: "This Nymph of ours" (l.11) brings forth "E ternall [*sic*] garlands of [her] flowers, / G reene garlands neuer wasting; / I n her shall last our State's faire Spring, / N ow and for euer flourishing, / A s long as / H eauen's lasting" (lines 12–16).[15]

Frances Yates stresses that in the Renaissance a signal for the return of this lush golden age was the descent of the divine virgin Astraea to the earth she had fled for the skies to escape the earth's fall into the iron age. One major source of this mythos for the Renaissance was in Book I of Ovid's *The Metamorphoses,* which reports the degeneration of the earth from the golden through two more eras into the iron age of treachery, labor, and disharmony between humanity and nature, as well as Astraea's flight to assume the heavenly identity of Virgo. Frank Kermode and Harry Levin trace this appropriation of Ovid's Four Ages through the medieval and Renaissance writers Boethius, the authors of *Roman de la Rose*, Danté, Guarini, Tasso, Spenser, and Sandys.[16] The second major source for the Renaissance penchant for the myth of Astraea is Virgil's Fourth *Eclogue,* describing the birth of a divine child sparking Astraea's/Virgo's return to earth and the rise of a new golden age. This eclogue drew strong approbation from early Church founders down through the Middle Ages and into the Renaissance, as the divine child and returning virgin were interpreted as intimating the Virgin Mary's giving birth to Christ, who would restore a spiritual golden age by redeeming humankind from the fall precipitated by Adam and Eve.[17] Clearly, then, during Elizabeth's reign the motif of the sacred virgin's return that signaled humankind's spiritual regeneration and the restoration of harmonious bonds with nature and the Divine was strongly embedded in the culture. Protestant apologists such as Foxe and Jewell modified this image of Astraea, even as they had the Catholic Virgin's, to embody Elizabeth's sacred role in restoring England to spiritual health by driving off the corruption of Catholicism. In prose and poetry,

Dee and Raleigh, for example, used this image to champion Elizabeth's extension of her golden rule throughout the world.[18]

Her association with Astraea/Virgo enabled Elizabeth to carry her power as redeeming Virgin a step further than her absorption and displacement of associations with the Catholic Mary. Where the Virgin Mary was seen as an intermediary seeking mercy for the faithful, Virgo was perceived as a goddess who drew on mercy when she administered justice or returned justice to the earth.[19] Consequently, Elizabeth figured herself, or was figured by others, as the merciful dispenser of justice, her decisions validated by her link with the sacred as the divine virgin head of Anglican Church and State. Thus Elizabeth says of herself in "A Doubt of Future Foes," "Our realm it brooks not seditious sects, let them elsewhere resort. / My rusty sword through rest shall first his edge employ / To poll their tops that seek such change or gape for future joy" (lines 14–16). Elizabeth's sword is "rusty," disused, implying she finds more merciful means than execution to maintain peace in her kingdom; but should she need to use it to protect her people's security she will have no hesitation "his edge to employ." In his *Hymns to Astraea*, Davies celebrated how Elizabeth, like a contemporary Astraea, wins her subjects' obedience, loyalty, and love by ruling with the perfect mixture of justice and mercy: " B y *Loue* she rules more than by *Law*, / E uen her great mercy breedeth awe; / T his is her sword and scepter" (lines 6–8). Additionally, the 1591 Sudely entertainments rewrite Ovid's *Metamorphoses* so that Elizabeth answers a nymph's prayer and saves her from Apollo's lust "simply by the power of [her] presence" and her words of: "I stay, for whether should chastety fly for succour, but to the Queene of chastety?"[20]

Especially significant to this study of the female pastoral guide, Elizabeth's portrayal as Astraea is frequently set in the pastoral. This is not surprising, considering that the two main sources for the Astraea mythos are firmly connected to pastoral tradition. Ovid's myth of the golden age strongly parallels the idyllic natural, human, and divine interrelations of the pastoral world, and Renaissance writers frequently draw on these lines to evoke a pastoral topos. Hence, Guarini's *Il Pastor Fido* and Tasso's *Aminta* both incorporate this passage from Ovid to establish tone and setting. Tellingly, in *As You Like It* Charles the wrestler evokes Ovid's setting and ambiance to demonstrate that Duke Senior has found a more idyllic pastoral existence in the forest of Arden, when he says, "Many young gentlemen flock to him every day, and fleet the time carelessly as they did in the golden world" (1.1.118–19).[21] So the pastoral world will come to prove an apt symbol for England's golden era, and the popularity of Elizabeth as the divine figure guiding her people back into that age and protecting them from the incursions of hostile outsiders will ultimately merge with the female pastoral guide as goddess to give this character a foothold in English literature.

One more pattern draws together the Queen as divine virgin guiding her subjects to redemption and the female pastoral guide: the courtly love defined in *The Courtier*. Chapter 1 touched on how the theory of courtly love posited that chaste, altruistic love of beauty in the beloved lady could enable the courtier to ascend a spiritual ladder to embrace Good or God. Unencumbered by the grossness of sexuality, selfishness, or infidelity, the courtier sees the goodness and beauty in the lady as an emanation of divine good that he will strive to attain by developing his talents as artist, political adviser, soldier, dancer, etc., to their utmost in service to the lady. All he does, he dedicates to the lady of goodness and beauty, so all his efforts must be pursued with unselfishness and devotion to spiritual purity. As the chaste goddess, Marian or Astraean, whose spiritual purity enables her to redeem the fallen world, Elizabeth proves an apt version of the lady whose mercy and justice accord favor to those who have served Good through serving her. Or, as Harry Levin relates, "All Englishmen found themselves engaged in a collective romance, since their sovereign was not merely a woman but a notorious virgin, whose courtiers acted out the rituals of courtship and made a mystique of her virginity."[22]

But this courtship carried high political stakes, for as Peter Hermann writes, "from the 1570s onward the rhetoric of love in the Elizabethan court became deeply entwined with the rhetoric of politics."[23] Illuminating the way in which "love lyrics" and "the language of love . . . could express figuratively the realities of suit, service, and recompense,"[24] Stephen Greenblatt describes how courtly pursuit of Elizabeth in a plethora of incarnations as sacred chaste lady consolidated her strength:

> Through the years, courtiers, poets, ballad makers, and artists provided many other cult images: in Raleigh's partial list, "Cynthia, Pheobe, Flora, Diana and Aurora," to which we may add Astraea, Zabeta, Deborah, Laura, Oriana, and, of course, Belphoebe and Gloriana [of *The Faerie Queene*]. The gorgeous rituals of praise channeled national and religious sentiments into the worship of the prince, masked over and thus temporarily deflected deep social, political, and theological divisions in late sixteenth-century England, transformed Elizabeth's potentially disastrous sexual disadvantage into a supreme political virtue and imposed a subtle discipline upon aggressive fortune seekers.[25]

Elizabeth, then, cleverly used courtly love to consolidate her own power and to distract those under her from challenging her. In a courtly motif, service to Elizabeth's political and religious goals became an ascent up the stairs of love to divine communion. Equally important, as a courtly lady meriting her courtiers' service, Elizabeth kept her nobles in line by channeling their energies and ambitions into striving to please her, often forcing then to dissipate their aggressions against each other rather than her, in hope of reward.

Still, Louis Montrose points out that in the courtly pursuit of Elizabeth the exchange of power was not all one way: "The cult of Elizabeth . . . also served the interests of her subjects by providing a flexible medium of address, at once refined and humble, in which they could supplicate and inveigle their royal mistress."[26] The forms of courting Elizabeth might be carried out within a work of art or through a combination of art and action. In the Earl of Hertford's pastoral entertainment for the Queen at his estate Elvetham in 1591, a "crescent-moon-shaped" body of water, before which the Queen sat in state, evoked her role as divine virgin. The defeat of Sylvanus, a "bestial God of the woods" who had declared his love for "Cynthia," by a sea god rising from the pond and dousing his "'wanton fire'" playfully conveyed her inspiration of the sacred and her purification of earthly corruption.[27] In a better known example, Spenser's *Faerie Queene* is a massive literary celebration of Elizabeth's great rule, but it is also a call for her financial support and consequent approbation of the Protestant virtues the poet endorses and the artistic form he uses to convey them.[28] Even other royalty used art to make their courtly addresses. Using a Petrarchan sonnet, in 1586 James IV/I wooed Elizabeth in the courtly mode for a guarantee in writing of her promised pension from the Anglo-Scots treaty to him and for his appointment as her heir.[29]

Her subjects casting Elizabeth as sacred virgin was far from problematic. The pattern did not work purely in Elizabeth's favor because she did not have complete control over the power this iconography invested in her. Those lower in the hierarchy could also use this role-playing to pressure her to work toward their ends. Further, Elizabeth could not freely resist this pressure because to maintain her authority she needed to consolidate the support of class and religious factions or to play one off against the other. Michael Leslie's study of this reflexive relationship in court entertainments illuminates the point especially well. He observes that Elizabeth might be able to turn away to control the efficacy of entertainments performed in court or set outside her window at an estate hosting her during her progress. However, when she made a progress into a city or took a walk or rode upon an estate, she had no such options and could be forced into participating in the pageant of allegorical representatives of political questions.[30]

Literature exerts much the same pressure when lauding Elizabeth as courtly lady and sacred virgin. As noted above, James VI/I's sonnet approaches Elizabeth as divine Petrarchan lady, but this method demands political capitol of her to keep his support.[31] Spenser's *Shepheardes Calendar, Colin Clouts Come Home Againe,* and *The Faerie Queene* praise Elizabeth's wisdom, largesse, and sanctity but also pressure her politics by equating her possession and application of such traits with her adhering to specific views on Protestant reform, providing court and artistic support, and rejecting Catholic marriages and alliances.[32] Sidney's "Letter to Queen Elizabeth touching her marriage with Monsieur" praises her as "the example of princes, the ornament of this age, the comfort of the afflicted, the delight of your people, the most excellent fruit of all your progenitors, and perfect mirror to your posterity," but his praise is linked to Elizabeth's rejecting her intimated plans for a marriage with the Catholic Duke d'Alençon that would undo Protestant reform and weaken the political power of Sidney's family.[33] Thus, in a culture where "[t]he nobility, gentlemen, and hangers-on of the court generated a variety of pressures that constantly threatened the fragile stability of the Elizabethan regime,"[34] the motif of a courtly service to the divine virgin did not leave all the power in Elizabeth's hands. With national stability, eternal damnation or redemption, and each individual's life at stake, she and her courtier subjects were under tremendous pressure to negotiate transactions of power carefully.

Another pressure was added to the mix that no male prince had to consider. Elizabeth was a woman trying to justify her reign in a social order that asserted complete male ascendancy over women based on divine fiat and medical learning. As Louis Montrose writes: "The political nation, which was wholly a nation of men, seems at times to have found it frustrating or degrading to serve a female prince—a woman who was herself unsubjected to any man. Late in Elizabeth's reign, the French ambassador observed that her government is fairly pleasing to the people, who show that they love her, but it is little pleasing to the great men and nobles; and if by chance she should die, it is certain that the English would never again submit to the rule of a woman."[35] As a result, Elizabeth and her social system negotiated different strategies to prevent granting such power to a female from undermining the patriarchy. One such strategy that Elizabeth and her apparatus of state used to allay concerns about allowing governance to women was in selecting acceptable explanations for the successful rule of a female. Pamela Benson points out that, on one hand, texts such as John Aylmer's 1559 *An Harborowe for faithfull and trewe Subjectes agaynst the late blowne Blaste, concerninge the Gouernment of Wemen* allowed for Elizabeth's successful reign by asserting she was proof of God's power, showing He was so great He could even make a woman a successful ruler.[36] Conversely, treatises such as George Whetsone's 1586 *The English Myrror* and Henry Howard's *A dutiful defense of the lawful regiment of women* that explained her expertise as disproving contemporary views of women's moral, intellectual, and emotional incapacity were condemned.[37] This way, Elizabeth and the patriarchal state mutually served each other: she by keeping her prerogatives within the parameters of contemporary definitions of power distribution and the State by de-legitimizing, even demonizing, queens like Mary Queen of Scots who threatened Elizabeth's authority.[38]

Both Elizabeth and the males she ruled turned to her image as a virgin to calm masculine concerns about being under the subjection of a woman, who by nature was supposed as far more prone to voracious sexuality and irrationality than a man. Elizabeth's enacting the role of courtly lady whose purity inspired courtiers could also serve to allay such concerns.[39] What makes these strategies particularly relevant to an understanding of the female pastoral guide as goddess are Louis Montrose's and Diane Purkiss's observations that this anxiety is played out in contemporary Renaissance literature. One text that Purkiss and Montrose both turn to in order to explicate tensions over a woman holding a prince's power is John Lyly's *Endymion*. Significantly, in this pastoral the incarnation of Elizabeth as divine virgin and recipient of courtly devotion, Cynthia, strongly resembles the Continental female pastoral goddess guides, with hints of the wise mage as well. Discussing this play's adaptation of the female pastoral guide shows how the cult of Elizabeth, as well as its attendant social and political concerns, gives the guide a foothold in English pastoral. Equally important, a study of *Endymion* illustrates how the divine female pastoral guide provides an apt vehicle for exploring these concerns.

II

The courtly practice of wooing Elizabeth for practical favor by portraying her as a divinity creating and maintaining England as golden pastoral realm is one that Lyly draws on in his adaptation of the pastoral guiding goddess for overlapping political and personal ends. There have been conjectures that Endymion's desire to earn Cynthia's favor was Lyly's attempt to help restore either the Earl of Leicester or the Earl of Oxford, master of Lyly's playhouse, to Elizabeth's favor after these men had provoked her ire through ill-advised liaisons and marriages.[40] However, David Bevington and Michael Pincombe have suggested that any pleadings for Oxford would relate to the more timely charges and countercharges that he was exchanging with Arundel and Henry Howard, Earl of Norfolk, concerning a conspiracy to aid Catholic plots to assassinate Elizabeth and restore Catholic control of England, including accusations of using witchcraft and prophecy to harm a prince.[41] Fears of a Catholic overthrow of Protestant England seem strongly to inform this play, for David Bevington points out that there are remarkable parallels between Cynthia's rival for Endymion, Tellus, and the strong Catholic threat to Elizabeth's power, Mary Stuart (Queen of Scots).

Bevington explains that both Tellus and Mary continually plotted to overthrow the power of the rightful queen, both were connected with witchcraft, both were charged with trying to seduce and corrupt the monarch's loyal courtiers with promises of marriage, both were connected to blasphemy (Tellus, witchcraft; Mary, Catholicism and witchcraft), both continued to do so even after being imprisoned, both were repeatedly "forgiven" by the monarch—although in real life Elizabeth's patience fatally ran out, where Cynthia was able to forgive an obedient, if grudgingly repentant, rival.[42] Another strong parallel, which Bevington does not address, is that the tapestry portraits Tellus wove during her imprisonment rather pointedly evoke a tapestry that Mary Stuart created during her imprisonment as a present to the Duke of Norfolk, whom she had hoped to marry. Both fictional character and real woman were equally defiant to their rulers in their needle work: Tellus by taking possession of the man she has been ordered to forget through recreating him in art and Mary by presenting her potential groom with emblems contrasting their marriage's probable fertility with Elizabeth's single childlessness as a hint that they would be the ultimate source of an heir to England's throne.[43] Another important point that Bevington does not discuss is that Tellus's embodiment of the unruly woman's disruptiveness in sexuality, action, and word mirrors the mainstream English Protestant views of Mary Stuart, particularly in the scandals surrounding the death of her second husband, Lord Darnley; her affair with and marriage to Bothwell; and the sudden death of his wife.[44]

Lyly's motives for trying to influence Elizabeth could have been personal as well as political. Both Bevington and Pincombe note that Lyly's association with Lord Oxford, alive when *Endymion* was probably written, left him vulnerable to being sucked into the imbroglio over the Catholic assassination plots. Consequently, Lyly insisted on his innocence in a letter to chief counselor (Lyly's relation and Oxford's father-in-law) Lord Burley: "Loth I am to be a prophett, and to be a whiche [witch] I loath."[45] The epilogue to *Endymion* especially brings home how this political plea intertwines with personal need, as Lyly asks his "[d]read sovereign" to turn against "the malicious that seek to overthrow us with threats" and, instead, "vouchsafe with [her] favourable beams to glance upon us" (lines 11–13).[46] For here, Lyly is not just playing the role of Castiglione's good courtier who respectfully seeks to give his prince advice for the kingdom's benefit.[47] Lyly may also have been suing the Queen for his own advancement, an attempt to rise from entertaining "court poet" to influential "courtier poet." Numerous critics have pointed out Lyly's belief that in the late 1580s the Queen had intimated she would make him Master of the Revels.[48] *Endymion*'s celebration of Elizabeth's wisdom, mercy, and justice in the form of the pastoral guide Cynthia would have proved a flattering and artistically deft nudging of Elizabeth to approve him.

The most notable evidence of Cynthia as a goddess guide is the fact that this play is pervaded by references to her divinity enabling her to direct not only the pastoral world but the humans inhabiting it toward pastoral perfection. "The eternal gods" give her "government" over natural, supernatural, and human forces (5.4.7–8), "time, fortune, destiny, and death are subject" to "divine Cynthia" (5.1.61–62). Her celestial preeminence over creation is implied by the fairies awarding her an appellation reminiscent of the Christian Mary and the pagan Isis, "Queen of Stars" (4.3.35). Illustrating her beneficence as a supernatural being, this divine goddess harmonizes nature and humanity. Dedicated to order, truth, justice, and mercy, Cynthia proclaims, "I have always studied to have rather living virtues than painted gods, the body of truth than the tomb" (4.3. 55–56). In the course of the play we see that she recognizes and seeks to develop the good qualities in Endymion (3.1.36, 5.4.177–87), feels for his suffering (3.1.60–63) as well as for that of Eumenides concerning Semele (5.4.204–45), searches out the cause and means to reclaim Endymion from the curse of perpetual sleep (3.1.48–66), and in the final act of the play conquers the curses of Tellus and Dipsas, reconciling warring lovers and disgruntled courtiers.

In the end, Cynthia ensures social harmony amongst her subjects by uniting the major characters in appropriate marital pairings. In earthly marriages, she rewards Eumenides with a Semele chastened of her scorn and matches Corsites with Tellus, to whom he is devoted. Cynthia places the comical Sir Tophas with the equally comical Bagoa and returns a repentant Dipsas to her husband Geron, whom the old woman had once abandoned in order to practice witchcraft (act 5). Cynthia allows Endymion the privilege of worshipping her, though as she is a Goddess above him their marriage is out of the question. The upshot of all her guidance is that the witchcraft of Tellus and Dipsas is neutralized, as is the political maneuvering of Tellus and Corsites, while the marital difficulties of all are turned to harmony by the mistress of "time, fortune, destiny, and death" (5.1.62).

Purity, wisdom, and mercy empower and guide this pastoral goddess. Geron points out that to Eumenides, Cynthia is "the perfectest" (3.4.177), "the most absolute" (179) in her physical manifestation, the moon, so that "Cynthia, whose virtues, being all divine, must needs bring things to pass that be miraculous" (190–2). Her purity both empowers Cynthia to cure Endymion and inspires her to express her fidelity by standing by him when he is in need. Her incarnations as "Queen of Stars" and of the moon underlines Cynthia's transcendence of the frailties of the mortal sphere. This seeming freedom from human jealousy, pride, and doubt gives Cynthia the power to shape her actions with wisdom, seeing into the hearts of all around her as well as into the heart of "destiny." Cynthia is wise enough to send Eumenides, the courtier with the purest heart (3.1.47–66), to Thessaly to search for a cure for Endymion. Her forgiveness of Tellus's and Corsites' court intrigues reveals that mercy merges with wisdom. The goddess guide tempers her punishment of Corsites because she knows he is not truly vicious and has recognized the folly of acting against her and the golden world order that she represents.

To the untrustworthy Tellus, Cynthia responds, not with blind fury or jealousy but with reason. Initially, Cynthia sends Tellus away to reflect on her vindictiveness and intemperate love (3.1.41–47). Then, after discovering Tellus's second plot, Cynthia still gives her rival the chance to explain her actions and listens to her claims that Endymion had sorely provoked her by leading her on before and after he had started his devotions to Cynthia (5.4. 36–196). Cynthia understands Tellus's assertion that though she is not a goddess like Cynthia, her love is still deep (143–45); accepts Tellus's repentance (194–95); then concludes by uniting Tellus with Corsites (250–68). Cynthia's decision can be seen as wise and compassionate for leaving Tellus with the choice of enjoying the love of the devoted Corsites or continuing to pine over a love that can never be more than a "picture" (5.4.264–65).

In most of these cases, Cynthia presents an extremely flattering portrait of Elizabeth as a pastoral guide like Venus, Lia, or Felicia letting some of her charges learn for themselves. For example, when it comes to Endymion, Cynthia does not automatically purify her courtier but requires him to work through the process on his own, standing above him as inspiration. However, Lyly's portrait cannot be read as straightforwardly flattering. There is something far more prickly in this female pastoral guide than in the divinely, joyously consuming Venus or the Lia and Felicia whose tests are tempered with pleasure, both mental and physical. Cynthia is not like these guides in speaking a message of equating and merging male and female, dark and light, earthly and heavenly. She may be a woman on top but she definitely does not use her position to level upper and lower strata of the power hierarchy. Instead, upon close examination, her words, methods, and goals assert the need to enforce a split in these dyads. And though Cynthia is a goddess, a female divinity, her message repeatedly conveys the idea that woman unconstrained by masculine authority is dangerous, unnatural.

Elizabeth Harvey's and Diane Purkiss's study of male early-modern writers "ventriloquizing" women's voice for their own agendas was touched on in the introduction. This concept is particularly helpful in understanding what Lyly is doing with his revision of the female pastoral guide in this play. Though Diane Purkiss and Elizabeth Harvey each approach the subject from different critical angles, both observe definite tendencies in male writers to co-opt what many in early modern culture would consider the naturally disruptive voice of woman unrestrained by patriarchal authority. One of Purkiss's points of discussion concerns the pamphlet wars kicked off by Joseph Swetnam's incendiary 1615 publication. Purkiss presents interesting internal evidence that the pertly argued pamphlets signed with the women's names of Esther Sowernam, Joan Sharp, Constantia Munda (all three 1617), and Mary Tattle-Well and Joan Hit-Him-Home (1640) were actually penned by young university men to whom their society had closed off prospects for social and economic advancement. She posits that the motivations for this ventriloquizing of the verbally and sexually unruly woman by men was a complex blend of the emotional, social, and economic. On one level, the scolding tone and worldly sexual knowledge of their texts, combined with cultural associations of their pen names (sour, sharp, tattling, or violent—or, in one case, the seductive woman warrior, Esther) actually undercut the legitimacy of their defenses of women and criticism of men. Even more interesting, as these writings link criticism of those who think like Swetnam with other social and artistic issues, they may also be construed as far more related to men's concerns that have little to do with women. The misleading cover of a woman's voice gives the writers whose education has not brought them the social, political, or monetary advancement they expected an opportunity not only to earn a living but the opportunity to show off their rhetorical prowess and to express their disgruntlement with the dearth of money, power, or position to which they feel their intellectual superiority and education entitle them.[49]

Elizabeth Harvey, who coins the term "ventriloquized voices" in the title of her book, turns to French feminist criticism to explore this appropriation of a discourse associated with women. Her study broadens the scope of Purkiss's observations, looking at works extending from the Middle Ages to the late seventeenth century: Erasmus, Donne, and Milton. Harvey's writings on Erasmus raise a similar point to Purkiss's study of the university wits, although she sees his using female garrulousness as providing protective cover for a less personal and more general moral and philosophical critique of religion and human self-awareness in *In Praise of Folly*.[50] For her examinations of Donne and Milton, Harvey looks at how both writers create metaphors to describe the process of their writing by drawing on contemporary views of women as passive receptacles in which the male's seed grows, then are later "gateways" opened to allow his fruit/child to "pass through her" into the world.[51]

Although all the adaptations may not have silencing and controlling woman as their main intent in appropriating her voice, this result is a definite by-product. For repeating the convention of garrulous, promiscuous woman, even only humorously, could re-inscribe this view in audiences of elite texts, of pamphlets, of drama, of ballads, or of popular custom. As Harvey writes, "ventriloquizations of women in the Renaissance achieved the power they did partly because so few women actually wrote and spoke, but the representations of feminine speech that were current in literary and popular accounts, as well as in ventriloquizations, fostered a vision that tended to reinforce women's silence or to marginalize their voices when they did speak or write."[52] John Lyly's Cynthia in *Endymion* is a female pastoral guide who has been ventriloquized, and to some extent the words put in her mouth do address political and personal issues not touching directly on views of gender relations: apologies for erring nobles, praise of a Protestant ruler protecting the nation from Catholic overthrow, a pitch for personal and artistic advancement. However, Cynthia's advice, punishments, and rewards for her female and male subjects are the voice of traditional masculine authority decreeing the necessity of female submission. Lyly's characterization of Cynthia's superiority in chastity, reason, and verbal precision to the other female characters as anomalous further marks her as a corrective to the standard woman, not carnival's debunker and destroyer of traditional restraining conventions. In both ways, Lyly uses Cynthia to "foster a vision that [would] reinforce women's silence" and "marginalize their voices when they did speak or write."

That Lyly should use a female character to school women, and men, in proper behavior is not as contradictory as it might seem. One trait of Elizabeth's mythos that Lyly draws on in his creation of his female pastoral guide is the accepted defense of the Queen's reign as an anomaly sanctioned by God. Cynthia is female, but she is a female goddess, not a mortal woman. Like Elizabeth, she is a heavenly being who is free of the flaws innate in daughters of Eve. Finally, even though Cynthia seems to transcend womanly defects and to displace fears about the feminine Other onto the beings that she defeats, Lyly's characterization of her still does not raise women equal to men in the hierarchy of creation. For several reasons, his depiction of Cynthia reinforces the necessity of patriarchy to maintain the stability of the natural order. Most obviously, as the moon Cynthia is definitely not of this earth; she is even part of the celestial realm. This play thereby indicates that no earthly woman can even aspire to Cynthia's reason, justice, mercy, wisdom, forgiveness, or purity of body and soul—let alone her supernatural status. Insisting on the uniqueness of Cynthia's virtue recalls justifications for Elizabeth's rule as a unique situation, reinforcing the hierarchy of power based on masculine ascendancy. Bringing this point home further is Diane Purkiss's observation that none of the other women in the play is, literally, in the same class with Cynthia.[53] Dipsas is a village cunning woman; Tellus, Semele, and Favilla and Scintilla are merely ladies in waiting; while Floscula is Tellus's servant. Equally important, Cynthia's final resolutions of the love conflicts not only reassert masculine control over earthly females but, as will be detailed later, teach men not to mistake any human woman for an ideal such as herself. By channeling these froward women's energies into socially approved restrictions, Cynthia allays anxieties about the threat of the sexually or verbally unconstrained female.

The most straightforward instance of Cynthia's words and actions "voicing" the conventional contemporary wisdom to train women to their proper role is her interaction with Semele. Lyly creates Semele as the very type of William Gouge's "scornful dames" with a free tongue, displaying the disruptive insubordination condemned by Philip Stubbes in 1591 as those who "scolde or brawle, as many do nowadayes for everie trifle, or rather for no cause at all."[54] She might also be carnival's woman of the tart tongue who mocks men's attempts to constrain her, but Semele's pert loquacity is her downfall not her culture's route to joyous rebirth. Her woman's lack of judgment renders her speech harmful not only to others, but to herself. Not recognizing her natural duty to be subject to masculine authority, Semele's pride makes her cruel to the men around her. She laughs "spitefully" (4.3.143) at Corsites's suffering from the fairies (90–143) and uses poisonous, stinging language to loose her inner fury, as Cynthia proclaims her "[t]he very wasp of all women, whose tongue stingeth as much as an adder's tooth" (5.4.206–8). And as contemporary theory holds, as a woman Semele is incapable of using reason to control her poisonous tongue. Semele repeatedly scorns Eumenides's love (3.1.1–25, 5.4.205–229), even though everyone and everything, from Cynthia to a magic fountain, recognize Eumenides as a faithful, unselfish man. Essentially, Semele lacks the judgment to distinguish a good man from a bad man. In fact, her judgment is so poor that she claims she would rather die than be married to her devoted suitor (5.4.220–23). Only Eumenides's promising to sacrifice his tongue for hers wins Semele's acceptance (241–44). Her pride and "spite" not only belie her inability to make wise and stable judgments on a personal level but on a larger social level as well. Cynthia's criticism of an exchange between Semele and Eumenides depicts the two as indulging in petty sniping that disrupts the harmony of Cynthia's court, not the witty badinage of a Beatrice and a Benedict, "What, have we here before my face these unseemly and malapert overthwarts? I will tame your tongues and your thoughts, and make your speeches answerable to your duties and your conceits fit for my dignity" (3.1.16–19).

Especially important about the tone of Cynthia's reprimand, there is not only absolutely no sympathy for Semele, but the wording emphasizes her failure to live up to her womanly duties. She is "unseemly" and "malapert." Semele needs to have "tongue" and "thought" tamed, to be "answerable" to her social "duties." True, Cynthia is also speaking to Eumenides in this scene, but she quickly forgives him and commends his anticipation of her order that he go in search of a cure for his friend Endymion (lines 20–65). Semele is allowed no more words until 5.4, her voice silenced, even her presence denied. When she does return to the play, Cynthia uses the same kind of language as the earlier Kramer and Sprenger and the later Joseph Swetnam to characterize Semele as the lowest of creatures, poisonous and vicious: "wasp" and "adder" (lines 206–8). Cynthia further condemns Semele's pertness as mindless, calling her "parrot," a creature perceived to have no understanding of what it says, merely repeating words for effect. This divine female guide's next pronouncement makes the lesson she seeks to teach her female charge a hard one indeed: if Semele does not choose to accept Eumenides as her husband and lord she will lose her tongue, perhaps even her head. Since the typical women can use neither wisely on her own, she might as well lose both. And Cynthia only voices her forgiveness and satisfaction when Semele turns her waspish tongue mild and accepts Eumenides as her husband. Thus Cynthia offers far different instruction than Lia or Felicia, who used discussion and conversation to teach their lessons. The woman on top in this play, Cynthia, does indeed use verbal abuse to teach but not to teach carnival's lessons. Instead, her mockery aims to condemn and kill the very verbal iconoclasm and independence carnival's eternal woman is supposed to propagate.

It might be argued that Cynthia's harsh pronouncement is a clever lesson designed to prompt the good Eumenides to offer to sacrifice his own tongue in place of Semele's, thus salving her doubts about his sincerity so that she can believe his love. However, there is no evidence to that end, no explanation, as Lia or Felicia offered, as to why she chose particular treatments or tests. No one in the court offers even a hint of a suggestion either. Lyly's play indicates that Semele's tongue was not sliced off only because Eumenides was altruistic and she finally learned to submit. Further, even though Cynthia does follow the pattern of Lia, Venus, and Felicia giving their charges a choice to learn from her guidance, Lyly's guide offers Semele a Hobson's choice. In contrast, Ameto or the shepherds and shepherdesses of *Diana* only risked losing a happy life not life itself.

Finally, even Eumenides' rescue of Semele does not so much suggest that she is a woman worthy of great sacrifice as it does that she is foolish. Lyly may have Semele reveal that her fear Eumenides' professed love was a lie, like that of other wooers, prompted her sharp tongue. Nevertheless, in Semele's misjudgment of Eumenides Lyly demonstrates that she lacks the reasoning capacity to distinguish seducers from a man who would sacrifice limb and life for her, proof that women need men to guide their judgment. Under these circumstances, the fact that Eumenides is a loyal friend to Endymion, subject to Cynthia, and suitor to Semele demonstrates less that men need to be kind to women or women need to be treated with understanding than that women need to hold men in higher regard and themselves in lower.

Cynthia's training of Semele treats on the struggle to tame the threat of female boundlessness on a human level. However, Cynthia puts the triumph of patriarchal convention on a much grander scale by battling, defeating, and reintegrating into society two characters (Dipsas and

Tellus) associated with witchcraft and its embodiment of the terrifying feminine Other's sexual and verbal power. And by associating the inconstancy, lasciviousness, and disruptiveness of carnival's eternal woman with the frightening, dangerous witch rather than with refreshing liberation, he seals the grave on carnival's spirit as a positive force in his play. As discussed in the previous chapter, medieval and Renaissance people saw the witch as giving a conquerable body to the forces of nature, fate, and politics normally beyond their control. As a witch, Dipsas incarnates the dangers of female intransigence at its most powerful. Practicing witchcraft, Dipsas is by definition in league with Satan and thereby infernal, rather than celestial as Cynthia is. Her age reminds us that she is decaying rather than eternal, as Sir Tophas's unintentionally mock blazon makes clear (3.3.55–64), evoking Hecate, the crone, death.[55] Abandoning her husband to pursue the power granted by witchcraft, Dipsas is inconstant rather than steadfast and obedient to her spouse (5.4.1–30). Dipsas is also vindictive rather than forgiving and rational, turning her recalcitrant servant into a tree as punishment for refusing to follow her satanic behests, and she exults in this power to be a destroyer or a perverter of nature and humanity rather than their preserver (1.4.20–31).

To undercut fear of women as embodied in the witch, Lyly turns Dipsas into a burlesque of that most feared of medieval and Renaissance sorceresses, Medea. David Bevington and Michael Pincombe note that Lyly's witch draws on portrayals of Medea from Ovid's *Elegies* and *Metamorphoses* and from Appollonius Rhodius's *Argonautica*. However, Diane Purkiss more accurately reads the effect of the witch's parallels with Medea when she observes that although "Dipsas's very first speech makes gargantuan Medean claims for her magic," in practice she is no more than a "cozene[r]." By turning the would-be powerful witch Dipsas into a weak parody of Medea, Lyly can work out his own and his audience's anxieties about lack of control through mockery. Cynthia easily overturns her magic, and the liberated female agency it represents, forcing Dipsas back into the constraints of marriage.[56] Furthermore, as noted above, this haggish witch is a far cry from the sexually potent and alluring Medea or Circe who threaten to melt men into beasts, doubly robbing the male of his rightful place in God's hierarchy above women and animals. Sir Tophas's unintentionally mock blazon of this old woman's low forehead, thin lips, "tall and stately nose," and sagging breasts and jowls (3.3.55–64) not only shows that age has long ago degenerated whatever allure she may once have boasted but underscores the misguided perception of women underlying the devotion of Corsites, Eumenides, or any man to a human mistress by carrying them to a ludicrous extreme.[57]

Furthermore, even though Dipsas as the crone may represent Hecate, the death aspect of the triple goddess, through Cynthia, Lyly completely undercuts her powers to destroy. She kills no one, only putting one person to sleep and turning another into a tree. Both of these acts are undone by Cynthia. And though she is a crone, a symbol of life in decay, Lyly presents that decay not as a power that devours men but as something at which men can laugh. In this context, Dipsas may recall the laughing pregnant hag figurines that Bakhtin cites as embodying carnival's joyous embracing of cycles of death and rebirth to shatter stifling conventions designed to allay fears by denying death.[58] However, what Lyly uses her for in this play is to mock that shattering of "protective" conventions. Once again, the play turns carnival itself upside down to restore and confirm the traditional hierarchy of power. So, as critics such as Purkiss, Pincombe and Bevington have observed,[59] Cynthia's disempowering of this witch negates the threats of the feminine in particular and the uncertainties of life and death in general that the witch incarnated for Renaissance society.[60]

The duel between Cynthia and Tellus is a far more serious matter, so that taming the latter becomes an especially crucial enactment of the need to enforce submission to the rules of traditional gender hierarchy. In Tellus's relationship with Cynthia, Lyly rewrites Boccaccio's goddess guide. Where Venus in *Ameto* embodied carnival grotesque's synthesis of earthly and heavenly, sensual and spiritual, reason and emotion to create something more profound than either half of the pairs, Lyly embraces traditional Christian doctrine and splits these dyads. His divine guide, Cynthia is transcendent only for her heavenly spirituality and rationality, while Tellus is portrayed as demonic for possessing earthly sexuality and passion. Splitting these traits off from Cynthia and imbuing Tellus with them, Lyly makes the latter solely a goddess of the earth; and consequently Tellus is driven, even possessed, by those flaws perceived by many as characteristic of the fallen, earthly daughters of Eve, but definitely not as the positive, re-creative ends of carnival's symbolic woman as abuser.

Her name meaning "earth" in Latin, Tellus demonstrates the seductions of the world,[61] which her self-description in 1.2.20–28 emphatically illustrates. In these lines, Tellus revels in the alluring power she believes she exerts over creation, claiming, "Infinite are my creatures, without which neither thou nor Endymion nor any could love or live." The source of that divine allure is an earthly rather than spiritual fertility and lushness: "Is not my beauty divine, whose body is decked with fair flowers, and veins are vines, yielding sweet liquor to the dullest spirits, whose ears are corn to bring strength, and whose hairs are grass to bring abundance?" In fact, Tellus's self-portrait evokes carnival's emphasis on delicious and bursting abundance bringing intense sensual pleasure. She declares her "vines [yield] sweet liquor to the dullest spirits," her "ears are corn to bring strength," and that "frankincense and myrrh breathe out of [her] nostrils, and all the sacrifice of the gods breed in [her] bowels."

Although in these lines Tellus presents herself as all that is beautiful and loving, the giver of vitality and joy, her serving woman Floscula deflates this vision as deluded pride. Floscula points out that the power to maintain natural and spiritual harmony comes from not the terrestrial but the celestial sphere, in the form of Cynthia, who "by her influence both comforteth all things and by her authority commandeth all creatures" (33–34). In a highly anti-carnival perspective, the earthly woman who sets herself as high as the celestial figure finds her pride checked by comparison to a Cynthia/Elizabeth, much as apologists for Elizabeth who tried to undercut views of women's inherent limitations were checked by insistence that the Queen was a heavenly exception to natural law.

Indeed, taking precisely the opposite tack to carnival's celebration of woman as comic abuser, Lyly shows that Tellus's very earthliness embodies the traits that classical, medieval, and Renaissance patriarchy condemn in women as requiring tight control to prevent moral, emotional, and social chaos. David Bevington's description of Tellus as "changeable, vengeful, spiteful, malicious"[62] seems to come straight out of Aristotle's *Historia animalium*. This characterization is clear in the play, for Lyly emphasizes that Tellus's inability to control her lust and emotions does not shatter suffocating, ill-conceived conventions but renders her destructive to herself and others. Cynthia's criticism of Tellus decisively conveys the views of patriarchal critics of women when she says, "Tellus, who is made all of love, [will] melt herself in her own looseness" (4.3.131). The imagery of moltenness and melting suggests an earthly, elemental nature that must be contained or solidifed, before it consumes itself and overflows to incinerate everything in its path. Tellus, herself, describes her passion for Endymion in volcanic terms: "a continual burning in all my bowels and a bursting in almost every vein" that "fl[ies] abroad of divers sparks" (5.4.87–90). This woman of the earthly plane can not experience love rationally, altruistically, or spiritually but is overwhelmed and will overwhelm others in the lava flow and flames of her passions.

Tellus's actions bear out Cynthia's warning assessment as her destructive vindictiveness not only consumes herself but those around her. When Cynthia sends Tellus into exile to weave tapestries of tales that should teach her about the need to govern her passions and her pride, all she can do is weave images of Endymion, icons of her obsessive lust (5.4.261–66). Indeed, so obsessed is Tellus, that she takes advantage of Corsites' deep but misguided devotion to seduce him into contributing to destroying Cynthia's order by helping her capture Endymion (4.1). Then she laughs with other women at her devotee's folly in giving governance to woman's deceit, manipulation, and callousness (4.1.79–88). Or as Lyly has Cynthia disapprovingly chastise Corsites, complete dedication to the plans of a woman of the earth corrupts and consumes a once great "warrior" into a "wanton" (4.3.125). Tellus's beauty may be inspiring, but it is merely a deceptive mask for the inferior soul within. Thus, Corsites finally learns that, as embodied by Tellus, woman is "too fair to be true and too false for one so fair" (4.3.116–17).

The love Tellus offers Endymion is also far from vitalizing and uplifting. Despite her claims to offer both life and "love," giving in to her would denigrate both mind and soul; subjugation to her passion will reduce the courtier to a woman's depraved, undisciplined state, making him prey to "his loose desires" and "dissolute thoughts." No reasonable suasion, no "hope of preferment, nor fear of punishment, nor counsel, of the wisest, nor company of the worthiest" would be able to free him from "languishing" under her "amorous devices" to pursue duty and honor as a noble courtier should (1.2.49–55). Thus, rather than carnival's liberation and purification, Tellus's mastery would be a tragic emasculation, for him as well as for the queen and kingdom that his nascent virtues would benefit. And, as in the case of Semele, even Tellus's threat to masculine power is defeated by Cynthia's forcing her to bow to masculine authority. Tellus ends by apologizing to Endymion for bewitching him into a perpetual sleep (5. 4.193–95) and by accepting Corsites as her husband as Cynthia's condition for pardon, though she hints at lingering desire for Endymion (lines 250–55). Again, Cynthia effectively contains, if not snuffs out, carnival's rebellious female spirit with marriage.

Cynthia's guidance of the male characters also confirms the legitimacy and necessity of male control over female agency. Though Eumenides loves the pert Semele steadfastly, he does not allow his devotion to interfere with his self respect or sense of duty. He returns her sharp words with equal wit, and puts thought of her aside to demonstrate his loyalty to his friend and to his monarch when ordered by Cynthia to discover cause and cure for Endymion's mysterious enchantment. For these actions and for his patience and generosity, Cynthia rewards him with a more submissive and appreciative Semele. Though Endymion had been dishonest in using Tellus to mask from other courtiers his devotion to Cynthia, the goddess does not severely punish him. Rather, she gives him a brief reprimand and, because his actions were motivated to earn her regard, promises that he may one day attain that favor if he continues in her service (5. 4. 130–92). Endymion is let off the hook for betraying the earthly version of woman, Tellus, because his service to Cynthia is to a heavenly ideal. And though Geron is perhaps not overjoyed with the return of his wife Dipsas, he is allowed to chasten further his already meek, repentant wife (lines 1–36).

Significantly, the two male characters whose love prompts them to hand mastery to women are portrayed as foolish, sometimes even dangerously so. Sir Tophas's ridiculous version of courtly devotion has already been discussed, but it bears noting here that Corsites is also portrayed as foolish for his blind dedication to his lady. He finds himself embarrass-ingly pinched by fairies not only to mark his treachery for Tellus's sake but because this treachery is a dangerous treason to Cynthia's reign. Thus, Lyly's depiction of carnival's pert woman on top (Semele, Tellus, and Dip-sas) confirms conventional beliefs about women's sexuality, verbosity, and irrationality in the vein of Jyotsna Singh's observation on the inefficacy of carnival's subversion in "leav[ing] the *categories of social representation* largely untouched."[63]

Still, though Lyly allows Cynthia the privilege of speaking the law of the patriarchy because she is an anomaly, he does not seem able to let even an anomalous female exist without some female flaws. Helen Hackett makes a similar point about Lyly's "Glass for Europe" in *Euphues and His England* (1580) when she notes that this panegyric to Queen Elizabeth seems to "praise her as an 'exceptional woman' whose excellence raised her miraculously above the implied general depravity of her sex," but is phrased to hint that the woman Elizabeth needs to strive to live up to the ideal he describes.[64] In both the "Glass for Europe" and *Endymion*, she still needs masculine direction.

Although Cynthia is perspicacious and magisterial enough to dig out the truth through examining others and delegating the right people to perform her searches, she is still not so omniscient that she automati-cally knows of Tellus's plotting, of Dipsas's and Corsites's help, or of the means to cure Endymion. Additionally, Endymion's dream symbolizing the court parasites who seek to exploit Cynthia/Elizabeth and corrupt the kingdom's general prosperity for their own gain (5.1.131–52) raises some interesting questions about exactly how "perfect" Lyly wanted his audience to perceive this queen. If Cynthia/Elizabeth were indeed omni-scient, would she need to be warned against "wolves barking at her"? Would not she see through "Ingratitude with an hundred eyes, gazing for benefits, and with a thousand teeth gnawing on the bowels wherein she was bred" or "Treachery . . . all clothed in white, with a smiling coun-tenance but both her hands bathed in blood"? Would she not be able to protect her State from "drones, or beetles, . . . creeping under the wings of a princely eagle [Cynthia/Elizabeth], who, being carried into her nest, sought there to suck that vein that would have killed the eagle"? Equally noteworthy, Pincombe's observation that the imagery here strongly recalls Lyly's respectful warnings directed toward Elizabeth in *Euphues in His England*[65] underscores that concerns about the limitations of the British Queen color this play's incarnation of the guide as goddess. Unlike Venus of *Ameto*, who sees all, the female pastoral guide here is strongly in need of input from her virtuous male courtiers.

Depictions of Elizabeth as divine virgin pervading British pastorals, especially as illustrated in *Endymion*, are a powerful force in establishing this guide in pastoral drama. Such anxieties of a patriarchal society about serving a woman prince, combined with those about woman in general, will come to shape presentations of this guide as goddess. Frequently, the goddess guide will not be formed as an incarnation of Elizabeth, but she will reflect related questions about the threatening power of the feminine Other. For some dramatists, the goddess guide will be a figure who must be diminished to re-establish masculine authority. Another play by Lyly, *Loves Metamorphosis*, is a particularly good example. In this play, Ceres presides over the pastoral realm, protecting and teaching her nymphs and punishing those who deface her subjects, particularly Erisicthon, who takes an ax to her nymph-turned-tree. However, Ceres is not written to gain favor from a monarch, and so she becomes very much an example of the worst in women, portrayed as punishing vengefully and connected only with the physical and earthly aspects of nature rather than with the transcendent. It comes down to the intervention of a male god, Cupid, to rein in Ceres' vindictiveness and rescue a human male from eternal starvation, as well as to whip her proud nymphs into womanly submissiveness by requiring them to give up their cruel scorn of the devoted foresters who woo them. Interestingly enough, Lyly's Cupid is not the delightful or mischievous child of texts ranging from Longus's *Daphnis and Chloe* to Daniel's *Muses' Elizium* but a wise and firm adult male, a king ruling over his pastoral realm. This trend of a male divinity or authority directing or deputizing the female pastoral guide, especially in her guise of wise woman, will take root in later pastorals. For example, Ralph Knevet's *Rhodon and Iris* (1631) shows Flora, also a Roman earth goddess, lacking the omnipotence of the celestial Cynthia or Venus. In fact, at the conclusion of the play she is reduced to a simple stock figure, a deus ex machina. And the import of her judicial decisions for settling human conflicts is considerably undercut by the fact that human men had already arrived at these conclusions and planned to administer justice before she passes judgment (5.6). *The Faery Pastorall* (1603), by William Percy, shows the Queen of Fairies, Chloris, as even more deferential to her Lord Oberon, emulating Ceres by instructing her magical female retainers not to flout their male suitors' authority. The adoption of this trait to the guide as wise woman in *The Faithful Shepherdess* (1608/9) will be studied in chapter 5.

For still others, however, the goddess becomes a vehicle for undercutting or questioning this view of male/female relations, supporting Phyllis Rackin's observations that "[t]he easy assumption of a broad, schematic opposition between [early modern] oppression and present equality ignores the variety, the complexity, and the contradictions of women's positions in our own world, not to mention those of a remote past."[66] Supporting this view, Shakespeare's Titania and Wroth's Venus evoke Bakhtin's spirit of carnival, inverting the social order of "seriousness," "rationalism," and "classicism" to reveal a liberating truth about the inadequacies of the gender hierarchy of the early-modern world.[67] The remainder of this chapter will focus on two of these plays, *A Midsummer Night's Dream* and *Love's Victory*, selected for their illustration of the most interesting variations on the guide as goddess.

III

In *A Midsummer Night's Dream*, Titania's precedence as a pastoral goddess-guide is also subverted by a masculine divinity, and at first glance this seems to support the view that patriarchy must conquer female "unruliness" to protect cosmic stability. In this play, the rebelliousness of Titania, Queen of the Fairies, comes to be tamed by her lord, Oberon. Nevertheless, the taming of this froward fairy is no straightforward assertion of the propriety of female submission to masculine direction. In Shakespeare's play, there are some intriguing differences that counter rather than confirm mainstream beliefs about woman's dangerous inferiority.

Superficially resembling Ceres in *Loves Metamorphosis*, Titania is a goddess associated with fertility. The duties on which she sends her subordinate fairies include decking nature in stylized images of fruitfulness typical of Arcadian pastoral:

> And I serve the Fairy Queen,
> To dew her orbs upon the green.
> The cowslips tall her pensioners be.
> In their gold coats spots you see;
> Those be rubies, fairy favors;
> In those freckles live their savors
> I must go seek some dewdrops here
> And hang a pearl in every cowslip's ear.
> (2.1.8–15)[68]

However, unlike Lyly with Ceres or Cynthia, Shakespeare does not divorce this pastoral deity's predominance over fecundity from human sexuality. Lyly's Ceres lectured her nymphs on chastity, even bringing them to Cupid for more influential tutelage.[69] Titania, in contrast, shows no such prudery. She happily "gossiped" "in the spicèd Indian air by night" (2.1.123–25) with her beloved "vot'ress," whose "womb [was] then rich with [her] young squire" (131). Later, in a carnivalesque blending of human and supernatural sexuality with nature's fecundity, she has her fairies convey Bottom to an idyllic retreat where she will "wind" him in her "arms" like "the female ivy [e]nring[ing] the barky fingers of the elm" (4.1.35–39). While cuddling with her new "lover," Titania instructs her fairies to delight Bottom with a pastoral bounty that recalls the garden of Chloe's parents in *Daphnis and Chloe* or the harvest home celebrations and carven images on shepherds' cups in the *Idylls* and the *Eclogues*: "Feed him with apricots and dewberries, / With purple grapes, green figs, and mulberries; / The honeybags steal from the humble-bees . . ." (3.1.140–42). In all cases, the descriptions of humanity's and nature's fertility are lush, sensual.

Further, as a friend to the pregnant votress, at whose death she keeps and succors her child, Titania's connection to human as well as natural sensuality seems far different than the threat of an all-consuming Tellus. Similarly, Titania's liaison with Bottom does not corrupt him as Acrasia's does the knights she enthralls in her bower of bliss in Book 2 of the *Faerie Queene*. Shakespeare's female pastoral guide, then, is not at all a goddess used to ventriloquize lessons in austere chastity and self-denial, like Cynthia, or confusedly mixing lessons of restraint and obedience while still unable to contain her own verbal and emotional vindictiveness, like Ceres. Instead, the convergence of lush sexuality, love, and elements of nature within her being is exactly representative of the joyous, fecund abundance of carnival: delightfully overturning a hierarchy of heaven over earth/nature; spirit over body; divine over human and animal (Bottom); and, as will be clear later with Oberon, female over male. Indeed, Bakhtin would probably be delighted with her elevation and worship of (the) Bottom over gods and kings represented by Oberon![70]

Shakespeare's depiction of Titania approaches then veers off from the harshness toward women of Lyly's portrayals of goddess-guides in other ways. On the surface, Titania seems to follow the pattern of Lyly's Ceres as pastoral guide, weakened to reflect contemporary conceptions about female sexual, emotional, and mental instability. Both playwrights display uncontrolled female power connected with disruption opposed by an attempt to restore order through the assertion of masculine dominance. Ceres' justice festers into vindictiveness and false pride in *Loves Metamorphosis*. In *A Midsummer Night's Dream*, Shakespeare does portray the dark, flip side of Titania's power to create pastoral harmony. The result of her refusing to give up her "vot'ress's" boy to be Oberon's "henchmen" (2.1.121) is a complete disruption of pastoral's ideal concordance amongst nature, humans, and the supernatural. Over this issue, the divine figures of Oberon and Titania are at odds with each other, and nature flails back its displeasure. As Titania, herself, oberseves:

> Therefore the winds, piping to us in vain,
> As in revenge, have sucked up from the sea
> Contagious fogs which, falling in the land,
> Hath every pelting river made so proud
> That they have overborne their continents.
>
> (88–92)

Even human attempts to commune with nature or to find solace with the gods through festival celebrations or prayers have been contaminated, for "nine-men's morris is filled up with mud" (98) and the "winter here . . . [n]o night is now with hymn or carol blessed" (101–2). This supernatural female's intransigence to her "lord" (63) even inverts the orderly run of the seasons to create rot, death, and strife:

> The seasons alter; hoary-headed frosts
> Fall in the fresh lap of the crimson rose,
> And on old Hiems' thin and icy crown
> An odorous chaplet of sweet summer buds
> Is, as in mockery, set. The spring, the summer,
> The childing autumn, angry winter, change
> Their wonted liveries, and the mazèd world
> By their increase now knows not which is which.
>
> (107–14)

Here, the goddess guide's refusal to acquiesce to the masculine authority does not just deprive her of her traditional abilities to create harmony, deepen understanding, and uplift but completely reverses the effect of her powers. The broils caused by her refusal to turn the child over to Oberon seem, indeed, to illustrate John Knox's 1558 declaration that "the empire of a woman," or even her resistance to male authority is "repugnant to nature and contumelie to God" and "the order of his creation."[71] Her resistance to masculine authority seems to make real the worst fears about the effects of freeing the unruly female.

Elizabethan beliefs about the upbringing of boys clarifies why this "unstringing" of natural order progresses from Titania's refusing to turn her child over to Oberon. The Indian child is seven years old, about the age at which male children of the upper classes would receive "a ceremonial first pair of breeches" and be moved from the woman's world of nurturing, "coddling" "nurses" and "mothers" into a more emotionally restrained and intellectually rigorous one of "schoolmasters" and "fathers."[72] As Sir Thomas Elyot instructs in *The Book of the Governor* (1531), "After that a child is come to seven years of age, I hold it expedient that he be taken from the company of women, saving that he may have, one year or two at the most, an ancient and sad matron attending him in his chamber. . ."[73]

Critics have looked at various ways this specific socialization of men would affect audience's receptions of the play. Gail Kerns Paster and Howard Skiles suggest that "for adult gentlemen in Shakespeare's audience, the memory of these separations was difficult and needed to be distanced through complex ridicule." So, although the Indian changeling never actually appears on stage, his presence is filled by the comical "indulgent care of women and fairies." In addition, Mary Ellen Lamb sees the maternal imagery of Titania's and the fairies' "indulgent care" of Bottom as a comically "safe" way for the adult upper-class male to recapture the attentions of a mother and nurses that he has been schooled to scorn as beneath his place in the class and gender hierarchy. Montrose's assessments are particularly relevant to discussing Titania as guide. He points out that not only do Puck and Oberon seem to perceive Titania's recalcitrance as retarding the boy's development, even emasculating him, but that Oberon sees Titania's greater attachment to the boy as a challenge to his authority over her. That Titania's attachment to the child derives from her attachment to his mother implies she is resisting the natural order by privileging loyalty to another woman over obedience to her lord.[74] Thus, Titania's refusing to give up the male child to masculine authority seems to make her doubly disruptive of God's order where, as William Gouge put it in *Of Domestical Duties* (1622), "Nature hath placed an eminency in the male over the female, so where they are linked together in one yoke, it is given by nature that he should govern, she obey."[75] She not only refuses her duties to honor Oberon, her natural superior, but she seems to be short circuiting the continuance of patriarchy by holding back the next generation, the Indian boy, from moving into that order. On the surface, then, Titania appears to be a dangerously disruptive example of female power. Louis Montrose's comment that her identification with Circe through a source familiar to many Elizabethans, Ovid's *Metamorphoses*,[76] might especially indicate that audiences would perceive Nature as fortunate to have Oberon rein in Titania.

Oberon, indeed, takes control of Titania and undermines her resistant pride even more forcibly than Cupid does that of Ceres in *Loves Metamorphosis*. And he does so with a facility that would seem to confirm man's placement above woman. Titania's fairy guards repeatedly proclaim "Never harm / Nor spell nor charm / Come our lovely lady nigh" (2.2.16–19, 28–30). Yet Oberon easily circumvents "One aloof stand[ing] sentinal" (32), to squeeze the juice of an enchanted flower on Titania's eyes that will bind her to love the first creature she sees, "[b]e it ounce, or cat, or bear, / Pard, or boar with bristled hair" (34–40). Further, Oberon seems to take charge of carnival abuse here as his curse reduces the pastoral goddess's glorious power to transform and purify into a burlesque when she winds up effusing her devotion and admiration to a weaver whose head Puck has transformed to match his mental and physical state. Like Venus's encouragement of Ameto and Cynthia's of Endymion, Titania promises Bottom "I am a spirit of no common rate" who "will purge [his] mortal grosseness so / That [he] shalt like an airy spirit go" (3.1.127,133–34). However, unlike her divine predecessor guides, Titania has markedly less success with her charge. Her attentions to the literally and metaphorically ass-headed weaver still cannot raise either his intellect or his soul above making bad puns on her fairies' names (153–67). Under punishment of Oberon's enchantment for her insubordination, Titania ostensibly demonstrates that delusion not insight is inherent in the female pastoral guide due to her gender. Where Cynthia, while appreciating Endymion's devotion, realizes he has only started his spiritual evolution, in contrast, Titania, under Oberon's punishment, is convinced that calling "large [donkey] ears" fair and a furry head "sleek" and "smooth" transforms her lover (4.1.3–4). Thus, Oberon appears to take charge of carnival abuse in imposing this grotesque juxtaposition on Titania in order to teach conformity to traditional dogmas of masculine preeminence by demonstrating how easily he can turn the female guide's power into an embarrassing display.

Oberon seems to usurp the power of the other forms of the pastoral guide, the mage, and the wise woman, as well. Like them, he is learned in the magic powers of specific herbs and how to use them, both love-in-idleness's power to cause love (2.1.155–174) and Diana's bud's power to cure it (3.2.367–68, 4.1.68–69, 2.1.184). Also like these other forms of the pastoral guide, Oberon uses his powers in attempts to untangle the crossed lovers who sojourn in his forest beyond Athens. So, in many ways, Oberon appears to portray a more socially acceptable transference of the guide's powers and ascendancy from female to male and a co-opting of carnival's abuse to consolidate rather than to overturn traditional order.

This being said, it is especially interesting to realize that if Oberon stands as a figure of patriarchy taming the unruly female and restoring authority to the appropriate gender, Shakespeare does not make him a particularly capable or admirable figure—and here the Bakhtinian reversal of the legitimacy of the "serious" order comes into play (literally and figuratively). Oberon prides himself on seeing further and deeper than others, thereby having the right and capability to direct their lives. For example, only he saw where Cupid's shaft landed and imbued a flower with magical powers to create love (2.1.155–72). Further, Oberon proclaims himself far above the dark aspect of the feminine Hecate, not bound by her limitations (5.1.361–63). More importantly, Oberon sees himself as wise and gracious enough to use his magic to make a cruel Demetrius love the Helena he scorns (2.1.245–46). So the King of the Fairies commands Puck to "[a]noint" the eyes of the "disdainful youth" with the love-kindling flower with the general instructions, "Thou shalt know the man / By the Athenian garments he hath on" (264–65).

In his self-assurance of his omniscience, Oberon gives instructions that he thinks are sufficiently clear. However, Oberon does not know all, as he believes, for another Athenian-garbed youth also roams the forest—Lysander. Following Oberon's insufficiently specific instructions, Puck anoints Lysander's eyes and disrupts true love when the young man opens them on Helena (2.2.109–11). Oberon's "omniscience" is the snowball that ends in an avalanche of strife, rather than producing the self-knowledge and satisfaction of Felicia's, Venus's, and Cynthia's guidance. Worse, discovering his mistake, Oberon reacts with all the dignity and maturity of Homer Simpson bawling out Bart for the results of his own stupidity:

> What hast thou done? Thou hast mistaken quite
> And laid the love juice on some true love's sight.
> Of thy misprision must perforce ensue
> Some true love turned, and not a false turned true.
>   (3.2.88–91)

Ironically, Oberon can not even see his own responsibility, blaming Puck completely ("What hast thou done?"). Puck has done exactly as Oberon ordered and anointed the man in "Athenian garments." But though the evidence is right before him that more than one bearer of Athenian fashion was wandering the forest, Oberon cannot figure out his own culpability in why Puck "hast mistaken quite."

Tellingly, the Fairy King's attempts to set right his mistake end up challenging the premise of his superiority even more pointedly. Oberon's commanding Puck to anoint Demetrius's eyes only worsens matters, causing Demetrius and Lysander then to battle over Helena; causing Hermia to bewail, alternately, Lysander's inconstancy and Helena's seemingly duplicitous stealing of her lover; and convincing Helena that all her friends are indulging in a major conspiracy to humiliate her for their amusement (3.2.1–344). The all-knowing Oberon's response? Once again to shift the blame and remain oblivious to his limitations: "This is thy [Puck's] negligence. Still thou mistak'st, / Or else committ'st thy knaveries willfully" (3.2.345–46). But Puck's response leaves no mistake about where the fault lies, "Believe me, king of shadows, I mistook. / Did not you tell me I should know the man/ By the Athenian garments he had on?" (3.2.347–49). Oberon's lack of control is firmly established when he is allowed to make no rejoinder here.

So, in Oberon's attempt to play the part of love-disentangling guide, Shakespeare brings to the fore that the Fairy King's ill-considered actions, his poorly articulated commands, and his bad temper render a bad situation worse. Oberon may eventually straighten out the mess, which he has created, but not before showing his ludicrous incompetence in handling the powers he tries to usurp from the female pastoral guide. Even more interesting, unlike Titania, Oberon cannot plead that an enchantment excuses his inadequate perception or control. *A Midsummer Night's Dream* may be addressing contemporary society's desire to tame female power, but unlike in Lyly's plays or in texts like Percy's *Faery Pastorall* and Ralph Knevet's *Rhodon and Iris*, this play does not locate security in completely affirming masculine ascendancy.

Also interesting is the fact that Oberon exhibits many of the negative traits that men were supposed to discipline in women. Rather than act with rationality and dignity, Oberon, himself, is a creature of jealousy, spite, and hot temper. When Titania chides that he seems still interested in his former "buskined mistress," the "bouncing Amazon" Hippolyta (2.1.68–72), he carps tetchily about her former relations with Theseus (76–80). Additionally, his response to Titania's refusing him the child is as waspish as any words from Lyly's Tellus: "Thou shalt not from this grove / Till I torment thee for this injury" (146–47). His anticipatory delight at the thought of Titania humiliated by love for something bestial only underscores that Oberon is not driven by reason but pride and revenge (2.1.177–87). Similarly, Oberon's blaming Puck for the imbroglio caused by his own poorly planned use of the enchanted flower demonstrates that his false pride blinds his perceptions and leaves him bad tempered when frustrated. All in all, Shakespeare's Oberon seems a clearer representative of John Knox's catalogue of women's flaws than does Titania: "weake, fraile, impacient, feble and foolishe, . . . unconstant, variable, cruell and lacking the spirit of counsel and regiment."[77]

So, although on the surface *A Midsummer Night's Dream* may initially seem to stay within the pattern of rewriting the guide in line with more conservative contemporary views of gender relations, the portrayals of Titania and Oberon actually work across the grain in a Bakhtinian sense. In Shakespeare's play, what carnival would define as the "classical" or "serious" patriarchal order that Oberon embodies and seeks to impose reveals its own inadequacies when the King of the Fairies actually ends up turning his realm over to the spirit of carnival he is trying to contain or direct. Oberon's attempts to force the irrationality of love into logical courses not only fail but actually set off carnivalesque verbal abuse and literally earthy results, with characters rolling in briars and mud. Ironically, as noted earlier, when Puck points out that the Fairy King's inadequate directions set the snafus in motion, this patriarch of the fairy world cannot even control his own temper. Oberon is reduced to the fool and the clownish Puck, who delights in carnivalesque pranks (1.2.32–58), ascends over him in wisdom. Thus, in his (mis)direction of the mischievous Puck, Oberon definitely illustrates that he and the order he represents lack the understanding and mastery of language to control let alone suppress the spirit of carnival.

There are other examples of Oberon being overwhelmed by the carnivalesque. Oberon's determination to rein in Titania's thoughts and actions through revenge not only reveals his own uncontrollable passions but, again, ironically, introduces the spirit of carnival into his realm. Oberon laughs as Titania lovingly delights in Bottom's embodiment of the grotesque, but he is unaware that the joke is also on him. Making her fall in love with an ass, Oberon misses the fact that he has arranged his own cuck-olding! More importantly, that he is responsible for Titania's lover having the head of an ass, a creature that is a major symbol of the reversal of social order in carnival in actual celebrations and literature,[78] further undercuts Oberon's masculine authority. He has literally and symbolically replaced himself with the spirit of carnival. Consequently, when Titania later muses, "Methought I was enamored of an ass" (4.1.72), the audience may conjecture whether Bottom is the only beloved whom the appellation fits.

In this light, though Shakespeare's female goddess-guide does reflect anxieties about women, *A Midsummer Night's Dream* suggests that addressing these anxieties merely by containing or degrading woman is a misapprehension of reality and a misdirection of energy. The juxtaposition of Oberon and Titania shows that displacing human frailty onto woman does not give humanity more control or protection but creates a dangerous illusion. Power goes into the hands of men who are just as vulnerable as women to misjudgment and to misusing power.

IV

Lady Mary Wroth's *Love's Victory*, written circa 1620 as a "private theatrical" for her literary and intellectual coterie, also challenges the trend to subvert the guide as a goddess in order to express or allay anxieties about the "unruly" feminine Other. Wroth's pastoral goddess-guide emphatically challenges the Jacobean perception that to maintain social order "husbands, parents, or frends . . . should have powre over [women] and make them pay for yt."[79] Angeline Goreau in *The Whole Duty of Woman* points out that "[a]fter the death of Queen Elizabeth, the misogynistic diatribes that had appeared off and on throughout the sixteenth century accelerated noticeably in frequency—and ferocity."[80] In a personal letter of 1620, John Chamberlain writes that the "insolence and impudence" of women is excoriated on all fronts. "Our pulpits ring," "players," and "ballades and ballad-singers" and "the King" make "theyre eares tingle." Josephine Roberts points out that James I did, indeed, "order . . . the Bishop of London that the clergy should 'inveigh vehemently and bitterly in theyre sermons against the insolencie of our women'."[81] Not surprisingly, then, Joseph Swetnam's popular and highly misogynistic *The Arraignment of Lewd, Idel, Froward, and Unconstant Women* was written about this time, 1615. Elaine Beilin, as well Angeline Goreau and Juliet Dusinberre, also notes that Swetnam's attack prompted vehement written ripostes, including a 1617 response from the respected female scholar Rachel Speght[82] and "a popular play called *Swetnam, the Woman-hater, Arraigned by Women*" in 1620.[83] Mary Wroth's Venus of *Love's Victory* can be seen as a like-minded private disputation with those who believed, like Swetnam, that woman's "aspiring mind," "wanton will," inner corruption, greed, profligacy, and venomous tongue "procur[e] man's fall."[84]

Where Shakespeare's *A Midsummer Night's Dream* contains a diminished version of the goddess guide, Wroth's theatrical returns her to full power presiding over love and life, humans and nature, in the pastoral world. Though some of the goddesses addressed in this chapter seem to reflect the take of critics such as Singh, Stallybrass, Russo, and Purkiss that this woman on top represented little in the way of a challenge to the hierarchy of gender, Natalie Zemon Davis's different perspective fits Wroth's play better. Zemon Davis relates that literary women on top not only could serve as a positive role for social critique but that women did have some power in the sixteenth- and seventeenth-centuries in effectively voicing social criticism in writing or even direct action.[85] Mary Wroth's pastoral drama can be said to fit more with Zemon Davis's views both by emphatically placing a female deity "on top" to untangle human folly and by showing that negative views of women stemmed from a lack of understanding. Still, Wroth's Venus is more what Bakhtin refers to as a "watered down"[86] version of carnival in Renaissance literature. Like Felicia and Boccaccio's Venus, she may invert women's place in the gender hierarchy, but she still does not follow the extent and intensity of true carnival's celebration of the sensual.

One of the most important ways Wroth returns the pastoral goddess-guide to power is by reversing the relationship between Cupid and Venus that Lyly portrayed in *Loves Metamorphosis*. Where Lyly reduces Venus to a mere honorable reference by a son who exercised wisdom and power in his pastoral demesne, Wroth creates a Venus who sees all, knows all, and directs all, while downgrading Cupid to Venus's henchman. Cupid's position as Venus's subordinate further establishes her as the "goddess" on top. Venus gives him directives to carry out in the scenes framing the action of the play (1.1, 1.4, 3.3).[87] And the goddess even righteously chides him for failing to implement her instructions effectively. For example, believing her son to be lax, Venus scolds, "Fie, this is nothing! What? Is this your care? / That among ten the half of them you spare!" (1.4.1–2). Cupid's responses are those of a loving lieutenant. In one instance, Cupid portrays himself entirely at Venus's command, his sole will to propagate her power and glory: "This will I do, your will and mind to serve, / And to your triumph will these rites preserve" (1.1.31–32). Another time, Cupid not only sues for his mother's approval but pleads for more work to do in her service: "Is this not pretty? Who doth free remain / Of all this flock, that waits not in our train? / Will you have yet more sorrow? Yet more woe?" (3.3.1–4). Even Venus's criticism does not prompt resentment from Cupid but a delighted explanation of how his method for carrying out her plans will bring high regard to them both, with his honor glorifying Venus: "Love's Victory shall shine, / Whenas your honour shall be raised by mine" (1.4.25–26). In her theatrical, Wroth has greatly shifted the balance of power from that shown in *Loves Metamorphosis*. Cupid takes rather than gives orders. He treats the goddess with respect rather than disparagement for daring to step out of the natural order of relations. In fact this goddess is portrayed as "outranking" him: she is his mother where Ceres was an incarnation of humanity's bestial, material nature, his "guts" (5.1.8–9). Equally important, Venus's responses to Cupid's devotion, such as pledging, "Thanks, Cupid, if thou do perform thine oath" (1.4.27) and showing appreciation of his "gracious favour" (3.3.32), indicate that her leadership is far more reasonable and temperate than Ceres' impertinent haranguing of Cupid or Oberon's squabbling with Puck.

Louise Schleiner argues that Wroth only empowers women in this play in a roundabout way. Claiming Wroth portrays Venus as "more peevish and arbitrary than her son" and "delegat[es] some of her authority to him," Schleiner suggests that Wroth is only creating the appearance of confirming masculine over feminine. Schleiner sees Wroth as actually awarding agency to females, though under the cover of making Silvesta, a woman, Cupid's "female human agent . . . who must carry out [his] task, and do it beneficently, not capriciously or destructively."[88] However, through Venus Wroth actually offers a more direct challenge to the assertions of the danger of independent women with power. Close study of Venus in the play reveals that she is not really "peevish and arbitrary" but displays an admirable balance of rationality, feeling, wisdom, and dignity. From the start, Wroth makes clear that Venus's plan to make humans suffer is not motivated by temper but by her desire to bring human and divine relations in the pastoral world back into harmony. Relating to her son why they must school mortals, she says: ". . . These people grow to scorn our will. / Mercy to those ungrateful breeds neglect; / Then let us grow our greatness to respect, / Make them acknowledge that our heavenly / power / Cannot their strength, but even themselves, devour" (1.1.2–6). In these lines, Venus explains that humans have egotistically taken divine mercy for granted, as their unearned due: human pride "scorn[s] our will," so human "neglect" becomes "ungrateful." And this neglect does not just wound divine pride but cruelly hurts other humans. For example, Lissius in scorning love wounds the nymph who genuinely adores him. Philisses defies love's power over himself by unkindly scorning Silvesta, then tries to protect himself from vulnerability to true love by hurtfully rejecting Musella under the pretense of jealously.

Later, when Venus instructs Cupid that making Lissius fall in love is an insufficient trial to humble the human's pride, her motivation is hardly vindictiveness. She explains to her son:

> Lissius is too soon blessed,
> And with too little pain hath got his rest;
> Scarce had he learned to sigh before he gained,
> Nor shed a tear ere he his hopes obtained.
> This easy winning breeds us more neglect,
> Without much pain, few do Love's joys respect;
> Then are the sweetest purchased with felt grief,
> To floods of woe sweet looks give full relief.
>
> (3.3.9–16)

To reward Lissius too easily would merely confirm his false egoism, would prevent him from recognizing the hard-won effort that must go into living up to one's place in the order of creation. Equally important, worshipping the divinities of love is coincident with treating humanity with compassion: humans' harmony with the sacred and with other humans converge. For Lissius's humbling will lead him to appreciate and reward the speaker of "kind-words" who "cure[s]" his "heart-wounds" (18).

Though, initially, she may seem to make these proud, misguided humans suffer, Venus is not acting viciously but helpfully. *Diana*'s Felicia had stressed that we learn by travail, and Boccaccio's Venus trained her nymphs and Ameto through suffering and tests. So, too, Wroth's Venus instructs her henchman son to prick the humans enough to make them think and learn but not to torture them maliciously, a carefully calibrated carnival abuse. So, under Venus's direction, the humans whose vanity "gave them cause on [Cupid] to make this scoff," Cupid "shalt discern their hearts, and make them / know / That humble homage unto [him] they owe" (1.1.10–12). However, though she says he must use his arrows to "[w]ound them," he must "kill them not" (17–18). Although she gives him freedom to "[s]hun no great cross which may their crosses / breed," Venus cautions Cupid to "let blessed enjoying them succeed." She insists that through "mercy" his "glory will shine bright" (19–22). Venus does not want merely to pain or humiliate humans. She wants them to learn through suffering how to appreciate love's value. As noted above, Venus only desires Lissius to suffer more so that he will develop the insight and tenderness to enjoy love more, and the greater devotion his suffering will cultivate in him will please his lady.

Clearly, then, the goal of Wroth's Venus is not to punish humans wantonly or spitefully. The reasoning behind her acts as ruler counters any who would support Swetnam's assessment that "by her aspiring mind, and wanton will, she quickly procure[s] man's fall" (70). Her goals are precisely the opposite, to deflate humans' vanity and to open their eyes to the power of love of others to restore concordance to their world. Once humans have realigned their perspective, she intends to act in the mode of Boccaccio's Venus by rewarding the humans to "let blessed enjoying [the crosses of suffering] succeed" (1.1.20).

Wroth even structures the play to underline the short-sightedness of envisioning a woman exercising power as invariably dangerous. Each act of the play and the contretemps contained within it is framed at either beginning or end by Venus and Cupid's plotting to teach the humans to love truly and unselfishly. Act 1 begins and ends with the two outlining the humans' flaws that require disciplining. Act 2 follows their planning, and the last scene of act 3 sums up their accomplishments as well as the need for more work. It also sets the tone for act 4, which Wroth closes with a scene of Venus and Cupid setting the direction for the following act 5. This last act ends with Venus's resolution of the play's conflicts. These frames create reasonable explanations and justifications for the sufferings that the characters endure. Without them, the vagaries of love in the main body of the play would have appeared to be as undirected, irrational, and capricious to the audience as they do to the characters. Of course, Wroth does not mean to imply that pagan gods direct human experience. However, by structuring her play to show a female god wisely directing what would seem random and uncontrolled fate only to the uninformed (audience or characters), she intimates that similar attacks on women's inconstancy and lack of discipline also reflect inadequate understanding. Women and love deserve more respect than either her play's self-absorbed lovers or a misguided patriarchal society affords them. Aristotle's, Galen's, Paracelsus's, Paul's, Augustine's, Vives's, James I's, balladeers' and playwrights' depictions of woman as flighty, vindictive, or irrational are as blind to the truth as the play's lovers who are unaware of the goddess's plans and motivation. Though not carnival in its purest Bakhtinian sense, the goddess on top inversion in Wroth's play, then, "purifies from dogmatism, from the intolerant and the petrified"[89] the contemporary definition of woman.

Wroth's human characters further subvert gender stereotypes. True, one woman, Dalina is inconstant and flighty (2.1.192–205). Nevertheless, rational, loyal, and generous women far outnumber her. Slivesta's disappointment in love leads her to dedicate herself to Diana and chastity; but her love is so pure, her character so strong, that she comforts and advises Musella, the woman who replaced her in Philisses's affections (3.1.23–103). Musella is also admirable. She wisely advises Simeana to reject the pejorative gossip of Arcas against her lover Lissius, as well as to forgive any transgressions Lissius might have unintentionally committed (4.1.232–92).

If the opposite of the woman being on top is the man on bottom, then *Love's Victory* completes the reversal with its male characters predominately demonstrating the jealousy, pride, and shallow intellect that Wroth's society attributed mainly to women. Philisses's jealousy prevents him from sharing love with Musella (2.1.100–116, 2.2.18–60, 3.1.44–78), and even somewhat undermines his friendship with Lissius (2.2.18–60). Lissius is blindly overproud, overestimating his ability to resist love (1.2.64–70, 226–35) and insensitive to the suffering he causes three young shepherdesses (3.2.1–188). Rustic is such a shallow simpleton that he can neither puzzle out a riddle (4.1.391–98) nor create beautiful loves song requisite for any self-respecting pastoral swain (1.3.55–72).

Arcas, however, blends two of the worst traits for which women were arraigned, destructive speech and hateful cunning. He exhibits the dangerous use of language in his plots to disrupt the love of Lissius and Simeana by spreading vicious rumors (4.1.233–300). This male's pettiness at Musella's rejection contrasts tellingly with Silvesta's altruistic and dignified response to Philisses's rejection. Arcas tricks Musella's mother into contracting the girl in marriage to the loathsome Rustic, slandering her and separating her from her heart's joy (5.5.126–35). He even exults in his revenge of humiliating Musella in this marriage when he sneers, "Now she that soared aloft all day, at night / Must roost in a poor bush with small delight" (5.2.22–23). His vindictiveness has far-reaching repercussions, for Silvesta is threatened with immolation for seeming to help the lovers commit suicide to escape the dread marriage (5.7.13–19).

More importantly, Venus, the goddess, sets aright the social harmony Arcas has disrupted on both a personal and a broader social level. It is Venus and her "instrument ordained" (5.7.71), Silvesta, who defeat and subdue Arcas in the pastoral world. Silvesta's potion forestalls the marriage by making the lovers appear to be dead. Rustic, believing he no longer has a bride, breaks his troth and leaves the way open for the lovers to unite when the goddess resuscitates them. Venus not only brings about the lovers' personal happiness by reviving then reuniting them, but her act frees Silvesta from the charges of murder requiring her execution (5.7.67–100). Further, Venus gives the Forester, who has pursued Silvesta with promises of chaste, altruistic love, the opportunity to prove his vows by offering to sacrifice his life for the woman he loves. In response to his sincere gallantry, once she is freed of her death sentence, Silvesta trusts the Forester's honor and promises him her "chaste love" and to "grieve only for [his] sake" (99–100). Finally, not only does Venus undo all of Arcas's disruptive plottings, but she keeps him in the pastoral world as a living example of male treachery (143–48). Neither capricious nor weakminded, Venus is not swayed by a man of "treachery" 's (156) claims of repentance but answers with firm majesty: "Your doom is given, it may not be recalled" (155).

Perhaps even more important, since Venus and Cupid have stated that they have given lovers "crosses" to teach the humans the value of love, the implication may be that Arcas is not a real threat to Venus's power to create harmony. Rather, she turns him into another instrument to promote it. His disruptions do not denote a male's power over the female, for Venus transforms the problems he creates into learning experiences for her charges. Musella's mother learns not to be gullible or to value empty honor over genuine feeling (5.6.120–33). Musella and Phillises learn the depth and legitimacy of their love when they realize that each is willing to give up life for the other (5.4). Silvesta learns the Forester is a true Platonic courtly suitor worthy of her chaste love (5.7.93–100).

Love's Victory is a powerful challenge to the orthodoxy of women's inferiority, even dangerousness, of Wroth's era. In her human characters, Wroth shows that women can be chaste without being hypocritical (Silvesta); loving without being demanding (Musella, Silvesta); and wise, insightful, courageous, and steadfast (Silvesta, Musella, Simeana). With the divine female pastoral guide, Wroth gives her audience a woman who seems to wield power capriciously only to those who are too egotistical, insecure, selfish, or short-sighted to recognize the wisdom and justice shaping her thoughts and behavior. Lady Mary Wroth's work restores the female pastoral guide to assert the potential of woman's power in reason, love, strength, and courage when unconstrained by prejudice and fear. This is not to imply that Wroth's use of the guide to challenge views about women effected change in her society or even in the social discourse on the subject. *Love's Victory* was written for private presentation, for Wroth's own coterie. According to S. P. Cerasano and Marion Wynne-Davies, the play itself survives "in only two manuscripts versions and one of those is incomplete," neither readily accessible to the public. As late as 1906, W. W. Greg's *Pastoral Poetry and Pastoral Drama* barely touched on the play and asserted the authorship was unknown.[90] Nevertheless, Mary Wroth's work is important to consider as a demonstration that though dissenting voices may not have predominated, they existed and would not be entirely silenced.

The plays on which this chapter focused show that the female pastoral guide as a goddess made the transition from Continental to English sixteenth- and seventeenth-century pastoral. Facilitating this move was the mythos of Queen Elizabeth as sacred virgin restoring a golden age in England in affinity with the divine guide's using wisdom, justice, and a bond to the sacred order, often through tests of her charges, to restore pastoral harmony. Tensions generated by interconnected political, religious, and gender conflicts of the era colored literary portrayals of Elizabeth, which in turn shaped the depiction of the guide as goddess. This is apparent in direct mergings of Elizabeth and the guide (*Endymion*) and in general usage of the guide as pastoral divinity (*Loves Metamorphosis, A Midsummer Night's Dream, Love's Victory*). The next chapters will explore how a version of the guide as learned woman, sometimes straddling human and supernatural as a mage, also partakes of some of the same revisions.

Once again, these versions of the guide will reflect a range of responses to views of woman's threat to order: from affirmation to questioning to disputation. Like Venus in *Love's Victory*, these guides will prove active women on top, "liberat[ing]" and "purify[ing]"[91] and healing their charges from constrictive, false worldviews with carnival tests and play, through their language and their actions, only not as goddesses with divine power but as scholars wielding their educations.

4

The Pastoral Guide:
The Mage and Female Scholar

I

PORTRAYALS OF THE FEMALE PASTORAL GUIDE IN DRAMA as more human than divine came to predominate with Elizabeth's death and control of England reverting to a male monarch. During Elizabeth's reign, the guide most frequently appeared as a goddess on the court, university, or general-public stages, most notably as Cynthia (*Endymion*), Ceres (*Loves Metamorphosis*), Juno (*Maydes Metamorphoses*), and Titania (*Midsummer Night's Dream*). Even two of Elizabeth's incarnations as a wise-woman guide, in *The Arraignment of Paris* and *The Lady of May*, had more supernatural than human associations, where she carried the semi-divine connotations of being monarch and head of the Church of England. With the ascent of James I, the need to shore up support for a female governor, or wrestle with anxiety over this situation, was no longer an issue. Elizabeth's death transferred the anxiety over female agency outside masculine control from centering on an individual, powerfully positioned woman to women in general. At the same time, the number of guides depicted as goddesses came to be drastically outnumbered by those portrayed as educated, scholarly human women, with or without magical powers.

From 1603 to the mid-seventeenth century, of sixteen notable examples of dramas with a female pastoral guide, eleven used the learned guide in the form of mage or wise woman. Only five pastoral dramas used the goddess guide, and when she did appear she often shared the stage with a learned woman (sometimes with magical powers) or had only a brief part. In fact, even though it can be argued that one of the most striking examples of the human pastoral guide, Rosalind of *As You Like It* (1599/1600), existed during Elizabeth's lifetime, the character's creation so close to the end of the Queen's life (1603) and the restaging of the play during James's reign suggest that the human form of the guide she embodies was more congenial to Jacobean and Caroline artists and audiences than the goddess guide. Strengthening Rosalind's positioning with Jacobean and Caroline learned-woman guides is another cultural influence: the preoccupation with the propriety and necessity of educating middle- and upper-class women. To understand how this form of the female pastoral guide could

137

reflect the shift in concerns, it is useful to review not only the traits of the guide as learned woman but to recall how contemporary views about the Neoplatonist mage shape the guide.

The figure of the mage is a particularly apt vehicle for exploring the ramifications of allowing women this kind of learning because in early-modern culture the mage was burdened with similar concerns about education's lifting humans out of their divinely appointed places in social and spiritual hierarchies. In fact the mage could be cited as possessing many of the same flaws that were supposed to make women liable to practicing witchcraft and were used to justify severely limiting their independent agency: gullibility, short-sightedness, and pride. So, despite the mage's claims to spiritual cleansing and only pious, altruistic use of his powers, orthodox religion, Catholic and Protestant, frequently interpreted this figure as either trying to usurp divine power, especially from the Deity's representatives in Church and State, or foolishly, egotistically misled by Satan, the Prince of Liars, into believing that there was a distinction between holy and demonic magic.[1] Marlowe's Dr. Faustus is the ideal literary representation of the view that human vanity, greed, and short-sightedness prevent the purification of which Ficino, Pico della Mirandola, Dee, and Paracelsus believed humans capable. In consequence, as the mage could be read as dangerous for trying to understand and control power beyond the natural capabilities granted him by God, the woman who attempted to step outside her proper intellectual and social sphere could be considered to have grasped a power that she was inherently incapable of wielding safely.

The creators of the female pastoral mages and wise women rejected this negative perception of the mage in shaping their guides, providing themselves with a useful vehicle for resisting the similar depiction of a scholarly woman. Clorin, Helena, Rosalind, Silvesta, and others were portrayed in line with the professed goals of mages to improve themselves in order to help others, not as dangerously misguided mages or women for stepping outside their God-given place. However, even the mage or wise-woman guides of pastoral drama were not entirely free to act too "frowardly": their scholarly wisdom only qualified them to teach the law of patriarchal control or their challenge of that law had to be masked by disguise, humor, or a co-opting of the discourse designed to contain them.

The female pastoral guide as mage does, indeed, disprove fears about woman stepping beyond her limitations, for she exercises power over the natural and supernatural through her virtuous pursuit of knowledge. Although the source of her powers is an outside divinity, she is not, herself, divine. Rather, a deity has granted her paranormal abilities due to her disciplined study of philosophy and natural science, or "art," shaped by her purity of mind, soul, and body. She has learned Pico della Mirandola's lesson to discipline away "[r]aging greed" and "the pride of life, the lust of the flesh, and the lust of the eyes," so she can recognize that "this our mind, to which even divine things are accessible, cannot be of mortal race, and will be happy only by the possession of divine things." Most importantly, the female pastoral guide as mage has shaped herself by Pico's instruction "that if we wish to be blessed, we must imitate the most blessed of all things, God, possessing, in ourselves unity, truth, and goodness."[2]

In alignment with these teachings, the guide uses her powers to uplift and save others, directing them to reach for the heavenly to sanctify the earthly, thereby restoring prelapsarian pastoral concord. Healing her charges, both physically and spiritually, she fits John Dee's 1570 description of the "Mathematicall minde" that "by good meanes [can] Mount aboue the cloudes and sterres . . . : and . . . Descend, to frame Naturall thinges, to wonderfull vses: and when he list, retire home into his own Centre: and there, prepare more Meanes, to Ascend or Descend by: and, all, *to the glory of God, and our honest delectation in earth.*"[3] Indeed, she matches John Dee's perception of himself as mage as one whose "sacred duty [was] to harness the occult forces of the universe . . . in order to ameliorate our earthly condition."[4] Like the mage ideally envisioned by Dee and Pico, as well as other Neoplatonists such as Marcillo Ficino and Giordano Bruno, the female pastoral guide has risen to be as close to God as humanly possible by virtue of her unselfish devotion to serving God through healing humanity of its spiritually fallen state.[5]

The learned woman as mage or wise woman can be found in Montemayor's *Diana* and in "the only complete translation," by Bartholomew Yonge, including within it Gil Polo's sequel *Enamoured Diana.*[6] Because Yonge's work expanded opportunities for English audiences to become familiar with Montemayor's 1559 original, it is an important source for the female pastoral guide. Felicia of *The Diana,* as discussed in chapter 2, clearly illustrates how the guide incarnates the ideal Neoplatonic mage of the fifteenth, sixteenth, and to some extent seventeenth centuries. Her role as guardian over the temple of Diana, goddess of chastity, demonstrates Felicia is not corrupted by physical desires. Known as the "wise" or "sage Felicia," she demonstrates the accuracy of these titles by healing lovers' suffering through magic, psychology, or a combination of both, depending on what is most appropriate. Proving she is a mage whose intentions are good and whose results are beneficial, Felicia only uses her powers to help lovers to learn for themselves or to expose the villainy of others, such as Alfeo. In both the original and Yonge's English translation of *Diana,* Felicia reflects Ficino's and Pico's conviction that "the highest levels of magical power could be obtained only by one who had been sanctified and whose motives were, consequently, entirely pure."[7] In sixteenth- and seventeenth-century pastoral poetry and prose, Felicia lives on in Spenser's

Coelia of *The Fairie Queene* and Lady Mary Wroth's Melissea in *Urania*, wise women whose sacred studies and personal holiness enable them to heal the bodies and souls of the injured brought to them.

Although the wise woman shares the traits of insight and virtue with the mage, she differs in lacking supernatural power. Instead, as solely a wise woman she gets her power to work good from her insight into human nature, her compassion, her rationality, her wit, and her learning. She follows Paracelsus's admonition to prove oneself worthy of knowledge of God's universe through purification and in altruistic devotion to understanding God's creation: "For nothing has been created that man could not explore, and it has been created so that man may not be idle but walk in the path of God, that is, in his works. Not in vice, not in fornication, not in gambling, not in drinking, not in plundering, not in the acquisition of goods nor the accumulation of riches for the worms. But to apply his spirit, his light, his angelic kind to the contemplation of divine objects."[8] She "walks in the path of God" and "appl[ies] his spirit" by eschewing vices while rejecting the self-aggrandizement of "the acquisition of goods [and] the accumulation of riches," in order to find the deeper insight that comes from "the contemplation of divine objects." The wise woman is also like Paracelsus's doctor who uses his powers to make others well in body and mind, solely out of devotion to God's laws of love and service to one's fellow humans.[9] As with the other guides, she may, herself, be a pastoral world visitor (Rosalind, Lady in *Comus*, Bellessa in *Shepherds' Paradise*) or native (Marian of *The Sad Shepherd*).

The guide as wise woman appears in varied forms on both public and private stages. On the surface, *As You Like It*'s Rosalind might seem almost to spoof the guide, with her empowering "old religious uncle" (3.2.335–36) and her own practice of conjuring (epilogue) existing nowhere but in her imaginative and playful humor. Yet, for all her jesting at the conventions of courtly love, pastoral idyllicism, and the guide's power, Rosalind expertly harnesses the wise woman's imagination and wit to help herself, the charges with whom she interacts, and those who interact with her charges. As a wise woman guide, Maid Marian in Jonson's unfinished *The Sad Shepherd* is no longer a mere bawdy fertility symbol of rural festivals. She has wit, insight, and independence to help her puzzle out the source of love-sickness; straighten out a love tangle; challenge a supernatural threat of chaos; and give as good, if not better, than she gets in verbal sparring with her love, Robin Hood. Several other examples from royal performances also feature the wise-woman pastoral guide. Queen Bellessa, of Montagu's masque *The Shepherd's Paradise*, is selected to rule for her beauty, modesty, and wisdom by her subjects and demonstrates the guide's insight, rationality, compassion, and virtuousness in reigning. In Milton's 1634 Ludlow Masque, also known as *Comus*, The Lady acts out a unique twist on the guide's attempts to maintain or restore the golden age within the individual's soul and in society. This work does not show the wise woman merely struggling with the folly or egotism of misdirected lovers but portrays her under siege and striving to use her wit, insight, and strength to save her own soul from damning corruption.[10]

As with the mage, an important source character for the wise woman is found in *Diana*. As discussed in chapter 2, Felismena demonstrates the requisite wit of a guide. The young man who woos her is sent by his father to court to separate them. Felismena has the loyalty and courage to set out after him in concern over his gradual failure to stay in touch, and the cleverness to preserve her chastity on her mission by disguising herself as a page.[11] Though she cannot preserve Felix's fidelity or prevent the object of his affection, Celia, from falling in love with her disguised persona, Felismena treats both with fairness, wisdom, and sympathy tempered with firmness.[12] Celia's death from unfulfilled love at discovering Felismena's true gender and Felix's despairing flight from court at that death[13] stem not from Felismena's "deception" but from the self-absorption, infidelity, and indulgence that led them to reject her good advice and pursue self-destructive goals. Though Felismena cannot guide these two characters away from their folly, this "failure" tellingly takes place in the court world where corruption typically prevails. What matters is that Felismena consistently demonstrates qualities essential to the guide: wit and learning, intelligence, discipline, rationality, compassion, and loyalty.

Once in the pastoral world, Felismena takes on the role of guide more effectively. Felismena single-handedly saves Selvagia, Syrenus, Silvio, and several of Felicia's nymphs from a pack of satyrs maddened by lust for the nymphs, a scaled down version of *Aithiopika*'s Chariklea defeating an entire army with her prowess as an archer. This presages later achievements that Felismena accomplishes when putting her wisdom and pluck at Felicia's service. As detailed in chapter 2, Felismena brings her own lover and Belissa's back to Diana's temple for loving reunions and reconciliation, and while on her mission untangles the fractious love lives of shepherds and shepherdesses whom she meets along the way.[14]

Interestingly, although Felismena's adventures in the court world disguised as a man have drawn scholars to link her to Viola's misadventures as disguised page with Duke Orsino and Olivia in *Twelfth Night*,[15] they have missed the stronger similarity between Felismena and the archetypal female pastoral guide, Rosalind in *As You Like It*. Felismena's independence and wit are more strongly echoed in Rosalind, sometimes humorously. Viola, on occasion, sauces Orsino and Olivia for their melancholy but does not aggressively school them on their follies in love as Rosalind does Orlando, Silvius, and Phebe. Particularly interesting are the strong similarities between Felismena's and Rosalind's roles in settling the love crises between shepherds and shepherdesses. Both Felismena and Rosalind listen in, unobserved, on the love-plagued pastoral denizens, and both decide that they must determinedly step forward to sort out the lovers' problems.[16]

When Amarillis tries to dash off before her lover can present his case to Felismena's judgment, Felismena "tak[es] hold [of the shepherdess] by her garment," admonishing, "It were not reason Shepherdesse, that I should receive this discourtesie at thy hands, who desires so much to serve thee." Later, in the process of "arbitrat[ing] the matter between [Duarda and Armia]," Felismena sharply gives the shepherd Armida the sound advice that honorable behavior and loyal respect are far more reliable signs of true service to a lover than "smooth and filed speeches" or fancy sonnets.[17] Doing some equally telling arbitration of her own in *As You Like It*, Rosalind chides Phebe and Silvius together, warning the former of the loneliness her pride will bring her (3.5.57–63), the latter of the failure his abject worship will bring him (49–52), and the world of the danger the marriage of such idiocy will bring: "'Tis such fools as you / That makes the world full of ill-favour'd children" (52–53).

Rosalind's closer resemblance than Viola's to Felismena's assertiveness and independence also comes into play in a humorous, self-deprecating instance. Felismena's first appearance, braining any lust-craze satyrs she does not fatally impale with arrows, anticipates Rosalind's promise in *As You Like It* of presenting "a swashing and a martial" mien (1.3.116). An even more playful variation on Chariklea than Felismena, Rosalind plans only to carry "[a] gallant curtle axe upon [her] thigh" (113), not use it to kill dangerous predators—human or otherwise. Still, Rosalind's boldness to all she meets in Arden and her earlier resistance to Duke Frederick's false charges of treason (1.3.52–84) reveal her to be no easy victim, even if she claims to be subject to "woman's fear" (1.3.114–15) and humanly faints at the sight of Orlando's blood (4.3.157–58). These comparisons and the reasons for Rosalind's variation from Felismena will bear deeper discussion in chapter 7.

These variations on the guide as wise woman or mage reveal an array of views on seventeenth-century debate over how much or what kind of education women should be allowed and what would be the consequences of such education. This debate over training women to take their place most effectively and properly in society generally turns on the answers to two conflicting questions. The first question would be: will education become dangerous power in the hands of weak daughters of Eve, easily led into temptation and dangerously adept at luring men after them? The second question, though not absolving women entirely of flaws traditionally associated with their gender, contradicts the negative implications of the first in suggesting that women can be taught to overcome these traits, querying, will education teach women the discipline to temper their "naturall towardnesse," as Richard Mulcaster suggests, and to "more diligently . . . cultivat[e]" their "wit" so that "nature's defect may be redressed by industry," as Thomas More puts it?[18] According to the second view, a more benevolent patriarchal perspective, tempering the inherent female tendency to pride, capriciousness, and flighty emotionalism through education will better prepare women, as Henry Bullinger writes, to "help and comfort" their husbands, "brin[g] up children in the fear of God," and save themselves from falling victim to or practicing "wantoness and niceness in words, gestures, and deeds, . . . unhonest games and pastimes [and] unhonest loves."[19]

Those who backed female education were not completely in accord with each other, though. On the one hand, Valerie Wayne points out that early-modern writers like Thomas Elyot and William Gouge would and did bridle at being identified with medieval thinkers who condemned women as inherently evil. On the other hand, she notes that their praises or defenses of women still strongly confirmed that women required patriarchal control.[20] An effective way to keep women under that control was to divert application of their education away from competition with men by containing it within the domestic sphere—over which the husband/father held ultimate control. Not surprisingly, then, the two main groups pushing for the treatment of women as educable beings, the Protestant reformers and the Christian humanists, "enjoined Englishwomen to exercise their newly developed understanding in private roles within the confines of their homes."[21] Thomas More, who so carefully cultivated the reasoning powers and classical learning in his daughters, wrote to his favorite, Margaret Roper, that she should be happily content for her learning to benefit no larger an audience than the two immediate patriarchs in her family, "your husband and myself."[22] W. P.'s popular 1598 translation of Bruno's *The Necessarie, Fit, and Convenient Education of a yong Gentlewoman* expressed the fears that classical studies would distract woman from her true duties to "the needle, the wheele, the distaffe, and the spindle," essentially "to govern[ing] our houses," or, worse, bring "great daunger to offend the beautie and glory of her minde" by teaching her to be a "subtil and impudent love[r]" crafting "verses, poetrie, ballads and songs."[23] Nearly fifty years later, in *The English Gentlewoman*, Richard Brathwaite was still warning that young women must "make choice of such arguments as may best improve [their] knowledge in household affairs, and other private employments. To discourse of State-matters, will not become [their] auditory: nor to dispute of high points of Divinity, will it sort well with women of [their] quality."[24]

In contrast to such reservations about educating women, learning in areas beyond the domestic sphere could also be seen as a way to enhance rather than degrade women's ability to perform the duties assigned their gender. Important educators such as Thomas More, Juan Vives, and Richard Mulcaster asserted that education in the classics would provide women with examples of morality, discipline, and self-denial that would be especially beneficial to their weaker moral; emotional; and, some would contend, intellectual natures.[25] The popular 1639 translation of Jacques Du Bosc's *The Complete Woman* disputes several traditional arguments against educating women outside the domestic realm, pointing out that learning in arts and sciences not only makes women more companionable and moral wives and mothers, but that this knowledge does not hinder the performance of wifely duties. Rather, such education keeps female minds too busy to be to be distracted by frivolity or immorality while women pursue their domestic responsibilities. Moreover, Du Bosc insists that if any woman does use learning destructively, it is because she is a corrupt individual not because women by nature are corrupt.[26] Bathsua Makin expresses related sentiments, writing in *An Essay to Revive the Antient Education of Gentlewomen* (1673) that when women were in classical times "Educated in the Knowledge of Arts and Tongues, . . . by their Education, many did rise to a great height in Learning." Consequently, she argues, "[w]ere women thus Educated now, . . . the advantage would be very great: The Women would have Honour and Pleasure, their Relations Profit, and the whole Nation Advantage."[27]

There were some writers in the sixteenth as well as the seventeenth century who even claimed that learning was valuable for women's moral development, regardless of its domestic value, with women apt learners because of their high natural intellectual and moral capabilities. Pamela Benson points out that in *Defence of Good Women* (1540), Thomas Elyot "reasons that one system of virtue exists for both sexes, that women participate in virtue equally with men, and that, as a consequence, educated women are as capable of governing nations [under extraordinary circumstances] and living moral lives as educated men."[28] Over one hundred years later, Samuel Torshell, in *The Woman's Glorie* (1645), declares that reading "what is printed in the whole volume," uncensored, is "as proper" "to the woman's sex as flying to a bird." A good education and "a good heart look[ing] out through modest eyes" "[keep] the scale of affections even. This teaches a denying and preventing behavior towards tentations [*sic*]. 'Tis much better than philosopher's wool to stop the ear with. It is the best guardian both of the eye and the ear."[29] Phyllis Rackin cites the practical applications of education, domestic and otherwise: aristocratic women often arranged marriages for female kin, administered country homes, and inherited estates; middle- and working-class women arranged their own marriages, ran the household economy, sometimes directed businesses, and supported themselves before marriage or after being widowed.[30]

By linking the female pastoral guide with the highly learned figure of the mage, pastoralists were using the guide to examine not merely the ramifications of educating women but more specifically the results of women entering into the intellectual and social fields opened to them by letting them become scholars in areas normally the purviews of men. How would a woman scholar have been defined? In many ways, surprisingly similar to a male scholar. Early-modern educators like Thomas More, Nicholas Udall, Richard Mulcaster, Thomas Elyot, and Roger Ascham, men highly regarded by their contemporaries, recommended a plan of study for scholarly women that, beyond the obvious ability to read and write, could include all or some combination of: rhetoric to facilitate clear thinking and persuasive writing and speaking skills; knowledge of classical and biblical texts, as well as contemporary writings on philosophy and art; and to that end, instruction in not only English but classical languages (Hebrew, Greek, and Latin) and the languages of contemporary art, philosophy, and religious thought (Italian, French, Spanish—possibly German and Portuguese).[31] Disputing the Judith Shakespeare mythos of a scholarly early modern woman as completely anathema to her society, a notable contingent of women excelled in all these areas.

Proof of women's rhetorical accomplishments suggesting their clear thinking, eloquence, and moral rectitude are not hard to find. Philip Stubbes praised his wife Katherine for her ability to cite and explain scripture to confound the heresy of misbelievers.[32] Elizabeth Askew drew on her knowledge of the Bible not only to outmaneuver her interrogators' attempts to trick her into heresy but also to turn their charges against them to suggest the inadequacy of their knowledge and faith.[33] After Parliament attempted to pressure Elizabeth I into marriage by criticizing her for neglecting to provide a successor, the Queen's Speech to the House of Commons, January 28, 1563, cleverly, ceremoniously rebuked them that if anyone knows her responsibilities, which she has fulfilled in protecting her critics repeatedly, it is she: "And so I assure you all that though after my death you may have many stepdames, yet you shall never have any a more mother than I mean to be unto you all"![34] Completely turning back on them their criticism of her for failing to provide the nation with a legitimate heir, she sharply reminds them that she is no cruel or selfish false mother, as "stepdames" were perceived to be. Instead, her devotion to governing her nation wisely and justly has made her a loving, protective "mother" to an entire nation.

Other women used their rhetorical skill in prose and poetry to defend their gender from misogynist attacks, arguing that the licentiousness, temper, dishonesty, and intellectual shallowness usually attributed to women are too often the provenance of men, and that men's vices corrupt women's virtue, not the other way around. In 1589, a writer using the pseudonym

Jane Anger answered a now-lost attack on women with "articulate anger." By "stand[ing] on their heads all the clichéd charges about women's pride of appearance, laziness, and dependency," she revealed that men's lust and duplicity preying on women's trusting innocence led to fallen women.[35] About twenty-five years later, Rachel Speght's *A Mouzell for Melastomus* (1617) also "stands on their heads" the charges of Joseph Swetnam's misogynist pamphlet with rationality, righteous indignation, and an impressive arsenal of examples from classical and biblical sources.[36]

In poetry, Isabella Whitney's *The Copy of a Letter . . . With an Admonition* (1567) and Aemilia Lanyer's *Salve Deus Rex Judaeorum* (1611) use similar rhetorical strategies to rescue women from men's criticism by asserting men's hypocrisy for making charges of which they are themselves much guiltier.[37] Margaret Tyler anticipates and reverses criticism that men would level at her as a woman for translating a Spanish romance into *The Mirrour of Princely Deedes and Knighthood* (1578). To those who say she cannot write of martial matters because women are untrained and unpracticed in this field, she counters that if men expect their writings about women to be accepted they had better not deny her equal capability to imagine outside her personal experience. Any who insist women expose themselves to impropriety by writing about romances, she counters with the question: why do you expose us women to romances by writing them with the expectation we will read them?[38]

Women's erudition was also demonstrated by their accomplishments as readers and translators of classical and modern-language texts. Thomas More's daughter Margaret Roper and her daughter Mary Bassett were both highly respected by More, Erasmus, and Juan Vives for their learning in Greek and Latin and for their translations of classical and contemporary texts in these languages.[39] Lady Joanna Lumley, "between 1550 and 1553[,] produc[ed] the first English version of a Greek drama," *Iphegania at Aulis*, as well as translated the Greek of Isocrates to Latin.[40] Many other women scholars were highly regarded for their ability to read and translate both modern and classical languages. Patricia Demers points out that Elizabeth I was respected by her educators, who included Roger Ascham, William Camden, and Thomas North, for "ease" in "French, Latin, Greek, and Italian." Her translations included not only a Latin to English *Consolation of Philosophy*, but various texts from Greek and Latin to English, as well as even from Greek to Latin.[41] Anne Cooke Bacon, one of several highly educated literary sisters, translated work by an Italian divine, Bernardo Ochino, in addition to Bishop Jewell's *Latin Apologia Ecclesiae Anglicanae*. Her sister Elizabeth Cooke Hoby Russell created poetry in Latin, Greek, and English as well as translated Bishop John Ponet's Latin religious work.[42] Lady Mary Herbert studied Greek, Hebrew, French, and Italian with her brother Philip Sidney and put those studies to work finishing his translations of the Psalms and translating and publishing Garnier's *Marc Antoine* under the title *The Tragedie of Antonie* (1595). Elizabeth Carey, who would be the first woman to write an original drama in English, also taught herself French, Spanish, Italian, Latin, Hebrew, and Transylvanian (!).[43] Both women were lauded by Sir John Davies as the ideal of scholarly womanhood, when he called them: ". . . The Most Noble, and no lesse deservedly renowned-Laydes, as well as Darlings, as Patronesses, of the Muses; . . . Glories of Women."[44]

Although translations might be viewed as uncreative exercises in transferring the masculine word from one language to another, and women might even claim this was their goal, this was not always the case. For example, Tina Krontiris and Patricia Demers note that Lady Mary Herbert's translation of Garnier's play radically changed and improved the language and use of verse, while also shifting emphasis to make Cleopatra more sympathetic. Her finishing the translations of the Psalms that she and her brother had started together allowed her to create a tour de force of varied poetic forms and evocative imagery.[45] In a different vein, Margaret Tyler's selection of *The Mirrour of Princely Deedes and Knighthood*, a romance that focuses on noble, thinking female characters who suffer at the unfairness of marriage laws for women, enabled her to put into circulation views of women that challenge some of the norms.[46]

As with Mary Sidney's Psalms, translations and religious works sometimes overlapped, allowing women to demonstrate that they could understand and interpret scripture; they had artistic talent; and they were not mere weak daughters of Eve using their tongues or pens to deceive and destroy.[47] Women could also put their intellectual and creative talents to work indirectly. Noble women such as Lady Mary Herbert, Margaret Countess of Cumberland, and the Duchess of Bedford presided over intellectual coteries on their estates where they fostered the work of the like of Aemilia Lanyer, Sir Philip Sidney, Samuel Daniel, Abraham Fraunce, and Nicholas Breton, exerting their own aesthetic and philosophical bents on these writers to varying degrees.[48]

Women could also be educated in science and the healing arts. Betty Travitsky writes that in addition to studying "classical authors," "the new testament," "church fathers," and "Christian poets," women could also be encouraged to study a "lofty science like astronomy" as well as a "useful science like the preparation of medicines." [49] In terms of "lofty" sciences, the schools that Mary Ward set up in the sixteenth century for girls across Europe, including her native England, added to the curriculum of "languages" and literary and religious studies, "mathematics, astronomy, [and] geography." Likewise, Anna Maria Van Schurman, known as "the Dutch Sappho and the learned maid of Utrecht," as Patricia Demers notes, wrote a treatise on female education, *The Learned Maid; or Whether a*

Maid May Be Scholar? A Logick Exercise (1659), asserting that women need not only study "Scriptural Theology," languages, *"Grammar, Logick,* [and] Rhetorick," history, and the arts but *"Physick," "Metaphysicks,"* and *Mathematicks."*[50]

Throughout the sixteenth and seventeenth centuries, the "useful" science of medicine was a particularly practical course of study for women, which they practiced regularly in caring for the health of spouses; children; and, depending on their economic class, their servants. As M. A. Katritzky points out, well into the sixteen hundreds, "Domestic management manuals still took it for granted that the 'compleate woman' should have sufficient knowledge in the realms of surgery, physic, pharmacy and cosmetics to oversee basic health and hygiene care in her own domestic sphere, whose size was determined by her station in life."[51] Lady Margaret Hoby's diary, running from 1599–1605, regularly records her treatment of animals and humans: "Mak[ing] a salve for a sore beast," "dress[ing]" one "poore mans [*sic*] hand," another "sarvants [*sic*] foot," and treating a miscellaneous collection of "sores." Lady Elizabeth Clinton's *The Countesse of Lincolnes Nurserie* (1622) instructs her daughter-in-law and other women on the benefits of nursing their babies themselves.[52] According to Charlotte Otten, Lady Grace Mildmay (c. 1570–1620) studied from "Dr. Turner's Herbal" and "books of physic" so that she could "ministe[r] to one or the other by the directions of the best physicians of [her] acquaintance and ever God gave a blessing thereunto."[53]

Women outside the nobility also studied and practiced health care, such as Dorothy Burton of the "landed gentry." In *The Gentlewoman's Companion* Hannah Woolley reports that her "thirty years' observation and experience" prove that her education in science, art, mathematics, estate management, and housewifery benefited not only the aristocratic family she served as governess and steward but the domestic needs of her family and community. Mary Trye, a latter-day Helena of *All's Well*, learned her craft in medicine from her father, Dr. Thomas O'Dowd, and successfully took over his practice when he died. And throughout the sixteenth and seventeenth centuries, women also earned their bread in conjunction with quacks and montebanks, practitioners scorned by the medical establishment though some of them provided help through psychology and herbal medications.[54] In fact, women even wrote down their recipes and medical advice for futurity. Some of these texts were actually published, though the women, themselves, were not always the ones who chose to publish. Elizabeth Clinton's guide for breastfeeding came out in 1622. Grace Mildmay "kept a book of prescriptions" to pass on to her descendents. In 1671, Jane Sharp was the first woman in England to publish a manual on midwifery for women.[55]

The physical treatments these women gave family and dependents was often seen working in conjunction with spiritual healing. Elizabeth Clinton's guide blends moral and bodily health in urging mothers to provide children with their own breast milk rather than a wet nurse's not only because God ordained this work for her but because the child will imbibe the mother's finer moral character and her better health this way.[56] Women like Lady Mildmay and Lady Margaret Hobey also attended to their servants' spiritual health by leading them in prayer. Women of all classes were expected to teach their children the proper religious faith and Christian behavior, deferentially guide their husbands, and set examples for and give advice to their servants. For example, in *On Domestical Duties* William Gouge advises wives to serve as "a good pattern" to "children and servants" because "the family is a seminary of the Church and Commonwealth. It is as a bee-hive, in which is the stock, and out of which are sent many swarms of bees: for in families are all sorts of people bred and brought up: and out of families are they lent into the Church and Commonwealth. The first beginning of mankind, and of his increase, was out of a family."[57] According to Gouge, moral wives, mothers, and mistresses not only shaped the spiritual well-being of their families but created a moral standard for the entire nation, as their husbands, children, and servants "len[d]" themselves "into the Church and Commonwealth."

However, all this is not to fall into Burckhardt's claim that the opportunities to put their education to use was identical for men and women. For the small percentage of women who received some kind of education, learning did not send them into the world but became another way to keep them in the private sphere. Where boys of several class levels could attend the universities, girls would usually be taught in the home by fathers (Maragert Roper by Thomas More, Elizabeth Carey by her father), mothers or mother figures (Elizabeth and Mary Tudor by Katherine Parr), or perhaps by tutors, sometimes their brothers' (Mary Herbert, Mary Wroth).[58] As touched on earlier, generally, the ends of women's education also were far different and more constricting than those for men, mainly designed to keep them out of the public spheres of politics, commerce, or literary fame and to channel them into the domestic realm of wives and mothers. Thus, Thomas Salter warns in 1579 that education should reflect the fact that "the governement of estates and publike weales are not committed into the handes of womene" nor are women capable to be trained as "professours of Science and facultie, to teache in Schooles the wisedome of Lawes and Philosophie." Instead, women's learning should fit them up for their proper role in society: "wholelie to be active and diligent about the governement of her housholde and familie." Educators of women should keep in mind that "how far more convenient the Distaffe, and Spindle, Nedle and Thimble were for [women] . . . then [*sic*] the skill of well using a penne or wrighting a loftie vearce."[59]

In fact, the public face of publishing, sometimes even just writing, was often seen as a form of immodesty. For a female to expose herself to an audience, especially a paying one, was to become a public woman, a charge following the traditional pattern of linking verbal and sexual immodesty. To put it another way, "a silent woman was also assumed to be chaste and obedient and a loquacious woman was perceived to be disobedient and sexually licentious. In this socio-cultural context, therefore for a woman to express herself [in writing] was simultaneously to bring her reputation into doubt." So, even Thomas More commends his daughter concerning her translations: "In your modesty you do not seek for the praise of the public."[60] Women who do write have to defend their modesty constantly by an array of devices: shielding themselves with a list of respectable patrons; invoking biblical and classical women who spoke out but were not immodest or rebellious; insisting that they do not claim to attempt to equal men; reasoning that their meager talents render them beneath the concern of men; stating that their works were published without their permission; or claiming that they are driven to speak by God's command to share their spiritual or medical knowledge for the benefit other humans.[61] In fact, the genres of writing that caused women the least amount of friction for expressing a public voice were those that could be seen as putting her voice under masculine control. Translations were acceptable because it could be claimed that the woman writer was not expressing her own ideas but merely repeating those of the male writer she was "Englishing." Religious meditations and prayers would be acceptable for harmonizing her "writing" voice with the teachings of God and His ministers. Of course manuals on household management, child rearing, and health care dovetailed neatly with woman's domestic roles, especially if they asserted that the ultimate authority in the house is the husband.[62]

Two of the most vital uses to which female scholarship was put were also important roles for the guide: educator and healer of her charges, spiritually and physically. Even more important, some of the same concerns over woman's innate capacity to carry out these roles, the propriety of her taking limited authority within the home or conversely the questions raised about the accuracy of views of woman as inferior in light of her success in these roles, are reflected in various versions of the guide.

As discussed in earlier chapters, the classical medical theory of Aristotle and Galen so influential in early-modern culture defined women as physiologically and psychologically inferior to men, her cold, moist, unstable, diffuse mind and body putting her at a disadvantage to man's heat and firmness. Perception of women's related physical and mental deficiency in relation to men shaped not only medical views on women but views on her ability to practice medicine. As touched on in chapter 2, most women's connection to health care was through folk traditions as herbalists and cunning women—sometimes with the stigma of being associated with witchcraft.[63] The descriptions of women as healers earlier in this chapter also shows that most of them were not involved in mainstream, formal medical studies but learned receipts and practices passed on, orally or in manuscript, from mothers or female elders. Even the work they did was limited either to gynecological care or tending to minor health problems such as sores, fevers, and broken bones. Formal training at the universities in the classical tradition of Galen and Aristotle, the more modern studies of the anatomists, or Paracelsus's chemical and psychological teachings were closed to them.[64] Cultural expectations created this practice of exclusion: why waste an education on women when they lacked the intellectual strength and rigor of men to hold up under intensive study and retain what they had learned? Furthermore, since university educations prepared men for their rightful place in public life in law, the ministry, commerce, the arts, or government service, women, whose rightful place was in the domestic sphere, would be receiving training ill suited to their place in society. In fact, would not the university be too public a sphere for a modest woman? After all, had not William Gouge, Henry Bullinger, Juan Vives, Thomas Salter, and many others warned that the Bible enjoined woman not to speak out publicly, not to raise her voice equally to man's, as she might with male students?

As the early modern era increasingly institutionalized and professionalized medicine through requiring university study and licensing, women found themselves increasingly marginalized in various ways from one of the few areas of health care in which they had been allowed to practice, gynecology and obstetrics. Women were caught in something of a Catch–22 as medical schools based their training in gynecology on anatomy studies, which would automatically exclude women due to demands of modesty and general skepticism concerning their intelligence. Doctors then claimed that women's knowledge in this area was inadequate and antiquated, based on superstition and ignorance, while contemporary cultural beliefs barred women from "modernizing" their medical education. In 1590 Johan Fischart expressed a representative contemporary European sentiment in characterizing midwives as "rusty old hags" and "female cow-doctors." Undermining women's rebuttal that their knowledge and practices were based on proven, successful experience, "learned" men translated and published books asserting the pre-eminence of an education that was denied women. Finally, although women had been licensed and registered as midwives as early as 1512 in England, the increasing control various doctors sought to implement through controlling licensure came to put more solidly under masculine medical and government authority women's methods of work, the legitimacy of their work, and even their ability to work at all.[65]

Women did speak out, insisting on the validity of their own expertise and experience and resisting attempts to subjugate themselves to the authority of doctors: witness Jane Sharp writing and publishing *The Mid-wives Book* (1671); Elizabeth Cellier's 1688 answer to an unnamed doctor to justify establishing a midwives college proving the expertise and morality of midwives; and midwives Mrs. Hester Shaw and Mrs. Whip successfully petitioning to prevent Peter Chamberlen's repeated attempts to have the government give his family a patent to regulate the work of midwives. However, their battle was ultimately a losing one. By the eighteenth century, men had supplanted women as what Elizabeth Harvey calls "the primary birth attendants."[66]

The female pastoral guide of English Renaissance drama, particularly in the cases of Clorin (*The Faithful Shepherdess*), Helena (*All's Well*), and Rosalind (*As You Like It*), provides an interesting variety of responses to her culture's conflicting views of medical (and psychological) care that can be best understood through the prism of Bakhtin's carnival. The playwrights invert traditional order by making these three female characters talented, effective "Doctor Shes" who display a remarkable understanding of the masculine realm of medicine in their knowledge and effective application of conforta-tiva and contraria, treatments of a major light of the educated Renaissance medical world, Paracelsus. More importantly, these female healers do not just reverse the dominant order of gender by giving women traits and background normally associated with men. They also embody Bakhtin's concept of the ambivalence of carnival, the holding of opposing forces in an enlivening communion, by using "masculine" intellect and advanced education in conjunction with "feminine" folk knowledge and magic. Clorin uses herbs, spells, and Paracelsian psychology to promote the restraint the patriarchal order seeks to impose on Otherness. Helena spices her learned receipts with the language of ritual for the King and frames her *contraria* and *conforta-tiva* in carnivalesque "abuse" of Bertram. Rosalind associates herself with a hermit magician, and also applies Paracelsian treatments by using carnival's verbal play and blurring of identity.

Interestingly enough, part of what these three pastoral guides help their charges discover through inversion is the inadequacy of the gender hierarchy to delineate human experience: for the male characters frequently exhibit precisely the flaws cited to justify the suppression of women, while these female guides' teachings, through trial and play, reveal their possession of many of the virtues traditionally assigned to men. In the cases of Helena and Rosalind, guides further demonstrate carnival's concept of ambivalence, of expressing the cosmic comic rather than the personal satiric, by mocking themselves as well as the charges whose hearts and minds they try to "liberate" from "static" oppressive, dead "dogmas" of love and gender relations. They embody the positive aspect of the grotesque that blurs boundaries rather than merely reversing the role of oppressor and creating a new but equally static hierarchal system.

This is not to say that the female pastoral guide is exactly Rabelais's Sybil of Panzoult, who throws her skirts over her head in a gesture that defiantly, joyously reveals her genitalia, freeing herself by challenging masculine control or the betrothed who Panurge fears will savagely expose the flaws and inadequacies of patriarchal dogma he embodies.[67] These guides are far less wild women on top, mirroring Bakhtin's observation that sixteenth- and seventeenth-century writing was increasingly toning down the spirit of carnival.[68] To some extent, the female pastoral guide as mage or wise woman reflects the warning that Peter Stallybrass and Mary Russo make against too naïvely reading carnival as a successful liberation from the intricate constrictions of social order. Still, Clorin, Rosalind, and Helena are not equally subdued, and one of the ways they can be compared deals with the concept discussed before, the ventriloquized voice.

Of the three plays, *The Faithful Shepherdess* presents the most conservative view of a pastoral guide as woman on top. Shepherdess Clorin channels the voice of the god Pan, ultimate male ruler of their pastoral realm, to guide her charges to align their lives with a world order that is not misogynistic but still privileges masculine ascendancy. Shakespeare's Helena and Rosalind are "cattle of a different color." Though they are created by a male author, these female characters ventriloquize a male voice to contrast the folly of the male characters with the wisdom and superiority patriarchy claims for itself. In these three plays, the conflicting views of women's roles and capabilities, particularly in terms of their scholarship as spiritual and physical healers, are explored as enlivening truths alternative to the dogmatism requiring female constraint. To make the contrast of their worldviews clearest, the next chapter will address the most straightforward and conservative, *The Faithful Shepherdess*, with the subsequent two chapters working toward the most challenging and nuanced, *All's Well* followed by *As You Like It*.

5

The Faithful Shepherdess:
Handmaiden of the Great God Pan

I

JOHN FLETCHER'S *THE FAITHFUL SHEPHERDESS* was likely first printed in quarto in 1609 or 1610, and indications in "the commendatory verses, printed with it" suggest that the play was written shortly before its publication.[1] According to Fletcher, the play initially received a negative reception for presenting the pastoral in philosophical, Arcadian terms rather than in the down-home form of "hired shepherds in gray cloaks, with curtailed dogs" and "Whitsun-ales, cream, wassail, and morris-dances."[2] However, *The Faithful Shepherdess* seems to have been more favorably received as the century progressed, with subsequent quartos printed in 1628, 1629, 1634, 1656, and 1665. In 1634, the play was "acted before the king and queen on Twelfe Night."[3] One point that makes this text especially interesting is that in adapting Guarini's 1590 *Il Pastor Fido* into an English play, Fletcher changed the faithful shepherd mage into a *shepherdess* mage—deliberately choosing to create his play around a female pastoral guide.

The choice of transforming a shepherd to shepherdess in *The Faithful Shepherdess* could well have reflected John Fletcher's concern with the reception of his work by the female members of his audience. Fletcher was one of the individuals whom Richard Levin frequently cites in "Women in the Renaissance Theater Audience" as a playwright especially interested in cultivating the "gender-loyalty" or addressing the "gender-concern" of "women spectators." The article does not specifically include *The Faithful Shepherdess* among its examples of Fletcher's work demonstrating the playwright's characteristic "sympathetic treatment of women characters," asserted in a 1638 Preface to *The Woman-Hater*.[4] However, there are several reasons *The Faithful Shepherdess* should also be considered along with the plays Levin sees offering appeals to the female members of the audience or readers of the plays in print. A general connection can be seen in the fact that the range of years during which *The Faithful Shepherdess* was staged or in print dovetails almost exactly with the late Elizabethan through Caroline eras in which Levin detects a notable interest of authors in women's reception of their plays. There are also more specific similarities between this play and the others cited in Levin's article. For instance, Fletcher's portrait of Clorin using her wisdom, learning, and virtue to help men and women to resolve their conflicts exemplifies Levin's observation that a playwright might attempt to win the approval and support of female audience members by "present[ing] a version of the battle of the sexes" that favored women.[5] Levin also suggests that one reason playwrights revealed they cared about how women received their plays was that they believed women would be influenced or "edified as a result of some lesson conveyed by the behavior or fate of female characters in the play." For example, Levin cites Thomas Heywood's claim that "chaste women in the audience are 'encouraged in their virtues' by the examples of noble heroines, and 'The vnchaste are by vs shewed their errors' in the persons of various fallen women."[6]

In *The Faithful Shepherdess*, "unchaste" and undisciplined women like Amarillis and Cloe do, indeed, demonstrate the dangerous error of uninhibited female agency. Even more notable is the portrayal of the play's main character, Clorin, as an "edif[ying]" "noble heroine" in being an effective female pastoral guide under the direction of a fatherly Pan. Though Clorin shares traits with earlier guides of both romance and drama, examining some of her differences from two in particular, *Diana*'s Felicia and *Endymion*'s Cynthia, is a useful starting point for exploring how Fletcher has revised his guide to teach women appealingly that if they, too, wish to be noble heroines they must accept the direction of masculine, but not misogynistic, authority.

Comparing Clorin's and her two predecessors' connections to divinity provides a good introduction to Fletcher's rethinking of the female pastoral guide. Although both Felicia and Clorin are portrayed connected to the goddess Diana, the difference in the relationships of these two guides to their patron divinity tellingly demonstrates how Fletcher decidedly limits his mage's independent voice and agency. Felicia presides over the Temple of Diana, but neither Montemayor nor Yonge in his translation emphasizes her dependence on Diana's patronage. In fact, no one in the romance ever mentions any god as the source of Felicia's power. She always knows what potion to use, what advice to offer, or what trials to give her charges. In contrast, Clorin is much more dependent on the sponsorship of higher powers. For example, although she also has a connection with Diana, unlike Felicia, Clorin explains she is entirely reliant on Diana to direct her search for herbs beneficial for healing her pastoral-world neighbors (2.2.2). A much more significant difference between Clorin's and Felicia's relationships with the divine is that Clorin gives the most credit for empowering and instructing her to Pan, a god rather than a goddess. This relationship with Pan in *The Faithful Shepherdess* is also the source of significant similarities as well as differences between Clorin and Lyly's Cynthia.

Like Cynthia, Clorin is ventriloquized by the voice of patriarchal authority determined to subdue the spirit of carnival in the "unruly woman." However, Fletcher's pastoral guide is portrayed even more decisively as the vehicle of a patriarchal voice than is Lyly's. Cynthia teaches the beliefs of the gender hierarchy and carries out trials, punishments, and rewards to guide her charges, male and female, forcefully into compliance. In Fletcher's play, however, it is much clearer that Clorin is no divinity like Cynthia but an agent of an actual patriarchal figure, Pan, the god presiding over her pastoral world. In several instances, Clorin insists that all her powers to cure, to guide, and to instruct come from this masculine deity. For example, when working to cure Alexis, Clorin credits her patron god with the ultimate power to heal the young man: "Then repent, and pray / Great Pan to keep you from the like decay" (4.2.114–15). She further explains that only with *Pan*'s blessing of the sincerely penitent Alexis will she, can she, "undertake [his] cure with ease" (116). Notably, the Priest of Pan tells the shepherds to kneel not to Clorin in thanks for the restoration of order and in prayer for maintaining it but to Pan, for whom she has only served as an instrument (5.5.196–99). Clorin's words even end the play with an assertion of Pan's, not her own, preeminence.[7] Stepping aside to join in honoring the masculine divinity she serves, she puts into practice the requisite womanly virtues of *"discretion, silence,* and *modesty,"* detailed by Robert Codrington in *The Second Part of Youth's Behaviour; or Decency in Conversation Amongst Women.*[8] Decidedly, the similarities between Pico's mage who can approach God and Fletcher's female pastoral guide who humbles and effaces herself diverge at the boundaries set by the contemporary gender hierarchy. Clorin's relationship to Pan falls in line with the organization of power approved by Anglicans and Puritans, and even Catholics, alike: princes over subjects, masters over servants, fathers over children, and husbands over wives.

Interestingly, Fletcher's ventriloquizing Clorin to speak the voice of patriarchy brings home the important point that, in limited forums and under the auspices of patriarchal authority (husband, father, minister, Church), women would not necessarily be charged with frowardness for expressing themselves. For example, Philip Stubbes, who praised his late wife's adherence to Paul's command that "women . . . be silent, and . . . learne of their husbands at home" also lauded her for challenging and defeating blasphemous "Papists, [*sic*] or Atheists": "for her whole heart was bent to seeke the Lorde, her whole delight was to bee conversant in the Scriptures, and to meditate upon them day and night. [. . .] And when she was not reading, she would spend her time conferring, talking and reasoning with her husband of the worde of God, and of Religion: asking him: what is the sence of this place, and what is the sence of that?"[9] Under a husband's guidance, a woman might read, meditate on, and discuss the

Bible. She might even correct heresies against the theology in which her husband has instructed her. Nevertheless, Stubbes's phrasing clearly sets boundaries on a wife's independent thought and speech. A woman should only talk about "Scriptures," "the worde of God," and "Religion." Even then, a woman still must depend on her husband's final word, for Stubbes only approves of "conferring, talking and reasoning," words implying consultation with, not correcting of, a husband, let alone offering new or divergent opinions.

Clorin's relationship to Pan, the masculine authority validating her voice and enabling her to work good, strongly resembles Katherine Stubbes's to her husband. Both females rescue others from wandering off the road to spiritual health. Both use verbal medicines that sting their patients into health, while exerting their powers to comfort and heal. But most important, both are empowered and educated by masculine authority. As Katherine Stubbes derives power and inspiration from the Christian God and the husband who directs her scriptural studies, Clorin derives the same from Pan. As with Philip Stubbes's praise of his wife Katherine, Clorin's voice is acceptable even laudable when she speaks the words her guiding patriarch has taught her. In both cases, the implication is that women are not inherently evil or dangerous; they just need masculine care to enable their minds and souls to flower to their full potential for good.

The verbal modesty with which Clorin defers to Pan dovetails with her sexual purity, as expected of a good woman.[10] In this respect, Clorin recalls *Endymion*'s Cynthia more than *Diana*'s Felicia. Like Cynthia, Clorin derives her knowledge of and power to draw on nature and the divine from this combining of the two definitions of modesty. In Clorin, Fletcher shows that the female scholar is valuable if she is chaste and humble, more serviceable than independent, affirming masculine ascendancy by accepting patriarchal direction. Where in *Diana* the sage Felicia's chastity is implied but never discussed, Fletcher emphatically asserts not only that Clorin is chaste but that her sexual purity is the source of her great power. Briefly touched on earlier, Clorin partly derives the power to help others as a follower of Diana, in the form of chaste moon goddess not lady of the beasts. This relationship bears deeper study here to explain how Fletcher's portrayal of his guide's purity allays cultural concerns of Otherness embodied by woman.

As discussed in chapter 3, the virginal form was associated with moon goddesses such as Cynthia or Diana; the Ephesian Diana would represent woman in fertile, mature sexual form; and Hecate, the sorceress, hag, and goddess of the underworld, figured death and corruption. In *Diana*, Felicia, as an old, wise, chaste woman has transcended concerns about the virgin declining into the threatening, disruptive sexual woman. The form of devouring death and chaos, embodied by popular Renaissance images of Hecate from Ovid and Virgil through Sannazaro's cunning woman to Dipsas and Poneria, is translated into a comforting, even uplifting being in Felicia, a woman whose age gives her dignity, wisdom, and temperance. Further undercutting associations of the aged woman with decay, Felicia's expertise in helping her charges to learn to balance feeling and reason in all their perceptions and actions leads not to death and disorder but to the death of disorder and to the rebirth of the soul in a higher form.

Clorin does emulate Felicia in defusing threats embodied in the triform Diana. Her vow of chastity to her deceased shepherd swain is the key to her achievement. Clorin introduces herself by revealing that she had chastely loved a shepherd, and with his death she will forever maintain her purity by renouncing the amorous pursuits of the fecund, sensual pastoral world (1.1.1–29).[11] Significantly, Clorin's devotion to her deceased lover merges virgin, lover, and old woman in a way that cancels out negative truisms about women's vices with positive ones about their virtues. Her love of the shepherd identifies her with one who has known love; her loss of that love to death identifies her with a widow, a status frequently associated with old age; and her pledge of eternal chastity to a love unconsummated also identifies her with the purity of the virgin. Conversely, the virgin's innocence also offsets the fearful stereotypes of the sexually mature woman or the widow addicted to desires of the flesh, described by Vives as "inflammed with vicious lust," after being spoiled of her chastity in marriage.[12] So Clorin possesses the virgin's purity, the lover's vitality, and the widow's wisdom. This translation of the triform Diana could be said to defuse the mage's threat to masculine ascendancy even more than does Felicia. The widow had a social status that often slipped through the net containing daughters and wives. However, by making Clorin a young virgin rather than a wise old woman, a widowlike figure, Fletcher creates a guide who exercises her powers but is inexperienced in areas that make women threatening. In consequence, Clorin must rely on patriarchal direction as what Richard Allestree would call "a probationer in the world, [who] . . . must take this time rather to learn and observe, than to dictate and prescribe."[13]

The mage's transcending earthly lusts in this play can be read as a charge to women to maintain their purity in order to best serve society. For Fletcher makes clear that virginity, not just sexual or material abnegation, is the source of his female mage's power, very much in line with contemporary thought on the source of women's contribution to society. This view of the positive force of a woman's chastity is most eloquently expressed in Juan Vives' pronouncement of a virgin's ability to please, even reform, all who encounter her purity: "Howe pleasaunt and dere to every body is a virgin? Howe reverent a thynge, even unto them that be yll and vicious them self."[14] Clorin expresses the same sentiments when she proclaims the efficacy that her sexual purity bestows on the herbs she uses to heal: "such secret virtue lies / In herbs applied by a virgin's hand" (1.1.39–40). In a similar vein, Clorin reflects that her mother had long ago advised her that her "virgin-flower uncropped, pure, chaste, and / fair" (113) protects her from, even gives her power over, the "goblin, wood-god, fairy, elf or fiend / Satyr, or other power" (114–15). Significantly, in *The Faithful Shepherdess* creatures that would carry out a carvnivalesque inversion are portrayed as depraved and vicious for degrading of the proper order with "vain illusion," physical violation, "wander[ing]," and "ruin" in material and spiritual "mires and standing pools" (1.1.114–20). Clorin's purity is a strong bulwark protecting a woman from their control and society from the damage of a woman out of control—a painful rather than liberating scenario that Clorin's female opposites, Amarillis and Cloe, will realize.

Clorin's uses of the supernatural powers granted her and the reasons for her success is a particularly significant expression of the belief that women must learn from patriarchal authority and accept its direction. One of her main accomplishments is to subdue the spirit of carnival given agency by two women of lascivious actions and words, Amarillis and Cloe. Like Lyly's Tellus and Dipsas, Amarillis is so beyond the pale that she practices witchcraft. In many ways, she exhibits the traits Bakhtin describes as "woman's image in the popular comic tradition" of carnival: "wayward, sensual, [with a] concupiscent character of falsehood, materialism, and baseness."[15] In contrast to the upright, chaste lovers Perigot and Amoret, Amarillis aggressively tells Perigot her passionate determination to "enjoy" him, unconcerned with his commitment to Amoret (1.2.191); uses witchcraft to take on Amoret's image and try to seduce Perigot; offers sexual favors to the Sullen Shepherd if he will help her split apart Perigot and Amoret, with no intention of keeping her promise; and lies to Perigot to make her disguised pursuit of him cast a darker light on the puritanical young man's judgment. Her refusal to be contained by modesty in word and action might evoke Bakhtin's vision of carnival inversion revitalizing, liberating a society by smashing repressive, stifling conventions. However, in *The Faithful Shepherdess*, Amarillis's inversion of world order is portrayed as the dangerous lust and vanity that patriarchy feared in the unruly woman. Fletcher depicts Amarillis's passionate desire for Perigot as pushing her to foist her love, not refreshingly, but immodestly, even ravenously, on the flabbergasted shepherd: "I love thee, Perigot; / And would be gladder to be loved again / Than the cold earth is in his frozen arms / To clip the wanton spring" (1.2.140–43). Furthermore, she is impelled by vanity and a cruel temper to court disaster and disrupt natural order by being a woman who would control a man: "I must enjoy thee, boy, / Though the great dangers 'twixt my hopes / and that / Be infinite" (191–93).

The anguish, not insight, that the froward Amarillis unleashes justifies Joseph Swetnam's warning that a woman's "aspiring mind, and wanton will . . . quickly procured" not just "man's" but everyone's "fall."[16] Amarillis is unable to control her initial plot and its various subplots, so that all of them spin out of her grasp. Instead of "free[ing] human consciousness, thought, and imagination for new potentialities," as Bakhtin might suggest,[17] Amarillis only entangles herself and others in misery. She cannot keep the Sullen Shepherd under her supervision long enough to prevent him from sexually assaulting Amoret and trying to kill her for resisting. She cannot control the Sullen Shepherd's lust when he turns on her to claim his reward for helping her (4.3.59–81). More tragically, Amarillis's wanton act in the guise of Amoret does not merely move Perigot to embrace her or reject his lover but drives him to try to take Amoret's life (3.1.301–19). When Amarillis discovers Amoret has survived the Sullen Shepherd's near fatal attack, she repentantly sends the girl to Perigot to undo her wrong, forgetting that he expects her to appear disguised as Amoret. Ironically, Amarillis's attempts to contain the passions that she unleashed actually lead Perigot mistakenly to try to murder the woman he loves in a flash of vengeful pride. Therefore, in her motivations, in her words and actions, and in her sources of power, Amarillis, acting independently of any masculine guidance, transforms the idyllic harmony of the pastoral to horrific nightmare. This "world inside out" is not the spirit of comedy making comic abuse and confusion a leveling experience liberating vitality and hope[18] but the tragedy and anguish of a world "out of joint."

The combination of Amarillis's desires and her magical means of attaining them through sorcery, coupled with her mendacity, incarnates the worst early modern fears about women's use of language and their sexuality embodied by the witch. Amarillis recalls Ann Usher, described in the 1566 Chelmsford witch trial pamphlet,[19] manipulating men with sex when she tries to take possession of Perigot through seduction and promises the Sullen Shepherd her body if he will be her henchman. Equally important, the source of Amarillis's power is not Bakhtin's pregnant hag combining the hopeful balance of life with death, but an aged witch, an archetype for fears about chaos and all-devouring death. In the tradition of many of the case histories propagated in the witch trial pamphlets, "The Chelmsford Witches" for example, an older witch passes her powers on through the generations to disrupt and corrupt the natural order.[20] In the same vein, a cunning-woman "grandam . . . [r]ight wise in charms" (2.3.83–84) showed Amarillis "[t]his holy well" that "[h]ath power to change the form of any / creature, / Being thrice dipped o'er the head, into what feature, / Or shape 'twould please the letter-down to / crave / Who must pronounce this charm too, which/ she gave / Me [Amarillis] on her death-bed" (84–89).

The power of the grandmother passed down to Amarillis degrades the "holy well" from sacred into a means to satisfy a woman's lust by enabling her control of men's sexual and emotional desires through deception.

Amarillis is not the only flawed female character in *The Faithful Shepherdess*. Cloe also is a creature controlled by lust and duplicity. On the surface, this shepherdess seems to be an amusing variation on the traits so dangerous in Amarillis. Fletcher paints her wantonness with a lighter stroke when he has Cloe deflate the "menace" of the Sullen Shepherd's threat to rape her with an enthusiastic confession: "It is impossible to ravish me, / I am so willing" (3.1.213–14). Equally amusing is her lament that in a pastoral world full of men, a lusty girl like herself can only come across representatives of the two extremes that leave her unsatisfied (1.3.147–52): Thenot is too cynical to view women without disgust (44–70) and Daphnis is too innocent and idealistic to do anything "disgusting" (124–45). Her deceptions prove amusing as well. She plots to meet both Alexis and Daphnis in the woods for romantic rendezvous (1.3.159–96); makes Daphnis hide in a tree when she thinks she has a better opportunity with Alexis (2.4.102–09); and then fishes out Daphnis, later, as a handy backup when Alexis is "retired to the bench" by the Sullen Shepherd (3.1.229–33).

Closer study of these situations reveals that Cloe's unconstrained freedom, though initially amusing, is not enlivening or liberating but has painful, dangerous repercussions. Cloe's wantonness leads Alexis into a wood where he is wounded by the Sullen Shepherd. Later, Clorin warns that the untempered passion that Cloe provokes in Alexis will keep him unsound in body and soul (5.2.1–14, 105–09) and even taint her attempts to heal the pure Amoret (45–49). Cloe, herself, is humbled because of her sexual and verbal immodesty when she fails the test of the sacred taper, being painfully burned in the process (91–98). Although Fletcher may show the lighter side of woman's imperfections, he never lets his audience take the effects of those failings lightly.

In this play, the female pastoral guide subdues the anarchic force of woman embodying the unfettered freedom of carnival, but a major reason she can do so is that she functions as the voice and hand of masculine authority. As noted earlier in the chapter, Clorin derives her powers mainly from the offices of male deity. In serving Pan, modesty of speech and action, combined with altruism, imbue her life. Her goals are to preserve Pan's law of temperance, and, in consequence, to serve humanity. As his deputy, she is able to bring back order and safety, dispelling the horrors that have been spawned by Amarillis's schemes and lies and Cloe's irresponsible lasciviousness: she heals Amoret's, Alexis's, and Daphnis's physical wounds, as well as the spiritual ones caused by Alexis's, Daphnis's and Cloe's lust and of Perigot's pride and anger through herbal medicine and psychology made efficacious by Pan. Especially significant, Clorin echoes John Lyly's Cynthia by taming and containing the most unruly of women in her play with the requirement of wifely obedience in marriage. A magic candle signifies that Cloe has at last been rendered free of her dangerous wantonness and will be taken in marriage by Alexis (5. 5.1–20). Amarillis, the fiercer rebel of the two, has been humbled into repentance, so tamed of passion that she has been "brought again / to virgin-state" and agrees to follow Clorin's stern injunction to relinquish her virginity only in faithful obedience to a husband. (158–65).

How Clorin uses her abilities as a scholarly woman, a mage, to guide her charges by healing their bodies and souls is perhaps the most intriguing means by which she reflects Fletcher's modification of the comic world of ambivalences. For, under mainly Pan's guidance, Clorin not only balances expertise in practicing both the lower stratum's female folk remedies (even white magic) with the upper stratum's Paracelsian medical theory, but her work also offers a restrained challenge to a strict reading of the rules of gender hierarchy. Like Cynthia, Clorin may treat women for their failure to meet conventional standards of behavior, but she also treats men for their pride, lust, vindictiveness, and anger, a view more in line with *A Midsummer Night's Dream* than *Endymion*. Since Clorin's synthesis of high and low culture's medical treatments is so tightly intertwined with her actual healing of her charges' physical and psychic wounds, both will be discussed together. In this respect, she is much closer to the wise woman and scholar of holy magic Felicia than to the goddess Cynthia.

Despite some earlier cited differences, Clorin does share important traits with Felicia in both *Diana* and *Enamored Diana*. Like Montemayor's and Yonge's versions of Felicia, Clorin adheres to the mage's code of wielding magic under Pico's virtues of "charity, faith and hope" for Paracelsus's "love for one's fellow creatures."[21] Felicia promises her dedication to healing the wounds of love, advising Felismena, "I knowe what thou art (without report of anie) and whether [whither] thy thoughts do leade thee, thou shalt in the ende perceive if I be able to help thee in any thing. Wherefore be of good cheere, for if I live, thou shalt see and enjoy thy desire, in pursuite whereof though thou hast passed much paine and travell [travail], there is nothing (as thou knowest) obtained nor gotten without it."[22] Her promise subscribes to Paracelsus's revelation that no complete healing can come without some purgative pain, as pain accompanies the joy of giving birth to a baby.[23] Thus, in the context of Paracelsus's childbirth metaphor, Felicia's using the term "travail" to convey the concept of trial, test, or suffering as necessary and beneficial links her even more closely to the tradition of medicinal mage.

Fletcher's Clorin emulates Felicia by resolutely acting to heal the sufferings of the pastoral dwellers who need her. Echoing Felicia's words,

Clorin outright states her determination to use her magic to help others, for example comforting the shamed Perigot with "What art thou that dost call? / Clorin is ready to do good to all: / Come near" (5.5.25) or offering the pained Thenot "If any art I have, or hidden skill, / May cure thee of disease or festered ill / Whose grief or greenness to another's eye / May seem unpossible to remedy, / I dare yet undertake it" (2.2.85–89). Clorin's determination "to do good to all," Felicia-like, pervades *The Faithful Shepherdess*. Fletcher's pastoral mage also echoes Felicia in knowing which type of cures are best suited for her charges: psychology (Thenot), the magic of applying herbs or washing bodies in sacred waters (Amoret), or a combination of both (Cloe, Alexis, Perigot, and Amarillis). Her goals are the same as Felicia's, to restore pastoral harmony by enabling the citizens of this world to guide their lives with a balance of reason and feeling to love deeply, devotedly, but not irrationally. So, Clorin guides Thenot away from the self-pitying cynicism that prompts him to pursue her as an unattainable ideal while scorning all other women as unworthy of him. Conversely, she teaches Perigot to see the dangerous error in his captivation by the opposite extreme view of love: his idealization of Amoret causing his almost fatal revulsion from her when he mistakenly believes her unchaste. Alexis, Cloe, and Amarillis learn through her words and magic to rein in their sexual passions that have led to confusion, deception, and near death. Again like Felicia, Clorin teaches these characters through "travell/travail," be it with the sting of her words or of her curatives.

Finally, like Felicia who peruses books of magic and learning and can wisely direct Socratic debate to cure others, Clorin is not only well-educated but relies on that education when healing others with wit and/or magic. In applying her learning, Clorin decidedly anticipates Bathsua Makin's assessment that through education women "would have Honour and Pleasure, their Relations Profit, and the whole Nation Advantage."[24] Clorin's treatments of Alexis and Thenot are two particularly striking examples of her familiarity with the theories of Renaissance mages. In the first case, after Alexis was stabbed by the Sullen Shepherd over the favors of the promiscuous Cloe, the Satyr finds Alexis and brings him to Clorin to save him (3.1.167–207). Drawing on her occult knowledge, Clorin, first, applies an "herb" to "stay the current" of bleeding and "restrain / Ulcers and swellings, and . . . inward pain" (4.2.67–69). Next, she guides her acolyte, the Satyr, to apply "[w]ater of a virtuous spring / On his temples; turn him twice / To the moonbeams; pinch him thrice; / That the laboring soul may draw / From his great eclipse" (75–79). However, the mage / guide also makes clear to Alexis that she cannot administer Pan's holy power to heal his body and keep it sound if he does not eradicate from his soul the poisonous festering "decay" of lust as well (109–16).

Clorin's prescription aligns with the Neoplatonic views on the correspondences between the body and the soul, as Pico in *Heptaplus* down to Paracelsus in *Diseases* agree.[25] Thus, like Felicia in *Diana*, Clorin intends to treat body, mind, and soul, to restore golden world order by promoting temperance against bodily excesses. Only with her work to "but still [calm] his mind" (5.2.108) does she completely cure Alexis. Only after Clorin's off-stage tutelage in "wise precepts" (5.2.7), do Alexis's physical and spiritual wounds cease festering and bursting (99–106), and can he honestly, rationally declare his genuine content with his spiritual and physical health: "I have forgot all vain desires, / All looser thoughts, ill-tempered fires: / True love I find a pleasant fume, / Whose moderate heat can ne'er consume" (5.5.13–16).

Clorin's treatment of Thenot shows that her learning in the writings of philosophers and medical men is a vital part of her ability to act like Hannah Woolley, making her knowledge and experience useful "within [her] own roof" and "among [her] neighbors, friends and acquaintances."[26] The shepherd Thenot, who misogynistically condemns women as inherently duplicitous, has dedicated himself to Clorin because he insists that her vow to remain a chaste consort to her deceased lover proves that she is the only decent woman in existence (1.3.20–66; 2.2.49–70, 142–59). Clorin is too wise to be taken in by Thenot's backhanded flattery, his praising her by denigrating all other women. When warning him that the ghost of her beloved will rise to defend her against him does not discourage Thenot (2.2.109–15, 138–41), Clorin turns to what Lynn Sadler Veach calls the Paracelsian overplus:[27] treating a mania with a dosage that strikes against the source of the illness, either through a specific or a contrarium. For an instance of a "specific," Paracelsus explains: "If a person is afflicted with an illness from cat's brain, the medicine should be such that it kills the cat's brain." Another example of Paracelsus's concept of contraria is his contention that if the moon, which "attracts all iron and steel" should cause mental illness, then the patient should be treated with oleum mercurii, which "will not be attracted by any magnet."[28] Especially germane to the case of the morose Thenot is Paracelsus's prescription of contraria for the melancholic, designed to draw overabundant mirth or sadness back to a middle ground: "If the melancholic patient is despondent, make him well again by a gay medicine. If he laughs too much, make him well by a sad medicine."[29] Clorin's treatment of Thenot draws on prescriptions of both specifics and contraria.

This pastoral guide throws herself at Thenot, promising him passionate love, insisting that her deceased lover means nothing to her in comparison to Thenot's charms (4.5.33–92). Using specific to destroy Thenot's false devotion to her chastity and fidelity, by feigning abandonment of the virtues that attract him to her, Clorin will kill Thenot's self-indulgent idealization of her. Simultaneously, her use of a contrarium, overwhelming Thenot with the opposite of traits he claims to desire, finally draws him back toward a less lopsided view of womankind. Once he can conclude that no woman is ideal, he decides that he may as well fall in love with anyone he sees (91–92). Although Clorin has not completely cured Thenot, she has at least purged him of a self-destructive (to him) and annoying (to her) "devotion" that benefits no one. Now, he has the chance at least to stumble onto a woman like the admirable Amoret or the reformed Cloe and Amarillis, all of whom could prove the falsity of his selfish and cowardly views on love.

Clorin's healing and guidance are a powerful illustration of the good that can be done by the scholarly woman whose character is shaped by chastity and restraint. This guide uses her knowledge of holy remedies and the human heart to purify Amarillis and Alexis of their sexual lusts. Through the same resources, she cleanses self-love and anger from Thenot and Perigot. The faithful shepherdess's reform of Satyr illustrates this point particularly effectively. In her interactions with Satyr, Clorin redeems a creature seen by contemporary audiences as possessed by uncontrolled lust. In appearance and action, satyrs seemed created in the image of their master Pan, a lustful god in mythological tales available during the Renaissance, such as Ovid's *Metamorphoses*.[30] The Satyr of Fletcher's play, however, becomes quite a different sort under Clorin's sanctifying influence.

When the Satyr first appears in the play, he displays the sensuality and wildness to be expected of his kind. This is a being unbounded, who "run[s]' and "trot[s]" freely across "plain" and "thick woods." His descriptive language bespeaks the unconstrained, vital sensuality coloring his perspective. For him, "spring" is "lusty" and in "these thick woods'" "bottom never kissed the sun." Satyr's mission is to seize the luscious fruits of the season for a feast where Pan will woo a "paramour" (1.1.47–56). His language, his mission, his movements are all of energetic sensuality. Yet Clorin's purity is so great and so beautifully compelling that at first sight of her, the stage directions read that the Satyr "stands amazed." Next, he immediately acknowledges her ascendance over him, "bend[ing his] "knee in worship of" her seeming "deity," before her "heavenly form and "awful majesty" over all earthly beauty or authority (58–67). The Satyr's first promise to serve Clorin here recalls Ameto's initial infatuation with Lia, focusing on the physical rather than the spiritual, although the Satyr is so awed that his material offerings are not sexual but the fruit of the earth: "grapes, whose lusty blood / Is the learnèd poet's good," "nuts more brown / Than the squirrel's teeth that crack them," "berries for a queen," "All these, and what the woods can yield, / The hanging mountain or the field, / [he] freely offer[s], and ere long / Will bring [her] more, more sweet and strong" (76–95). This determination to serve Clorin even inspires him to participate actively in restoring social order. Discovering a wounded Alexis, the Satyr is ecstatic at having found someone to bring to Clorin for help. More importantly, this reaction shows that under Clorin's influence the Satyr does not merely follow Pan's commands to maintain order but takes the initiative to display compassion (3.1.200–207). Later, he repeats the act of compassion upon finding Amoret injured (4.4.184–94).

Clorin's rewarding admiration of the Satyr confirms the goodness she has inspired in him. Seeing he has gently bound Alexis's wounds and tenderly carried the injured boy to her, she pronounces: "Satyr, they do wrong thee that do term / thee rude; / Though thou be'st outward-rough and tawny–/ hued, / Thy manners are as gentle and as fair / As his who brags himself born only heir / To all humanity" (4.2.62–65). Clorin gives him further inspiring guidance when she redirects the Satyr's service away from ephemeral forms of earthly delight ("the nimble wind," "[s]hadows," supernatural "beauty" [133–38]) to that which will help other humans find spiritual as well as bodily health: "I thank thee, honest Satyr. If the / cries / Of any other, that be hurt or ill / Draw thee unto them, prithee, do thy will / To bring them hither" (139–41).

In following these instructions to serve her by serving others, the Satyr later brings Clorin the wounded Amoret, whose salvation eventually leads to the restoration of Perigot. Further, the Satyr's altruism and kindness sufficiently purify him so that he can visit Clorin's bower without tainting it with "uncleanness" (5.2.47). Indeed, the Satyr becomes so imbued with purity through his dedication to Clorin that she can even entrust him with "[p]urg[ing] the air from [Cloe's] lustful breath"(61) and administering the test of chastity to shepherds and shepherdesses with the sacred taper (91–98). Service to this pastoral mage transforms an earthy, though not evil, creature into a being whose compassion, purity, diligence, and fidelity contribute to restoring the golden world balance internally to the souls of humans and externally to human romantic relations. In this sense, Clorin's relationship with the Satyr also recalls the courtly tradition permeating the pastoral of the lady inspiring the courtier to transform himself through service to her, similar to the influence of Lia on Ameto and Cynthia on Endymion; and, as will be addressed in chapter 7, Rosalynde on Rosader and Rosalind on Orlando. As Clorin has tamed the wild, disruptive energies of Amarillis and Cloe, she has channeled the energies of another being associated with carnival impulses of social disruption into kindly "responsibility."

Clorin's purification of the Satyr and Thenot prefigures her reformation of the other characters flawed in their love relations. Alexis, Cloe, Amarillis, and Daphnis, in differing ways, reflect the Satyr's undisciplined potential. Daphnis's too trusting naïveté; Alexis's, Cloe's, and Amarillis's lust; and Amarillis's vanity and selfishness all require the restraint and direction that reason provides to better enable each to love faithfully, self-lessly, and chastely. Perigot, on the other hand, is closer to Thenot in the lesson he must learn. He not only overly idealizes Amoret but wraps up his own ego, rather than her well-being, in this idolatry. Like Thenot, Perigot must be shaken and humbled by Clorin, as she does when she exposes him to the shining innocence of Amoret and gives him the opportunity to humble himself before his wronged lover. Thus, Clorin's treatment of her courtly suitors, Thenot and the Satyr, figures the extremes of love in all her other charges, whom she must bring into a state of moderation. Her freedom from contaminating sexuality or ego enables Clorin to teach all that love will not endure when ego or lust infect perception but only where compassion, humility, and reason mediate over feeling.

This play does not criticize only women for not living up to conventional responsibilities assigned by gender. Men are taken to task, as well, for failing miserably at their responsibilities atop the gender hierarchy to provide and care for women. Even proponents of women's obedience insisted that man must not rule tyranically. William Gouge, whose *Domestical Duties* pounds home the lesson that by God's law a wife owes her husband obedience in all things as his natural inferior, is equally adamant that the husband owes her respect, love, and protection as head of the house: "If the inferiour must give honor, and by virtue thereof perform such duties as appertain thereto, then must the superiour carry himself worthy of honour, and by virtue thereof perform answerable duties."[31] Just as important, Gouge does not believe that a superior's neglecting his duties justifies the disobedience of inferiors, but that he harms his soul by turning from the model of Christ that stands as spiritual salvation:

> These words [and he is the Saviour of the body] as they do declare the office of Christ, and the benefit which the Church reapeth, so they note the end why an husband is appointed to be the head of his wife, namely that by his provident care he may be as a saviour to her. It is here noted rather to show the benefit which a wife reapeth by her husband, than the duty which he oweth: for that the Apostle declareth afterwards, verse 25, etc. The meaning then is, That as Christ was given to be an head of the Church which is his body, that he might protect it, and provide all needful things for it, and so be a Saviour to it, even so for that very end are husbands appointed to be head of their wives.[32]

The law of God, then, requires men to protect, respect, and provide for the women depending on them. To abuse these women is to blaspheme. Abusing a woman's submission or seeking to lead her into evil costs a man his place in the holy Christian order of family, Church, and society.

The play's critical treatment of men who fail to live up to the responsibilities assigned by Christian ideals reflects Richard Levin's point that playwrights sometimes revealed a sensitivity to women's feelings on gender conflicts. A play might address women's "gender concerns" by conveying the message that they were not always the cause of strife, that men bore their own share of responsibility through abusing their power over women or misjudging them. "Gender loyalty" certainly could be elicited from women by emphasizing that on these counts men needed to be "edified." Clorin's work to make several of the male characters aware of the ramifications of their failings and to cure them is a significant criticism in that same spirit.

The suffering of Amoret who plays by the rules assigned women underscores the validity of Clorin's insight into the failings of this system when men do not play by the rules assigned them. In her inspiration of admiration and compassion from supernatural creatures and of penitence from her proud lover, Amoret seems to match Clorin in taking to heart injunctions that women be modest, charitable, and obedient to their lords. That Amoret's unconditional forgiveness of Perigot eventually inspires and uplifts him echoes contemporary advice to women never to judge their spouses but to reclaim them with forgiveness, kindness, and good example.[33] Unlike Clorin, however, Amoret is highly vulnerable to the social disorder resulting from others' intemperance.

Amoret's vulnerability carries weight concerning the play's portrayal of gender relations. Even though Amoret follows the exhortations of Church, State, and popular opinion on female decorum, she is not only the victim of unrestrained female power (Amarillis), she is also at the mercy of unscrupulous (Sullen Shepherd) and irresponsible (Perigot) masculine power as well. The Sullen Shepherd tosses her in a well to hide his complicity in Amarillis's shameful deceptions so that he may enjoy the dangerous woman's sexual favors. His sexual desire overrides any shred of morality that ought to protect Amoret. Perigot also allows baser emotions to override rationality and forgiveness. His disgust with Amoret when he is tricked into believing her to be wanton leads him to stab her once; his vengeful fury leads him to stab her again when he thinks he is exacting revenge on a disguised Amarillis. In his relations with Amoret, Perigot inarguably falls down on the job of being what Gouge has described as the man's role of "saviour" to the women over whom he has power. Perigot's un-Christ-like inability to forgive another, to contain his temper, or to harness his pride is evident in his violent resentment with Amoret's seeming imperfections and his fury at Amarillis. This young man's ego and passions undeniably overwhelm his duty to offer "provident care," to "protect," to "provide all needful things," as he, instead, leaves the woman under his charge prey to the Sullen Shepherd and makes her a victim of his own tyrannical passions. By these demonstrations that the worst of men can overpower the best of women, Fletcher's play may not overturn the gender hierarchy, but it makes clear to those at its top the grave results if they do not discipline their own flaws before they exercise power.

Thenot and the Sullen Shepherd are completely oblivious to this concept of "provident care." When Thenot believes all women are immoral, rather than be the "savior" of one, he rejects them all. The Sullen Shepherd is even worse. He delights in leading women to perdition, reveling in seducing them to break faith with their lovers and to surrender their chastity to him (2.3.1–20). Both seem good examples of the evaluation of men in "Esther Sowernam's" response to Joseph Swetnam, where she charges that the Bible reports that from the beginning of history the male has been more malevolent and deceitful than woman ever was: "the Serpent of the masculine gender; who maliciously enuying the happinesse in which man was at this time [in Paradise], like a mischieuous Politician, hee practised by supplanting of the woman, to turne him out of all: For which end he most craftily and cunningly attempteth the woman; and telleth her, that therefore they were forbidden to eate of the fruit which grew in the middest of the Garden, that in eating, they should now be like vnto God."[34] Turning one of the most traditional archetypes of women's mendacity on its head, the author raises the question, how can men be trusted, how can women be safe, when it was Satan, a "Serpent of the masculine gender," not Mother Eve, that caused humanity's fall from paradise? Much like the conniving, persuasive "Serpent of the masculine gender" that seduced humankind, the Sullen Shepherd's abuse of his powers to reason and of his responsibility to guide women leads them into giving up "the jewel / Maidens so highly praise" (2.3.18–19). His agreeing to support Amarillis's plans to seduce Perigot, shame Amoret, and give herself to him proves this character to be what Esther Sowernam pronounces a "Schoole-master . . . abundant in mischiefe."[35]

Thenot reflects Sowernam's accusation against misogynist men via Adam even more precisely. In Adam, Sowernam finds another of the "masculine gender," in addition to the "Serpent," as the true culprit of humanity's fall from grace rather than Eve:

> It was no good example in *Adam*, who hauing receiued his wife from the gift of God, and bound to her in so inseperable a bond of loue, that forthwith he being taken tardie would presently accuse his wife & put her in all the danger; but the woman was more bound to an vpright iudge, then to a louing husband: it would not serue *Adams* turne, to charge her, therby to free himselfe: It was an hard and strange course, that he who should haue beene her defender, is now become her greatest accuser. I may heare say with Saint *Paul, by one mans sinne, death,* &c. so by the contagion of originall sinne in *Adam,* all men are infected with his diseases; and looke what examples he gaue his wife at the first, the like examples and practises doe all men shew to women euer sithence.[36]

The author shrewdly justifies shifting blame from Eve to Adam by charging Adam with failing to be his wife's savior, as divines such as Gouge had charged. Adam criticizes Eve for her weakness to temptation, yet he fails in his duty to protect her from temptation or to enlighten her of her sin and how to amend it. He exercises his sense of superiority but not his insight and care. Thenot, indeed, also seems "infected with [Adam's] diseases," blindly characterizing all women as corrupted by "appetite," "desire," and "fancy" (2.2.146–48). His wholesale rejection of women to wallow in self-pity, rather than finding an Amoret to marry, shows that "he who should haue beene [woman's] defender, is now become her greatest accuser." And, of course, Perigot's knee-jerk assault on Amoret when Amarillis's ploys fooled him into thinking his lover was not entirely chaste places him in the same category.

Thus, *The Faithful Shepherdess* retreats from a harsh condemnation of woman as a dangerous force needing to be tightly reigned in to maintain social harmony and does not entirely reject the innovating spirit of carnival. Instead, Fletcher's play expresses a milder form of carnival spirit, for to a limited extent it inverts the "dogma" of patriarchal ascendancy in showing that men share many of the same frailties of women so that the masculine gender cannot automatically assume a mantle of moral superiority. Men, too, must examine their own natures and discipline themselves as Perigot, Alexis, and Daphnis learn to do with varying degrees of success. As Pan was revised to match virtuous leaders of Church, State, and family, these characters must remake themselves as temperate, responsible, rational, and compassionate if they expect women to be modest, wise, and generous helpmeets. Yet, even with its critique of men who abuse the power God and State have given them over women, *The Faithful Shepherdess* still does not portray women as equal, let alone superior, to men. Woman's virtues can empower her to offer men support, as writers such as More, Stubbes, and Makin suggest; however, this play insists that woman is still rightly subject to man's direction. The Priests of Pan act with restraint and wisdom, while their god presiding over this pastoral world is portrayed as an enforcer of reason and virtue. In *The Faithful Shepherdess*, the ultimate source of stability and knowledge, the ultimate bulwark against chaos is patriarchy.

Other pastoral plays follow a similar pattern in using the mage or the wise-woman guide to show that under patriarchal guidance woman's education will make her more serviceable to the needs of society, will curb her innate vices and enhance her virtues. As in *The Faithful Shepherdess*, these plays often pit the guide as mage or wise woman against a witch or similar type incarnating the destructive sexuality and duplicity informing the feminine Other. John Lyly's *Loves Metamorphosis* contains a guiding mage, Protea, who uses the power to transform herself to help her espoused free himself from the clutches of the sexually alluring but voraciously devouring Syren and to help her father find the money to survive Ceres' curse of insatiable hunger. Marian of Jonson's uncompleted *The Sad Shepherd* (1640) is a wise woman rather than a mage. Nevertheless, she uses her wit and warmth to set up pastoral feasts, ease the suffering of frustrated lovers, and thwart a witch who uses malicious magical disguises to disrupt pastoral's feasting, love, and camaraderie. More importantly, though, she needs her lover/husband Robin and a wise old male hermit, Alken, to save her when Maudlin the witch undoes Marian's reputation and power while magically disguised as Marian. Thus, Jonson's play even more directly than Fletcher's suggests that protection and determination of a woman's identity lies with masculine authorization.

Walter Montagu's court masque *The Shepherds' Paradise* (written 1632) similarly uses the guide to suggest that even the best of women needs masculine guidance. In the play, Bellessa escapes an immature fiancé to take on the role of guide as learned woman, presiding over the pastoral enclave of the title, settling political and romantic disputes, and schooling her suitor in the traditions of courtly love. Still, this admirable Bellessa chooses to rely on the guidance of mythology's dubious romance expert Echo, rather than her own insight or learning, to make decisions about love (5.1.3283–3345).[37] Further, the play insists that women are allowed to vote for their queen, not because women are wiser but because men's decisions may err on the side of compassion while women's would on the shallow ground of cattiness (2.1.872–79). These points are two amongst others in the play suggesting that women without the guidance of men's judgment are liable to error. Finally, in her concluding acquiescence to marriage with Basilino/Moramonte, Bellessa gives governance of herself entirely over to her father and her husband (5.2.3591–96), affirming the power of masculine authority in terms of kings, fathers, and husbands. Unlike as will be shown with Rosalind at the conclusion of *As You Like It*, Bellessa's "disposeing" (2.3594) herself to the will of her father and her new husband portrays the appropriateness of a guide being completely compliant to patriarchal direction.

As a human, the learned female pastoral guide, whether mage or wise woman, is a character whom women could emulate or with whom they could identify more readily than with a goddess. Rather than reflecting concerns about investing power in a unique woman, this form of the guide is colored by concerns about investing everyday women with the intellectual and actual power and freedom that come through scholarship. In some respects, the guide as learned woman might appear to symbolize a desire to reconcile the drive to educate women with the requirements of the gender hierarchy, especially when these guides can be shown functioning beneficially under the direction of some masculine authority. Her magic or wisdom stemming from study, this version of the guide revealed that audiences and writers could accept that educating women might better serve their roles as dutiful daughters, wives, and mothers. Still, there are other versions of the mage or wise-woman guide that embody much more iconoclastic, more carnivalesque perspectives on the goals of female education and the nature of woman. Some of these pastorals use the female guide even to question or challenge the belief that woman inherently requires masculine guidance. The next two chapters will explore the differing degrees of such a challenge, touching on Mary Wroth's *Love's Victory* but mainly examining the more nuanced approaches to the subject in *All's Well That Ends Well* and *As You Like It*.

6

Subversive Wise Woman:
The Doctor She of *All's Well That Ends Well*

I

ALL'S WELL THAT ENDS WELL AND *AS YOU LIKE IT* PROVIDE VERSIONS of the female pastoral guide as mage or wise woman that are much further outside the parameters of female submission than Clorin in *The Faithful Shepherdess* offers, versions that give freer reign to the iconoclastic spirit of carnival. To best understand the subtly and intricacy that public stage presentations such as *All's Well* and *As You Like It* must use to do so, it helps, first, to look at the directness of a private drama, *Love's Victory* (1620). Ostensibly, Mary Wroth's guide Silvesta is like Clorin in deriving strength from her purity and acting as the "instrument ordained" (5.7.71) of divinity for righting the miseries, injustices, and misapprehensions that disrupt pastoral harmony. Yet there is a marked difference in how their creators depict these character-istics in their guides. For example, Clorin's virginity is portrayed as a kind of sacred deprivation; she is allowed no suitors but worships at the tomb of her deceased swain. Silvesta's chastity, on the other hand, seems much closer to that of some of the heroines of ancient romances, giving her power to preserve her own body from exploitation by fathers and husbands on the marriage market and giving her control over her emotions and thoughts by liberating her from the spiritual turmoil of unrequited love (2.1.41–52, 3.1.53–58). In fact, her chastity helps her maintain authority over a suitor rather than drive one off, for the Forrester who pursues her with courtly devotion agrees to serve her with affection and loyalty without expecting the sexual or social control of a husband or lover (5.7.99–104). Especially signifi-cant, where Clorin's power stayed firmly within cultural bounds by being directed by a higher masculine authority, the god Pan, Silvesta's sponsoring divinity is Venus, a female. This relationship establishes a powerful resis-tance to the traditional definition of women according to the contemporary hierarchy of genders. As discussed in chapter 3, like Boccaccio, Wroth re-envisions Venus as a wise and just pastoral guide rather than giving her the standard characterization of promiscuous and fickle. In fact, a male divinity, Cupid, even serves Venus. Also, as seen in earlier works with a pastoral guide, the human women mirror Venus by tending to act more reasonably, honorably, and compassionately than the males.

This play's extending the refutation of beliefs in women's inferiority from the divine to the human is particularly noteworthy. The implications move in the opposite direction from those of *Endymion*, where only the divine, not the everyday, female resisted woman's tendency to weak self-government. As illustrated by the partnership of Venus and Silvesta, the wise, thinking, learned, and self-possessed woman is not a supernatural anomaly. In carnival fashion, the woman on top proves the norm, existing on both the everyday human as well as on the elevated divine strata of the world to teach men like Arcas, Lissius, Lacon, and Rustic to rein in their vindictiveness, pride, jealousy, and lust; to appreciate and respect women rather than scorn or control them; and to reform the laws of a society that sacrifice young women in marriage to the decisions of unthinking parents or loutish, unappreciative husbands. In this respect, the wise woman/mage of *Love's Victory*, Silvesta, presents an especially straightforward justification of female independence of patriarchal rule.

Written for the enjoyment of Lady Mary Wroth's private coterie, *Love's Victory* did not enjoy the broad display of either a royal entertainment or a public theatrical presentation that many of the other plays covered in prior chapters could claim. *Love's Victory*'s obscurity, as well as later near disappearance, indicates that Wroth's direct expression of her ideas on gender relations in the play was perhaps not congenial to many in her society. This point is reinforced by that fact that in giving voice to various social criticisms with the assurance of a Silvesta or a Venus in *Urania*, Wroth, herself, earned sufficient enmity to contribute to her exile from the court of James I.

As performances in the public sphere, *All's Well That Ends Well* (1602/3) and *As You Like It* (1599/1600) bring the wise-woman guide's carnivalesque challenge to gender conventions to a much wider audience.[1] The indirection of these plays' presentations of such views also suggests that there was also still too much uneasiness over the froward woman to permit the kind of boldness Wroth's closet drama portrayed. Though Wroth's private drama may have appealed to the gender concerns of the men and women in her circle, both of Shakespeare's comedies had a broader audience of men and women to address. Helen Hackett points out that even many sixteenth- and seventeenth-century women would not be all that comfortable with a heroine who stepped too far beyond the conventions of female behavior to which early-modern women had become acculturated.[2] Still, the respect these plays accord their heroines, the way they address and resolve gender conflicts, and the "edification" they offer men on their duties and on women's value suggest that they would appeal to the concerns and elicit the loyalty of women, and perhaps sympathetic men. It is the more complicated, less direct subversion that Helena and Rosalind wield that frees them to speak to those who already share their views to varying degrees and to evade the censure of those who do not. Thus, these characters stealthily, humorously, not-too-threateningly are able to question the status quo.

Surprisingly, though Shakespeare's two guides' addressing of gender issues is less direct, it is in some ways still more assertive than Wroth's. Both Helena and Rosalind must leave behind their homes and identities as daughters, virgins, and/or wives to set to work guiding their charges. Further, they can only act undercover, behind the scenes, in disguise. Still, once in motion, Helena and Rosalind have remarkably greater independence than either Clorin or Silvesta. Rather than acting as instruments of a clearly defined divinity to heal and reform others, these wise women create a carnival ambiance by melding the lower stratum of women's folk cures with the upper of men's learned Paracelsian medical treatments. Further, Helena and Rosalind create a joyful cosmic community by drawing on the traditions of carnival abuse with their use of disguise and inverted identities; riddles, teasing, and tricks; and mockery of misguided, stultifying conventions constraining human relations. Particularly interesting, these wise-woman guides of Shakespeare are strongly attuned to the cosmic, diffuse spirit of carnival because, unlike either Wroth's Silvesta or Fletcher's Clorin, they mock themselves.[3] Moreover, this self-mockery is not a denigration of women but, as Bakhtin describes in carnival, more of a dissolution of any one group's ascendancy. Perhaps the most intriguing way Shakespeare's two wise women beneficially invert the social stratum is by becoming ventriloquizers of patriarchal voice. In the forms of Helena and Rosalind, women take over men's discourses of control, be they courtly, medical, misogynist, or paternal, and use them either seemingly seriously as verbal shields to slip by a subversive thought or mockingly to reveal a convention's shortcomings.

All's Well That Ends Well is not, strictly speaking, a pastoral. However, neither is Anthony Dawson correct to insist "there is no pastoral here."[4] Specific interrelated characteristics of setting, character, and plot, along with Helena's function as a female pastoral guide, connect this play to the genre. The contrasting settings of the Rossillion estate and the King of France's court evoke the juxtaposition of green world and court characteristic of the pastoral. A typical example of this contrast between pastoral and court worlds is Sir Philip Sidney's "Disprayse of Courtly Life." In this poem, Sidney commends the estate of his sister Lady Mary Herbert and her husband as a pastoral refuge of simplicity, honesty, artistry, and natural beauty (lines 27–47) from a "servile Court" (line 12) filled with "many pufft in minde" (line 50) and "false, fine, Courtly pleasure" (line 48).[5] The Great House poetry of Lanyer, Jonson, Marvell, and Herrick similarly celebrates the stewardship of a lord over his country seat (or in Lanyer's "On Cooke-ham," a lady over her estate) through some or all of the following traditional pastoral motifs: lush nature serving a worthy aristocrat by providing spiritual and/or material comforts for him/her and his/her charges; harmony of humans, nature, and divine under the auspices of the lord or lady; a genuine, unselfish bond of responsibility and guidance from the superior and loyalty and reverence from the inferiors; and, frequently, a fecund harvest-home celebration of the estate's ideal social relations.

The estate of Rosillion, a noble's country property and a place of womblike security, strongly recalls the rural green-world's escape from the pressures of the court. When the play opens, The Countess describes sending her son Bertram from Rossillion to the court in terms of releasing him from the soft, infantine protections and comforts of her womb to the contentions of the court: "In delivering my son from me, I bury a second husband" (1.1.1).[6] In fact, her linking "delivering" (giving birth and handing over) with death (burying) intimates a movement from the pastoral's world of eternal rebirth and renewing nature to the world of mortality in the court. Rossillion carries other associations with the genuine hospitality, love, and comfort of the pastoral world as well. Here, Helena has been unquestioningly welcomed into her lord and lady's family at her father's death, the sting of mortality muted by the sympathetic comfort from pastoral denizens. Also significant, as in the Great House poems, not all laudable pastoral citizens are lowly shepherds. In both Great House poems and in *All's Well*, the aristocratic ruler of the estate cares lovingly and responsibly for his or her servants. The Countess describes how she happily took in, raised, and educated Helena when her father "bequeath'd" the girl to the woman's "overlooking" on his death (39–41). The older woman also keeps the clown, Lavatch, to honor her husband's promise that he would always have a safe haven (4.5.64–67). Later, when Helena is deserted by Bertram, the Countess comforts the girl at this country estate (3.2.46–95). So, although flower-enameled meadows may not be emphasized, Rossillion plays the role of pastoral world by serving as a simple, hospitable, compassionate refuge from the stress, competition, and dishonesties of court life.

Rossillion also possesses another notable trait of Renaissance pastoral, exposing court corruptions. The Countess playfully echoes Felicia's Socratic interviews with the shepherds when quizzing her charges to undercut the warped values of the court. Or perhaps the humorous mode of Shakespeare's character aligns her more with the witty challenges of one of his younger pastoral heroines: Rosalind working on Touchstone, Jaques, and Orlando. The Countess's two witty interchanges with the clown at Rosillion reveal the folly inherent in the court's fad of blaming women for the world's iniquity (1.3.8–97) and following the popular lead in responding to all circumstances without thinking through the consequences to one's self and others (2.2.1–63). All told, these exchanges undercut a superficial understanding of human relations.

The court world in *All's Well*, in this case that of the King of France, is as corrupt as the clown's reports imply. Despite Lafew's promise to the Countess of Rossillion that her son will be safe to mature under the King's supervision (1.1.6–10), much about its inhabitants and their descriptions of their world reveals that vitality, morality, and wisdom have sickened there. First of all, the King himself, the human incarnation of the land, suffers from a fistula, an ulcer (1.1.34), symbolically eaten away from within by corruption. Anthony Brennan observes that the King's physical illness reflects his spiritual state, writing that he "is dangerously unstable, crotchety, all-forgiving, irascible, indulgent by turns."[7] The King's behavior bears out Brennan's point, for this monarch wallows in self-pity and despair (1.1.13–16, 1.2.65–67); marries Bertram off to Helena without mulling over the advisability of the match (2.3.105–76); and throughout act 5, scene 3, in dizzying succession, forgives then condemns Bertram for Helena's death. With the exception of the usually mordant Lafew, the other inhabitants of this court world generally follow their King, some even outdistance him, in falling into corruption.

The "Love . . . cloak[ing] Disdaine" (l. 40) of the court world that Sidney decried in "In Dispryase of Courtly Life" can be seen especially in Parolles' feigning love and esteem to Bertram's face (2.3.267–300), then deriding him when Parolles is tricked into believing himself captured. Parolles' decrying Bertram to the girl his master woos, not to protect her but to seduce her himself (4.3.212–31), equally illustrates his courtly hypocrisy. Early in the play, Parolles' "learning" in courtly honor hides what Philip Sidney had described as an "inward will of harming" (lines 41–42), manifested in calling Bertram "sweet heart" repeatedly (2.3.268, 271) while urging the young noble to prove himself "admirable" through behavior that violates the courtier's obligations of serving king and lady. Insisting "the King has done you wrong" (300), inverting the hierarchy of social relations, Parolles convinces Bertram he must satisfy desire to find adventure and to build his martial reputation rather than to obey their sovereign's order to stay at court and be Helena's husband (271–300). Once in Florence and at the wars, Parolles' influence grows worse, abetting Bertram's illicit attempts to corrupt the honorable virgin Diana (3.5.15–18). He is teaching Bertram to be as "pufft in minde" as he is himself.

Particularly illuminating of court conditions are the King's observations on how the ideal courtiership, embodied in his friend, Bertram's father, has degenerated in this world of "goers backward" (1.2.48). The earlier Count of Rossillion knew the value of obedience and duty, "look[ing] far / Into the service of the time" (1.2.26–27). Not only tactful, Bertram's father was never so "pufft" with vanity that he set indulging his pride over serving his society. The Count of Rossillion, though clever, never used his wit cruelly or egotistically but disciplined himself to warn and correct only with a severity proportionate to the offense, treating people of all ranks with courtesy (36–45). The present day "courtiers" are just the opposite, according to the King. Their tendency to seek great achievement or unleash their "wit" out of vanity, not their responsibility to serve, exposes their inadequacy: "But they may jest / Till their own scorn return to them unnoted / Ere they can hide their levity in honor" (33–35). These faux courtiers lack the wisdom and constancy to do anymore than seek fame by chasing fads, the ephemeral nature of which degrades them and society: "Younger spirits, whose apprehensive senses / All but new things disdain; whose judgments are / Mere fathers of their garments; whose constancies / Expire before their fashions" (61–63).[8]

Helena's use of wit, knowledge, and magic to heal society through its prince, his subjects, her husband, and herself shows her functioning in the same vein as Felicia and Clorin as a mage pastoral guide. Shakespeare's choosing to adapt the tradition of the female pastoral guide would certainly be an important part of explaining why "Shakespeare, like his model Boccaccio, departs from tradition in making the King's healer a woman."[9] However, this mage/wise woman differs from both Clorin and Felicia by embodying carnival's ambivalences not only in her merging of folk magic with medical scholarship but in subversively ventriloquizing masculine discourse. With these "medicines" she invades the world of conventional order to expose and heal its autocratic and capricious rulers, sham "courtly" lovers and backbiting courtiers with a carnival wit that she will also have to direct toward herself.

Concerning Helena's healing abilities, on the one hand, there is plentiful evidence linking her with the lower level expertise of the cunning woman. Helena's verse speeches to heal the sick king and revise Bertram's rejection of her into a pledge binding him to her have been described as rooted in the folk and romance narratives "The Healing of the King" and "The Fulfillment of the Tasks." Various critics have noted that the phrasing of Helena's interchanges persuading the King to allow her to heal him create the impression of casting a spell. Regina Buccola specifically links Helena with "white witches" and "fairy midwives."[10] However, Helena's efficacious healing skill is not limited merely to the woman's sphere of folk remedies; she draws on the masculine sphere's scholarly learning as well, even if her education is less formal than theirs. When she reveals to the Countess of Rossillion her plan to cure the King in order to win Bertram in marriage as her reward, Helena does not just credit supernatural forces, "th'luckiest stars in heaven," but her training and education in applying her "father's skill" and "his good receipt" (1.3.242–46).

With all her sacred, scholarly power to cure, Helena still must disguise her breaking conventions in healing the king by describing her actions and goals in terms that play to contemporary expectations of a virtuous women's submissiveness to masculine authority, divine or mortal. In fact throughout the play, characters across the spectrum of the class hierarchy insist on defining and explaining Helena with words that reduce her to an obedient woman, passively subject to the highest patriarchal authority, God. The court adviser Lafew sees her as a kind of chess piece moved by "the very hand of heaven" (2.3.31). For the middle and lower classes, a ballad lauding her curing of the King illustrates popular sentiment by characterizing Helena as an "actor" not a creator, playwright, or source of "heavenly effect" (24). She is only God's instrument, with the implication that God, not she, cures the King. Helena will deftly exploit these sentiments, offering a subtle but mordant carnival inversion of such dogma by choosing to ventriloquize this discourse of patriarchal ascendancy to hide that she is actually undercutting the very authority she is citing.

Although Bakhtin's concept of heteroglossia was originally posited in terms of the novel, it is extremely useful for understanding Helena's ventriloquizing the discourse of patriarchy to camouflage her subversion of its control. Heteroglossia describes how within a culture the language spoken is woven with discourses that shift across the numerous social groups of its constituents: "The internal stratification of any single national language into social dialects, characteristic group behavior, professional jargons, generic languages, languages of generations and age groups, tendentious languages, languages of the authorities, of various circles and of passing fashions, [and] languages that serve the specific sociopolitical purposes of the day."[11] In describing herself and her actions in terms of submissiveness, self-effacement, and humility, Helena deploys the languages "of the authorities" (patriarchal Church and State) and of "specific sociopolitical purposes" (maintaining an economic and political status quo between men and women) to "translate" her subversiveness into seemingly compliant behavior. By mastering the language of the social stratum above her, Helena is able to curb its power over her, even reverse the direction of flow of power to some extent.

To persuade the King to allow a woman the presumption of trying to cure him, Helena asserts her credentials in terms of the male Almighty sponsoring her power to heal: "He that of the greatest works is finisher / Oft does them by the weakest minister" (2.1.136–37). Calling herself "the weakest minister" of the masculine "finisher" "of great works," Helena masks the frowardness of daring to enter the male world of medical learning by portraying herself as only the handmaiden of the ultimate masculine authority, God. She makes palatable her insistence that the King defer to her desire that he accept the cure she offers with, "Of heaven, not me, make an experiment"

(154). By presenting heaven, not herself, as the active force, Helena leads the King to believe that he "makes experiment" of "heaven" not of a woman. When she declares that "[t]he greatest grace lending grace" (160) will establish that "[h]ealth shall live free, and sickness freely die" (168), Helena again cloaks her assertiveness with a modest deferral of credit to the Almighty. For she seems to be declaring that "greatest grace" is only *lent* her by God; and that force of God, not she, cures the King. By portraying herself as merely an instrument of God, Helena turns arguments against a woman acting with her independence on their heads in two important ways. First, by claiming God empowers and directs her, Helena shrewdly invalidates any condemnation of her based on biblical and patristic demands for woman's silence, submission, and limited learning. Second, she inverts claims of women's susceptibility to Satanic influence as witches by identifying her magic with heavenly rather than infernal power.

Covering all bases, Helena also claims patriarchal authorization on the mortal as well as divine level to legitimize what many in the Renaissance would have read as an "indecorous" claim by a woman to learning.[12] As noted above, in 1.3.242–46, Helena simultaneously credits God and celebrates her late father, Gerard de Narbon, a master physician who could almost cheat death, sentiments echoed by the Countess and Lafew (1.1.17–31). She is especially adept at drawing on her father's reputation to legitimize her frowardness as a scholarly doctor when she explains to the King how her father provided her with the knowledge, training, and medicines that she will use to cure him :

> On's bed of death
> Many receipts he gave me; chiefly one,
> Which as the dearest issue of his practice,
> And of his old experience th'only darling,
> He bade me store up, as triple eye,
> Safer than mine own two, more dear. I have so,
> And hearing your high Majesty is touch'd
> With the malignant cause wherein the honor
> Of my father's gift stands in chief power,
> I come to tender it, and my appliance,
> With all bound humbleness
>
> (2.1.104–14)

Helena is at great pains in this speech to make herself an instrument of her father's greatness, much as she has been to make herself that of the other great father, God. She emphasizes that the "receipt" that will cure the King is her father's possession and creation. She outmaneuvers the upholders of tradition by explaining she now holds it because her father gave her permission to use it, his "gift." Furthermore, Helena makes clear that she does not claim to have invented the receipt, but merely to have read it and learned to value it at her father's advice (ll.104–9). Thus, she does not present herself as having the in-depth education of the mage described by Pico, delving into classical, Hebrew, and patristic texts, nor, as the doctor described by Paracelsus, traveling the world to find new compounds and recording the results of his experiments on their usefulness against various illnesses.[13] Her father is the mage; she is an obedient and less educated apprentice. Further, Helena's phrasing erases any sense that she is trying to demonstrate her power in learning or medicine. She proffers her "father's gift" "humbly." She states that she only offers this gift to help the King, not for her own benefit. In this wording, Helena's offer seems entirely an exercise in serving patriarchal figures (her father, by honoring him; a king, by curing him). So ventriloquizing sixteenth- and seventeenth-century views that women are educable, but that education does best by society when men control it and the outcomes are used to serve masculine authority, Helena gains the chance to cure the King, which will give her opportunities not supposed to be available to women, such as traveling on her own and choosing her husband.

Another means by which Helena manipulates the discourse of masculine authority on female behavior is by emphasizing her modesty and chastity in her endeavor to heal the King. She shows the requisite modesty by not only referring to herself as humble but in presenting her actions as deferring honor and authority to her father and God. The Countess's characterizing Helena as "a poor unlearned virgin" (1.3.240) reveals that this guide has created the reputation of purity that will confirm her claims of heaven's support. Helena draws on that characterization to persuade the King that her cure has the social and divine authorization to work. She wagers her good name to convince the King of her good faith in her being worthy and capable to serve as God's minister (2.1.170–74). In depicting her ability to heal and restore society to order in terms of the "discretion" and "modesty" that seventeenth-century writer Robert Codrington praised,[14] Helena attempts to neutralize fears that knowledge and power make women disruptive forces.

Helena, however, is definitely not Clorin's twin in illustrating woman as an obedient, chaste instrument for good entirely in the hands of masculine power. Much more active and assertive than not only Clorin of *The Faithful Shepherdess* but even Felicia in *Diana*, Helena is more like Felismena, a guide who does not exist above the fray but plunges into adventure to battle the problems, frustrations, and instability of human existence. What proves particularly interesting about Helena's closer proximity to Felismena is that her adventurous motivations and actions reveal that her initial professions of humility and service do, indeed, camouflage a subversive potential.

Not surprisingly, then, critics have noted that despite the modesty of speech and deference with which Helena conveys her intentions and undertakes her actions, close examination of both reveals she violates Renaissance norms of obedience and chastity. As noted in more detail earlier, Helena presents her attempt to cure the King as an active embodiment of serving patriarchy. However, Helena's motivations for curing the King, which she reveals only to the Countess when she is pressed, violate female decorum. She actually sees her father's art and God's power as a means for possessing the man she desires in marriage, as she admits to the Countess: "My lord your son made me to think of this; / Else Paris, and the medicine, and the King, / Had from the conversation of my thoughts / Happily been absent" (1.3.231–34). Helena's reflections on her determination to possess Bertram underscore that she refuses to perceive her life entirely circumscribed by her gender or her class, though fully aware that these constraints exist. She laments class boundaries: "[T]h'ambition of [her] love plagues itself" because she is "not in [Bertram's] sphere." She acknowledges the seemingly insurmountable danger of challenging class and gender boundaries with "the hind that would be mated by the lion / Must die for love" (1.1.89–92). However, Helena emphatically does not see those barriers as so central to the essential order of creation that they cannot, should not, be leaped over:

> Our remedies oft in ourselves do lie,
> Which we ascribe to heaven. The fated sky
> Gives us free scope, only doth backward pull
> Our slow designs when we ourselves are dull.
> What power is it which mounts my love so high,
> That makes me see, and cannot feel mine eye?
> The mightiest space in fortune nature brings
> To join like likes, and kiss like native things.
> Impossible be strange attempts to those
> That weigh their pains in sense and do suppose
> What hath been cannot be. Who ever strove
> To show her merit, that did miss her love?
> The King's disease—my project may deceive me,
> But my intents are fix'd, and will not leave me.
>
> (1.1.216–29)

Obedience and modesty do not even enter into Helena's consideration in this speech. The only impediment to a woman's happiness is timidity ("slow designs") and lack of motivation or ambition ("when we ourselves are dull"). "Fortune," not modesty or gender or ambition, is the obstacle Helena feels she must overcome. Helena's speech reveals no concern with or even acknowledgment of her society's conventions that the right to choose a mate rests only with the man, that a woman's only option is to serve the man who chooses her with modesty of body, tongue, and demeanor. To Helena, a woman's virtue lies in actively pursuing her desire and asserting control of herself and her "mate." In fact, she sees this line of behavior as only bringing a woman success, stating "Who ever strove / To show her merit, that did miss her love?" And notably, as the next line of the speech indicates, thought of curing the King only occurs to Helena when she needs a means to satisfy her desire to possess Bertram's love.

In fact, Helena's challenge to the status quo on womanly subservience informs her entire pursuit of Bertram. The reward of selecting her own husband that she requires for curing the King makes both men, one a prince, subject to her desire, as her laying out of terms with the King illustrates: "Then thou shalt give me with they kingly hand / What husband in thy power I will command" (2.1.193–94). She ventriloquizes the King's voice to subvert what her culture would consider the natural order, manipulating this patriarchal figure into using his masculine authority to "command" what she cannot demand, even request, directly. Later, Bertram, her choice, may relegate her to awaiting his return at the estate of Rossillion (2.5.63–69), but Helena violates the wife's duty to obey even a bad husband.[15] Instead, she disguises herself and pursues him to Florence (3.2.126–30, 3.5.35). As David McCandless writes, Helena transforms Bertram's charge that she can never have him into a "scenario of acceptance" through the consummation of their marriage using a bed trick.[16] Utilizing carnival's abuse of repressive and cruel authority with this trickery, Helena not only takes control of their sexual relationship but the Rossillion family past (ring) and future (child). In Helena's hands, comforting a husband seems to become a means to chastise or even establish mastery over him, rather than a manifestation of wifely obedience.

From this perspective, the sexual modesty that Helena had striven to impress on other characters to legitimize her less than conventional behavior might be questioned. David McCandless argues that although in her early interchange with Parolles Helena parries the scurrilous fellow's attempts to trick her out of her virginity, her words at the end of their conversation reveal that she does not perceive her own sexuality as wanton in and of itself. Only a man's abuse of it would be. Rather, she talks of sexuality as something a woman might enjoy with the husband of her choice rather than as a "commodity," as Parolles calls it (1.1.152), to be bartered between fathers and husbands-to-be. In McCandless's view, Helena is less afraid of losing her virginity than of losing control over it.[17] In a related vein, when Helena does lose her virginity, it is part of her plan to assert her claim on Bertram.

In light of this behavior, Helena might be read as an incarnation of the worst fears about unleashed female power (sexual, verbal, emotional).

Many of her acts and attitudes seem of the same stripe as the manipulations that Amarillis, Tellus, Poneria (*Rhodon and Iris*), and Syren (*Loves Metamorphosis*) practice on men through lies, lust, and magic. Many of the results might even seem similar. Helena's boldness in plotting to capture Bertram and then in obligating the King to turn Bertram over to her does trigger a chain reaction of problems. To escape Helena, Bertram runs off to war, rejecting his responsibilities to his mother and the King. In Florence, where he feels Helena's impertinent claim has driven him, Bertram seeks to quench his "sick desires" by "pervert[ing] a young gentlewoman" (4.3.14–15). Consequently, Helena's stepping outside her natural place in the social hierarchy to wield her powers of magic, wit, knowledge, and sexuality might be aptly described by Lisa Jardine as "threateningly unruly and disorderly in her indecorous articulateness and sexual 'knowingness'—in her wearing of the breeches."[18]

However, critics have also noted that much in the text mitigates harsh assessments of Helena. On the subject of her overstepping contemporary restrictions on female sexuality and assertiveness, both David McCandless and Lisa Jardine note that as Helena meets repeated social resistance to her independence, she tends to bring her approaches and ends more in line with accepted female decorum—though never entirely so.[19] McCandless's and Jardine's similar views of Helena are related to those of earlier critics who also see her as a character whose experiences mold her to better fit sixteenth- and seventeenth-centuries expectations for women. For example, although Alexander Leggatt does not focus on Helena's becoming a less socially threatening female, he explores how Helena must temper her ambition and self-preoccupation to function positively within her society. Leggatt argues that Helena learns that idealizing her love blinded her to the rights of others: "The enchantress-heroine has been rebuffed and told, in effect, that she has gained her husband by means that are not really valid. . . . She seems disturbed by what she has done; she recognizes that the law provides an external sanction for her marriage, but that until the internal sanction— the consent of her husband—is provided, she is no better than a thief if she tries to claim his love, for that love is not rightly hers."[20] In other words, she must learn to respect the feelings and desires of others rather than run roughshod over them to get what she wants. An interpretation of Helena's needing to "mature" into the role of effective guide, rather than taming herself to meet social expectation, is worth pursuing. For Helena and Bertram's final interchange does not so much show that "[h]er dominance of Bertram ultimately enables her to submit to him in marriage"[21] as that Bertram has finally learned the lessons of awareness that Helena has already achieved and toward which she has been trying to guide him.

Although Helena's initial attempt to win Bertram could be seen as a sign of her flawed character, it actually underscores an important point of this play: all are human and can learn from experience. Her poorly considered method of achieving a valid end more accurately illustrates that she herself has to mature and learn that wanting is not sufficient; one has to adjust desire to make it viable within the constraints of society. When her illusions about herself and Bertram are stripped away, she responds— not cynically or selfishly—but responsibly and compassionately. Helena's early mistaken perceptions concerning Bertram and herself are, therefore, not valid criteria on which to condemn her actions throughout the play. In fact, Helena's "imperfection" further aligns her with carnival spirit. As she acknowledges her mistakes and resolves to do better, this guide's self-chiding captures the spirit of empathy and bonding with others in recognizing a shared imperfection. Helena does "not exclude [herself] from the wholeness of the world" but sees herself as on a mission to awaken others to the same vision, not to repress them as they had tried to repress her.[22]

Helena does, indeed, come to acknowledge and give up the delusions of her own "dogma" of control. After Bertram rejects her, Helena, no longer deluding herself, releases him from his obligation to her and requests the King do the same (2.3.148). She does not hang on to Bertram when she feels she has no right but adjusts to the loss of her ill-founded dream. Later, when Bertram calls her before him prior to his departure, Helena does not fool herself into believing all is well or ignore that she has forced him into an unwanted match. Refraining from taking a high hand with him, as would be expected of a scold, Helena instead tries to soothe her husband's hurt pride and feelings. She apologetically refers to herself as "a timorous thief" who "would steal" his love rather than allow him the ability to choose whether to grant it (2.5.79–82). When Bertram later flees, Helena even takes responsibility for driving him off and any harm that could consequently befall him (3.2.102–16). Helena learns, albeit painfully, that she can not gain a loving husband by wishing or through a clever trick.

This final point must be kept in mind to understand why Helena's "bed trick" is more than just a sly maneuver. As an individual with the insight, derived from experience, to accept disenchantment without being conquered by it, Helena proves an effective agent for educating Bertram that he need not fear accepting the roles of husband and father that his society requires for his spiritual progress and the social order's continuance. Helena will not force her will on Bertram but will try to strip him of the misconceptions that have prevented him from seeing the terrible results of his behavior. She makes him see for himself why he is wrong before she tries to prove to him that she is right, giving her spouse the choice of accepting the comfort, as well as the difficulty, of maturity. This gentler version of Bakhtin's carnival mocker who is "naturally opposed" to a self-aggrandizing "senile" or unthinking, repressive "presumptuousness,"[23] degrades Bertram and kills his old worldview of himself and others in order to give him a happier, truer renewal and rebirth.

Bertram is inarguably a character who needs to experience a carnival inversion of his "intolerant" and "petrified"[24] worldview. For his proud solipsism leads him to spend the body of the play "seeing" but not accurately perceiving. Like Parolles, most likely influenced by him, the young man's perception of others is superficial, creating what Bakhtin would call a dangerous combination of "didacticism" based on the sandy foundation of "naïveté and illusion."[25] Because Helena's social status is lower than his, Bertram cannot recognize that Helena cultivates nobility of character. That such nobility is not to be scoffed at and that Helena possesses it is stressed by Lafew's and Countess Rossillion's lauding this trait in her (1.1.36–45). Ironically, Bertram cannot see that his perception of his own "nobility" pales when his actions are compared with Helena's. When Helena is faced with the undesirable and painful, Bertram's rejections, she responds unselfishly and reasonably, telling the King that she is willing to free Bertram (2.3.147–48). In contrast, when Bertram confronts the undesirable prospect of a forced marriage, he irresponsibly and selfishly runs away, causing himself deserved and others undeserved anguish. Like a child, Bertram acknowledges only how he feels, how circumstances affect him. For one who claims to be concerned with class restrictions and privileges, he is quick to ignore the ultimate prerogative enjoyed by the king who ordered his marriage to Helena. He is a failure at social integration into a Renaissance court world, serving neither his prince, his lady, nor his family as an ideal, even savvy, courtier ought to do.

David McCandless characterizes Bertram's immature irresponsibility and egocentrism, particularly in regard to sex and marriage, as a "male sexual dread" of being emasculated by devouring female sexuality and aggression.[26] From a Bakhtinian perspective,[27] Bertram seems to suffer a fear much like Oberon's. Accepting the fluidity around constraints of language, sex, life, and death with which his culture associates woman requires him to accept that he cannot control either the metaphor or what she represents. From his fearful perspective, women's power must be denigrated or denied if he is to maintain a sense of self that denies a world of ambivalences and change rather than cope with it bravely through carnival laughter. Thus, he sees his wife is as a "clog" (2.5.53), a duty that weighs him down. Conversely, he sees Diana as a toy to be enjoyed, carnal recreation without commitment: she is wooed from a grab bag of clichés and discarded without a second thought, a "nicer nee[d]" "dispatch'd" amongst "sixteen businesses" (4.3.85–92). Particularly relevant to this argument are the conditions of Bertram's challenge to Helena to try to lock him into a mature sexual and family relationship: she must win from him the family ring, with all its connotations of matrimony and female sexuality, and produce a child by him

(3.2.57–60). His smug confidence that Helena will never be able to fulfill these conditions reveals that he sees marriage and family as completely alien to his existence. Bertram's association of these family-oriented conditions with Helena and his subsequent flight from both show his distaste for, and even fear of, moving to a stage of maturity requiring the acceptance of the responsibilities to perpetuate society through family. Or from a Bakhtinian perspective, he is not willing to participate in the cycle of life, death, and renewal that marrying and creating a family propagates. Like the self-centered and fearful Panurge, Bertram "does not want to accept his fate. He believes that he can somehow escape his doom. . . . He wants to be the eternal king, the eternal new year and youth."[28]

Bertram, however, is not portrayed as either too villainous or too dense for regeneration. Bertram never deliberately seems to plan to be vicious. It just never occurs to him that others can be hurt by his actions. A particularly representative example that clarifies the root of his destructiveness is his farewell letter to his mother.

> I have sent you a daughter-in-law; she hath recover'd the King, and undone me. I have wedded her, not bedded her, and sworn to make the 'not' eternal. You shall hear I am run away; know it before the report come. If there be breadth enough in the world, I will hold a long distance. My duty to you.
> Your unfortunate son,
> Bertram (3.2.19–27)

Bertram complains that he is "undone," yet he is blind to the fact that he is detailing how he has "undone" the expectations and hopes of others: abandoning a wife, abandoning a mother (the only other member of his noble family), and fleeing the command of his king in cowardly fashion. Still, this young man's words do not imply that he mocks his mother, that he is telling her of his flight to antagonize her. In fact, his assured tone indicates that he expects she will perfectly understand that he is responding with due indignation to his "persecution." His description of outwitting the King and Helena even has a jesting tone, punning on "not" and "knot." Oddly enough, Bertram even seems to be trying to cushion the blow for his mother in his own obtuse way, warning her of his departure before someone else shocks her with the news (22–23). Bertram closes his letter with "My duty to you," revealing that he truly seems unaware that indulging his hurt pride is an affront to his duty to his family and to the State in the form of the King.

More germane to the argument that Bertram's immaturity hampers him from properly orienting himself to his place in the social order is his inability to use words accurately. Marjorie Garber notes that in many of Shakespeare's plays the ability to wield language in a constructive manner and to describe or accurately "mirror" reality denotes intellectual and emotional maturity: "For the most part, however, the capacity to compare, contrast and discriminate is highly valued in the plays, and becomes a further rite of passage for the Shakespearean protagonist. Far from being odious, the act of comparing takes on the status of a trial or test, which marks the initiate as successful—or not—in his relationships with himself, with other persons, and with history."[29] Conversely, those who either cannot accurately portray their environment and experience or who use their wit to maneuver language destructively exhibit an inability to comprehend the world with maturity and wisdom.[30]

In this vein, Bertram's inability to see that his letter to his mother does not recount that he has outwitted unfair persecutors, but that he has cruelly and stupidly hurt and offended those to whom he is obligated, demonstrates an effective "self-protective plo[y]" to "distance the speaker from the events or persons he is describing" or with whom he is interacting.[31] The hollow phrasing of his protestations of love to Diana also demonstrates his refusal to connect emotionally or intellectually with those around him, to acknowledge the existence of anything beyond lust as a basis for relations between the sexes. Bertram's insistence on what he perceives to be the truth concerning the ring he has received from his bedmate perhaps most strikingly exhibits his failure to portray experience accurately in words.

Functioning as pastoral guiding wise woman as well as mage, Helena successfully uses insight into human nature to open Bertram's eyes, to heal him through teaching. Viewed through the perspective of carnival, she can be said to "unmas[k]" his views as "senile presumptuousness." Still, though carnival's "cuckoldry, thrashing, and mockery"[32] come into play in her treatment of Bertram, they do so in a tamed, but still powerful, version. First of all, Helena's perception of Bertram's potential for insight is the foundation for her attempts to spur him to save himself through accepting maturity and responsibility. For example, Helena acknowledges Bertram's resentment at being required to marry her by approaching him, not as if he were a prize she had just won, but by treating him as a person whose feelings she values and whose right to control his actions she respects (2.5.56–96). In the final scene of the play, Helena promises to explain clearly to Bertram how she enacted her miracle so that he can decide whether they should remain together. In fact, Helena is, arguably, the *only* character who ever gives Bertram a choice. Bertram is ordered to be a ward of the King, to stay away from the wars, and to marry Helena. In contrast, Helena ultimately gives him the choice in the final scene whether to hear her story and accept her as his wife. She grants that Bertram has the ability, no matter how underdeveloped, to think when she grants him the choice of accepting her story with her words: "If it appear not plain and prove untrue, / Deadly divorce step between me and you!" (5.3.317–18).

In using her bed trick, Helena distinguishes herself from Clorin in a particularly interesting way. For Helena can do her work as a sexual being.

Clorin must repress her sexuality, subdue her desires in a form of chaste widowhood to access the supernatural power to shape and serve others that Pan grants her. In contrast, Helena trades away her virginity to shape Bertram for the better—and she owes her power over him mainly to her wit. In this way, this guide's purity is more in tune with that of her ancestresses in antique-world romance, defined by her devotion to and protection of the love of her choice rather than in emphasizing physical chastity and obedience to one's ruling patriarch, be he father or husband.

Yet Helena is not completely out of the bounds of her social norm, for in taking charge of her body within marriage she turns back accusations of the witch's, and woman's, disruptive promiscuity. She does not merely scheme to ensnare a man or indulge her own sexual desires like Tellus or Amarillis. On one level, her successfully answering Bertram's challenge to be bedded and impregnated by him literally brings Bertram to maturity by initiating him into what his society would consider moral sexuality and fatherhood. And in tune with carnival's insistence on the ambivalences of life, death, and renewal, her endeavor also metaphorically enables Bertram to attain emotional maturity. First, by substituting herself, the legitimate wife, the pastoral guide transforms Bertram's seduction into a socially sanctioned, appropriate act, even though he does not yet realize this. Helena's description of the intended bed trick to Diana and her mother demonstrates this point:

> Let us assay our plot, which if it speed,
> Is wicked meaning in lawful deed,
> And lawful meaning, in lawful act,
> Where both not sin, and yet a sinful fact
> (3.7.44–47)

Helena's subterfuge becomes a method for transforming Bertram—her method may seem underhanded, but her end of helping her husband and the fact that Bertram is her husband validate her act. Though Bertram's "meaning" is wicked, his action is redeemed by Helena's enticing him into what is actually a "lawful act." Only according to Bertram's myopic perception is it a "sinful fact" that he has seduced Diana. In view of all the actual facts, Helena's motivation is a "lawful meaning" that renders Bertram's action a "lawful act" due to her status as his wife and the epiphany she hopes she can consequently bring to him. Thus, carnival's conception of truth as born of embracing ambivalence, that one convenient belief cannot suppress all inconvenient possibilities, beautifully informs the double meanings of Helena's riddle. Helena's bed trick and its complicated unraveling eventually lead Bertram to revelation by forcing him to confront the consequences of his actions in order to shake his faith in his solipsistic worldview, to enlarge his limited perspective.

In her wielding the power of carnival's abuse, Helena demonstrates her adeptness as a wise woman/Doctor She who knows the most effective "receipt" to teach and thereby heal both her subject and the society he wounds. As when she restored the King's health, Helena's combining both folk and scholarly medical practices to treat Bertram displays carnival's grotesque blurring of boundaries. Her use of riddling, incantatory language, her "magical resurrection" from the dead, and her satisfaction of a seemingly impossible task evoke the folk and magic traditions. This folk "magic" is the vehicle she uses to deliver what Lynn Veach Sadler describes as a sort of Parascelsian physic: "It seems possible that Shakespeare is using on Bertram . . . the technique of a Parascelsian overplus: Bertram is doused with evidence of his faulty vision and of his judgment of Helena by external values until he surfeits and is purged."[33] In the thorny unraveling of the bed trick, Helena attacks and abuses Bertram's unawareness by putting him in a position where the painful consequences of his actions do not occur at some distant date or to some other person, but land squarely on him. In fact, the more Bertram insists, sometimes wittingly, sometimes not, on twisting reality to suit his ends, the deeper he sinks into trouble. Thus, Bertram's unintended "lies" or "untruths" about receiving the "controversial" ring from Diana instigate the King and Lafew to turn further from him, even causing the young man's own mother to doubt him. Bertram's intentional distortions of reality draw equally prompt punishment. His lie that Diana threw him the ring as an enticement that he manfully attempted to resist inspires the King to question all of the young man's honor (5.3.92–112). Through her intricate plot of carnival abuse, Helena "purifies" and "completes"[34] Bertram's understanding of his place in the world by forcing him to recognize the pain abandonment causes when both intended and unintended lies turn the King and Lafew dangerously against him, when even his mother questions and suspects him. Now he must comprehend the King's fury at finding his expectations shortchanged. Stripped of the "didactisim" in his "naïveté" and "illusion," Bertram finds himself suffering as much as he has made Helena and his mother suffer earlier.

Helena's scheme not only challenges the wisdom of Bertram's irresponsible perspective by forcing him to recognize that his way of life is ultimately destructive even for him, but her plan even enables her to demonstrate why his superficial perspective is debilitating. In the early part of 5.3, Bertram's convinced insistence on his truth symbolizes his blindness. True, as far as he knows, he did sleep with Diana; but Bertram's conclusion is based on inferences drawn on perceptions limited by ignorance of all the facts. Diana promised to sleep with him in the dark. Diana promised to exchange rings with him. Therefore, since he slept with and exchanged rings with a woman in the dark this woman can only be Diana. Subtle or unusual conclusions, facts that contradict his desires do not occur to Bertram. They have no place in his worldview. How could Helena slip into the picture when he has already made up his mind that he has escaped her and is free to enjoy Diana? At this point, Bertram does not dig beneath surface appearances to search for the truth.

As Helena's trick plays out, however, Bertram can be nothing but aware that his actions have repercussions. He is forced to deal with the fact he does not live in a vacuum, that ignoring his responsibilities will only cause the resulting pain and disruption to boomerang back to him. On a domestic level, he must accept his society's directive to a husband, put into writing in *Domestical Duties*, to "carry himself worthy of honour, and by virtue thereof perform answerable duties" if he would have his wife "honour" him.[35] On a political level, he must behave with honesty, honor, and justice toward his Prince, setting a good example and helping him see the truth, rather than setting him an example of selfishness and dishonesty to "corrupte [him] and to straye [him] from the way of vertue and to lead them to vice."[36]

That, in spite of himself, Bertram instinctively makes "such sweet use . . . of what [he] hate[s]" (4.4.22) also illustrates that delusion shapes his rejection of marital and familial duty. He must learn that the world of social responsibility does have pleasure, perhaps a more fulfilling kind than what he was originally seeking. Thus, Helena's final "magical" revelation makes possible Bertram's recognition of the superficiality of his perceptions by forcing him to perceive that there is a world beyond the boundaries set by his self-centeredness—a world from which he cannot distance himself. When he stops trying to limit reality to merely what he wants to perceive, Bertram is able to understand that Helena can outwit him so that she both beds him and bears their child. Most important, he can understand that his appropriate place in the world cannot be avoided but still need not be feared. He may even find happiness there, as he did in his night with Helena. He may no longer be debilitated by fears of death or lack of control, like Rabelais's Panurge or Shakespeare's Oberon and may be able to embrace and enjoy the freedom of carnival's world of continuous becoming.

Has Bertram learned or is he unregenerate? Bertram's response in 5.3.314–15 has provided ammunition for arguments on both sides of the question: "If she, my liege, can make me know this / clearly, / I'll love her dearly, ever, ever dearly." In the context of this discussion, the quotation suggests there is hope for Bertram. For the first time Bertram is willing to ask questions and look for answers before making a decision. He is no longer hanging onto Parolles' every word or rejecting opinion solely because it does not tally with what he wants to hear. By allowing Helena to explain, Bertram is for once granting that someone else may know something that he does not. Furthermore, because Helena has given him a choice, it would be inaccurate to claim that Bertram is listening to her only because she ordered him to do so. He is now trying to think for himself.

Critics such as Ian Donaldson and Gerard Gross claim that Bertram has not improved because his response is such blandly bad poetry.[37] Still, as bald as his words are, they certainly lack the detachment, triteness, and exaggeration of his formal address to the King and his sonneteering to Diana. Should Bertram be expected to wax eloquent here, anyway? Bertram has, in a way, been reborn—moved to a new stage of maturity after being stripped of his delusions. Is it not natural for the neophyte to stumble over words or express himself simply? It seems as if Bertram, for the first time, is not hiding behind false bravado or detached formality but perceiving the world clearly and expressing himself honestly, succinctly, and thoughtfully, free of the dogmatisms of courtly love or misogyny.

In light of this analysis of Helena's bed trick and its effect, her appearance at the end of the play becomes an illustration of a literal and metaphorical opportunity presented to Bertram to prove he has changed sufficiently to accept his society's requirements of young men to become dutiful husbands, fathers, and subjects. By asserting the family bond and by appearing with child at the conclusion, Helena literally saves Bertram from himself and his lies by showing that he has not killed her; there is no need to execute him. She metaphorically saves Bertram by giving him the opportunity to choose to free himself from the sterility and destructiveness of his narcissistic worldview; she provides him with a chance to choose the comfort and hope of rebirth and renewal in the form of wife and family. Consequently, Bertram can be reintegrated into society on two levels: he can be forgiven by the powerful figures at Court, and he can actively strengthen himself and society through accepting his family. Finally, Helena brings the salvation of family to completion by acknowledging Bertram's and her own bond to the older generation through her loving words to the Countess: "O my dear mother, do I see you living?" (5.3.319). Thus, to make an even more detailed application of Paracelsus's theories than does Lynn Veach Sadler, one can say that Helena treats Bertram by applying a "specific" in the form of contraria to drive out his illness and a confortativum or "sedative" to restore him.

Paracelsus explains that mental illness can stem from various causes: food and drink, planetary influences, animal bites, and inherent internal imbalances.[38] The medicine he prescribes to cure such illness comes under two forms, contrarium and confortativum. As explained in chapter 5, contraria are treatments that work under the principle that "one force expels another." You must find the force causing affliction of reason and apply an equal and opposite force to drive it out. Confortativa, also called sedatives, have the power to "soothe" harmful elements; they "change . . .

and redirect . . ." the "humors" of the mentally afflicted so that "the new make-up may be stronger and more powerful than the old."[39] The "specific" of experiencing the pain of people judging him with perceptions as limited as his own have been and of treating him with as much unjust disdain and harshness as he had exercised is the contrarium that will kill and purge these traits in Bertram. Next, Helena's confortativum of forgiveness and granting him the opportunity to exercise his judgment, now purged, soothes Bertram's battered psyche and restores him by giving him the chance, even encouraging him, to make a responsible decision.

Through the healing powers of the teaching mage Helena, all does "end well" in this play, if ending well is defined in the play's own terms of carnivalesque ambivalence: no assurance of an easy perfect life, just hope that compassion and responsibility toward fellow members of society will enable individuals to remain unconquered, if not unscathed, by adversity. Still, like *The Faithful Shepherdess*, this play far from completely asserts superiority for women. Helena helps cure her society through her treatment of the King and Bertram, but she does so to take on, ultimately, the accepted roles of dutiful subject, wife, mother, and daughter-in-law. However, though Helena pledges obedience to her lord at the conclusion, Bertram must prove himself worthy of her pledge, showing awareness of and repentance for his past lapses. As the Anglican *Homily on the State of Matrimony* instructs husbands, Bertram must also cherish and honor his wife to prove he lives up to his responsibility as head of the family.[40] Further, unlike with Clorin, Helena's sexual desire does not have to be suppressed for her knowledge and power to work, but merely harnessed. As Jay Halio and David McCandless point out,[41] Helena's sexual energy as much as her purity vitalizes her power to cure the King. Notably, Lafew characterizes the King's recovery in terms of sexual revitalization: "*Lustick*, as the Dutchman says. I'll like a maid the better whilst I have a tooth in my head. Why, he's able to lead her a coranto" (2.3.41–43). It is also this desire for Bertram that sets off a chain of events that finally enables her to help him grow through trial.

In her independence of mind, Helena also strongly varies from Clorin, who exists only to serve others. Helena's serving her own needs does not render her selfish or destructive. Rather, with the insight of carnival's wise mockers, Helena acknowledges her mistakes and becomes more reflective and sensitive, and, as a result, more successful in her pastoral guidance. Although Helena's disobedience of Bertram's unwise order (stay in Rossillion until he commands otherwise); her taking the initiative in directing the widow, Diana, and Bertram through the bed trick; and her complicated unveiling of the truth, on the surface, might be interpreted as dangerous plotting, the end result is not. As Ian Donaldson writes, "[t]he play is . . . much concerned with ends and means as well as with endings and beginnings."[42]

Thus, though Helena's means would seem to violate the strictures for womanly modesty of mind and body, her ends (marriage, motherhood, keeping her husband moral, serving her king), in both senses of the word, do not disrupt the stability of the social order. Shakespeare's play seems to agree with Fletcher's in calling for accountability in men but to differ in intimating the possibility of allowing women greater flexibility in living up to the social roles assigned them.

7

"Curing by Counsel":
Rosalind of *As You Like It*

IN CONTRAST TO *ALL'S WELL That Ends Well*, *As You Like It* seems a typical pastoral play. The "time" is seriously "out of joint," in its court world of an usurping younger brother (Duke Frederick) and an abusive older brother (Oliver). But since this is a pastoral comedy, not a tragedy, it can be set right by a sojourn to the festive green world under the auspices of a female pastoral guide rather than by a brooding, doomed tragic hero. The pastoral realm of Arden proves an apt refuge for the regeneration of the corrupt and the persecuted, a place to "live like the old Robin Hood of England" and where "many young gentlemen flock to [Duke Senior] every day, and fleet the time carelessly as they did in the golden world" (1.1.115–19). Here, footsore and hungry travelers can find simple but sustaining hospitality from green-world dwellers, be they shepherds (Corin to Rosalind, Celia, and Touchstone) or lords in exile (Duke Senior and his retinue to Orlando and Adam). Venerable old shepherds offer wise advice to calm the passions of love (2.4.19–29). Pastoral *otium* prevails: "There's no clock in the forest" (3.2.295–96). In time-honored tradition stretching back to Virgil's *Eclogue* 9 (lines 52–54) a lover festoons a tree with expressions of his passion for his beloved (3.2). And at the conclusion, lovers, brothers, parents, cynics, governors, and subjects all "[a]tone together" (5.4.109) so they can reform themselves and purify the court from which corruption had driven them. Pertinent to the argument of this book, Rosalind, as Lady rather than Lord of Misrule, uses witty game playing to guide these individuals away from views that warp their self-knowledge and their bonds to each other, enabling them to "atone together."

As typical of pastoral as the play seems on the surface, it decidedly does not treat the genre's conventions in a straight-faced way. Though C. L. Barber notes that pastoral conventions in this play offer the opportunity for harsh social rules to be "mocked and flouted" in a safe, festival setting removed from the workaday world,[1] *As You Like It* provides distinctly carnivalesque twists to festive comedy and pastoral. For example, the love poems in this play hung on trees with the intention of immortalizing, even deifying, Rosalind, are excruciatingly bad, "honoring" Rosalind with a "very false gallop of verses" (3.2.111). The compliments to her are trite, bland. She is a "jewel"; she makes all paintings look "black" in comparison to her. Everybody is supposed to keep her

195

"face" in his "mind." No evocative, subtle metaphors here. Just as bad, she is fêted with a monotonous rhyme that does not change for eight lines (86–93). Inarguably, Orlando is not quite up for the intricacies of Petrarchan, Shakespearean, or Spenserian sonnets. Even Rosalind, herself, shudders at the awkward, irregular rhythm of the lines, commenting, "For some of them [verses] had in them more feet than the verses would bear," and those overabundant "feet" "stood lamely in the verse" (3.2.161–63, 166–67). An audience's expectations of courtly love poetry elevating their object and creator to the sublime through the writing's artistic excellence are playfully turned upside down, even deflated, by the poet's bland incompetence.

The play's very ending spoofs pastoral convention with special verve, working in the mode of carnival's playful use of "[e]xaggeration, hyperbolism, excessiveness" to expose the absurdity of an ordered world.[2] On top of three tidily married couples, we also have Jaques giving up cynicism to learn from the realm's resident holy hermit (5.4.183–84). But wait, there's more. Not only does Orlando and Oliver's missing brother show up just in time for their weddings, but he also happens to carry the news that Duke Frederick, who had been murderously bearing down with his armies to kill them, was met by this same holy hermit just before hitting the forest and was miraculously converted to spiritual studies with the holy man forthwith (150–64). Shakespeare rewrites the detailed battle of Rosader, Saldyne, and the Duke Gerismond against the evil Duke Torrimond's forces in his source, Thomas Lodge's *Rosalynde*,[3] into one more last-minute impossibility. The audience can hardly catch its breath for the plethora of happy endings playfully tossed in, mocking conventional comic resolution and reconciliation.

As You Like It's tongue-in-cheek take on the traditional pastoral debate between court and country further employs carnival's rejection of any dogma, shifting the vertical hierarchy of right over wrong into a horizontal balance of neither stand taking precedence over the other in wisdom or folly. In the pastorals of Sidney, Spenser, Virgil, Drayton, and others, either two shepherds or a shepherd and a court dweller square off over whether the cultivation of the court world is superior to the superstitious, uneducated country or whether pastoral simplicity and humility are superior to society's ambitious, vain, and cruel search for political and personal power. Each speaker presents his opponent's world as the Fallen one and his own as closer to God's divine order. Does learning enlighten man spiritually and thus draw humanity away from the Fallen world closer to God or does the natural world, as God's creation, purify humans of learning that is based on limited human perceptions and corrupted by human desires? Touchstone in *As You Like It* takes part in such a debate with Corin, but the juxtaposition of the clown's frivolous sarcasm with the simplisticness rather than simplicity of Corin's observations completely undercuts the seriousness of the verbal duel.

First of all, Touchstone refuses to play by the rules and gives only playful answers in chop logic, the tone and content of which undercut the seriousness of both sides in the debate. Touchstone mocks Corin's praise of the simple, unambitious pastoral life (3.2.23–30) with the pun of calling the shepherd a "natural philosopher" (31)—a philosopher of the natural world and simultaneously, according to an additional meaning for "natural," a fool. That is only the beginning. Hearing Corin's admission of never being to court, Touchstone pounces with "Truly thou art damned" (36), again based on a play on words. Never having been to court, Corin lacks "good manners." Equating two different meanings of "manners" (good breeding and "moral character" [62n41]), Touchstone concludes "thy manners must be wicked, and wickedness is sin, and sin is damnation" (41–43). Corin responds with the affable pastoral compromise of valuing different customs according to the environments that create them (44–49). However, Touchstone's response is even more flamboyant and devoid of logic. The clown insists that lack of court manners will damn one because now he posits that court world customs are *less* wholesome than country ones (50–67)! But in this play, pastoral simplicity does not cut through courtly flummery; Corin is too flummoxed to see the logical fallacy before him and relents with "You have too courtly a wit for me, I'll rest" (68). Of course, the rascally Touchstone will not let Corin rest "damned" and teases the shepherd further. Corin responds with a catalogue of pastoral virtues: "Sir, I am a true labourer: I earn that I eat, get that I wear; owe no man hate, envy no man's happiness; glad of other men's good, content with my harm; and the greatest of my pride is to see my ewes graze and my lambs suck." (71–75). Yet this answer is less a dignified assertion than a desperate falling back on typical saws about the pastoral world that neither answer Touchstone' charge that Corin is damned (69–70) nor silence the clown. For Touchstone goes on for another seven lines turning Corin's defense into the sin of pandering sheep to sheep (76–83).

The point is not that Touchstone defeats Corin. He does not. He just out-talks him. Neither side, neither conventional view, can claim superiority. Touchstone demonstrates the intellectual trickery for which the pastoral criticizes the court, while Corin displays the lack of sophistication that the court criticizes in the pastoral or rural world. *As You Like It* playfully shows that neither extreme is viable. In a true expression of carnival ambiguity, both are equally ridiculous.

This comic abuse of reductive pastoral convention challenges the efficacy of these conventional beliefs. In other areas, the play continues to spoof the audience's expectations about not only art but the perceptions of human nature and experiences that art seeks to portray. The play's treatment of the female pastoral guide is particularly interesting in this light. In Rosalind, the guide becomes a vehicle to re-examine expectations about the inherent characters of man and woman, delivering a serious challenge under the pleasing cover of wit. Much as a flavorful sauce might make more palatable an usually distasteful medicine, a "saucy lackey" might use humor to cure Orlando, Jaques, Phebe, and Silvius of their misperceptions. In this respect, Rosalind is the ideal conveyor of "[t]rue ambivalent and universal laughter [that] does not deny seriousness but purifies and completes it."[24]

Rosalind possesses exactly the traits expected of a wise-woman pastoral guide. She shares with Felicia, Felismena, Spenser's Coelia, Wroth's Melissea, and Clorin compassion for the sickness and suffering of others supplemented with a desire to cure them. Like these other female pastoral guides, Rosalind also has insight into human nature enabling her to find the middle route between cynicism and idealism, which in turn empowers her to calibrate wit and compassion to best help others find this same inner harmony of reason and feeling and an outer harmony in their relations with others. Finally, as with guides from Boccaccio's Lia and Venus down through Montemayor and Yonge's Felicia and Felismena, Rosalind leaves up to her charges the responsibility of deciding for themselves whether to embrace the perspective she helps them discover.

Still, with all these shared essential traits, Rosalind is quite different from most of her predecessors, and even many of her successors, like Clorin in *The Faithful Shepherdess* or Marian in *The Sad Shepherd*. Typical characteristics of the guide are modified in this play in ways that decidedly could pique an audience to question how innate certain traits are to each gender alone. Perhaps the most basic variation is that this guide is entirely human, neither goddess nor mage with supernatural powers. Here the pattern Elizabeth I shadowed over literature of legitimizing female power by making the female authority an "exception" no longer holds true. Rosalind is not a goddess in the mode of Boccaccio's Venus, Lyly's Cynthia, or Ralph Knevet's Flora. Pretending to have magical tutelage, Rosalind is not a secluded, learned virgin like Felicia or Clorin, the latter approved by a masculine divinity. More resembling Helena in *All's Well*, as a human woman who wields language and wisdom deftly suiting her severity, levity, or gentleness precisely to the needs of her charges, Rosalind refutes the major anxieties of patriarchal order concerning women's wit and tongue. This guide's use of slightly ribald wit to guide Orlando away from wild emotion and toward reason in love undercuts related anxieties about women's uncontrolled passions and tongues loosing disruptive sexuality on society. Rosalind embodies Bakhtin's eternal woman whose carnival abuse challenges patriarchy's denying its own weaknesses and fears by demonizing her wit and sexuality, though she is still inhibited enough by convention not to display the same ferocity.

One particular revision of the female pastoral guide in *As You Like It* sets the tone for how this play stealthily but decidedly challenges views that woman's education best serves them and society by inculcating deference in them. As has been discussed earlier, female pastoral guides frequently exercise their power under the auspices of a patriarchal authority. Some examples spanning drama and poetry include the following: Ceres and Protea under Cupid, Clorin under Pan, Chloris under Auberon in *Fairie's Pastorall*, and the nymphs under Apollo in *The Muses Elizium*. Sometimes, the role of guide or mage even falls to a man, for example Enareto in Sannazaro's *Arcadia*, the "Hermite" in Book 6, Cantos 5 and 6 of the *Faerie Queene*, or Alken in *The Sad Shepherd*. Even the learned Helena of *All's Well That Ends Well* still derives her knowledge and the efficacy of its effects from the combined authorizations of human (her father) and divine (God) masculine agency. In *As You Like It*, Rosalind manipulates this expression of masculine ascendancy, the authorization of the benevolent patriarch, to cloak from the other characters her actual independent agency.

In explaining the source of her magical powers and medical knowledge, Rosalind claims to have been trained by a benevolent patriarch, her "old religious uncle" (3.2.335–36) who is "a magician . . . and yet not damnable" (5.2.61–62). This is a socially acceptable explanation for Orlando of how a rustic youth could be wise and eloquent, as well as for the audience of how a woman in a page's disguise could possess these qualities. Legitimized by a holy man while she appears to be a boy, Rosalind no longer seems to be acting or speaking independent of masculine authority, and her magical powers can no longer be associated with the terrifying, disruptive symbol of female Otherness, the witch. Here Rosalind plays on the discourse of patriarchy, manipulating "language of authorities,"[5] to tap into others' mistaken beliefs in conventions, pastoral (magical guides) and social (women can only function constructively under male guidance) to help them learn in spite of themselves. The catch, though not trumpeted in the play, is that there is no old religious, magician uncle. As the uncle only exists because Rosalind created him with her imagination, she actually controls the male figure whom others would expect to authorize her. There is no magic, either, only Rosalind's actual articulateness, wit, wisdom, rationality, compassion, and understanding of human nature. This situation goes much further than Helena's ventriloquizing the discourse of masculine control to cite God and father as legitimizing her power. Unlike in Rosalind's case, neither audiences nor characters are given any definite implication that Helena's patriarchal sponsors do not actually exist. In *As You Like It*, however, only Rosalind, the human woman, is the agent who actually possesses and deploys these traits to her own credit and for clearing the minds of her companions. This is, indeed, a subtle dismantling of the gender hierarchy, its definite subversion softened but still there for those who will see it.

Rosalind even ventriloquizes the voice of a god, Hymen, leveling hierarchies of gender and divinity in one move. For, despite asserting that he will "bar confusion" to "make conclusion" (5.4.124–25), the play clearly depicts Hymen as at most Rosalind's ally, certainly not her lord. Unlike the Apollos, Cupids, Pans, and other gods constantly invoked and sometimes appearing in other pastorals, Hymen is never mentioned until he suddenly appears in the play's last scene when Rosalind wants him. Consequently, the last-minute appearance of an actual divinity seems completely alien to the environs of *As You Like It*'s pastoral, or even court, world. Rosalind alone plans and carries out the untangling of the lovers, while Hymen merely confirms what she has already decided and worked out. Even more important, the figure of Hymen may not even be intended to be perceived as an actual god but as a rustic decked out to enact symbolically divine blessings on the marriages that Rosalind has arranged.[6] The fact that the only other supernatural elements of the play, Rosalind's magical transformation and her magician uncle, were both fictitious makes it likely that Hymen may be one more imaginative creation of Rosalind's—a performer under her direction aiding her "magical" transformation and reconciliation of lovers.

The fact that Rosalind is a human woman, neither goddess nor mage empowered by some masculine divinity, serves as much more of a challenge to the authorized contemporary views on gender roles than the other depictions of female guides discussed previously. Peter Erickson would argue that this humanity signals Rosalind's female inferiority: "[a]s the disguise [of Ganymede] begins to break down before its official removal, Rosalind's transparent femininity takes the form of fainting—a sign of weakness that gives her away ... The capacity for love that we find so admirable in Rosalind is compromised by the necessity that she resume a traditional female role in order to engage in love."[7] More accurately though, *As You Like It*'s female guide, possessing human frailties that provide her with empathetic insight, is an example of carnivalesque's wise fools who "do not exclude themselves from the wholeness of the world," who realize that "he who is laughing [at the world] also belongs to it."[8]

Belonging to the world in which she teaches others to laugh, Rosalind does faint at the sight of her lover's blood (4.3.156–57), broods over the unfairness of separation from her father (1.2.1–6) and from a putative lover (1.3.1–25), and even lapses into giddiness (4.1.195–207) or frustration (3.4.1–35) as she falls deeper in love. Nevertheless, the play does not, overall, portray Rosalind as Juan Vives' "fraile thynge, and of weake discretion."[9] Instead, unlike the other characters, Rosalind has the carnivalesque perspective to see that the extremes of cynicism and idealism are both delusions that people impose on experience in order to exclude the disappointment and lack of control created by their own and others' human frailties. By recognizing that she cannot exert complete control over herself or others by imposing an order that suits her desires, Rosalind learns to make the best of human weaknesses, while rejoicing and taking comfort in inherent virtues like forgiveness, fidelity, sympathy, and humor. Her insight into her own failings and strengths, as well as into those of others, enables her to recognize a mean between the extremes of giving up on virtue (the cynicism of Jaques or Touchstone) or blinding oneself with delusive expectations of human perfection (Orlando's, Phebe's, and Silvius's beliefs in the ideal of courtly love).

A good guide, Rosalind uses her self-knowledge to understand and sympathize with others, then tempers this insight with wit that she calibrates from playful (Orlando) to mordant (Jaques, Phebe, and Silvius) according to the condition of her charges. Thus, she uses game playing, in the mode of Barber's festive Lady of Misrule or Bakhtin's carnival abuser, to liberate them from their delusive dogmas of control and to open them up to the hopeful possibilities of adaptation that she has learned to use to guide her own life. Then it is to be expected that with the play's emphasis on the guide's humanity, Rosalind's insight and power do not come mainly from arcane studies (Silvesta, Felicia, Clorin), her own divinity (Cynthia), or under the aegis of a masculine deity (Clorin), but from an understanding of human nature growing out of her own self-awareness. The female pastoral guide in the form of a wise, reasonable, self-aware, and faithful independent human like Rosalind refutes the definition of woman as innately inferior to males. This human woman needs patriarchal authorities neither to rein in her irrationality, changeableness, promiscuity, or garrulousness nor to protect her from her weaker understanding, tender feelings, and inability to withstand temptation.

There are many examples of Rosalind overcoming her own suffering by accepting her lack of complete control and drawing on camaraderie and humor, carnival laughter and equality, to help her escape becoming oppressed by a dogmatic world-view as either a cynical victim of circumstances or an idealist denying reality. The play introduces Rosalind brooding over her father's exile: "Unless you could teach me to forget a banished father, you must not learn me how to remember any extraordinary pleasure" (1.2.3–5). Yet Rosalind is far from a helpless victim of suffering. She responds with good-will of her own to her cousin Celia's promptings of deep sympathy and loyalty (6–13, 16–22), including Celia's infectious humor and promise to return the kingdom when she comes to power (17–20). The two cousins end up mocking the very "Fortune" that had brought Rosalind to a sorry pass (30–45). Even when Rosalind finds the frustrations of a lover's vagaries plaguing her, she does not fool herself with idealizing him or her own unhappiness. Neither does she cynically give up on love for its bumpy moments. Instead, Rosalind wryly mocks the importance of the disappointments human frailty brings to love. Suspecting Orlando will once again come to her late, Rosalind uses only "pretty oaths that are not dangerous" to punish her imperfect lover. The worst that she will condemn Orlando with is being a "pathetical break-promise," even if he is guilty of the high crime of "com[ing] one minute behind [his] hour" (4.1.178–81). Unlike Silvius (3.5.1–6) and Orlando (4.1.104–5), she knows that disappointment in love does not kill: "Men have died from time to time and worms have eaten them, but not for love" (4.1.101–2). Unlike Touchstone, Rosalind knows that although the clown is right to say "nature in love [is] mortal in folly" (2.4.52–53), she also knows that he is wrong to conclude cynically that infidelity is inevitable in marriage (3.3.45–58).

The key to Rosalind's ability to help others lies in her refusing to become embittered by adversity but instead turning that experience into insightful self-awareness that engenders in her sympathy for others, not a sense of superiority over them. In her relations with others, she constantly reveals carnival's sense of the cosmic, the ultimately comforting blurring of barriers in comic grotesque. In fact, Rosalind's observation on the whippers of lovers and madmen demonstrates how her understanding enables her to teach others to acknowledge that though they cannot control they still need not be victims. Disguised as the page Ganymede, Rosalind informs Orlando, "Love is merely a madness, and I tell you, deserves as well a dark house and a whip as madmen do; and the reason why they are not so punished and cured is that the lunacy is so ordinary that the whippers are in love too. Yet I profess curing it by counsel" (3.2.388–93). Essentially, whippers, the authorities, are as much victims of love as the lovers/madmen. Recognizing they have no more control than (indeed they are at one with) the madmen whom they are supposed to control, the whippers treat lovers with forbearance, enacting carnival's shifting of human relations from the vertical to the horizontal. For, logically, if they did not do so they would have to whip themselves for being as flawed as their charges. Here is a playful echo of Rosalind's earlier sympathy with Silvius's devotion to Phebe: "Alas, poor shepherd, searching of thy wound, / I have by hard adventure found mine own" (2.4.41–42). Though she may not abase herself as Silvius comes to do, Rosalind does not scorn him for she recognizes herself in his suffering over unfulfilled love. Thus comparing Rosalind and keepers of madmen shows that this guide's wisdom and compassion give her greater power than those who respond harshly to imperfection. Where the whippers are immobilized by the defect they share with their charges, Rosalind is empowered by it so that she can "cur[e] . . . by counsel" her charges and "restore . . ." them to "ambivalent wholeness."[10]

In what form does Rosalind counsel her charges? Many critics have seen Rosalind as a teacher. Carol Thomas Neely describes her as such in her use of disguise to "educate [her] beloved. . . ." Marjorie Garber observes "that Rosalind's intention is to teach her lover to 'speak to her in the natural language of men and women'."[11] However, Rosalind also casts herself as a healer of sickness, "quotidian," bringing to mind another influence on her embodiment of the female pastoral guide: the Paracelsian physician. Anticipating Helena and Clorin, Rosalind uses a "cure" that strongly follows Paracelsus's directives for curing "Diseases that Deprive Man of His Reason" with contraria and confortativa. Rosalind's learned expertise "turns the world upside down" by showing her well-thought-out, efficacious administering of the medical knowledge her culture declares to be the provenance of only the higher, masculine strata of the gender hierarchy.

These cures can be administered as materials that are applied internally or externally (vitriol, oleum mercurii, herbs) or as actions by individuals (counseling, kindness, moderate beating, or throwing someone in cold water).[12] To decide when to use the former or the latter, Paracelsus instructs, "Each sickness requires different treatment" so that "[a]gainst material diseases material remedies should be applied; against spiritual diseases, spiritual remedies." He also points out that "[i]f someone falls in love through a potion, that love should be destroyed in the same way, so that the potion be driven out."[13] Rosalind combines all three of these instructions from Paracelsus, driving out cynicism, pride, self-abasement, or mere naïveté with doses of mockery, respect, humility, and realism, which she carefully prescribes, measures, and mixes to match the degree and type of "infection" in her charges. Thus, Rosalind's "oleum mercurii" against Touchstone's and Jaques's jaded world-views is biting wit. She douses Orlando's faux idealization of what to expect from himself and her with the contraria of equally extreme skepticism of either men's or women's ability to fulfill that ideal. Her mocking of Silvius's piquing himself on his abjection and Phebe on her sense of superiority are the "cat poison" that should drive out the "cat madness" of their false pride.

Equally important, Rosalind also uses confortativa where applicable. This choice reflects Paracelsus's paramount belief that medicine, as a gift of knowledge from God, "require[s] . . . love for one's fellow creatures" to work.[14] The pastoral guide of *As You Like It* is rarely harsh and never cruel. Thus, Rosalind follows Paracelsus's warnings to moderate all treatments so as not to destroy what is healthy with too strong a dosage.[15] For an Orlando who is essentially intelligent, witty, loyal, and reasonable, but just troubled by inexperience,[16] Rosalind dilutes her wit with tenderness and playfulness to confront him with a misogyny so unrealistic that it is as laughable as its opposite extreme in courtly love.

Rosalind's Paracelsian treatment of the cynics Touchstone and Jaques on the limitations of their worldviews is to "counsel" them on the folly of their perspectives with a wit sharper than their own. However, her outspokenness is far from what Richard Brathwaite in 1631 will describe as a woman's "[v]olubility of tongue" that "argues either rudeness of breeding, or boldness of expression."[17] Instead, the insight behind her wit is squarely on target and designed not to plump her own ego but to bring others awareness of the folly in their unreasonable perspectives. Rosalind shows Touchstone and Jaques that they are not the wise fools debunking hypocrisy and folly that they think they are, for their cynicism is too devoted to "single meaning" to hold congress with "true ambivalent and universal laughter." Their humor, self-involved and satirical, is just another form of "intolerant and petrified" dogmatism.[18] Touchstone mocks Orlando's love poems, recasting the young man's divine Rosalind as the opposite extreme of promiscuous whore (3.2.99–110). In response, Rosalind verbally clips the clown, pronouncing him a "medlar": "rotten ere you be half ripe, and that's the right virtue of the medlar" (117–18). In other words, she asserts that his perception of love leaps from callow (barely ripe) to cynical (rotten), skipping over, oblivious to, a middle, ambivalent, ground of wise acceptance (ripe).

With both Touchstone and Jaques, Rosalind does not just debunk cynicism but the "intolerant and dogmatic seriousness" insisting on women's limited intellect, eloquence, and virtue. That Rosalind, a human woman, not an exceptional goddess or mage or female authorized by masculine agency, can hold her own rhetorically and morally with males challenges the convention that woman lacks the judgment and self-control to expend her wit wisely. Though he considers himself witty while he's at it, Jaques's preening over his ability to wallow in melancholy and pessimism is actually what Bakhtin calls an "intolerant, dogmatic seriousness."[19] Consequently, he also receives apt deflation from a Rosalind who has had to defeat her own demons with humor and understanding. She exposes the pretentiousness of his sententious, solemn "'tis good to be sad and say nothing" with "Why then 'tis good to be a post" (4.1.8–9). Having known true suffering herself, Rosalind flouts the folly of Jaques's determined pursuit of "designer" melancholy (10–24) when she informs him: "I had rather have a fool to make me merry than experience to make me sad, and to travel for it too!" (25–27). Whether or not Jaques wants to acknowledge it, Rosalind shows him that there is dubious merit in being able to "suck melancholy out of a song, as a weasel sucks eggs" (2.5.12–13). But Rosalind does not challenge only the vision of cynics. She points out that any extreme is dangerous and irrational: "Those that are in extremity of either [joy or melancholy] are abominable fellows, and betray themselves to every modern censure, worse than drunkards" (4.1.5–7). Clearly, then, Rosalind's forthright speech is far from "mere chatting, prattling humour, which maintains itself at the cost of . . . neighbors,"[20] but a voice that humorously yet tellingly works to deflate the ego and make sense of the irrationality that disrupts social amity.

The characters whom Rosalind guides at the other end of the extreme are Orlando, Silvius, and Phebe. Their problem is creating the opposite dogmatic "illusion" of idealizing love and its suffering. But their version of the Neoplatonic vision of courtly love is equally out of touch with reality, variously mistaking abasement for self-sacrifice, believing love requires them to be ideals, or worshipping an ideal rather than loving an imperfect human. C. L. Barber's description of what he sees as the intent of Shakespeare's general wit in *As You Like It* nicely characterizes Rosalind. Where a "satirist presents life as it is and ridicules it because it is not ideal," she "represents or evokes ideal life, and then makes fun of it because it does not square with life as it ordinarily is."[21]

Rosalind's treatment of Orlando and Phebe and Silvius follows essentially the same patterns, so to discuss all three in detail would be redundant. As Rosalind's vis-à-vis, Orlando receives the greatest attention from her; and her work with him serves as the most interesting example of how she adapts the role of female pastoral guide. This relationship, then, will receive the most attention. Rosalind's treatment of Orlando is highly different from Rosalynd's of Rosader in Lodge's romance, the play's source, where "the unqualified Petrarchan sentiments of the pair [Rosalynd and Rosader] are presented as valid and admirable."[22] In *As You Like It*, Rosalind will challenge the constrictive, inaccurate "seriousness" or dogmatism of courtly love, exposing how it dehumanizes women by imposing on them an ideal of virtue, beauty, and influence impossible for any human to achieve, setting the stage for unavoidable failure in women and disappointment in men. These differences underscore a break from conventions, social and aesthetic.

Lodge's Rosalynd and Shakespeare's Rosalind have markedly different attitudes toward themselves and their lovers' adherence to the role of courtly lover. Rosalynd delights in Rosader's casting her as the inspiring courtly lady when he woos her. Using her disguise to get Rosader to compliment her so she can bask in his adoring love, Rosalynd eggs him on to celebrate her as the traditional ideal: "Much have I heard of thy mistress' excellence, and I know, forester, thou canst describe her at the full, as one that hast surveyed all her parts with a curious eye; then do me that favor to tell me what her perfections be."[23] Lodge's heroine even goes on to persuade her "lover" to return to her so she can enjoy more of that adoration and reciprocate as a gentle, but moral, ideal courtly lady would.[24] *As You Like It*'s pastoral guide proves "a Rosalind of" a different "leer"

(4.1.63–64)—and that difference proves a vehicle for subverting expectations about not just the pastoral but the nature of men and women.

As You Like It's Rosalind is far less demure and compliant with courtly standards. Rather than nudging her beloved to strive to fill the idealized requirements of courtly love, she acts as a variation on carnival's wise fool, C. L. Barber's Lady, if not Lord, of Misrule. Shakespeare's Rosalind treats conventions of courtly love as the aspects of society that must be "flout[ed] and fleer[ed]" so that Orlando is "released" from his delusion and achieves the "clarification" of vision concerning how love can be successful in the everyday social relations of the Elizabethan world.[25] Rosalind's use of her disguise in comparison to Rosalynd's brings this point home. Where Lodge's heroine uses her disguise to enjoy more easily Rosader's enacting the role of courtly lover, Rosalind turns her disguise into a means to flout the ideals that Orlando is building up in place of his and her true characters. Rosalind sets the tenor of her actions when she informs Celia before initiating her first pastoral encounter with Orlando, "I will speak to him like a saucy lackey and under that habit play the knave with him" (3.2.290–91). In the rest of the scene of this first pastoral encounter, Rosalind proceeds to "play the knave" by mischievously debunking the very conventions about love that Rosalynd sought to cultivate in Rosader. Both may spur their lovers with a variation on the challenge "there is no true lover in the forest" (3.2.297), but Rosalind does so in a gentle exercise of comic abuse of the shallowness, the unreality of lovers' conventions.

Rosalind's later instruction of Orlando in 4.1 proves a neat blending of Paracelsian medicine and carnival play. Here, Rosalind adeptly demonstrates the folly of Orlando's casting himself and his "very very Rosalind" (4.1.67–68) as courtly ideals. Perhaps the most essential problem with Orlando's trying to love according to the book is the fact that the book's "patterns of love" do not even fit the prescribed ideal, let alone bring happiness in love. Rosalind deftly rebuts Orlando's belief that one can die from love by cataloguing how several of "the patterns of love" (94) really died. She humorously reveals that love had nothing to do with their demises: Troilus was killed by his characteristic recklessness in battle and Leander ignominiously lost his life to a less than romantic "cramp" while swimming (89–103). Reality is prosaic: "Men have died from time to time and worms have eaten them, but not for love" (101–2). The placement of "for love" after both "men have died" and "worms have eaten them" downgrades the ideal even further: is love to be associated with dying men or munching worms?—the latter an image directly opposed to the transcendence courtly love promises. Rosalind even demonstrates that convention deprives love of its joy and spontaneity when she drolly likens a lover trying to win a kiss to a boring, empty headed orator: "Nay, you were better speak first [before kissing], and when you were gravelled for lack of matter, you might take occasion to kiss" (70–72). In fact, when reduced to convention, a kiss becomes not just boring but only the slightly more sanitary of two options: "Very good orators when they are out, they will spit, and for lovers lacking—God warr'nt us!—matter, the cleanliest shift is to kiss" (72–74).

Still, throughout this flouting of courtly love ideals, Rosalind intersperses sufficient tenderness and humor so that Orlando is neither frightened nor hardened into rejecting women and love. To Orlando's "I would not have my right Rosalind of this [cynical] mind, for I protest her frown might kill me" (104–5), Rosalind not only promises to commit no such fatal act but softens the "vitriol" with further confortativa: "But come, now I will be your Rosalind in a more coming on disposition; and ask me what you will, I will grant it" (106–8). Still, this Rosalind has not thrown away her physic to urge Orlando back into courtly mode. She skillfully cools the ardor of his blunt "Then love me Rosalind" with promising not only to love him "Fridays and Saturdays and all" but to love "twenty such" because "can one desire too much of a good thing?" (109–17). Yet she will not let this jest rankle in him, immediately calling her "sister" to act the priest and lead them in a play marriage (117–18). In her participation in the "mock marriage" with Orlando, Rosalind continues administering the contraria mixed with confortativa. Though she does tease him with reports of the extremes of female emotional instability and promiscuity, she also counters this generalization about women with the specific of Rosalind's own feelings: "but I do take thee Orlando for my husband. There's a girl goes before the priest, and certainly a woman's thought runs before her actions" (130–33). Once again, the genuine feelings of the genuine Rosalind reveal the true woman that Orlando cannot quite see for the disguise of convention on women and of a page's ensemble on Rosalind.

Particularly important in this scene, Rosalind's "treatment" of Orlando guides him toward an acceptance of carnival ambivalence, a realization that neither men nor women can live up to ideals set up for them. The "sky" may "chang[e]" for May maids "when they are wives," but men also are "April when they woo, December when they wed" (139–41). Neither gender is more changeable, unstable, or promiscuous than the other. That this statement of imperfection in both genders directly precedes Rosalind/Ganymede's description of herself as "jealous," "clamorous," "newfangled," "giddy," and contrary (142–48) may even imply that Rosalind's admission applies to Orlando's character as well. She is the representative of women here, and, reciprocally, Orlando is the representative of men.

A related point can be discerned in Rosalind/Ganymede's carnivalesque assertion of women's lust, dishonesty, and lack of discipline corrupting their moral character, "the wiser, the waywarder" (4.1.152–53). On the surface, Vives's statement that "[w]omans [*sic*] thought is swyfte, and for the most parte unstable, walkyng and wandrynge out from home, and soone wyl slyde, by reason of hit [*sic*] owne slypernes, I wot nat howe far"[26] might seem to be echoed by Rosalind's "[m]ake the doors upon a woman's wit, and it will out at the casement; shut that, and 'twill out at the keyhole; stop that, 'twill fly with the smoke out at the chimney" (4.1.153–56). However, Rosalind's and Orlando's carnivalesque verbal abuse of this view of women undermines the legitimacy of its power to define and consequently control women.

In contrast to Vives's furious, frightened condemnation of the dangers of a woman's freewheeling wit and body, Orlando playfully charges the woman's wandering wit and virtue, "Wit, wither wilt'" (4.1.158). Rosalind continues the abuse of the sentiments Vives expresses by indulging in mischievous, even slightly ribald, verbal sparring with Orlando that undercuts unjust, inaccurate views about gender relations: "You shall never take her without her answer, unless you take her without her tongue. O that woman that cannot make her fault her husband's occasion, let her never nurse her child herself, for she will breed it like a fool" (162–67). Ironically, though in this characterization of women Rosalind might appear to confirm the anxiety over women's danger to themselves and society if their tongues and bodies are unconstrained by masculine discipline, her tone in expressing this "dogma" turns it on its head. Rosalind playfully undercuts the standard conclusion that controlling wayward women will protect the world from Satan wreaking disruption through women's freedom to speak and move, when she insists that such constraint will only lead to stupid children, "breed[ing] . . . fool[s]." Rosalind's lighthearted exchange with Orlando demonstrates that a woman may be knowing about sex without knowing sexual liberties. She may speak of her knowledge without corrupting those around her; rather in doing so, she will liberate them from, purify them of their misguided, narrow-minded fears.

Finally, Rosalind closes the lesson with a playfully exaggerated threat to Orlando that if he fails to live up to his professed ideal by being "one minute behind [his] hour" that she will curse him with "pretty oaths that are not dangerous." Thus, falling short of the ideal may be disappointing, but it is human and to be dealt with by generosity and humor. Rosalind demonstrates that allowing woman to express her displeasure with her mate will not automatically result in a shrewish disruption of marital harmony but a reprimand tempered with humor.[27]

What is Rosalind's success with Orlando? As shown above, Rosalind persuades Orlando by the end of the scene to abandon his ineffective perspective and join her holiday game playing. Throughout the remainder of the play, he no longer bombards her with faux idealization. Further, it is significant that Orlando finds it within his heart to forgive and save Oliver only after Rosalind has twice schooled him in accepting himself and another as humanly flawed.[28] Finally, after this last interchange and after seeing his brother united with a lover, Orlando responds to Rosalind's offer to "serve your turn for Rosalind" with "I can live no longer by thinking," with pretending to love an ersatz Rosalind (5.2.48–50)—an ideal even falser than the disguise of Ganymede. Rosalind has trained him to see the difference between a false image and "her that [he thinks] is not here, nor doth not hear" (109). Paul Alpers suggests that this instance reveals Rosalind is no longer in control, that circumstances have forced her hand to end a charade she would enjoy continuing.[29] However, the longing Rosalind reveals to let slip her disguise in the mock wedding of 4.1.125–136 and her delight in love after Orlando leaves (191–207), combined with her alacrity in coming up with a scheme to use an imaginary magician uncle to justify her transformation into Rosalind for Orlando (58–68), indicate that she eagerly anticipates shedding her disguise when her lover has put aside his delusive expectations about love. That Orlando accepts her hand under these conditions (5.4.118) and that with this change Hymen agrees, "You and you no cross shall part" (130), testifies to the efficacy of Rosalind's blend of contraria and confortativa in treating her suitor for the "quotidian" of his superficial understanding of courtly love. Under the pastoral guide's carnivalesque treatment, Orlando has found a "joyous truth" in embracing a worldview of "laughter [that] . . . seeks and hopes," "liberated from fear" of woman empowered and from debilitating "piousness" toward courtly tradition.[30] The social stability Rosalind establishes between lovers subverts the belief that female wit unconstrained by masculine guidance destabilizes society. Demonstrating carnival's laughter that "heals and regenerates,"[31] Rosalind's wit, though caustic at times, enables her to strike the perfect balance between confortativum and contrarium in her dealings with Jaques, Touchstone, Phebe and Silvius, and Orlando.

There is a body of criticism holding that no matter how much independent agency Rosalind seems to exhibit in the play, the character is actually secured tightly within the traditional boundaries masculine authority sets for women. Clara Claiborne Park and Peter Erickson assert that one of the ways Rosalind is limited is that her influence never extends into such territories of men as politics or philosophy but is only active in the feminine spheres of interest, love and marriage.[32] Erickson, in addition to Paul Alpers, Carole Thomas Neely, and Louis Montrose, also contends that even within the domestic sphere, Rosalind's power is severely limited by mainstream expectations of wifely deference. As Neely puts it, Rosalind is a prime example of one of Shakespeare's "strong, articulate women" who is "subdued at the [end] of [her] comed[y]" by marriage. These critics hold that when Rosalind puts off her disguise as a saucy boy to return, literally and figuratively, to her female identity for her marriage, the character relegates herself to the control of two of the most common forms of patriarchal authority, father and husband.[33] Erickson and Park further contend that the character is por-trayed as even happy to give up her power and retire into this role.[34] Finally, Erickson and others argue that Rosalind has been under masculine control throughout the play because she is only a female character that owes her life, movement, and voice to a boy actor.[35]

Countering these points clarifies just how subversive Rosalind is to conventional views of women's submissive role. In truth, she turns on its head the dogma of the gender hierarchy by subverting its views of women, sometimes with adept and delightful subtlety. Turning back the first contention that Rosalind is contained and controlled within the domestic sphere is the fact that her influence pervades decisions made out-side of what Clara Claiborne Park calls "love matters."[36] Jaques decides that "[t]here is much matter to be heard and learn'd" from the hermit and the "convertites" (5.4.183–84) only after a pastoral experience that has featured Rosalind's raillery of his studied melancholy. Additionally, Orlando acts with forgiveness of human failings and saves his brother, after a struggle of conscience (4.3.127–30), but only after his idealistic views of himself and others have been challenged by Rosalind in their two pastoral meetings.

Interestingly enough, Rosalind, without the protection of a male disguise, does acquit herself in the political sphere with more wit and integrity than does a man, her uncle, Duke Frederick. This encounter turns the world inside out by reversing the conventional beliefs of male rationality, eloquence, and integrity in opposition to female irrationality, "chydyng and scoldyng" tongues, and moral weakness, when Rosalind honestly, reasonably, and tact-fully turns back her uncle's charges against her of treason. Duke Freder-ick starts the duel by calling Rosalind as untrustworthy as "all traitors" and ordering her to leave the kingdom because he "trust[s her] not" (1.3.49–51). Rosalind first disproves the legitimacy of his charges by countering his judg-ment of her with the accurate assessment that biased thinking cannot change her good character: "Yet your mistrust cannot make me a traitor." She then reasonably undercuts his attack by asking him to provide valid proof to sup-port his claim: "Tell me whereon the likelihood depends" (52–53). Frederick, again, imperiously tries to silence her with the faulty syllogism that because Rosalind is a blood relation of Duke Senior, his enemy, she will automatically plot against him: "Thou art thy father's daughter, there's enough" (54). At this point, Rosalind outwits her uncle by subtly, calmly turning his challenge to her loyalty into not only an assertion of her integrity but an intimation of his own betrayal of her father:

> So was I when your Highness took his dukedom,
> So was I when your Highness banish'd him.
> Treason is not inherited, my lord,

> Or if we did derive it from our friends,
> What's that to me? My father was no traitor.
> Then good my liege, mistake me not so much
> To think my poverty is treacherous.
>
> (1.3.55–61)

Rosalind carefully brings back into the conversation the fact that her father is only Duke Frederick's enemy because Frederick was a traitor in overthrowing him. She concludes with a reassuring but not servile assurance of her loyalty, so that her observations on her father's behavior tactfully bracket Duke Frederick's guilt of the very crime her presses on her. Like a Rachel Speght, Isabella Whitney, Aemila Lanyer, or Margaret Tyler, Rosalind's virtuosity with phrasing and rhetorical technique proves that a woman's reasoning ability is hardly light and can actually be more insightful and logical than that of a male to whom society grants authority over her. Further reversing traditional views of the genders, Duke Frederick seems to display the irrationality and light intellect so often attributed to women. He angrily bursts in upon Rosalind and Celia (1.3.36–41) and for no clear reason declares that his subjects are plotting to overthrow him to restore his brother's direct line to power through Rosalind (73–75). Additionally, Frederick's chiding his daughter to turn on Rosalind as an opportunity to shine more in the eyes of the people (76–78) and threatening Rosalind with death if she "outstay the time" (84) of "ten days"(39) displays the vindictiveness, jealousy, and vanity so often associated with women.

True, one might argue that Rosalind loses this round when she is exiled anyway. However, the fact that Duke Frederick was not only clearly wrong but almost hysterical in exercising his power questions the conception that masculine authority over female will and voice is inherently a sound belief. And as the play concludes, it is Rosalind who will be returning to court while her uncle must remain behind with a holy hermit to ponder life lessons that she already knows and has been teaching.

Examination of the play also disputes the next two arguments made to support a view of Rosalind as completely subdued by masculine power in marriage, and glad to accept that control. Paul Alpers states that "Rosalind's taking off her disguise . . . means that she is handed over to the Duke as a daughter and to Orlando as wife." Clara Claiborne Park adds that Rosalind "gladly and voluntarily relinquish[es]" her masculine disguise to submit herself to "merely a nice young man."[37] Nevertheless, Phyllis Rackin is closer to the mark when she observes that not only does Rosalind, not her father, arrange her marriage, but she arranges all the marriages at the conclusion of the play.[38] Further, although father and betrothed may lay claim to her with "If there be truth in sight, you are my daughter" and "If there be truth in sight, you are my Rosalind" after her promise to "give" herself as theirs (5.4. 115–18), Rosalind is not "casting herself in the role of male possession."[39] Rosalind may, as Clare Kinney notes, "speak . . . only once more in the main action,"[40] but she still has the decisive last word in claiming these men for *herself*: "I'll have no father, if you be not he. / I'll have no husband, if you be not he" (5.4.121–22). Thus, if Rosalind does not get *her* choice, she will not have to take anyone. These are not the words of a mere "male possession."

Still, Rosalind's disguise as a male does stand as an intriguing method for legitimizing the figure of an authoritative woman, although perhaps not in exactly the ways Park and Erickson set out. First, since only the characters do not know that Ganymede is actually a woman, the disguise can act as a mild palliative only for more conservative members of the audience. Second, there is an added dimension to the irony of Rosalind's disguise, for the Elizabethan audience knows that a boy plays the female character of Rosalind. The gender disguise consists of several layers. Perhaps, the best way to examine the significance of how Shakespeare handles these three layers of identity is to study the portion of the play directly addressing this issue, the Epilogue. Mark Shapiro's main interest is with "the epilogue as theatrical play rather than social polemics," but he does neatly sum up two opposing interpretations of the Epilogue's address of the layering of gender identities. Shapiro points out that some critics see this level of disguise, the male beneath the female as "a dilution of Rosalind's female power." The masculine authority is re-asserted as underlying female power in the form of the actor rather than a god or wise man in the play. However, Shapiro also notes the opposite reading, best illustrated by Juliet Dusinberre's belief "that the return of the play-boy is really the return of Rosalind 'as insouciant as ever in her breeches'."[41] Examination of the Epilogue shows Dusinberre much closer to the mark.

First, as Shapiro points out this is the "only [epilogue] we have for Shakespeare's five plays with a cross-dressed heroine."[42] Even in *All's Well That Ends Well*, where Helena also functions as Paracelsian guide, the Epilogue goes to the King of France. In fact, though Duke Senior gets the last word in the play proper, Rosalind gets the last word with the audience. The woman is the bridge between the play and the audience leaving for the world outside the playhouse. Also significant is the organization and content of this speech.

Peter Erickson's take on the Epilogue is a good example of reading emphasis on the boy actor playing Rosalind as evidence that the female has been subsumed under the male: "in spite of the disarming of Rosalind, resistance to women remains. It is as though asserting the priority of relations between men over relations between men and women is not enough, as though a fall-back position is needed. The Epilogue is, in effect, a second ending that provides further security against women by preserving on stage the image of male ties in their pure form with women absent. Not only are women to be subordinate; they can, if necessary, be imagined as nonexistent."[43] However, by focusing only on the identity of the text's actor, Erickson does not accurately reflect all the information contained in and implied by the Epilogue itself. The words that the speaker uses and the identity that the speaker offers in the Epilogue decidedly do not "absent" women. Instead, by proposing to talk as both male and female, by desiring to appeal to both males and females, this speaker actually establishes a parity, a merger of the two as equally balanced in one. As Clare Kinney puts it, "the 'I' represented here (Rosalind? Ganymede? The actor? Shakespeare?) may be construed as a celebration of plurality and a continuing interrogation of socially constructed gendered identities."[44] Here we have an evocation of carnival's beautiful grotesque ambivalence, embracing the universal, the cosmic. This is mostly apparent in lines 208–17:

> My way is to conjure you, and I'll begin with the women. I charge you, O women, for the love you bear to men, like as much of this play as please you. And I charge you, O men, for the love you bear women—as I perceive by your simpering none of you hates them—that between you and the women the play may please. If I were a woman, I would kiss as many of you as had beards that pleased me, complexions that liked me, and breaths that I defied not.

In contrast to Erickson, Richard Levin cites this Epilogue as an example of a playwright's appealing to the gender loyalty of women in his audience.[45] Levin only makes a brief reference to this passage, but a deeper examination of it suggests that his interpretation is on the right track. For in the Epilogue, if an auditor wanted to argue that the balance tips in favor of either gender as proper administrator of power in social relations, the scales actually seem to favor women. First, the plea begins with the statement "My way is to conjure you," and in the pastoral tradition the conjurer is usually not a disruptive witch but a wise woman, especially in this play. More important, consider that, as previously demonstrated, "Rosalind's" ability to "conjure" does not derive from the auspices of masculine authority. Rather, magical masculine authority is not only an imaginary construct but, as Rosalind's invention, under female control. Thus, even while showing the man behind the woman, this same "man" balances that view with references to the woman behind the man. But especially important, the final voice with which the figure chooses to request the audience to "bid me farewell" is definitely feminine. The speaker makes "curtsey," not a masculine bow, and promises to kiss the men with trim beards, likeable "complexions," and "breaths that I defied not" (215–17). So, this may not be a pure version of carnival's ambivalence where the vertical hierarchy has been flattened in completely horizontal relations; still, the variation favors the subversion of the traditional order by giving women the edge.

Significant as well, is the fact that in this passage Rosalind/the player's charge to women, while acknowledging their love for men, decidedly grants them the independence to choose however much of the play they want to accept: "I charge you, O women, for the love you bear to men, to like as much of this play as please you" (209–11). However, the speaker's advice to men playfully, but decidedly, impinges on their ability to guide their decisions rationally or act independently. Men are not only charged "by the love they bear to women," but unlike with the charge to women, they are twitted for their silliness, their irrationality "as I perceive by your simpering none of you hates them [women]" (212–13). Clare Kinney concurs that this "asymmetry of the speaker's commands" indicates that women have free choice to "selectively applaud (as they like it) what they have just seen. They are free, for example, to prefer the author's representations of Rosalind and Celia's wit over his representations of Touchstone and Jaques's."[46] However, the significance runs even deeper. Where the speaker allows women to make their decisions independently, she/he requires men to act in partnership with women: "Between you and the women the play may please" (213–14). In this context, the speaker's bid to get audiences to break conventions about wine (good ones need no bush) and Epilogues (ladies do not speak them and good plays do not need them) might subtly extend to other conventions as well. As the pastoral is spoofed in this play, so are expectations about gender relations.

All in all, Rosalind is an even more subversive female pastoral guide than Helena. Both stand in direct disputation to that incarnation of fears about the female Other, the witch with her diabolical sources and uses of "magical" power. These two guides function as healers of physical and spiritual ills and, in consequence, bring society back to order rather than lead others into sin and society into chaos. Both are Paracelsian doctors who are intellectually and morally purified. However, while Helena must insist that her power derives from patriarchal authorities (God and father) in order to get away with healing and directing other representatives of masculine ascendancy (king and husband), Rosalind answers to no such powers. The magician uncle who "trained" her in psychology, medicine, and magic is completely her creation. Thus, the patriarchal authority expected by audiences to control a woman (and by characters to control a young boy) is revealed to be an illusion. Further undercutting this illusion about natural patriarchal ascendancy in *As You Like It* is Rosalind's ease in manipulating her supposed superiors. Significantly, however, this power to manipulate in the play is not another example of witches like Dipsas, Tellus, Poneria, Syren, or Maudlin wreaking social havoc through woman's inherent tendency toward vicious deception. Instead, the playful carnival abuse of Rosalind's disguises, riddles, games, and humor are designed not only to promote the reason, fidelity, and self-discipline that men are usually credited with bringing to women, but her illusion actually frees Orlando, Jaques, Touchstone, Phebe, and Silvius from the destructive delusions misdirecting them into pain and folly.

Nevertheless, Rosalind is a guide whose character is not a completely straightforward challenge. As other critics have pointed out, she does her work only when hiding that she is female. Still, this condition does not indicate that Rosalind is completely subservient to male domination. The fact that this female pastoral guide adopts a disguise, combined with the circumlocution of the Epilogue, suggests that the character is not a gauntlet thrown down against traditional beliefs about gender. More accurately, this pastoral guide who asks audiences to choose as much as pleases them to applaud is a carefully coded assurance to those who already agree with the play's sentiments. A perceptive audience could recognize that underneath the disguise is a woman, without need of masculine control, healing and teaching others, and in consequence society. The Epilogue she speaks may even allow those in the audience who support a more traditional view of women's social roles to comfort themselves with the belief that a male actor lurks under the guise of the character speaking. Nevertheless, those in the audience unthreatened by or even receptive to female agency could instead focus on the fact that in this speech female identity is positively privileged.

8

"And Afterwards"

WITH THE RESTORATION AND INTO THE EIGHTEENTH CENTURY, the female pastoral guide's representation of women's place in society fades from the stage. There are many reasons for her disappearance. First, the pastoral, itself, as a dramatic form became both less respected and less popular as a literary genre. In Elizabeth's and James's reigns, the pastoral was valuable for portraying the monarch's claim of restoring a golden age to England, and, as Leo Marx points out, extending that golden reign to the New World.[1] In both reigns, it could be used to chide social failings, with the monarch receiving more criticism during the reigns of James I and Charles I.[2] Although pastoral masques may have remained highly favored by Charles I's royal consort Henrietta Marie,[3] W. W. Greg's thorough study of private and public pastoral dramas shows that most productions of pastoral drama at the time were limited to court masques or to university entertainments. On the Restoration and early eighteenth-century stage, Greg observes that pastorals had largely fallen out of favor, their main refuge "under the wing of the fashionable romance of France."[4] Indeed, of the pastorals studied in depth in this book, few enjoyed revival later than the reign of Charles I. Although reprinted as late as 1665, *The Faithful Shepherdess* was presented in a royal entertainment only as late as 1634. *As You Like It* was reportedly revived for James I in 1603 but was not re-staged again until 1723 in the drastically revised and "less popular adaptatio[n]," *Love in the Forest*.[5] Jean Marsden observes that "[t]he various adaptations of *A Midsummer Night's Dream* [1745, 1755, 1763] most clearly embody the [play's] shift from mainpiece to entertainment."[6] Conjointly, the influential literary critics of the era tended to see the pastoral, at best, as no more than a genre on which to cut poetic baby teeth before moving on to more laudable work (Pope) or, at worst, as vulgar and silly (Johnson).[7] If an artist had a social or political critique to offer, pastoral drama was no longer a venue providing either sufficient audience or respectability.

Ironically, the startling change of allowing women actors to perform regularly on the public stage during the Restoration could have provided a blow to the female pastoral guide's place in drama. Carol Barash relates that "[a]lmost as soon as Charles II granted patents to Thomas Killigrew and Sir William Davenant to reopen London's theatres [*sic*] in 1660, actresses began to appear on the stage," with the king officially "decree[ing] that only women should perform women's roles on stage" in 1662.[8] That women

216

had been given dispensation to public expression as actresses might lead to the expectation that the female pastoral guide, as a woman who uses her voice to good ends, would be a popular dramatic figure, perhaps becoming even more outspoken. Silvestas, Helenas, and Rosalinds would flourish on stage. However, as numerous stage and social historians have pointed out, this "liberation" of women on stage created complex repercussions for women. Insisting that women play women on stage was less a granting women more freedom and more an attempt to control gender identity. Carol Barash explains that in order to "appeas[e] Puritans' residual distrust of theatres' licentiousness," Charles "claim[ed] to be authorizing women to appear on stage in order to minimize homosexual 'Abuses' associated with boys' cross-dressing to play female roles."[9] As Juliet Dusinberre explains, preserving heterosexual ascendancy, was the King's true concern not acknowledging female equality.[10] Indeed, Barash notes in declaring that "'women's parts shall be acted . . . by women, [Charles II] suggests at once the need to enforce and regulate women's complicated new roles, their public status as sexual and linguistic subjects, in the larger process of establishing and maintaining political order."[11] Thus, Charles's ruling insisted that the natural, sacred order demands that gender identity is not interchangeable and that women's voice must continue to be authorized by masculine authority: king and God.

Because late seventeenth-century concern with "preconceptions not only of a woman actress, but of the audience, about what it was proper for a woman to say whoever she might be acting,"[12] the guide's tendency to challenge masculine precedence might not sit well. Putting the female pastoral guide's words of authority in the mouth of an actual woman would undermine the buffer that their having been spoken by a male playing a female had once created. Or as Dusinberre puts it, "Once there is really a woman on the stage the playwright feels the need to bow to the male idea of female modesty. . . . Shakespeare and his contemporaries . . . had no social inhibitions to overcome because their women's jokes were racy . . . [but were] spoken by boy actors."[13] One more reason that a woman playing the pastoral guide could hasten the character's disappearance from the stage was that perceptions of actresses as immodest, public women would discredit the guide's claim to blending purity with outspokenness. Further, the public titillation caused by women playing breeches roles[14] might confirm the fear about the dangerous strength of women's sexuality if it were combined with the independence, wit, and outspokenness of the female pastoral guide. Note that a form of *As You Like It* does not reappear until 1723, nor does a feisty Rosalind until 1740.[15]

Jean Marsden raises another point about changing tastes in theatre that would bode ill for the continued presentation of female pastoral guides, "the popularity of the pathetic drama in the late seventeenth century."

Marsden explains that "[t]he pathetic plays strive to provoke the sympathy of their audience and depend for their effect on the sufferings of oppressed and helpless virtue," with "[t]he object of this pathos almost . . . inevitably a woman."[16] Although some of the guides covered in this book endure painful adversity and even defer to masculine authority, they certainly are not so "oppressed" that they or their virtues could be called "helpless." In fact, most of these guides actively endeavored to re-establish virtue in their societies by freeing characters from the oppression of their or others' selfishness, folly, or cruelty. Clearly, then, changing taste and values concerning public theater leave little place for the female pastoral guide on the stage after the mid-seventeenth century.

Even in this atmosphere, the female guide of the pastoral does not so much disappear as shift venues. Less palatable to the appetites of the general public, the guide seems to migrate off the stage and settle in a more quasi-private, educated, artistic milieu: the poetry of women of the aristocracy or gentry who circulated their work mainly within their private coteries or, if they did publish, it was mainly under the auspices of male authority (fathers, husbands, critics). Carol Barash sees the French femmes fortes or Frondeuses as the progenitors of the personae through which women poets could critique society and redefine their place within it. This conception of intellectual, artistic females waging war against social ills with their poetry was transplanted to England by translations of French women writers, Royalists returning from exile in France at the Restoration, and intellectual consort-queens Henrietta Maria and Mary of Modina.[17] When the concept of the femme forte, the warrior-poetess, was combined with the pastoral's own female defined by her bond with the Divine, her powerful intellect, her mordant but not immoral tongue, and her moral probity, the result was the poet becoming a kind of guide, herself. One could, in fact, conclude that Katherine Philips, Aphra Behn, Jane Barker, Anne Killigrew and others became female pastoral guides as their poetic personae, replacing the plays' fictional characters, challenging and guiding their readers with pastoral healing and insight into matters of social order, love, art, self-knowledge, and faith. Interestingly, Jane Barker seemed literally, as well as literarily, to have taken up the role of a Felicia, Rosalind, Helena, Clorin, or Silvesta in her *Poetical Recreations*, where she depicts her life as a "healer"[18] and "herbalist" in the countryside. In this poem, Barker "renounces poetry in favor of studying Galen and Hippocrates,"[19] much as Silvesta and Clorin (and perhaps Felicia) have renounced love to pursue medicinal and magical treatment of the bodies and souls of their charges.

Carol Barash notes that the groundwork set for such writing rests on a combination of factors. First, the shifts of power from absolute monarchism toward more republicanism over the seventeenth and eighteenth centuries triggered questions about the relations between genders that for many centuries had been defined as parallel: "Should subjects obey kings as wives obey husbands or children fathers, or are both political and domestic relationships mutually and contractually negotiated?"[20] Second, the value Puritans and Quakers placed on individual prophecy was sometimes taken to authorize leeway for female prophets to express themselves even when "at odds with masculine authorities on the basis of a spiritual authority that rested outside themselves, in the will of God"[21]—not that these women might not still meet with, literally, violent resistance from men.[22] Such a legitimization of female voice was seized upon by Royalist women as well to justify their own "political and religious obligation to break rules that required women's public silence." Thus, a poet such as Katherine Philips could depart from obedient compliance to her Puritan husband's political and religious beliefs because God obliged her to assert her support of Royalist sympathies.[23] Jane Barker's celebration of female friendships is justified by its presentation as an example of the golden society created by James II and Mary of Modena, as is her harsh critique of those who try to steer her away from the salvation of political and religious allegiance with these two monarchs.[24] The third important factor is the foreign influence of powerful societies of women, imported by Charles's consort Queen Henrietta Marie from France and by James's Mary of Modena. Henrietta Marie brought to England the concept of the femme fortes or the Frondeuses: political, artistic, and intellectual women warriors. Though the English versions were not nearly as politically empowered as their French antecedents, women in connection with or influenced by the climate created by Henrietta Marie, such as Margaret Cavendish and Katherine Philips,[25] seized on this opportunity for intellectual and artistic development and freedom to give voice to a golden world of female friendship, assert the ascendance of female artistry, or challenge oppressive or immoral social mores. Later, "Mary of Modena re-created at the English court a sense of the female community associated with European convents," promoting female education, intellectual exchanges, and creative endeavors (poetry, masques, performance, and painting). Among those poets who were a part of this circle, some even following her into exile, were Jane Barker, Anne Killigrew, and Anne Finch. In addition, Aphra Behn dedicated poetry in praise of the deposed queen.[26]

However, women writers still had not found complete liberation from traditional social constraint. It was Katherine Philips, not a flamboyant Margaret Cavendish or a sexually adventurous Aphra Behn, who was awarded the crown of "matchless" and set as the standard for future women writers. Why Philips in particular? Because the version of Philips that was "culturally sanctioned" was based on perceptions of her and editions of her poetry that could be viewed as aligned with views that credited women with some intelligence and talent but did not challenge masculine superiority.[27] Similar points can be made about how masculine readers interpreted what Finch wrote, while Killigrew and Barker made their points under the veil of indirection.[28]

Particularly germane to the guide, Carol Barash asserts that Philips, Killigrew, Behn, Barker, and Finch repeatedly utilized the pastoral to legitimize expressing their voices on issues of faith and politics or for exploring how the relationships amongst women could assert female intellectual and moral legitimacy.[29] Thus, Katherine Philips reworked the courtly tradition of pastoral love to provide a vehicle to convey the purity and transcendence of the love in female friendships through her poetic rendering of her relationships with Mary Aubrey and Anne Owen as Orinda's wooing and bonding with Rosania and Lucasia, respectively.[30] Philips, thereby, undercut traditional views of women's mental, spiritual, and moral superficiality. Anne Killigrew and Anne Finch saw "the pastoral topos" as a "political retreat" for a community of women.[31] Aphra Behn's pastoral love poems, through strategies ranging from blurring the sexual identity of her narrators or subjects to reversing sexual stereotypes, undercut her society's cultural norms for the genders, and thereby "multipl[ied] and confound[ed] cultural narratives of gender and sexuality . . . to create positions from which the woman writer can challenge the literary codes she inherits."[32] Jane Barker not only symbolized James II's reign with the pastoral world but also drew on the tradition of one's grief (here the deposing of her King) alienating her from pastoral otium surrounding her. Her pastorals also could not just evoke the pleasures and pains of female friendships and question the virtue of "[f]eminine innocence" from knowledge but reveal her own experiences as an authority in the pastoral world,[33] relating "her career in medicine," "healing her rural neighbors and . . . support[ing] herself through meaningful work."[34]

So, though the female pastoral guide slips from the stage, she is too powerful a literary vehicle for exploring gender relations to be entirely lost. Moving out of the seventeenth and into the eighteenth century, writers focus far more on poetry for further, though still limited, latitude in using the guide to grant woman political and social voice. In fact, the guide will continue to shift venues for at least a century to come. Eventually she will become a useful means for addressing the Woman Question in rural and pastoral Victorian novels by authors such as Elizabeth Gaskell, Thomas Hardy, George Eliot, William Morrison, and Anne and Emily Brontë, making her sojourn in the Victorian novel a subject rich enough for another book.

Conclusion

IN THE INTRODUCTION, THE IMPORTANCE OF NOT overgeneralizing views of woman's place in sixteenth- and seventeenth-century society was emphasized as one of the main thrusts of the last thirty years of scholarship. A fundamental basis for this perspective is to avoid falling into an extreme of insisting women were either completely subjugated and degraded or enjoyed equal respect, education, and power with men. Instead, researchers such as Betty Travitsky, Tina Krontiris, Elaine Beilin, Pamela Benson, Diane Purkiss, Natalie Zemon Davis, Joan Gondal Kelly, Patricia Demers, Lorna Hutson, Lisa Jardine, and Margaret Ezell have uncovered, studied, and published writings, and related art work, by men and women suggesting that although there may be some truth to these two extremes posited by Virigina Woolf and Jacob Burckhardt, respectively, the reality of actual views and practices stretches across the points in between. A related problem that these critics have sought to overcome is the tendency to pass judgment on the views of women in early-modern writing based on whether they dovetail with twentieth/twenty-first-century sensibility rather than understanding how ideas expressed in early modern literature fit into their cultural context.

One innovative way of finding and better understanding women's own voices revealing their education, philosophy, and artistry, including thoughts on their place in the world, was the opening up of the literary canon to include texts in which women were allowed to write (mother's guides, meditations, samplers), while rediscovering and re-evaluating women's translations, romances, drama, and poetry that had come to be dismissed as an inadequate incursion on the territory of the masculine intellect. Scholars have further based their conclusions on the breadth of early-modern opinion on woman, especially as an artist or scholar, on the work they have uncovered of contemporary male and female educators, clerics, artists, and pamphlet writers. This research has yielded sixteenth- and seventeenth-century perspectives ranging from outright misogyny to varying degrees of respect for women's innate virtues, requiring matching degrees of direction and support from patriarchal guardians, to assertions of women's equal capability and challenges to masculine superiority. However, even these challenges tended to reflect another important point that scholars have noted informing the writings of early-modern women: negotiation with rather than direct challenges to social authority.

Poetry or prose by Isabella Whitney, Aemilia Lanyer, or Rachel Speght might turn back accusations against women's innate morality or intellect, but they do so while denying a direct challenge to the hierarchy of gender in politics or economics. Translations may give women a venue to discuss their take on issues or to exercise their artistic talents, but these female authors often frame their views and express their creativity in terms implying they are only repeating the thoughts of a wiser man. In addition, women were also given weight as audiences by writers of the time, pointed out in Richard Levin's, Phyllis Rackin's and Jean Howard's writings concerning reception of plays and by Sasha Roberts's, Mary Ellen Lamb's, and Valerie Wayne's writings concerning reception of printed texts. Cited in previous chapters, critics such as Betty Travitsky and Helen Hackett have helped keep the conclusions of this interest in women's reception of texts in its cultural context by warning that though the sixteenth- or seventeenth-century woman's desire to see herself portrayed in a positive light could put pressure on writers, her views of female strengths would not necessarily include all the same traits that appeal to twentieth- and twenty-first century readers.

Through her heyday on the stage, ranging from the late sixteenth to mid-seventeenth century, the female pastoral guide proves an important vehicle for exploring the breadth of these complicated views on the place of women in society. As covered in this book, the guide's presence in a venue that addressed so many individuals of different classes and educations, as well as both genders, reveals not only that she reached a large audience, but the fact that she steadily appeared on the stage from the pen of so many different playwrights for such an extended period of time indicates that she was popular with those audiences. Perhaps one of the reasons she was so popular was that her traits enabled her to address issues deep-rooted in early-modern society. Her carnivalesque healing of a split between Self and Other, mind and body, reason and passion, man and woman provided a comfort to a psychic wound that we have seen traces its way back through medieval to late antiquity romance, back through the medieval and late antiquity Christianity to ancient-world societies. In more contemporary terms, her healing and uplifting use of magic and or supernatural powers counteracts fear of chaos and vulnerability to nature and social upheaval embodied as the female Other in the sexuality, agency, and voice of the witch so powerful in the Middle Ages and Renaissance. Similarly, her ability to deploy her education to help others answered concerns whether a woman could be safely allowed an education, and, if yes, what kind. And in a case peculiar to the political situation of sixteenth-century England, the guide provides a way to deal with dis-ease over the "unnatural" situation of a woman rising to the top of the gender, political, and religious hierarchy when Elizabeth I reigns.

As the examinations of the various guides of this book have shown, the female pastoral guide is not by any means a straightforward endorsement of either Woolf's or Burckhardt's views of women's place in the

Renaissance. Depictions of the guide reveal a rich variety of responses to the question of what is the true nature of woman and, in consequence, what is her place in her society. For example, as seen in chapter 3, John Lyly presents the extreme of reinforcing the misogynist views of women underlying a belief in the necessity of strict masculine control of women. In *Endymion*, the majority of the female characters illustrate the folly, vindictiveness, lasciviousness, and vicious garrulity that women's severest critics preached, while the virtuous Cynthia, herself, is portrayed as an anomaly. Her making permanent the order she has restored by defeating these froward women by consigning them to meek penitence in marriage reaffirms contemporary preaching that harmony ensues when woman accepts her duty to submit to her husband. Further, even though Lyly might flatter Elizabeth I through his portrait of Cynthia's preeminence, he also hints at her own need for masculine guidance from wise courtiers—like himself? Significantly, when his plays are not designed to earn Elizabeth's patronage, Lyly creates a goddess guide in Ceres who needs a father or a husband figure, Cupid, to hold her vindictiveness in line.

At the opposite pole, Venus and Silvesta from Lady Mary Wroth's *Love's Victory* assert a view of woman's wisdom and virtue over men's vanity, superficiality, and even viciousness. Wroth reverses the traits traditionally assigned men and women by her society and shows that women can effectively rule themselves and others for the good of their worlds. Rather than creating chaos because of lasciviousness, vengefulness, or weak intellect, Wroth's Venus designs lessons to teach humans to love unselfishly and humbly, undoes the evil plottings of men, and rewards the good. Her human assistant, Silvesta, aids in implementing her plans. To elevate women, Wroth actually reverses some of the techniques Lyly had used to degrade them in either *Endymion* or *Loves Metamorphosis*: Venus lacks the tetchiness of Cynthia and the downright vengefulness of Ceres; rather than making only a goddess capable of maintaining order, Wroth has both a divine and a human guide representing woman's ability to bring the world to harmony; and Cupid becomes the servant of the goddess rather than her director.

More importantly, the pastoral guide on the stage decidedly reveals an array of nuanced views between these two extremes. Shakespeare's *A Midsummer Night's Dream* questions the innate superiority used to justify masculine authority over women. While the play allows that its goddess guide is not able to rule on her own, it also shows that its god does not automatically possess the traits justifying masculine control over women. *The Faithful Shepherdess* overlaps Lyly's work in some ways but is closer to the views in Shakespeare and Wroth in others. Like Lyly's plays, Fletcher's pastoral is not shy in presenting the necessity of reining in female agency: portraying the social disorder set off by women who are sexually and verbally froward, asserting that containing their energies in submissive marriages will retain order, and suggesting that the woman who can restore order is extraordinary for her purity. Clorin is also admired for her obedience to masculine authority, Pan. However, Fletcher is far less hard on women than Lyly. Clorin may be an extraordinary woman, but she is still human. Further unlike Lyly, but more like Shakespeare and Wroth, Fletcher is willing to set before men their responsibility to be patriarchs who are benevolent, just, compassionate, and respectful when directing women.

Chapters 6 and 7 examined how two of Shakespeare's later plays, *As You Like It* and *All's Well That Ends Well*, also address the responsibility of men to live up to their roles in the gender hierarchy, although, as these chapters demonstrated, the plays present a far more radical view than *The Faithful Shepherdess*. Rosalind and Helena answer to or rely on no Pan, and succeed. What is particularly interesting in these cases, additionally differentiating them from *Love's Victory*, is how their attempts to negotiate mainstream views forced them to present challenges under physical and verbal disguises for both characters and audiences. This situation connects to earlier discussions about audience reception. The more iconoclastic *Love's Victory* was a private theatrical, designed to entertain Wroth's own circle, but plays like *The Faithful Shepherdess*, *As You Like It*, and *All's Well* had to face the judgment of a broad audience much more representative of general taste and values. They also had to pass the judgment of the State censor. Their limited or indirect challenge to conventional views of women's inferior place or man's right to a superior one reflects the need and opportunity to negotiate acceptance carefully. Still, though they needed to be coded and could not push too many too far, questions might be raised and answers might be suggested to modify traditional views.

As rulers, scholars, doctors, potential wives, daughters, and/or subjects, the Venuses, Cynthias, Clorins, Rosalinds, Helenas, and Silvestas of the early-modern stage were important figures for addressing concerns about conflicting views about the gender hierarchy. They might be portrayed as admirable for acting like obedient daughters or wives, as well as for being independent, self-directing, even saucy, teachers and healers. These guides could be goddesses or rulers who need the guidance of male wisdom; are no better or worse than their male counterparts; or are perfectly competent on their own, even wisely directing male mortals and divinities. They might use carnival abuse to mock others who challenge the traditional order or they might mock a dogmatic adherence to traditional order in others. As this book has shown, this variety of incarnations and interactions with fellow characters is firmly rooted within the beliefs of culture in which the guide was created, revealing the range and complexity of beliefs on the nature and role of woman in the sixteenth and seventeenth centuries.

Notes

Introduction

1. Philip Sidney, *An Apology for Poetry*, ed. Forrest G. Robinson (1595; repr., Indianapolis: Bobbs-Merrill, 1970), 42–43; George Puttenham, *Arte of English Poesie*, ed. G. D. Willock and A. Walker (Cambridge University Press, 1936), 38–39, quoted in Frank Kermode introduction. *English Pastoral Poetry: From Beginnings to Marvell* (Toronto: George G. Harrap & Co., Ltd., 1952), 29–30; John Fletcher, "To the Reader," *The Faithful Shepherdess*, in *Typical Elizabethan Plays*, ed. Felix E. Schelling and Matthew W. Black (Harper and Brothers, n.d.), 609.

2. Samuel Johnson, "From Milton," in *Rasselas, Poems, and Selected Prose*, 3rd ed., ed. Bertrand H. Bronson. (New York: Rinehart, 1971), 335, 336; Alexander Pope, "A Discourse on Pastoral Poetry," in *Poetry and Prose of Alexander Pope*, ed. Aubrey Williams (Boston: Houghton Mifflin, Riverside Edition, 1969), 3–7.

3. William Wordsworth, preface to the Second Edition of the *Lyrical Ballads* (1800), in *English Romantic Writers*, ed. David Perkins (Fort Worth, TX: Harcourt College Press, 1995), 424.

4. Wordsworth, 1850 *The Prelude* 8, 121–221, in *The Prelude 1799, 1805, 1850. Norton Critical Edition*, (New York: W. W. Norton, 1979).

5. George Eliot, "The Natural History of German Life," in *Selected Essays, Poems and Other Writings* (London: Penguin, 1990), 110–11.

6. John Ruskin, "Of Queens' Gardens," in *Sesame and Lillies* (New York: John W. Lovell, n.d.), 82–84, 100–101; Sarah Stickney Ellis, *The Women of England*, ed. Perry Willett, in Victorian Women Writers Project. February 5, 1999, Indiana Univeristy. http://www.indiana.edu/~letrs/vwwp/ellis/womeneng.html#p9, 231–32, 306; Coventry Patmore Prologue I and II to "The Angel in the House," in *The Poems of Coventry Patmore*, (London: Oxford University Press, 1949); Walter Pater, "The Child in the House," in *Victorian Literature 1830–1900*, ed. Dorothy Mermin and Herbert Tucker. (Fort Worth, TX: Harcourt College Press, 2002), 960–67; R. H. Horne, "William and Mary Howitt," in vol. 1 of *A New Spirit of the Age*. (New York: Garland, 1986), 188–89.

7. Paul Alpers, *What Is Pastoral?* (Chicago: University of Chicago Press, 1997), 81.

8. Ibid, 93.

9. Definitions of the term "natural" clearly shift with the aesthetics of the era in which a pastoral would be created. As Frank Kermode, 11–12, and Harry Levin (*The Myth of the Golden Age in the Renaissance*, [New York: Oxford University Press, 1969], 106–9) point out, the concept of "natural" for a sixteenth- or seventeenth-century pastoral writer implies showing the world as a Platonic ideal, before the "unnatural" corruption of the Fall, or as Sidney writes, the poet's job is to "deliver a golden" world (*Apology* 15). In contrast, nineteenth-century realist George Eliot, 110, defines her pastoral world as natural for *depicting* the actual harsh conditions of rural life: "Art is the nearest thing to life; it is a mode of amplifying experience and extending our contact with our fellowmen beyond the bounds of our personal lot. All the more sacred is the task of the artist when he undertakes to paint the life of the People." Despite their differences in defining "naturalness," writers of both eras still hold that the pastoral's "naturalness" hinges on its portrayal of

Nature (human, divine, and otherwise) as it truly is, uncorrupted by misapprehensions of human-made civilization.

10. Sidney, *Apology*, 42–43.

11. Wordsworth, 1850 *Prelude* 8, 161–63.

12. Sarah Way Sherman, *Sarah Orne Jewett, an American Persephone* (Hanover, NH: University Press of New England, 1989), 16–18.

13. Sherman, 19.

14. Vera Norwood, *Made from This Earth* (Chapel Hill: University of North Carolina Press, 1993), 8–24, 28–53, 98–111, 133–39.

15. Sherman, 103–17.

16. Alpers, 28, 93; C. L. Barber, *Shakespeare's Festive Comedy: A Study of Dramatic Form and Its Relation to Social Convention* (Princeton, NJ: Princeton University Press, 1959), 3–73; and François Laroque, *Shakespeare's Festive World: Elizabethan Seasonal Entertainment and the Professional Stage*, trans. Janet Lloyd (Cambridge: Cambridge University Press, 1993), 3–73, 179–281.

17. Wendy Wall, *The Imprint of Gender, Authorship and Publication in the English Renaissance* (Ithaca, NY: Cornell University Press, 1993), 8, 12–19, 31–34; Margaret Ezell, *Writing Women's Literary History* (Baltimore, MD: Johns Hopkins University Press, 1993), 34, 37–38, 53–57; Heidi Brayman Hackel and Catherine E. Kelly, ed, Introduction, *Reading Women, Literacy, Authorship, and Culture in the Atlantic World*, 1500–1800 (Philadelphia: University of Pennsylvania Press, 2008), 7; Helen Hackett, *Women and Romance Fiction in the English Renaissance* (Cambridge: Cambridge University Press, 2000), 102–04; Tina Krontiris, *Oppositional Voices: Women as Writers and Translators of Literature in the English Renaissance* (London: Routledge, 1992), 22, 64–68.

18. For women's reading involved with domestic responsibilities, see Frances Teague, "Judith Shakespeare Reading," *Shakespeare Quarterly* 47, no. 4 (1996): 366, 369–71. For general information on low percentage of literacy, especially for women, see Teague, 362 n. 3, 365–66; Patricia Demers, *Women's Writing in English Early Modern England* (Toronto: University of Toronto Press, 2000), 23; Krontiris, 13 n. 46, 150; Hackett, 6–9; Hackel and Kelly, introduction, in Hackel and Kelly, 1.

19. The following critics discuss the wide audiences of class and gender to whom the stage was available and exerted a strong influence: David Kathman, "Grocers, Goldsmiths, and Drapers: Freemen and Apprentices in the Elizabethan Theater," *Shakespeare Quarterly* 55, no. 1 (2004): 1–49; Phyllis Rackin, *Shakespeare and Women* (Oxford: Oxford University Press, 2005), 75–76; Jean Howard, "Scripts and/versus Playhouses: Ideological Public Production and the Renaissance Public Stage, in *The Matter of Difference: Materialist Feminist Criticism of Shakespeare*, ed. Valerie Wayne, (Ithaca, NY: Cornell University Press, 1991), 221–25, 227–29, 233–34; Sara Eaton, "Defacing the Feminine in Renaissance Tragedy," in Wayne, 181–98.

20. The pastoral plays and masques I found that showed some version of the guide as I have described her extend from the 1580s to the 1640s, or the 1660s if restagings of earlier written texts are to be included. Below is a list of plays that have some version of the guide, organized by type of guide (goddess, mage, wise woman) and citing the name of the guiding character as well as the play's date. Since some works have more than one version of the guide, some plays are listed under more than one category. There could well be other examples of the guide that I have not yet discovered, but my survey is extensive. Only a select group of these plays will be discussed or referenced in this book.

Goddess: *Lady of May* (1578, Queen Elizabeth); *Arraignement of Paris* (1581, Eliza/Zabeta/Elizabeth I and Diana); *Gallathea* (1584, Diana, Venus, nymphs); *Endymion* (1584/5, Cynthia); *Love's Metamorphosis* (1588/89, Ceres); *A Midsummer Night's Dream* (1595/6, Titania); *Maydes* [sic] *Metamorphosis* (1600, Graces); *The Faery Pastorall*

(1603, Chloris); *Love's Victory* (1620, Venus); *Rhodon and Iris* (1631, Flora); *Comus* (1637, Sabrina).

Mage: *Loves Metamorphosis* (1588/89, Protea); *All's Well That Ends Well* (1602/03, Helena); *The Queen's Arcadia* (1605, Urania); *The Faithful Shepherdess* (1608/09, Clorin); *Careless Shepherd* (1629, Sylvia), *Love Crowns the End* (1632, Claudia).

Wise Woman: *As You Like It* (1599/1600, Rosalind); *Hyman's Triumph* (1614, Lamia); *Love's Victory* (1620, Silvesta); *Rhodon and Iris* (1631, Clematis); *Shepherd's Paradise* (1632/33, Bellessa and Sabina); *Comus* (1637, Lady); *Love Crowns the End* (1632, Florida) *Argalus and Parthenia* (1639, Queen of Corinth); *Sad Shepherd* (1640, Marian).

21. Burkhardt quoted in Krontiris, p. 3. See also Lorna Hutson, introduction, *Feminism & Renaissance Studies* (Oxford: Oxford University Press, 1999), 1–3, 7–8; Betty Travitsky, *The Paradise of Women, Writings by Englishwomen of the Renaissance* (New York: Columbia University Press, 1989), 244 n. 21; Joan Kelly, "Did Women Have a Renaissance?" in Hutson, 21–23, 46 n. 1; Demers 27.

22. Judith Shakespeare makes her appearance in Woolf's *A Room of One's Own*. Critical commentary discussing its insufficiently nuanced portrait of the early-modern woman includes: Krontiris 1–3; Margaret Ezell, 43–50; Suzanne Trill, Kate Chedgzoy, and Melanie Osborne *Lay by Your Needles Ladies, Take the Pen: Writing Women in England, 1500–1700* (London: Arnold, 1997), 2; Travitsky, *Paradise* 118, 254 n. 25; Elizabeth H. Hageman and Sara Jayne Steen, From the Editors, *Shakespeare Quarterly* 47, no. 4 (1996): v–vi.

23. Valerie Wayne, "Historical Differences: Misogyny and Othello," in Wayne 157, 159; Hackett, 28–32. See also Trill, Chedgzoy, Osborne, 2–4; Hackett, 30–32; Travitsky, *Paradise*, 35–36, 92–93.

24. Travitsky, *Paradise*, 36.

25. Ezell, 44. See also 9, 19, 24–26, 32, 43–65.

26. Trill, Chedgzoy, and Osborne, 2–7, 8–17; Demers, 5–16, 24–26, 63–194; Betty Travitsky and Anne Lake Prescott, "Studying and Editing Early Modern Englishwomen: Then and Now," in *Women Editing/Editing Women*, ed Ann Hollingshead Hurley and Chanita Goodblatt (Newcastle-on-Tyne: Cambridge Scholars Publishing, 2009), 20–22; Gibson and Wright, in Hurley and Goodblatt, 155–73; Travitsky, *Paradise*, 10–13.

27. Bianca F.–C. Calabresi writes that in sixteenth- and seventeenth-century England the needle and pen were not always instruments used for different skills, but often both were instruments for "writing." Using needle and thread like pen and ink, women wrote their histories, asserted their identities, and demonstrated their learning. Inscriptions made with needle and thread could be read literally or symbolically, as the pieces they worked (book covers, tapestries, samplers) frequently blended metaphorical imagery with script. In fact, women who could only "sign" an X on paper could still write their names or convey a verbal message with needle and thread. See "'you sow, Ile read': Letters and Literacies in Early Modern Samplers," in Hackel and Kelly, 70–104. For a related discussion on women's literary needle work, see also Demers, 16–19.

28. Mary Ellen Lamb, "Inventing the Early Modern Woman Reader through the World of Goods: Lyly's Gentlewoman Reader and Katherine Stubbes," in Hackel and Kelly, 15–35; Sasha Roberts, "Engendering the Female Reader: Women's Recreational Reading of Shakespeare in Early Modern England," in Hackel and Kelly, 36–51; Hackett, 38, 42–54, 70–75, 76–100.

29. Rackin, *Shakespeare*, 76. See also Rackin 75–76; Richard Levin, "Women in the Renaissance Theater Audience, *Shakespeare Quarterly* 40, no. 2 (1989): 165–74; Valerie Traub, in Wayne, 104–6; Jean Howard, in Wayne, 223–26, 234; M. A. Katritzky, *Women, Medicine, and Theatre, 1500–1750* (Aldershot, Hampshire, England: Ashgate, 2007), 148, 165–67.

30. Travitsky and Lake Prescott, in Hurley and Goodblatt, 11–14; Gibson and Wright, in Hurley and Goodblatt, 155, 159–62.

31. Ezell, 44. See also Trill, Chedzoy, and Osborne, 2–3 and Gibson and Wright, in Hurley and Goodblatt, 157–59.

32. Travitsky, *Paradise*, 12; Hackett, 29–32. See also Trill, Chedgzoy, Osborn, 2–4; Travitsky, *Paradise*, 35–36, 92–93.

33. Ezell, 18–19, 21–23. See also Trill, Chedgzoy, Osborn, 2–3; Gibson and Wright in Hurley and Goodblatt, 157–59.

34. As views of women's reading, writing, and medical knowledge prove particularly relevant to studying the female pastoral guide, they will receive deeper discussion in Chapter 4, which will explore contemporary views of women as scholars.

35. Hackett, 30–32. These examples of women's negotiations within the patriarchal system for voice and agency will receive detailed discussion and documentation later in this book, especially in chapter 4.

36. Trill, Chedgzoy, Osborne, 2–3, 14–17.

37. Diane Purkiss, "Material Girls: The Seventeenth-Century Woman Debate," in *Women, Texts, and Histories 1575–1760*, ed. Clare Brant and Diane Purkiss, (Routledge: London, 1992), 71–92.

38. Elizabeth Harvey, *Ventriloquized Voices: Feminist Theory and English Renaissance Texts* (London: Routledge, 1992). See introduction and chapters 1 and 2 in her book.

39. Richard Levin, 174.

40. For the quotation, ibid., 171. See also 167–173.

41. For references to both Shakespeare and Fletcher, see Richard Levin, 168–70, 171–73. For Fletcher's positive reputation treating women favorably, Richard Levin, 172.

42. Mikhail Bakhtin, *Rabelais and His World* (Bloomington: Indiana University Press, 1984), 10–17, 21–23, 26, 49–50, 72–73, 90–95, 121–23.

43. Ibid., 49.

44. Ibid., 81–82, 363–67.

45. Ibid., 4–12, 21–29, 81–82, 105–7, 114, 162–80, 240–44, 309–12.

46. Ibid., 19, 30–35, 39, 42, 48–53, 211–12, 234, 239–42, 363–67.

47. Ibid., 122–23.

48. Ibid., 21–26, 51–53, 147–52, 317, 355.

49. Ibid., 25–26.

50. Ibid., 240.

51. Ibid., 51–52, 89–103, 105–9, 117, 120, 127 n. 67.

52. Ibid., 240–41.

53. Jyotsna Singh, "The Interventions of History: Narratives of Sexuality, " in *The Weyward Sisters: Shakespeare and Feminist Politics*, ed. Dympna Callaghan, Lorraine Helms, and Jyotsna Syngh (Cambridge, MA: Blackwell, 1994); for the quotation from Singh, see 38; Peter Stallybrass, "The World Turned Upside Down," in Wayne, 211–16; Diane Purkiss, "Material," 84–91; Mary Russo, "Female Grotesques: Carnival and Theory," in *Feminist Studies Critical Studies*, ed. Teresa de Lauretis (Bloomington: Indiana University Press, 1986), 216–17;

54. Natalie Zemon Davis, "Women on Top," in Hutson, 171–72, 160–65.

CHAPTER 1. "LIGHT IN THE SKY"

1. Judith Kennedy, introduction, *Diana*, trans. Bartholomew Yonge (London: Oxford University Press, 1968), xix–xx, xli, liv–vi; Judith Serafini-Sauli, introduction, *L'Ameto* (New York: Garland Press, 1985), xiv, xvi–vii, xx; RoseAnna Mueller, *The Diana*, by

Jorge de Montemayor, (Lewiston, NY: Mellen Press, 1989) 10; and Helen Hackett, 114, 148, 160.

2. Kennedy, xix–xx.

3. Kennedy, xix–xx; Judith Serafini-Sauli xiv, xvi–vii; Anthony K. Cassell and Victoria Kirkham, introduction, *Diana's Hunt*, by Boccaccio (Philadelphia: University of Pennsylvania Press, 1991), 30–32; W. W. Greg, *Pastoral Poetry and Pastoral Drama: A Literary Inquiry, with Special Reference to the Pre-Restoration Stage in England* (London: A. H. Bullens, 1906), 40–43; Helen Cooper, *Pastoral: Medieval into Renaissance* (Ipswich, England: D. S. Brewer, 1977), 102–3.

4. Paul Turner 10–11, introduction. *Daphnis and Chloe* by Longus; Margaret Doody, *The True Story of the Novel* (New Brunswick, NJ: Rutgers University Press, 1996), 251.

5. Paul Turner, 11; Helen Cooper, 201; Margaret Doody, 240.

6. Alpers 323–74; Paul Turner 6–7, 12–13; Mueller 10, Margaret Doody, 48–50, 207, 251.

7. Margaret Doody also observes that Lyceanion (47–48) instructs Daphnis in the art of love, in a physical and an emotional sense; nevertheless, she does not note that Lyceanion and the Nymphs are the foremothers of a character that will become an important, but unremarked, convention in pastoral literature in centuries to come, the female pastoral guide.

8. Longus, 20–22.

9. Ibid., 58–63.

10. Ibid., 88–89.

11. Ibid., 19–20.

12. Ibid., 118–21.

13. Ibid., 45.

14. Ibid., 80.

15. Doody, 48.

16. Longus, 81–82, 120–21.

17. Knowing Theocritus directly or in translation would have been unlikely for most Renaissance writers since Latin was preferred over Greek as the language of scholarly study. More importantly, translations from Greek or even extensive copies of the Greek texts were scarce on the continent or in England. See Helen Cooper, 2–3, 26, 124, 153; Greg, 17–39, Robert Wells, introduction, *The Idylls* by Theocritus, 50. Particularly relevant to the study of the British Renaissance pastoral, Helen Cooper points out that "Theocritus was not even partially translated [into English] until 1588, when *Sixe Idillia* (not all in fact genuine Theocritus) was published at Oxford; and no Greek edition was printed in England for another half a century" (124). Instead, most would have either known Virgil's *Eclogues*, only having some familiarity with the conventions and motifs of Theocritus via Virgil's adaptation of them. See Kermode, 24–28; Alpers 137–38, 153–55, 174–84; and Edmund K. Chambers, introduction, *English Pastorals*. London: Blackie and Son, n.d., xii–xiii). Consequently, studying Virgil's text is more appropriate to the focus of the study of a Renaissance pastoral guide.

18. Virgil, *Eclogue* 8. All future references to the *Eclogues* are from this text.

19. This is not to assert that the pre-Christian pastoral was innocently and completely devoted to unfettered sexuality. In *The Virgin and the Bride*, Kate Cooper explains that such sexuality was ultimately harnessed to serve the social needs of the greater community. As a matter of fact, she uses *Daphnis and Chloe* as a prime example of how the romance in the early Common Era was used to do so. Cooper points out that the frame initiating and closing the tale reveals that Daphnis and Chloe have become responsible country gentry, funding the arts as well as the religious and social needs of their community. The adventures and romance of the main body of the work bring them together in an exotic, sexually charged setting so that they can ultimately accept the duties to the community that many of their class were shirking for want of money or interest. Thus, the romance acts

as delicious lure that leads to upholding social tradition. See Kate Cooper, *The Virgin and the Bride: Idealized Womanhood in Late Antiquity* (Cambridge, MA: Harvard University Press, 1996), 23–24, 30–32, 36–44. In a related vein, both Margaret Doody and Baring and Cashford observe that the pressure to "cleanse" the sensual from the spiritual was part of a psychic split that originated with the overwhelming of Great Goddess worship during the Bronze Age by invading herdsman societies favoring a patriarchal deity, ranging from Aryans to Dorians to Hebrews to Romans. However, the conflict and evolution of Western spiritual thought is far too complex to delineate in a footnote and will be discussed in more detail, where appropriate, later in this chapter. Anne Baring and Jules Cashford, *The Myth of the Goddess: Evolution of an Image* (London: Penguin, 1993).

20. Longus, 45–47.

21. Castiglione, *The Courtier*, trans. by Hoby, Book 4. 37.

22. Ibid. 38,

23. Ibid. 37.

24. Ibid. 38.

25. Ibid. 47–48, 49.

26. Ibid, 41.

27. Ibid. For quotations, see 47 and 48, respectively. See also 45–49.

28. Kermode, 35.

29. Baez paraphrased in Mueller, 34–35.

30. Joan Gondal Kelly and Marina Warner both note that the earliest forms of courtly love literature, sung by Troubadours of southern France toward the conclusion of the eleventh century through the early thirteenth, did not initially rewrite the earlier pastoral joys in sensuality. For Warner, see *Alone of All Her Sex: The Myth and the Cult of the Virgin Mary* (New York: Alfred Knopf, 1976), 136, 134. For Kelly, see "Did Women Have a Renaissance?" in Hutson, 24–25, 29–31. Still, both also write that a shift in the courtly tradition came over time when political and religious changes brought southern France, which had patronized this form of pastoral, under control of Church factions with stricter religious views (Warner, 137–48) and when across Europe changes in the socio-political structure from feudalism to capitalism reduced women's rights to control their property and destiny (Kelly, 31–45). Kelly looks to Castiglione's *The Courtier* as a major example of how courtly love was purged of sensuality in favor of a "Neo-Platonic notion of spiritual love" (39).

31. Bakhtin, *Rabelais*, 122–23.

32. See Erich Neumann, *The Great Mother*, trans. Ralph Manheim, (1963; repr., Princteon, NJ: Princteon University Press), 1991.94, 268–71, 290–91, 305–11 and Joseph Campbell, *Occidental Mythology* (New York: Penguin, 1988), 21–22, 61–62 on the Great Mother. Barbette Stanley Spaeth, *The Roman Goddess Ceres* (Austin: University of Texas Press, 1996), xiii sums up the problems of a "theory that in the ancient past there existed one great Mother Goddess from whom all other goddesses derived, . . . [a] female divinity [who] was the supreme power in a society that was both egalitarian and peaceful, and if not actually matriarchal, certainly matrifocal," "combined with another problematic assumption: that the goddesses of ancient society were archetypes, models for the behavior and personality of women both in the past and today." In *The Myth of the Goddess*, Baring and Cashman avoid what Spaeth (xiii) describes as "obscur[ing] what the ancient goddesses meant to the people who actually worshipped them and ignor[ing] the basically patriarchal structure of ancient society" by instead observing that the Great Goddesses ranging from paleolithic to classical times functioned in conjunction with a masculine deity consort; that the emphasis on individualism and reason of the patriarchal gods was not so much inferior to goddess worship as inadequate to face human spiritual needs without the goddesses' emphasis on the earthly, the sensual, the feeling.

See also in Lotte Motz, *The Faces of the Goddess* (Oxford: Oxford University Press, 1997), 5–38 and Marina Warner, 283–84 on misapprehensions about ancient societies produced by ill-founded insistence on the existence of Great Mother cults predominating a matriarchal ancient world.

33. Anne Baring and Jules Cashford, 152–69, 182, 440–48, 492–95.

34. David Leeming, *Goddess: Myths of the Female Divine*, 60. See also Betty De Shong Meador, *Inanna Lady of the Largest Heart*, 12–22.

35. Harris, quoted in De Shong Meador, 19. See also Baring and Cashford, 192–205.

36. The Epic of *Gilgamesh*, translated by N. K. Sanders, (1960, repr.; Harmondsworth, Middlesex: Penguin, 1985), 92; Leeming, *Goddess*, "Inanna," 62–66.

37. *Gilgamesh*, 3.84–86.

38. De Shong Meador, 161.

39. Enheduanna, quoted in De Shong Meador, 19.

40. De Shong Meador, 151. See also Baring and Cashman, 145–48, 169–70, 201–5.

41. De Shong Meador, 33–35, 47, 185. Baring and Cashman do note that Dr. Samuel Noah Kramer found evidence that there was some degree of equality when it came to owning property or serving in the priesthood in Sumeria c. 2400 BCE; however, they go nowhere near claiming the presence of a matriarchal society, and they continue to point out that the later influence of Akkadian Semitic invaders supplant even that degree of parity (159, 182).

42. R. E. Witt, *Isis in the Ancient World* (Baltimore: Johns Hopkins University Press, 1971), 81–87, 121–29; Leeming, *Goddess*, 77; Baring and Cashman, 224; Doody, 67–68.

43. Baring and Cashman 232–39, Warner, 256–57, Witt 123, Lewis Spence, *Ancient Egyptian Myths and Legends* (1915; repr., New York: Dover, 1990), 81–84.

44. Apuleius, *The Golden Ass*, trans. by Jack Lindsey, (Bloomington, IN: Midland, 1965), 237–38.

45. For these myths of Isis see the following: Spence, 63–70, 81–84; Witt, 38–45; Geraldine Pinch, *Magic in Ancient Egypt* (Austin: University of Texas Press, 1994), 144–46; and David Leeming, *The World of Mythology: An Anthology* (New York: Oxford University Press, 1990), 148–53.

46. Witt, 22–23, 49–50, 186–87; Pinch 140–41.

47. Witt, 22.

48. Ibid.

49. Pinch, 30; Spence, 259–61.

50. Spence, 68–69; Leeming, *World*, 149–50.

51. Bakhtin, *Rabelais*, 123; Leeming, *World*, 151.

52. Apuleius, 237.

53. Stanley Spaeth 13, 41–42, 60, 103–5; Baring and Cashford, 146–48, 368–72, 403–4.

54. For the Demeter/Ceres mythos see Baring and Cashford, 364–90; Leeming, *Goddess*, 68–71; Neumann 305–25; Hesiod, *Theogony*, in *Theogony, Works and Days, Shield*, trans. by Apostolos N. Athanassakis (Baltimore, MD: Johns Hopkins University Press, 1983), (ll. 912–14); and Michael Grant, *Myths of the Greeks and the Romans* (New York: Meridian, 1995), 126–34. Witt gives a useful discussion of the relationship between these myths and the antecedent Isis/Osiris mythos (20, 67, 127–28).

55. Baring and Cashford, 116, 366. See also 145–46, 364–69 and 403–5.

56. Baring and Cashford, 157–59, 442–43; 461–69, 612–14; Campbell, 72–92, 144–77.

57. Jacques Lacan, "The Function and Field of Language in Psychoalanlysis," in *Écrits*, trans. Bruce Fink (1966; New York: W. W. Norton, 1999), 65–67; Jyotsna Syngh, "Narratives of Sexuality," in Callaghan, Helms, and Syngh, 59–101; Valerie Wayne, introduction, in Wayne, 1–26; Carol Leventen, "Patrimony and Patriarchy in *The Merchant*

of Venice," in Wayne, 59–79; "Historical Difference, Misogyny in *Othello*" Wayne in Wayne, 153–79.

58. Doody, 67–68.

59. Stanley Spaeth, 13. See also Doody, 68–73.

60. Baring and Cashford, 404–5.

61. Jaroslav Pelikan. *Mary through the Centuries: Her Place in the History of Culture* (New Haven, CT: Yale University Press, 1996), 57–58.

62. Erich Neumann, 312–15 provides an image of the Virgin Mary holding the Christ Child for the Magis' admiration in an impression of a stone ring from Naples in the sixth century CE called "Adoration of the Three Kings" (Figure 70) that is strikingly similar to the positioning and number of characters, as well as symbols, in a Minoan signet ring image from Boetia ("Adoration of the Divine Son," Figure 69) and two Akkadian seals. See also in Warner Plates 32 (Isis) and 33 and 34 (Mary) and Baring and Cashford linking the Black Virgin with images of Isis, Cybele, and Artemis of Ephesus on page 587.

63. Marina Warner, 208–9 notes strong parallels between the depiction of Isis "with the miniature mummy of the dead Osiris across her knees, of which there are examples in the British Museum" with "countless Gothic and Renaissance treatments of the Pièta." The comparable images of Isis and Mary holding their divine sons sacrificed to death are Plates 35 (Isis) and 36 (Mary). See also Cashford and Baring, 584–86, linking the images of the Pieta with the laments for Dumizi, Tamuz, and Osiris. In a slightly different comparison, see Figures 20 and 21 for the similarities between and Etruscan Mother Goddess cradling a lion like a child and a fourteenth-century statue of Christian Mary holding the Christ child and supported by lions.

64. Warner, 276. Warner also cites other related examples on 193, 195. See also Baring and Cashford, 550–51, 586–88. Witt (275) further details the startlingly extensive co-opting of Isis's sacred sites and images into those of Mary.

65. Warner, 276, Neumann, 262, 308; De Shong Meador, 53.

66. Neumann, 261. See also Baring and Cashford, 577.

67. Warner, 278–81; Baring and Cashford, 575–79.

68. Witt, 44. See also 272.

69. Warner, 323. See also Baring and Cashford, 146–47. Baring and Cashford, 598–601 further note the similarities between the crucifix as symbol of the Tree of Life for bringing humanity spiritual salvation and the tree that grew around Osiris's body and came to be worshipped as a pillar of life.

70. Witt, 263, 266, 272–73, 272–74, 276–77; Warner, 266–68.

71. Witt, 263, 272–73; Neumann, 258; Warner, 255–69. Many of the titles and images are also shared amongst Inanna /Ishtar, Isis, and Mary (Baring and Cashford, 175–77, 554).

72. Baring and Cashford, 192. According to Bakhtin, carnival's conception of the beautiful grotesque in which human, natural, and supernatural blend into each other can be seen as an attempt to recover that unity. Further, in carnival the states of living, death, and rebirth reflect the grotesque worldview by merging in an eternal cycle, embodied by ancient, terra cotta laughing, pregnant hags as "pregnant death, a death that gives birth." See *Rabelais*, 25–26. More importantly, in the world of carnival the eternal female does not reflect women's corruption in the freeness of her words and sexuality, anymore than did Inanna or Isis. Instead, carnival's female icon of spiritual rebirth returns the vitalizing Goddess to power by "represent[ing] in person the undoing of pretentiousness, of all that is finished, completed, and exhausted. She is the inexhaustible vessel of conception, which dooms all that is old and terminated." See *Rabelais*, 25–26, 240. See also *Rabelais*, 31–35.

73. De Shong Meador, 85. See also Baring and Cashford, 168, 442–46, 465, 514–18, 531–32, 553–56.

74. Charlotte Otten, introduction, *English Women's Voices* 1540–1700 (Miami: Florida International University Press, 1992), 1–3; Jardine, *Still Harping on Daughters: Women and Drama in the Age of Shakespeare* (New York: Columbia University Press, 1989), 40; Warner, 177–82. See also Baring and Cashford, 503–4, 509, 520–22 and especially Ian Maclean, "The Notion of Women in Medicine, Anatomy, and Physiology," in Hutson, 127–55.

75. Isis's and other comparable goddesses' role as fertility divinities to the ancient world (mother of the god, bringer of the crops) is reflected in some of the epithets bestowed on Mary "the freshe tuft," "the earth," or calling her a "young heifer" or "fructification." See Witt, 272. Church fathers still tended to emphasize that such fertility only confirmed woman's role as giving her husband children and caring for them for him or suggested that the fertility Mary brought was spiritual rather than physical (Warner, 274–78).

76. Luke 1:35.

77. Ibid., 1:38.

78. Warner, 184. See also, Warner, 179, and Baring and Cashford, 551–52.

79. Elaine Beilin, *Redeeming Eve, Women Writers of the English Renaissance* (Princeton, NJ: Princeton University Press, 1987), xiv.

80. Introduction, *The Instruction of a Christen Woman*, by Juan Luis Vives, trans. Richard Hyrde, ed. Virginia Walcott Beauchamp, Elizabeth Hageman, and Margaret Mikeskell (1529; Urbana: University of Illinois Press, 2002), xlii–xlvi, lxxviiixciii.

81. Juan Vives, trans. Richard Hyrde, 62–63.

82. Beilin, xix.

83. The Christian Mary does not completely erase the pricklier traits of the Great Goddess. Traditions persisted into medieval times and the Renaissance where the Christian divine virgin exhibits anomalous links to fertility and ferocity. Diane Purkiss (*Witches*, 155) notes the persistence of charms and spells of pagan tradition cited by practitioners as prayers to Mary. Marina Warner (322–25) points out that there are also popular tales from the Middle Ages of the Virgin acting not merely to intercede for mortals but actively thwarting the devil, unjust humans, and even "circumventing God's justice altogether" for "her justice is loyalty to her own." However, these were not the traits of the Virgin Mary that predominated Western thought.

84. Baring and Cashford, 448–69, 487–546, 551, 555, 574, 611.

85. Quotation from Baring and Cashford, 162. See also 168, 465–66, 469, 514–15, 531–32, 553–56.

86. Bakhtin, *Rabelais*, 9–11; Singh, 35–36, 38; Stallybrass, 211–16; Purkiss, "Material," 84–91.

87. Baring and Cashford, 404–5.

88. Doody, 35, 64–69.

89. Ibid., 58, 88, 91, 95, 104.

90. Ibid. In *Chaireas and Kallirrhoé* see 36 and 42–45; in *Kleitophon and Leukippé* see 54; in *Apollonious of Tyre*, 83–84; in *Aithiopika* see 92, 95–96, 102–4; in *Paul and Thekla*, see 74.

91. Ibid. In *Chaireas and Kallirrhoé* 38–39; in *Aithiopika*, 90–92, 99, 103, in *Leukippé*, 54–59.

92. Ibid., *Kallirrhoé*, 38; *Leukippé*, 54, 57–58; *Thekla*, 75–76; Tharsia in *Apolonoius*, 84, 86; Chariklea in *Aithiopika*, 90–92.

93. Ibid., In *Apolinius*, 85–89; in *Paul and Thekla*, 75–76, in Leukippé, 58–59.

94. Doody explains that, though much material was lost in western Europe with the fall of Rome, not only were many manuscripts preserved in the East but through trade and conquest they made their way back across Europe. In fact, manuscript copies of several of these romances were found in Italy and France throughout the Middle Ages.

She discusses the similarities in plot and character of these romances with eleventh-century Byzantine romances, the *Chanson de Roland*, and the work of Chrétien de Troyes and Marie de France (late twelfth century), to name a few (175–92). Furthermore, Helen Hackett, 148–49 notes that versions of *Daphnis and Chloe*, *Aithiopika*, and *Kleitophon and Leukippé* survived to be translated into Latin and French early in the sixteenth century and into English in the second half of the century. This is not to say that translations to the vernacular did not edit or revise to align the texts more with Renaissance Christian thought, as Doody explains, 239–50.

95. Doody, 180.

96. Hackett, 148–50; Doody, 243–44.

97. Doody, 192–99.

98. Cassell and Kirkham, 38, 37.

99. Giovanni Boccaccio, *L'Ameto*, trans. Judith Serafini-Sauli (New York: Garland, 1985), 145.

100. Ibid., 5–6.

101. Ibid., 7.

102. Campbell, 476; Leeming, *Goddess*, 139.

103. Baring and Cashford, 331–32.

104. Bonnefoy, *Greek and Egyptian Mythologies*, trans. by Wendy Doniger, (Chicago: University of Chicago Press, 1991), 133; Baring and Cashford, 331.

105. Neuman's description of Artemis as an incarnation of the Lady of the Beasts dovetails with the interpretation of this myth representing a fear of the feminine as a fear of the animal-like or the uncivilized controlling and wreaking chaos on the world of order: "Artemis has been characterized as a goddess of the 'outside', of the free wild life in which as huntress she dominates the animal world. This is a symbolic projection of her role as ruler over the unconscious powers that still take on animal form in our dreams— the 'outside' of the world of culture and consciousness" (276–77). See also Leeming, *Goddess*, 139.

106. Boccaccio, *Ameto*, 6–7.

107. De Shong Meador, 85.

108. Boccaccio, *Ameto*, 7.

109. Quotation from Boccaccio, *Ameto*, 11. See also 5–11, 14–15.

110. Ibid., 8.

111. There is a definite parallel here to the concept in courtly love where in a world of divine perfection a beautiful body must reflect a beautiful soul. However, in *The Courtier* the beloved lady's physical and spiritual beauty are only an initial inspiration that drives the courtier to pursue the higher, purely spiritual beauty of God alone. As the rest of this chapter will show, Boccaccio's *Ameto* never completely separates the earthly from the spiritual, with the latter making the former sacred in Lia—or subjugates the female to the masculine, with the perfection of divine Christian love borne directly from the goddess Venus to Ameto.

112. Ibid., 8.

113. Ibid., 9.

114. Serafini-Sauli, 149n6.

115. Cassell and Kirkham, 31.

116. As the Creed is spoken after the baptismal initiation of an individual into the Christian community of faith, Lia pledges her creed in conjunction with the baptism of Ameto into her community of worshippers of Venus. For use of the creed for baptismal initiation see Kirkham and Cassell, 81–82 and William H. Anderson, "Nicene Creed, The," 381 CE, Ancient Creeds, 12/11/2008, http://www.creeds.net/ancient/nicene.htm.

Significantly, what might be called "The Creed of Venus" in *Ameto* (130–31) draws on and adapts four important points from the 381 CE Nicene Creed, maintaining notably similar phrasing: recognizing the omnipotence of God the Father in creating the world; acknowledging the son's sacrifice of entering this world through virgin birth, dying for our sins, and harrowing hell before resurrection; asserting the pervasive inspiration of the Holy Spirit; and requiring belief in the legitimacy and strength to save of the "Church Militant" (*Ameto*, 131) or the "holy catholic and Apostolic Church" (Nicence Creed). The structuring and phrasing of the Creed of Venus makes drawing out specific passages for comparison too lengthy for an endnote.

117. Boccaccio, *Ameto*, 12–16.

118. Ibid., 16–17.

119. Ibid., 42.

120. Ibid., 44, 129.

121. For example, the tale of Acrimonia/Fortitude gives him strength to accept that though he cannot have these nymphs sexually he can still delight in both their physical and spiritual beauty. Influenced by the earlier nymph, Adiona/Temperance "with a more moderate desire" (85), he "banished his vain fancies" and can now appreciate being admitted to their presence, which bestows on him "blessings of which no living man has ever witnessed the equal" (85–6). After these two tales comes the final story, of the nymph Fiametta, Hope: a hope that his temperance and fortitude have readied him to attain the harmony of earthly and heavenly desires represented in divine love, Venus (114–15).

122. W. W. Greg, 41–42; Serafini-Sauli, xvii; and Cassell and Kirkham, 31.

123. Cassell and Kirkham, 31.

124. Boccaccio, *Ameto*, 104.

125. Ibid., 45, 51–52, 88–89, 77–80, 89–91.

126. Ibid., 80–83, 94–95, 47–48.

127. For examples in literature of a medieval tendency to portray gross unnaturalness in the pursuit of a young woman by an old man see the following: Chaucer's *Merchant's Tale*, *Wife of Bath's Tale*, "Cherry Tree Carol." See also, Robert O. Payne, "Canterbury Tales," in *Geoffrey Chaucer, Second Edition*, (Boston: Twayne Publishers, 1986) and Kenneth Bleeth, in "Joseph's Doubting of Mary and the Conclusion of *Merchant's Tale*," *Chaucer Review* 21 (1986): 58–66.

128. Bakhtin, *Rabelais*, 240.

129. Boccaccio, *Ameto*, 90–91.

130. Ibid., 91, 93.

131. Ibid., 94.

132. Ibid.

133. Bakhtin, *Rabelais*, 240–41

134. Boccaccio, *Ameto*, 21–23, 29–30, 38–39, 50, 61, 74.

135. Ibid., 50, 61.

136. Ibid., 114

137. Ibid., 115.

138. Ibid., 129.

139. Ibid., 134–42.

140. Ibid., 27–28, 37–38, 50, 61, 74.

141. Ibid., 115.

142. Ibid., 134.

143. Cassell and Kirkham, 31. See also Serafini-Sauli, xvii.

144. Cassell and Kirkham, 11, 17, 52, 56.

145. Cassell and Kirkham, 11, 52; 191, fn. 34; Serafini-Sauli, xiv, xiv–xvii.

146. Bonnefoy, 147–48, 151.

147. Danté Alighieri, *The Paradiso*, trans. John Ciardi (New York: Signet Mentor, 1970), Canto 23. line 73.

148. Baring and Cashford, 332, 407, 145–46, 192.

149. Danté Alighieri, *The Paradiso*, 33.10–12, 16–18, 3–9.

150. Boccaccio, *Ameto*, 136–37.

151. Ibid., 133.

152. John (Catholic Bible, Confraternity of Christian Doctrine and the Challoner/ Douay Texts), 1:4–5; 1:1–3.

153. Matthew (Catholic Bible, Confraternity of Christian Doctrine and the Challoner/ Douay Texts), 18:20.

154. Boccaccio, *Ameto*, 52, 82.

155. Ibid., *Ameto*, 137.

156. Ibid., 80–83.

CHAPTER 2. MAGES AND SAGES

A version of the portions of this chapter comparing Enareto with the cunning woman and discussing Felicia's wisdom in exercising her powers was previously published in my article "The Sage Felicia and the Grave Melissea: *Diana of George Montemayor*, An Inspiration for Wroth's Defense of Women in *Urania*" in *ANQ: A Quarterly Journal of Short Articles, Notes, and Reviews*, 16, no. 2 (Spring 2003): 5–14. I am grateful to *ANQ* and Heldref Publications for allowing me permission to draw on this material for my book.

1. De Shong Meador, 85.

2. Keith Thomas, *Religion and the Decline of Magic* (Oxford: Oxford University Press, 1997), 5, 4–50, 51–109.

3. Robin Briggs, "'Many Reasons Why': Witchcraft and the Problem of Multiple Explanation," in *Witchcraft in Early Modern Europe*. ed. Jonathan Barry, Marianne Hester, and Gareth Roberts (Cambridge: Cambridge University Press, 1998), 61.

4. These examples of bizarre and seemingly inexplicable disasters that were chalked up to witchcraft can be found in almost all the pamphlet accounts of bewitchments. The quotation is from "Witches at St. Osyth" (1582), in *Witchcraft in England 1558–-1618*, ed. Barbara Rosen, (Amherst: University of Massachusetts Press, 1969), 131. Other pamphlets, in addition to "Witches at St. Osyth," that recount some of the most extensive varieties of such attacks are "Witches at Windsor" (1579) and "Witches at Chelmsford" (1579). Barbara Rosen provides some informative medical and psychological explanations for bizarre occurrences in humans, animals, and housewifery on 43–49. Linda Woodbridge also addresses how in these times people saw magic as a bulwark against natural, emotional, and political forces threatening them. See *The Scythe of Saturn: Shakespeare and Magical Thinking*. (Urbana: University of Illinois Press, 1994), 15, 46–52, 57.

5. Thomas, 5–21; Rosen, 40–49.

6. See Thomas, 184–87, 206–8, 249, 265, 544, 548–50; Rosen, introduction, viii, 4, 7; Woodbridge, *Scythe*, 5; and Diane Purkiss, *The Witch in History: Early Modern and Twentieth-Century Representations* (London: Routledge, 1996), 123–24, 159–60.

7. Carlo Ginzburg, *The Night Battles: Witchcraft and Agrarian Cults in the Sixteenth and Seventeenth Centuries*, trans. John and Anne Tedeschi. (Baltimore: Johns Hopkins University Press, 1992), 22–23, 30–32.

8. Thomas, 31; Briggs, "Reasons," 61.

9. Thomas, 30.

10. Thomas, 47–48, 62–65; Woodbridge, *Scythe*, 5–6, 162–64; Ginzburg, 23.

11. Purkiss, *Witch*, 120–25, 94–95.

12. John S. Mebane, *Renaissance Magic & the Return of the Golden Age: The Occult Tradition and Marlowe, Johnson, and Shakespeare* (Lincoln: University of Nebraska

Press, 1989), 11. Also see in Mebane, 1–21, 25–35, 36–72, 80–92. Other related background is found with Thomas, 223–27; Ernst Cassirer, *The Individual and the Cosmos in Renaissance Philosophy*, trans. Mario Domandi. (Philadelphia: University of Pennsylvania Press, 1983), 59–71; and Noel Cobb, *Prospero's Island: The Secret Alchemy at the Heart of the Tempest* (London: Coventure, 1984), 39–41.

13. Thomas, 268–69.

14. Mebane, 106; Thomas, 254–55; Rosen, 5–9.

15. Mebane, 99, 105.

16. Mebane, 98–99; Paul J.W. Miller, Introduction, *On the Dignity of Man*. By Pico della Mirandola (Hackett, 1998), xxix–xxx.

17. Mebane, 99.

18. Frances A. Yates, *The Occult Philosophy in the Elizabethan Age* (London: Routledge, 1999), 167; Mebane, 78–80.

19. Barbara Rosen, 7, provides a succinct summation of the tale of the notorious Dr. Lambe: "Dr. Lambe, 'The Duke's Devil,' was a wizard in the service of the Duke of Buckingham at the beginning of the seventeenth century. He not only cured diseases and found lost things by the aid of familiar spirits, but used magic to bring about death by poisoning. Sentenced to death for this, and then again for rape while in prison, he escaped both sentences by the influence of his master; but the London mob caught him in the streets and beat him to death."

See also Purkiss, *Witch*, 147 and Thomas, 303, 346–47.

20. Thomas, 283–322, 324–37.

21. For the entire statute, see Rosen, 56–57. For more discussion of the illegality of casting the monarch's horoscope see Rosen, 22 and Thomas, 344 and 348.

22. Thomas, 117, 128–50, 389–432.

23. Peter Elmer, "'Saints and Sorcerers': Quakerism, Demonology and the Decline of Witchcraft in Seventeenth-Century England," in Barry, Hester, and Roberts, 163.

24. Thomas, 479–92; Rosen, 35–42.

25. "Witches and Fairies," in Rosen, 64.

26. Rosen, 305. For more on Catholic plots to overthrow the government see: Rosen, 40; Elmer, 160–63; Purkiss, *Witch*, 185; Woodbridge, *Scythe*, 8–10, 102, 117–118. On Catholic plots against social and moral order in general because the Church is an instrument of Satan: Thomas, 92–93, 542, 559–60; Woodbridge, *Scythe*, 102, 117–18; Elmer, 160–63; and Roberts, 201–2, 203–4. On Catholic ritual linked with incantations: Rosen, 39, 172; Thomas, 52–68, 72–77; and Purkiss, *Witch*, 154–59. Jane Dunn's *Elizabeth and Mary: Cousins, Rivals, Queens* (New York: Vintage, 2005) gives a through depiction of the complexities of plotting by Catholic loyalists and nations either to depose Elizabeth or at least to offset her political influence by supporting the claims to the British throne by Mary Queen of Scots.

27. Gareth Roberts, "The Descendants of Circe: Witches and Renaissance Fictions," in Barry, Hester, and Roberts, 201–2.

28. Thomas, 37–38, 55–74, 114, 620–21, 313–15.

29. Ibid., 74, 479–80, 484–87.

30. Peter Elmer, in Barry, Hester, and Roberts, 149–55; Thomas, 469–87.

31. For primary accounts of attempts to murder aristocrats through witchcraft, see "The Witches at Windsor," 83–91; "The Death of a Queen," 310–12; and "The Death of an Earl," 305–9, all in Rosen.

32. Rosen, 7; Purkiss, *Witch*, 145–48; Thomas 346–47.

33. Purkiss, *Witch*, 215–25; Thomas, 234; Rosen, 307n6.

34. Malcolm Gaskill, "Witchcraft in Early Modern Kent: Stereotypes and the Background to Accusations," in Barry, Hester, and Roberts, 268–69.

35. Briggs, "Reasons," in Barry, Hester, and Roberts, 54. See also Ginzburg, 55–56; Briggs, *Witches and Neighbors: The Social and Cultural Context of European Witch-craft*, (London: Penguin, 1996), 55–56, and Brian Levack's article "State-Building and Witch Hunting in Early Modern Europe," in Barry, Hester, and Roberts, 96–115.

36. Jim Sharpe, "The Devil in East Anglia: The Matthew Hopkins Trials Reconsid-ered," in Barry, Hester, and Roberts, 252.

37. Ibid., 240–50, 252.

38. Purkiss, *Witch*, 166–67.

39. "Witches and Fairies," in Rosen 68–71.

40. Quoted in Ginzburg, 88–89.

41. Purkiss, *Witch*, 181–87, 180, 207–5, 232–47.

42. Sharpe, in Barry, Hester, and Roberts, 250 and Purkiss, *Witch*, 153.

43. Briggs, in Barry, Hester, and Roberts, "Reasons," 59.

44. Rosen, 20; Purkiss, *Witch*, 92–94, 145–54; Briggs, *Neighbors*, 28–31; Sharpe, in Barry, Hester, and Roberts, 247–54; and Wendy Wall, *Imprint of Gender*, 161.

45. Thomas, 5.

46. Briggs, *Neighbors*, 143, 149–54. See also Rosen, 38–39.

47. Briggs, *Neighbors*, 140.

48. Thomas, 552–69; Briggs, *Witches and Neighbors*, 140–41 and Rosen, x–xi. In their studies of witchcraft accusations on East Anglia and Kent, Jim Sharpe, 242–43 and Mal-colm Gaskill, 258–59, respectively, note that charges of maleficium also tend to reflect guilt over turning away the needy. Both Sharpe and Gaskill are in Barry, Hester, and Rob-erts. For specific examples from contemporary pamphlets, see "Witches at St. Osyth," 113–14 and "Witches at Windsor," 86, both in Rosen.

49. Briggs, *Neighbors*, 140. See also Rosen, 48 and Lyndal Roper, "Witchcraft and Fantasy in Early Modern Germany," in Barry, Hester, and Roberts, 224–36.

50. Thomas, 568.

51. Briggs, *Neighbors*, 241–42.

52. Purkiss, *Witches*, 134–36. Also Rosen, 17–18, 30. Questions about and searches of suspected witches for their hidden teats are rife in pamphlets of witch trials. See especially "The Devil in the Nursery," in the *Witches of Warboys* (1589) in Rosen, 296–97.

53. Purkiss, *Witches*, 91–112.

54. Ibid., 110–112.

55. "Chelmsford Witches," in Rosen 96.

56. Briggs, *Neighbors*, 79–80.

57. Purkiss, *Witches*, 109–10.

58. "The Devil in the Nursery," in Rosen, 240–97.

59. Purkiss, *Witches*, 97, 96.

60. Briggs, *Witches and Neighbors*, 22, 260–65; Sharpe, in Barry, Hester, and Roberts, 240; Gaskill, in Barry, Hester, and Roberts, 258–63; Roper, 211–36; Woodbridge, *Scythe of Saturn*, 125–27; and Marianne Hester, "Patriarchal Reconstruction and Witch Hunt-ing," in Barry, Hester, and Roberts, 288–94.

61. Roper, 233.

62. Thomas, 568.

63. Purkiss, *Witch*, 96–112; Roper, 209–13; Rosen, 8–9; 43; Hester, in Barry, Hester, and Roberts, 300–1.

64. Hester, in Barry, Hester, and Roberts, 301, 302–3.

65. Ibid., 303–4.

66. Ibid., 306, 301.

67. Baring and Cashford, 528–29.

68. Patricia Parker, *Shakespeare from the Margins: Language, Culture, Context* (Chicago: University of Chicago Press, 1996), 263.

69. Lisa Jardine, *Harping*, 40. See also Charlotte Otten, 2–3; Ian Maclean, "The Notion of Woman in Medicine, Anatomy, and Physiology," *Feminism and Renaissance Studies: Oxford Readings in Feminism*, ed. Lorna Hutson, (Oxford: Oxford University Press, 1999), 128–33.

70. Maclean, 132.

71. Purkiss, *Witch*, 121.

72. Aristotle quoted in Jardine, *Harping*, 40.

73. For views on Paracelsus's importance, see Otten, 3; Parker, 340n23; Regina Buccola, *Fairies, Fractious Women, and the Old Faith: Fairy Lore in Early Modern Drama and Culture* (Selinsgrove, PA: Susquehanna University Press, 2006), 186; Gregory Zilboorg, introduction. *The Diseases That Deprive Man of His Reason, Such as St. Vitus' Dance, Falling Sickness, Melancholy, and Insanity, and Their Correct Treatment*, in *Paracelsus: Four Treatises*, ed. Henry E. Sigerist, (Baltimore, MD: Johns Hopkins University Press, 1996), 130–31. The quotation from Paracelsus is found in *The Diseases That Deprive Man of His Reason, Such as St. Vitus' Dance, Falling Sickness, Melancholy, and Insanity, and Their Correct Treatment*, trans. Gregory Zilboorg, in Sigerist, 181.

74. On diseases peculiar to women due to their physiology, see Maclean, 131–47, in Hutson, and Harvey, 53, 65–66, 106. On views of women's bodies as not being an inferior copy of the male body but a separate form, perfect in itself but not on par with the male body, see Maclean, 135. See also, 134–47.

75. Vives, 49.

76. Heinrich Kramer and James Sprenger, *Malleus Maleficarum: The Classic Study of Witchcraft*, trans. Montague Summers (London: Bracken Books, 1996), 44.

77. Ibid., 43–44.

78. Ibid.

79. Purkiss, 121–22.

80. Hester, in Barry, Hester, and Roberts, 293–94.

81. Gareth Roberts, 196–202; Hester, in Barry, Hester, and Roberts, 294–96, 302–6.

82. Hester, in Barry, Hester, and Roberts, 294.

83. Jacques Lacan, "The Function of Speech in Psychoanalysis," in *Écrits a Selection*, trans. by Bruce Fink (1966; New York: W. W. Norton, 2002), 65–66.

84. Kramer and Sprenger, 44.

85. "Witches of Windsor," in Rosen, 85. Also of relevance in Rosen are "Witches at Windsor" (85), "The Fairy Queen in Hampshire" (pamphlet on Judith Philips) (215–18), "Witches Abroad" (a 1601 pamphlet translating into English reports on German witches) (316–22), "The Swimming Test" (1618 London pamphlet) (338, 340), "The Northamptonshire Witches (346–48). See also Briggs, *Neighbors*, 250.

86. Quoted in Sharpe, in Barry, Hester, and Roberts, 246 and 248. For more on unnatural couplings see Thomas, 444–45.

87. "Chelmsford Witches," in Rosen, 74–75. For more on sex with Satan, see Thomas, 521, 569; Roper, in Barry, Hester, and Roberts, 211, 213, 215; Sharpe, in Barry, Hester, and Roberts, 246–48; Brigg, *Neighbors*, 223, 250, 390–91; and "Witches' Sabbath" (James's 1591 examination of witches), in Rosen, 190–203. Oddly enough, though the succubi would seem most clearly to represent unrestricted female sexuality threatening masculine power, this image of the witch does not appear as blatantly as might be expected. In discussing both Continental and British accusations, Robin Briggs, in *Neighbors*, 250, does not see succubi as pervasive. Nevertheless, the actions of the succubus do color anxieties about the debilitating effect of female sexual potency and aggressiveness on patriarchal control.

88. Hester, in Barry, Hester, and Roberts, 294.

89. Ibid.

90. Briggs, *Neighbors*, 250.

91. Roper, in Barry, Hester, and Roberts, 226.

92. Hester, in Barry, Hester, and Roberts, 304–5.

93. Quotation from Gareth Roberts, in Barry, Hester, and Roberts, 200. See also 186–96, 199–203.

94. Purkiss, *Witch*, 260.

95. Gareth Roberts, in Barry, Hester, and Roberts, 199, 201–3, 194–99.

96. Quotation from Purkiss, *Witch,* 260. See also, 259–61.

97. Ibid., 258–61.

98. Reginald Scot, *The Discoverie of Witchcraft* (1584; New York: Dover, 1972), 37.

99. Ginzburg, 28.

100. Briggs, *Neighbors*, 37–38.

101. F. Elizabeth Hart, "Cerimon's 'Rough' Music in Pericles, 3.2." *Shakespeare Quarterly* 51, no. 3 (2000): 317–31.

102. John Milton, *Comus: A Mask*, in *John Milton, Selected Poems*, ed. Stanley Appelbaum (New York: Dover Press, 1993), 1.1.60–76.

103. Jacopo Sannazaro, *Arcadia and the Piscatorial Eclogues*, ed. and trans. Ralph Nash (Detroit, MI: Wayne State University Press, 1966), 91.

104. Ralph Knevet, *Rhodon and Iris, a pastorall, as it was presented at the florists feast in Norwich, May 3. 1631.* London: Printed [by J. Beale] for Michael Sparke, at the blew Bible in Greene-Arbour, 1631. (Homer Babbidge Library. University of Connecticut: Early English Books Microfilm), 2.3, p. 36. Note, since this copy of the play provides only act and scene but not line numbers, I will designate act, scene, and page number. I will repeat this format for any other plays that do not provide line numbers in the rest of my text.

105. Ibid., 3.2, p. 43.

106. Joseph Swetnam, from *The Arraignment of Lewd, Idel, Froward, and Unconstant Women; or the Vanity of Them, Choose You Whether With a Commendation of Wise, Virtuous, and Honest Women*, in *The Whole Duty of a Woman: Female Writers in Seventeenth-Century England*, ed. Angeline Goreau (1615; Garden City, NY: Doubleday, 1985), 73. In "Material Girls, The Seventeenth-Century Woman Debate," Purkiss makes a convincing argument that whoever wrote this pamphlet under the name of Swetnam may have been more interested in proving his rhetorical skill or even making a tidy profit from his writing than in actually defaming women. Nevertheless, Swetnam's pamphlet bears citing because its tremendous popularity for over many years and the responses from a legitimate writer like Jane Speght suggests that not everyone was necessarily in on the joke. Rather, the author appears to have touched a nerve that resonated tensions underlying, as well as produced by, views of women's dangerous inadequacies that justified holding them under masculine control.

107. Kramer and Sprenger, 44, 42, 44.

108. Hester, in Barry, Hester, and Roberts, 294.

109. Lynda Boose, "Scolding Brides and Bridling Scolds: Taming the Woman's Unruly Member," *Shakespeare Quarterly* 42, no. 2 (1991): 184. Interestingly, Boose's profiles of many of those persecuted as scolds make even clearer the similarity of their crime in the minds of their accusers with witchcraft. Citing David Underdown, she begins, 211: "women who were poor, social outcasts, widows or otherwise lacking in the protection of a family, or newcomers to their communities, were the most common offenders [of scolding]. Such women were likely to vent their frustration against the nearest symbols of authority. And, we might add, such women were also the most likely to have the

community's frustration vented against them." This list of traits strongly resembles Keith Thomas's description of witchcraft accuseds as marginalized. For in both cases, the preferred victims are "women who were poor, social outcasts, widows or otherwise lacking in the protection of a family."

110. Hester, in Barry, Hester, and Roberts, 298.

111. "The Devil in the Nursery," in Rosen, 255. Agnes Samuel's riposte is even feistier: "she answered that she was 'born in a mill, begot in a kill, she must have her will', she could speak no softlier." Unfortunately, Samuel's feistiness was no match for the class and gender forces that crushed her will, forced a confession from her, and ultimately executed her, her husband, and her daughter, 255.

112. Vives, 97.

113. Ibid., 23, 27–29, 47–50, 97–100.

114. Iibid., 16.

115. Warner, 57–59, 73–78; James Grantham Turner, *One Flesh: Paradisal Marriage and Sexual Relations in the Age of Milton* (Oxford: Clarendon, 1999), 98–106, 116–117; Hilmer M. Pabel, "Reading Jerome in the Renaissance: Erasmus' Reception of the Adversus Jovinianum." *Renaissance Quarterly,* 55 no. 2 (2002): 477.

116. Turner, *Flesh*, 16, 26, 107.

117. Otten, 1.

118. Ibid., 2.

119. Vives, 23–24.

120. Ibid., 25–26.

121. Turner, *Flesh*, 26, 25–27; See also Warner, 178–79.

122. William Whately, *The Bride-Bush*, quoted in Jardine, *Harping*, 106.

123. William Gouge, *Of Domestical Duties.* 1622. Fire and Ice: Puritan Reformed Writings. http://www.mountzion.org/text/gouge-duties.rtf, Third Treatise section 65 part 2.

124. Richard Allestree, *The Ladies Calling.* 1673, in Goreau, 55.

125. This is not to say that there were no insistent and powerful voices disputing or at least tempering views of women's language as dangerous, if not downright Satanic. In the late fifteenth and early sixteenth centuries Agostino Strozzi and Bartolomeo Goggio set out "the defense of the natural capacity of [women] to perform virtuous actions," although they do not seek to shift the distribution of power within their social structures. See Pamela Benson, *The Invention of the Renaissance Woman* (University Park, PA: University of Pennsylvania Press, 1992), 45, 47. In fact, Goggio argues that many of the softer qualities cited as women's flaws actually make them morally superior to men, while Strozzi points out that these qualities have been deemed faults because men not women get to set the value on character traits. Ibid., 56–57, 53. James Turner writes that many Protestant sects valued women as man's equal if not superior—often through emphasizing either the creation story where Eve is formed equal with Adam from the elements or by interpreting her formation from his rib as showing she is not sprung directly from the lowly earth as he is. See *Flesh*, 107–113. John Calvin does assert the necessity of woman's subordination to her husband, the reverse "invert[ing] the order of nature" as set out by the paradigmatic Adam and Eve where the latter was "subject to her husband," quoted in Turner, *Flesh*, 121. However, when he adverts to Paul's injunction that women remain silent, Calvin adds the qualification that there Paul was criticizing a specific group of "prat[ing] and babbl[ing] women in "the Church of the Corinthians," and more importantly, there will be instances that "require the voice of a woman." From "A Commentary upon St. Paul's Epistles to the Corinthians," quoted in Turner, *Flesh*, 440. Juliet Dusinberre similarly notes that the Puritans' religious reforms undercut traditional perceptions of women as innately oversexed and irrational by redefining purity to emphasize marital chastity for both partners, stressing the importance of a companionate

marriage, and asserting that women's consciences and moral strength could be equal to men's (32–33, 75–76, 82–83, 87–95). Nevertheless, theirs was not the predominating voice, and as Timothy Reiss points out about mid to late seventeenth-century British and French thought, though women might be credited with reason, that reason was still frequently defined as designed for nurturing rather than leading men. See "Corneille and Cornelia: Reason, Violence, and the Cultural Status of the Feminine: Or, How Dominant Discourse Recuperated and Subverted the Advance of Women," in *Renaissance Drama as Cultural History: Essays from Renaissance Drama 1977–1987*, ed. Mary Beth Rose (Evanston, IL: Northwestern University Press, 1990), 195, 198–99. There will be deeper discussion of some of these writers and others on this topic in chapter 4.

126. Sannazaro, 91, 93.

127. Bruno Bettelheim, *The Uses of Enchantment: The Meaning and Importance of Fairy Tales* (New York: Vintage, 1989), 66–69; Sandra Gilbert and Susan Gubar, *The Madwoman in the Attic. The Woman Writer and the Nineteenth-Century Literary Imagination* (New Haven, CT: Yale University Press, 1984), 28–44; Roper, 224–25.

128. Purkiss, *Witch*, 202–6, 215–25, 187–89.

129. Sannazaro, 91.

130. Ovid, *Metamorphoses*, trans. Rolfe Humphries (Bloomington: Indiana University Press, 1955), 7. lines 199–208.

131. Sannazaro, 91.

132. Ibid.

133. "The Devil in the Nursery," in Rosen 255.

134. Sannazaro, 91.

135. Lacan, "Function of Speech," 64–69 and "Letter," 163; Terry Eagleton, *Literary Theory, an Introduction* (Minneapolis: University of Minnesota Press, 1983), 164–64, 173.

136. Sannazaro, 91.

137. Ibid.

138. Ibid. Quotation found on 102. See also 91–95.

139. Ibid., 94, 107–9.

140. Ibid., 94, 106–7.

141. Ibid., 92–93, 102–3.

142. Ibid., 102–6.

143. For primary written text descriptions of witches' sabbats see *The Witchcraft Sourcebook*, ed. Brian Levack (London: Routledge, 2004), 53–55, 84–86 and 105–8 and *Witchcraft in Europe 400–1700*, ed. Alan Charles Kors and Edward Peters (Philadelphia: University of Pennsylvania Press, 2001), 115–16 and 360–61. For visual renditions of traveling to the Sabbath or of the event itself, see Figure 6 in Levack and Figures 8, 15, 18, 20, and 23 in Kors and Peters. For scholarly commentary and descriptions of the witches' sabbat see Kors and Peters, 153; Levack, *Sourcebook*, 52; Rosen 17; and Bengt Ankarloo and Stuart Clark, *Witchcraft and Magic in Europe: The Period of the Witch Trials* (Philadelphia: University of Pennsylvania Press, 2002), 75 and 165.

144. Sannazaro, 42.

145. Ibid., 45.

146. Ibid., 39, 88, 95, 101–5, 115.

147. Ibid., 102.

148. Ibid., 88.

149. Ibid., 39, 88, 102–5.

150. Ibid., 42–43.

151. Ibid., 131.

152. Ibid., 132.

153. Ibid., 131.
154. Ibid., 132.
155. Ibid., 109.
156. Ibid., 135.
157. Ibid., 135–38.
158. Boccaccio, *Ameto*, 10, 23.
159. Sannazaro, 135.
160. Ibid., 135, 137–38.
161. Ibid., 134–35, 138.
162. Jorge de Montemayor, *The Diana*, trans. RoseAnna M. Mueller (Lewiston, NY: Edwin Mellen, 1988), 151–53.
163. Ibid., 156–58.
164. Ibid., 68–69.
165. Ibid., 69.
166. Ibid.
167. Ibid., 177.
168. Bakhtin, *Rabelais*, 240.
169. Montemayor, 179, 180, 197.
170. Mueller, 28.
171. Montemayor, 186.
172. Ibid., 172.
173. Ibid., 106.
174. Ibid., 145.
175. Ibid., 140.
176. Ibid., 150.
177. Ibid.
178. Ibid., 165–66.
179. Ibid., 166–67.
180. Ibid., 168–70.
181. Ibid., 171.
182. Ibid., 172.
183. Ibid., 104–5.
184. Ibid., 106–22
185. Ibid., 190–97, 211.
186. Ibid., 212.
187. Ibid., 146, 169, 172, 212.
188. Ibid., 168.

Chapter 3. Queens and Goddesses

1. Marian Wynne-Davies, introduction, *Love's Victory*, by Lady Mary Wroth, in *Renaissance Drama by Women: Texts and Documents*, ed. S. P. Cerasano and Marion Wynne-Davies (London: Routledge, 1996), 93; direct quotation on Lyly from Michael Pincombe, *The Plays of John Lyly* (Manchester, England: University of Manchester Press, 1996), xiv; David Bevington, introduction, *Endymion*, by John Lyly (Manchester, England: University of Manchester Press), 49–50; R. Warwick Bond, introduction, *Loves Metamorphosis*, by Jonh Lyly, in *The Complete Works of John Lyly*, vol. 3 (Oxford: Clarendon Press, 1967), 295–96; Alfred Harbage, *Shakespeare's Audience* (New York: Columbia University Press, 1941), 86–90. The dates on *Loves Metamorphosis* are a little uncertain. Editor R. Warwick Bond, 296, suggests that most likely "... the Paul's Boys

first produced the play before 1591, and that the Chapel Children after the removal of their inhibition revived it in 1598–1600." For the dates on *A Midsummer Night's Dream*, see Paster and Skiles's introduction to *A Midsummer Night's Dream* (New York: St. Martins, 1999), 4 and Wolfgang Clemen, introduction, *A Midsummer Night's Dream*, by William Shakespeare (New York: Signet, 1998), lxv.

2. The goddess form of the female guide even made an appearance in Ralph Knevet's lesser known pastoral *Rhodon and Iris*, written and performed "at the Florists' feast on May 3, 1631, and . . . printed the same year," according to W. W. Greg, 351. The guide as goddess was so pervasive that she was a component of the pastoral even for bourgeois craft guilds.

3. Louis Montrose, "Eliza, Queene of Shepherdes," and the Pastoral Power," *English Literary Renaissance*, no. 10 (1980): 165, 164.

4. Steven Greenblatt, *Renaissance Self-Fashioning: From More to Shakespeare* (Chicago: University of Chicago Press, 1980), 230.

5. Montrose, "Eliza," 165; Roy Strong, quoted in Montrose, "Eilza," 165. See also Frances Yates, *Astraea: The Imperial Theme in the Sixteenth Century* (London: Pimlico, 1975), 78; Carole Levin, *The Heart and Stomach of a King: Elizabeth I and the Politics of Sex and Power* (Philadelphia: University of Pennsylvania Press, 1994), 18, 26–31.

6. Yates, *Astraea*, 78. For the rose as a symbol of Mary's purity and perfection in Christianity in general, see Neumann (261, 262). On Danté's use of this symbol for Mary, see Warner (169) and Neumann (326). Other symbols, see Yates, *Astraea*, 78.

7. Elizabeth I, quoted in Greenblatt, 168; Katherine Duncan-Jones, *Sir Philip Sidney: Courtier Poet* (New Haven, CT: Yale University Press., 1991), 16.

8. Quotation from Yates, *Astraea*, 44. See also Yates, 40–44; Warner, 244–47; Pelikan, 26–27.

9. Yates, *Astraea*, 48–50.

10. Warner, 206–23; 285–90; 315–31; Pelikan 125–36.

11. Anne Somerset, *Elizabeth I* (New York: St. Martin's Press, 1991), 121. For more detail, see Somerset, 120–22 and Yates, *Astraea*, 40–41. Sir John Hayward provides a contemporary representative of this view in his 1603 *An Answer to the first part of a Certain Conference*, in *Macbeth*, by William Shakespeare, ed. William C. Carroll (Boston: Bedford/St. Martin, 1999), 203–4.

> If they [monarchs] abuse any part of their power, we do not excuse, we do not extenuate it; we do not exempt them from punishment: let them look unto it, let them assuredly expect, that God will dart His vengeance against them with a most stiff and dreadful arm. In the mean season, we must not oppose our selves, otherwise than by humble suits and prayers: acknowledging that these evils are always just for us to suffer, which are many times unjust for them to do. If we do otherwise, if we break into tumult and disorder, we resemble those Giants of whom the Poets write, who making offer to scale the skies, and to pull Jupiter out of his throne, were overwhelmed in a moment with the mountains which they had heaped together. . . . rebellion produceth more horrible effects than either the tyranny or insufficiency of any Prince.

12. Quoted in Yates, *Astraea*, 41.

13. For connections between Elizabeth and Astraea, see Yates, *Astraea*, 30–32. For the direct quotation from Yates, see 43. For more detailed discussion of the symbolism of the "C" in Foxe and Dee, see 48–49, 42–43.

14. Ibid., 67.

15. Quoted in Yates, *Astraea*, 67.

16. Yates, *Astraea*, 129–32; Kermode, 240 n. 9, 241 n. 11 and 14, 27; Harry Levin, 18–23, 32–54.

17. Harry Levin, 18–19; Kermode, 27.

18. Yates, *Astraea*, 38–59; Somerset, 354–55.

19. Yates, *Astraea*, 33–35.

20. Elizabeth I, "The Doubt of Future Foes," ed. Gilbert and Gubar, *Norton Anthology: Literature by Women*, 2nd ed. (New York: W. W. Norton, 1996.); Sir John Davies, quoted in Yates, *Astraea*, 68; Montrose, *The Purpose of Playing: Shakespeare and the Cultural Politics of the Elizabethan Stage* (Chicago: University of Chicago Press, 1996), 158; 1591 Sudely Entertainments quoted in Montrose, *Purpose*, 158.

21. William Shakespeare, *As You Like It*. The Arden Shakespeare, ed. Agnes Latham, (London: Arden, 2000). All subsequent quotations from this play will be from this edition.

22. Harry Levin, 99.

23. Peter Hermann, "Authorship and the Royal 'I': King James VI/I and the Politics of Monarch Verse," *Renaissance Quarterly* 54, no. 4.2 (2001): 1499.

24. Arthur Marotti, quoted in Hermann, 1499.

25. Greenblatt, 168.

26. Montrose, "Of Gentlemen and Shepherds: The Politics of Elizabethan Pastoral Form," *English Literary History* 50 (1983): 441.

27. Somerset, 383.

28. Levin, 99–107; Katherine Duncan-Jones, *Sir Philip Sidney: Courtier Poet* (New Haven, CT: Yale University Press), 17.

29. Hermann, 1495–1501.

30. Michael Leslie, "Something Nasty in the Wilderness: Entertaining Queen Elizabeth on her Progresses," in *Medieval and Renaissance Drama in England*, vol. 10, ed. John Pitcher (Madison, NJ: Farleigh Dickinson University Press, 1998), 49–58.

31. Hermann, 1501–5.

32. Greenblatt, 168, 185–92; Richard McCabe, notes to *The Shepheardes Calender*, 514–16 and notes to *Colin Clouts Come Home Againe*, 549–50, both in *Edmund Spenser: The Shorter Poems*, ed. Richard McCabe (London: Penguin, 1999).

33. Philip Sidney quoted in Duncan-Jones, 163; See also Duncan-Jones, 162–63.

34. Montrose, *Purpose*, 156.

35. Ibid., 153. All this being said, Phyllis Rackin cautions against assuming that the predominant reaction to being ruled by Elizabeth, a woman, was anxiety. Rackin cites the genuine excitement and commitment in celebrating Elizabeth's ascension, her leading the defeat of the Northern rebellion of 1569, and the reports of contemporary foreign visitors and rulers, as well as of native historians, as evidence of satisfaction with Elizabeth I as a monarch. See 30–33.

36. Benson, 232–35, 329, 245–50. See also Travitsky, *Paradise*, 92, and Carole Levin, *The Heart and Stomach of a King: Elizabeth I and the Politics of Sex and Power* (Philadelphia: University of Pennsylvania Press, 1994), 11–13.

37. Benson., 232–33, 239–40; 247–50.

38. Ibid., 232–34.

39. Montrose, *Purpose*, 153–54, 158–59 and Purkiss, *Witch*, 186.

40. Pincombe, 81–82 and Bevington 9, 27–28.

41. Pincombe, 81–82; Bevington, 9, 27–28. For specific detail on the Arundel, Oxford, Howard charges and countercharges, see Bevington, 28–33, and Pincombe, 84–85.

42. Bevington, 33–35, 144 n. 72, 170 n. 143–46.

43. Travitsky, *Paradise*, 187–92; Demers, 132–34; Jane Dunn, *Elizabeth & Mary: Cousins, Rivals, Queens* (New York: Vintage, 2005), 179, 287–303, 355.

44. Demers, 16–17.

45. Lyly, quoted in Pincombe, 85. See Bevington, 31, 34–35; Pincombe, 84–85.

46. John Lyly, *Endymion*, ed. David Bevington (Manchester, England: Manchester University Press, 1996).

47. Castiglione, *The Courtier*, trans. by Hoby, Book 4. 4–7.

48. Steven W. May quoted in Pincombe, 86. See also, Pincombe, 85–86; Bevington, 8–9; Somerset, 341.

49. Purkiss, "Material," 73–91.

50. Harvey, 63 writes: "The borrowing of a female voice allows Erasmus to say with impunity what he might otherwise not be able to articulate openly. Folly functions as an enabling source and also as a shield; she lends Erasmus a freedom of subject and style, while always providing the very excuse that produced the voice in the first place: 'But if you think my speech has been too pert or wordy,' he says at the end of *Folly* and then reminds us again in the letter to Dorp, 'keep in mind that you've been listening to Folly and to a woman'." For the entire discussion of Folly as a ventriloquized text, see Harvey, 58–66.

51. Quotation from Harvey, 101. See also, 77, 96–106, 110–15.

52. Ibid., 5.

53. Purkiss, *Witch*, 187–88.

54. Gouge, *Domestical Duties*, Third Treatise, "Particular Duties of Wives," Section 11; Philip Stubbes, from *A Christal Glasse for Christian Women*, in Trill, Chedgzoy, and Osborne (New York: Arnold, 1997), 58.

55. Renaissance writers and audiences were keenly aware of the type of the "triplex," "triform" Diana, or, looking at the same grouping of goddesses from another perspective, "the triple Hecate." See Pincombe, 97; Purkiss, *Witch*, 186; and Montrose, *Purpose*, 167. See also, Jean Addison Roberts, "Shades of Triple Hecate in Shakespeare," *Proceedings of the PMR Conference* 12, no. 123 (1987–88): 54–55. In pre-Christian tradition, a powerful goddess of nature was incarnated in three forms, the lunar/celestial (Selene/Cynthia), the earthly (Diana), and the infernal or demonic (Hecate). The goddess's three forms roughly corresponded with the cycles of human life: the celestial, pure and above the earth, was associated with the virgin; the earthly with the sexually active and fecund woman; and the infernal with death in the form of the devouring hag. In fact, the triple goddess informed human understanding of all the cycles controlling nature. This mythos "was ubiquitous not only in Roman mythological poetry and drama but in the Renaissance mythography that pervaded the learned culture of Elizabethan England." See Montrose, *Purpose*, 167. For an excellent book-length survey of the Triple Goddess's prevalence and evolution through pre-Bronze age and Bronze Age, classical, medieval, and Renaissance cultures see Robert Graves *The White Goddess* (New York: Noonday, 1948). For more on her influence in scholarly and popular writings and drama during the Renaissance, see Pincombe, 98–97; Hart, 321–24; Montrose, *Purpose*, 167–68; and Addison Roberts, "Shades," 53–59.

56. Bevington, 18; Pincombe, 105–6; Purkiss, *Witch*, 188.

57. For more on the burlesque of the relationship between Sir Tophas and Dipsas, see Montrose, *Purpose*, 171 and Pincombe, 102–5.

58. Bakhtin, *Rabelais*, 25–26..

59. Pincombe, 103–5; Purkiss, *Witch*, 187–89; Bevington, 22–23, 33–34. For those who see Dipsas as a coded figure for various anxieties about the rule of an aging Elizabeth, see Montrose, *Purpose*, 167–69, 176–78; Purkiss, *Witch*, 187; Pincombe, 104–5.

60. The displacing evil qualities onto a witch figure standing in opposition to the guide is a pattern that continues in other pastorals. In Knevet's *Rhodon and Iris, a pastorall, as it was presented at the florists feast in Norwich, May 3. 1631* (Early English Books Microfilm. Homer Babbidge Library, University of Connecticut, n.d.), Poneria is the Dipsas figure, an embodiment of independent and powerful woman as disrupter of natural, political, and

personal order that predominates this play. Making the implications about unconstrained female power obvious, her name even means "Wickedness." See Greg, 352. As Lyly does with Dipsas, Knevet links Poneria to the two witch icons of women's destructive powers, Circe and Medea. Poneria compares herself to Circe (3.2, p. 43) and exults Medea-like in the moon's evil, occult influences (1.1, pp. 1–2). Thus, Poneria embodies the worst conventional fears about the disruption of natural order that a woman uncontrolled by man would perpetrate. And, although the playwright mocks her power somewhat by referring to her aged ugliness (4.5. p. 57, 5.5. p. 65) and her "terrifying" plot of trying to wreck a feast more important than "Olympian games," the Florists annual festival (1.1, p. 12), she is still a more threatening figure than Dipsas. Power in her hands is frightening because she perversely uses it only to "satisfie" her henchman's "wrath" and her own "displeasure" (1.1, p. 2). In fact, uncontrolled, Poneria corrupts virtue. On *her* female form, virtue is only a "robe" or "veille" (2.1. p.27) that she dons to disguise a core of evil motivated to destroy social harmony. A similar figure also opposes the guide as wise woman in the form of Maudlin in Ben Jonson's *The Sad Shepherd*. Maudlin imprisons a nymph in a tree for the lusts of her dense son, breaks up the feast of Robin and Marian, and generally causes dissension among lovers.

61. Pincombe, 97; Bevington, 16–17, 19–20; Purkiss, 188. In ancient Roman mythology, Tellus was a fertility goddess of the earth, either linked to or merged with Ceres (Stanley Spaeth, 34–36, 44). Bevington, 18 points out: "Tellus's association with the earth and with chthonic powers is in evidence throughout the play," so that "she relies upon the substances of the earth, especially those with alchemical properties." But rather than utilize Tellus's associations with rebirth in Roman mythology, Lyly treats her connection with the earth in terms of fecundity that quickly decays, be it life, love, or the soul. See Bevington, 18. In that respect, she is the opposite of Cynthia, dragging down through the death of the physical body rather than uplifting through the immortality of the purified soul. See ibid., 40. For similar discussions of this last point, see Pincombe, 7–98.

62. Bevington, 16.

63. Singh, "Interventions," 38.

64. Hackett, 83.

65. Pincombe, 83–84. For a detailed discussion of the dream, see Bevington, 26–27 and Pincombe, 83–85.

66. Rackin, 27.

67. Mikhail Bakhtin, *Rabelais*, 101. See also 10–11, 34, 49, 73–74, 101–9, 123.

68. William Shakespeare, *A Midsummer Night's Dream*, ed. Gail Kern Paster and Howard Skiles (New York: St. Martin's, 1999). All future quotations from this play will be from this text.

69. John Lyly, *Loves Metamorphosis*, ed. R. Warwick Bond, in *The Complete Works of John Lyly*, vol. 3 (Oxford: Clarendon, 1967), 2.1. 38–45, 135–36.

70. Bakhtin, *Rabelais*, 19–27, 30.

71. John Knox, "The First Blast to Awake Women Degenerate," from *The First Blast of the Trumpet Against the Monstrous Regiment of Women*, 1558, in Trill, Chedgzoy, and Osborne, 33.

72. Paster and Skiles, "Making," in *A Midsummer Night's Dream*, 167. See also Mary Ellen Lamb, "Taken by Faireis: Fairy Practices and the Production of Popular Culture in *A Midsummer Night's Dream*, *Shakespeare Quarterly* 51, no.3 (2000): 307. Mary Ellen Lamb (305) sets the age of separation at "[b]etween the ages of eight and ten," while Paster and Skiles (167) set the date "at around the age of six," so the distinction is not that great. Phyllis Rankin and Beatrice Gottlieb follow Steven Mullaney in setting the "canonical age of reason" and move to "gender specific clothing," away from realm of women to the that of men, at about seven. Quotation from Mullaney, "Mourning and

Misogyny: The Final Progress of Elizabeth, 1600–07," *Shakespeare Quarterly* 45, no.2 (Summer 1994): 155. See Rankin, 29 and Gottlieb, *The Family in the Western World: From the Black Death to the Industrial Age* (New York, Oxford: Oxford UP, 1993); 154–57. See also Michael Shapiro, 40.

73. Thomas Elyot, from *The Book Named the Governor*, in Paster and Skiles, 171.

74. Paster and Skiles, "Making," 167–68; Lamb, "Fairies," 302–8; Montrose, *Purpose*, 135, 137–39.

75. Gouge, *Domestical Duties*, Third Treatise, Of Wife's Particular Duties, 3. "Of the Husband's Superiority Over the Wife."

76. Montrose, *Purpose*, 166–67, 168.

77. John Knox, "Blast," in Trill, Chedgzoy, and Osborne, 33.

78. Bakhtin, *Rabelais*, 78–79, 351–52.

79. John Chamberlain, quoted in Josephine Roberts, critical introduction, *The First Part of the Contess of Montgomery's Urania*, ed. Josephine Roberts (Binghamton, NY: Medieval and Renaissance Texts and Studies, 1995), xv.

80. Goreau, 67.

81. Chamberlain quoted in Josephine Roberts, critical introduction, *Urania*, xv; Roberts, xv.

82. Beilin, 110–11, 248–66; Goreau, 68; Dusinberre, 179–82.

83. Goreau, 68.

84. Swetnam, in Goreau, 70. See also, Swetnam, 69–73.

85. Natalie Zemon Davis, 156–85.

86. Bakhtin, *Rableais*, 27. See also 33–35.

87. Lady Mary Wroth, *Love's Victory*, in *Renaissance Drama by Women: Texts and Documents*, ed. S. P. Cerasano and Marion Wynne-Davies (London: Routledge, 1996). All future references to the play are from this text.

88. Lousie Schleiner, *Tudor and Stuart Women Writers* (Bloomington: Indiana University Press, 1994), 146.

89. Bakhtin, *Rabelais*, 123.

90. Cerasano and Wynne Davies, 94; Greg, 367–68.

91. Bakhtin, *Rabelais*, 123.

Chapter 4. The Pastoral Guide

1. For mages' views of the purification of their pursuits, see Paracelsus, *Seven Defensiones, the Reply to Certain Calumniations of His Enemies*, ed. Sigerist, trans. C. Lilian Temkin, 14–15; Keith Thomas, 223–37, 268–72; Temkin, 4–5; Ernst Cassirer, 40, 63–69, 169–70; and John Mebane, 9–13, 73–98. For the established churches' insistence that these beliefs were blasphemy leading to personal and social danger, see Mebane, 97–108, Thomas, 230, 255–58, 437–41, Miller, xxix–xxx.

2. Giovanni Pico della Mirandola, *On Being and the One*, in *Pico Della Mirandola: On the Dignity of Man*, trans. Charles Glen Wallis, Paul J. W. Miller, and Douglas Carmichael (Hackett, 1998), 61.

3. John Dee, quoted in Mebane, 85.

4. Mebane, 85.

5. The theories of these philosopher scientists were not entirely interchangeable. Mebane (85–86) points out that Dee thought power could be harnessed by certain mathematical principles, though he still insisted on the practitioner's devotion to God. Though both Ficino and Pico looked for correspondences of sound and movement amongst humanity, earth, and the heavens that could be accessed through study of arcane pagan, Hebrew, biblical, and patristic texts, Pico differs in seeing man as actually able to refine himself into partaking of divinity. See Mebane, 22–52; Thomas,

224–25; Paul Miller, introduction, *On the Dignity of Man*, by Pico della Mirandola, xiv–xvi; and Ernst Cassirer, 61, 69–70, 84–87, 115–20. Paracelsus comes closer to what is perceived as modern scientific thinking. Rather than studying magical texts, he looked for knowledge and power through the data he gained from experimentation—although he did believe in the influence spirits exerted over the natural world, the celestial bodies, and the mind. See Mebane, 91–92, Buccola, 186–87, and Cassirer, 110–11.

6. Kennedy, xxxi. Yonge's version of *Diana* will be cited from now on since his translation would have been available to more members of the English audience.

7. Mebane, 57.

8. Paracelsus, *A Book on Nymphs, Sylphs, Pygmies, and Salamanders and on Other Spirits*, in Sigerist, 224.

9. See the following for Paracelsus on the mage physician empowered by God to serve humanity by restoring the body/soul harmony of good health: "The Fifth Defence," in *Seven Defensiones*, 29–33 and *The Disease That Deprive Men of Reason*, 187, 193–94. On the interconnection between physical and spiritual health, see *The Diseases That Deprive Men of Reason*, 142, 146–62, 168–70.

10. Also in drama, the Queen of Corinth heals a disfigured shepherdess in *Argalus and Parthenia* (1639); the nymphs Claudia and Florida nurse the physically and psychologically injured back to health in *Love Crowns the End* (1640); the shepherdesses govern their pastoral enclave in Jane Cavendish and Elizabeth Brackley's *A Pastorall* (1645); and in a much smaller role Lidia, the nurse/cunning woman, provides healing in *Hymen's Triumph* (1613). In poetry and prose, see the various nymphs in Drayton's *The Muses Elizium* (1630) who critique corrupt court life, drive off the subversive Venus and Cupid, and praise pastoral virtue; the Countess of Cumberland who presides over the Great House idyll in Aemilia Lanyer's "Description of Cookeham" (1611); and Mary Fairfax, who sanctifies the landscape of the estate of Appleton House with her purity and learning in Marvell's "Upon Appleton House" (written c. 1652, published 1681).

11. Bartholomew Yonge, trans. *Diana of George of Montemayor.* 1598, ed. Judith M. Kennedy (London: Oxford University Press, 1968), 87–88.

12. Ibid., 83–103.

13. Ibid., 103.

14. Ibid., 77–78; 184–85, 189; 195–97; 237–42; 212–17, 228, 233–37.

15. Ibid.; Kennedy, l–liii.

16. Ibid., *Diana*, 191–97, 232; *As You Like It*, 2.4.40–58, 3.4.43–55, 3.5.1–80.

17. Ibid., 212, 237, 235.

18. Richard Mulcaster, quoted in Beilin, 11–14; Thomas More, quoted in Beilin, 22.

19. Henry [Henriech] Bullinger, from *The Christian State of Matrimony: Wherein Husbands and Wives May Learn to Keep Home Together with Love*, 1541, in Paster and Skiles, 255, 254.

20. Wayne, "Historical Differences," 156–59.

21. Travitsky, *Paradise*, 5. See also, Travitsky, *Paradise*, 5–11, 49–51; Krontiris, 5–8, 12–14; Demers, 28–37; and Trill, Chedgzoy, and Osborne, 3, 5; Beilin, 14–15, 273–75, 282–84; Jardine, *Harping*, 53–54; and Otten, 3–4.

22. Thomas More, quoted in Krontiris, 6.

23. W. P., quoted in Beilin, 15, Bruno, quoted ibid., 14.

24. Richard Brathwaite, from *The English Gentlewoman*, in Goreau (1631; repr., 1641), 39.

25. Beilin, 12–14, 16–27; Benson, 157–203; Beauchamp, Hageman, and Mikesell lxii–lxiv.

26. Jacques Du Bosc, from *The Complete Woman*, in *The English Renaissance: An Anthology of Sources and Documents*, ed Kate Aughterson, (London: Routledge, 1998), 472.

27. Bathsua Makin, from *An Essay to Revive the Antient Education of Gentlewomen*, in Trill, Chedgzoy, and Osborne, 240.

28. Benson, 183. See also 183–203.

29. Samuel Torshell, from *The Woman's Glorie; A Treatsie Asserting the Due Honour of That Sex and Directing Women Wherein That Honour Consists*, in Goreau, 42.

30. Rackin, 19–23, 34–37.

31. Krontiris, 9–10, 13; Demers, 16–20, 28, 34–36 ; Travitsky, *Paradise*, 5–7, 19, 90–91; Benson, 158–66.

32. Philip Stubbes, *Christal Glasse*, in Trill, Chedgzoy, and Osborne, 57–58.

33. Demers, 99, 101–3; Travitsky, *Paradise*, 168–73; Beilin, 32–47.

34. Quotation from Elizabeth I, "Speech to the House of Commons, January 28, 1563, in *Norton Anthology of English Literature*, vol. b, ed. Greenblatt et al. (New York: W. W. Norton, 2006), 692. See also, 691–92.

35. Quotation from Demers, 40. See also, Demers, 39–40, 46; Travitsky, *Paradise*, 103–4; and Krontiris, 118.

36. Travitsky, *Paradise*, 30 and 105, Demers, 41–42.

37. On Aemilia Lanyer, see Krontiris, 111–18; Demers, 149–53; Schleiner, 27–29. On Isabella Whitney, see Krontiris, 28–31, 33–44 and Demers, 130–31.

38. Margaret Tyler, from *The Mirrour of Princely Deedes and Knighthood*, in Travitsky, *Paradise*, 145–46. See also Demers, 89–91; Hackett, 60–61; Trill, Chedgzoy, and Osborne, 5–6, 38–39; and Krontiris, 44–48.

39. Demers, 69–73, 76–77; Travitsky, *Paradise*, 35–36.

40. Demers, 79. See also Demers, 79–83 and Krontiris 157n26.

41. Quotation in Demers, 74. See also 74–76 and 77–78.

42. Demers, 83–89; Travitsky, *Paradise*, 23, 143; Trill, Chedgzoy, and Osborne, 28.

43. On Lady Mary Herbert, see Krontiris, 64–69; Travitsky, *Paradise*, 21, 116; and Demers, 91–92; 195–96. On Elizabeth Carey, Lady Falkland, see Travitsky, *Paradise*, 209–11; Demers, 93–95, 208–9; and Krontiris, 78–80.

44. Sir John Davies, quoted in Krontiris, 78.

45. Krontiris, 69–78; Demers, 91–93, 196–202; Travitsky, *Paradise*, 21, 116.

46. Krontiris, 44–62; Demers, 90; Hackett, 70–75.

47. Trill, Chedgzoy, and Osborne, 7–11; Otten 270–88; Demers, 103–6; Travistsky, *Paradise*, 19, 34–36, 38.

48. Demers, 195–96; Krontiris, 64–68; Schleiner, 23–24, 52–55, 60–69.

49. Travitsky, *Paradise*, 6. See also, n17, chapter 1 above.

50. On Mary Ward, see Demers, 35. On Anna Maria Von Schurman, the quotation from Demers is on 36 and the quotation from *The Learned Maid; or Whether a Maid May Be a Scholar? A Logick Exercise* is in Trill, Chedgzoy, and Osborne, 209–11. For more on Von Schurman, see Trill, Chedgzoy, and Osborne, 209; Demers, 36–37; and Goreau, 163–64.

51. Katritzky, 139. See also Katritzky, 135 and Otten, 173–82.

52. Lady Margaret Hoby, from her *Diary*, in Trill, Chedgzoy, and Osborne, 73–75. Lady Elizabeth Clinton, from *The Countesse of Lincolnes Nurserie*, in Trill, Chedgzoy, and Osborne, 119–24. See also Trill, Chedgzoy, and Osborne, 119; Travitsky, *Paradise*, 57.

53. Otten, 174.

54. On Dorothy Osborne, see Katritzky, 139. Hannah Woolley, quoted in Goreau, 232 and from *The Gentlewoman's Companion*, in Trill, Chedgzoy, and Osborne, 263, also 262–64. On Mary Trye, see Otten 177–178. On women working as professionals

connected with montebanks and the legitimacy of their work, see Katritzky, 5, 9–10, 135, 163–65, 173.

55. For the quotation on Grace Mildmay, see Otten, 174–75. For more detail on women's preserving and sometimes publishing their medical work, see Otten 175, 178–79.

56. Clinton, in Trill, Chedgzoy, and Osborne, 120–24.

57. Gouge, *Domestical Duties*, Treatise 1, Section 11 Section 8; See also, Demers, 51–52; Krontiris, 4–5; and Benson 158–61, 165–66.

58. Otten, 3–6; Demers, 34; Tina Krontiris, 15–17, 78; Goreau 5–6; and Patricia Demers also address the fact that some women did receive educations when allowed to use the libraries in the houses they may have worked as upper-level servants.

59. Thomas Salter, from *A Mirrhor Mete for all Mothers, Matrons, and Maidens, Intituled the Mirrhor of Modestie*, in Trill, Chedgzoy, and Osborne, 46–47.

60. Trill, Chedgzoy, and Osborne, 4. Thomas More quoted in Krontiris, 6. See also Krontiris 5–7, 17, 123–26; Otten, 2–3; Goreau, 1–15; Trill, Chedgzoy, and Osborne, 2–7; and Travitsky, *Paradise*, 114. Although Wendy Wall raises the point that the "stigma of print" also haunted male aristocratic writers who sometimes saw exposure of their work to the masses rather than to just a select circle of other intelligentsia as degrading, the issue of women's degradation through the immorality of their public exposure renders the situation doubly troubling for them. See Wall, "To Be A Man in Print," 132–33, in Hurley and Goodblatt.

61. Demers, 25–26, 39–40, 63–64, 103, 176–94; Krontiris, 21–23, 32–34, 60–64, 105–8, 141–45; Trill, Chedgzoy, and Osborne, 14–15; Otten, 85–86, 283–84; Purkiss, "Material," 91–95.

62. On the acceptability of doing translations, see Travitsky, *Paradise*, 18; Krontiris, 17, 20–21; Demers, 64–65; Trill, Chedgzoy, and Osborne, 5. On the acceptability of women's religious writings, see Travitsky, *Paradise*, 9, 18, 89; Trill, Chedgzoy, and Osborne, 5–11; Otten 277–89; Demers, 99. On the acceptability of women writing on household management, childrearing, and other domestic topics, see Travitsky, *Paradise*, 9; Josephine Roberts, "Editing the Women Writers of Early Modern England," 23; and Demers, 176–80.

63. Harvey (82) and Katritzky (143) note that women healers in general and midwives in particular could be demonized as practitioners of witchcraft.

64. Otten, 173; Katritzky, 137, 150; Trill, Chedgzoy, and Osborne, 228.

65. Fischart, quoted in Katritzky, 137; Harvey, 83. See also Harvey, 78–93, Demers 60–61; and Katritzky, 136–37, 141.

66. Harvey, 83. For more detail, see Harvey, 84–88; Otten, 178–82. Jane Sharp, from *The Midwives Book*, in Otten, 197–205. Elizabeth Cellier, "To Dr.———An Answer to His Queries Concerning the College of Midwives," in Otten, 206–11.

67. Bakhtin, 240–43.

68. Ibid, 105–9, 115, 118–19.

Chapter 5. *The Faithful Shepherdess*

1. Felix E. Schelling and Matthew Black, introduction, *The Faithful Shepherdess* by John Fletcher, ed. Felix E. Schelling and Matthew W. Black, (Harper and Brothers, n.d.), 607. All subsequent references from *The Faithful Shepherdess* will be from this text.

2. John Fletcher, "To the Reader," from *The Faithful Shepherdess*, 609.

3. Schelling and Black, introduction, 607.

4. Richard Levin, 171, 172.

5. For the quotation, ibid., 171. For more detail, 171–72.

6. For the quotations, ibid., 169, 170, respectively. For more detail, 170–71.

7. There are other notable examples. When Clorin attempts to cure Amoret's wound with holy herbs, the guide gives credit for their efficacy to Pan not herself: "May Pan bless this my cure" (5.2.45). Even when she uses her wit, rather than magic, to cure Thenot, Clorin gives Pan precedence for inspiring and directing her: "Tis done: great Pan, I give thee thanks for it!" (4.5.77) and "Blest be ye powers that gave such / quick redress, / And for my labors sent so good success!" (92–93).

8. Robert Codrington, *The Second Part of Youth's Behaviour; or Decency in Conversation Amongst Women*, in Goreau, 40.

9. Stubbes, in Trill, Chedzoy, and Osborne, 57–58.

10. To emphasize further the importance of sexual purity, Fletcher in the vein of Sannazaro's *Arcadia*, almost completely re-characterizes Pan as a god intent on preserving human chastity to forestall the violence and disorder of uncontrolled lust. Pan does not appear in the drama, but all references to him in the text either play down his traditionally randy reputation or describe policies he has enforced in the pastoral world to curb humans' lust and encourage their responsibility: protecting nymphs from rapists, punishing those violators of chastity (3.1.170–91), and purging both shepherds and shepherdesses of passions leading them astray (1.2.1–42). He teaches them to protect their flocks from literal wolves and themselves from the metaphorical wolves of irresponsibility, vanity, and lust. This Pan "keep'st [them] chaste and free / As the young spring" (1.2.38–39).

11. Elsewhere in the play, Clorin abjures other material indulgences as well, purging herself like the mages described by Pico in *On the Dignity of Man* and Paracelsus in his *Defensiones* of the grossness of feeding on flesh: "My meat shall be what these wild woods / afford, / Berries and chestnuts, plantains, on whose / cheeks / The sun sits smiling, and the lofty fruit / Pulled from the fair head of the straight-grown / pine" (1.1.41–44). Thus, purified of gluttony and empowered by self-abnegation in her choice only to help others (28–40), Clorin has followed Pico's direction and "spurn[ed] earthly things," "struggl[ed] toward the heavenly," and "put in last place whatever is of the world" to make herself worthy to "touch the ladder of the Lord." For quotations from Pico della Mirandola, see *On the Dignity of Man*, in *Pico Della Mirandola: On the Dignity of Man*, trans. Charles Glen Wallis, Paul J. W. Miller, and Douglas Carmichael (Hackett, 1998), 7 and 9, respectively. See also in *Dignity*, 5–13, 17; For Paracelsus, see *Seven Defensiones*, in Sigerist, 28–33.

12. Vives, 176. See also Roper 220–21, 226; Hester, in Barry, Hester, and Roberts, 304–05; Vives, 170, 177, Jardine, *Harping*, 128–30.

13. Richard Allestree, *The Ladies Calling*, in Goreau, 43.

14. Vives, 30.

15. Bakhtin, *Rabelais*, 240.

16. Swetnam, in Goreau, 70.

17. Bakhtin, *Rabelais*, 49.

18. Ibid, 11.

19. "Witches of Chelmsford," in Rosen, 74–75.

20. Ibid., 73–74.

21. Pico della Mirandola, *Dignity*, in Wallis, Miller, and Carmichael 29; Paracelsus, *Diseases*, in Sigerist, 193.

22. Montemayor, trans. Yonge, 79, 132.

23. Paracelsus, *Diseases*, in Sigersit, 196.

24. Bathsua Pell Makin, from *The Antient Education of Gentlewomen*, in Trill, Chedgzoy, and Osborne, 240.

25. Pico della Mirandola, *Heptaplus*, trans. Charles Glen Wallis, Paul J. W. Miller, and Douglas Carmichael, in *On the Dignity of Man*, 124–25; Paracelsus, *Diseases*, in Sigersit, 146, 148–61, 168–70.

26. Woolley, in Trill, Chedgzoy, and Osborne, 263.

27. Lynn Veach Sadler, "Eye Imagery in *All's Well That Ends Well*: A Neglected Problem," *Literatur in Wissenschafft und Unterricht* 10 (1977): 166.

28. Paracelsus, *Diseases*, in Sigerist, 178, 176.

29. Ibid., 179.

30. In *The Faerie Queene*, satyrs "euery one as commune good . . . handeled" a willing fugitive wife in festive, sexual orgy (3.10 stanzas 36–42, 43–52). In *Diana*, satyrs assaulted and attempted to carry off Felicia's nymphs for rejecting their advances. See Montemayor, trans. Yonge, 76–77. The visual arts also emphasized the rampant sexuality of the satyr, depicting lustful fairies and male fertility deities such as Puck in the image of satyrs: horned heads, goat-furred legs and hooved feet, and exaggerated genitalia. Furthermore, see the wood cut illustration from *The Roxburghe Ballads*. See Figure 2, 297 and the frontispiece from *Robin Goodfellowe, His Mad Prankes, and Merry Jests . . .* in Mary Ellen Lamb's article "Taken by the Fairies: Fairy Practices and the Production of Popular Culture in *A Midsummer Night's Dream*." See also Figure 3, 299. See also the illustration from the title page of *Robin Goodfellowe, His Mad Prankes and Merry Jests* in Paster and Skiles's edition of *A Midsummer Night's Dream*. See Figure 20, 318.

31. Gouge, *Domestical Duties*, First Treatise, section 10.

32. Ibid., section 15.

33. For a sampling of contemporary instruction on this belief, see Gouge's *Domestical Duties*, Third Treatise, "Of Wife's Particular Duties," section 5, part 2 and section 8; Vives, 98–101, 105–20, 140–41, 160; Tilney's *The Flower of Friendship*, in Aughterson, 445; Dod and Cleaver's *A Godly Form Of Household Government*, in Aughterson, 449–50; Brathwaite's *The English Gentlewoman*, in Goreau, 36; and Savile's *The Lady's New-Year's-Gift*, in Goreau, 45–46.

34. *Esther Sowernam, Ester Hath Hanged Haman: or, An Answere to a Lewd Pamphlet, Entituled The Arraignment of Lewd, Idel, Froward, and Unconstant Women; or the Vanity of Them, Choose You Whether With a Commendation of Wise, Virtuous, and Honest Women. London* 1617. Chapter 2, p. 9. Renascence Editions. 1998. https://scholarsbank.uoregon.edu/xmlui/bitstream/handle/1794/817/ester.pdf?sequence=3.

35. Ibid., chapter 7, 21.

36. Ibid., 22.

37. Walter Montagu, *The Shepherds' Paradise* (The Malone Society Reprints, Oxford: Oxford University Press, 1997), vol. 159. All references are from this source.

Chapter 6. Subversive Wise Woman

1. *As You Like It*'s staging for public and royal performances was discussed in Chapter 4. The stage history of *All's Well* is sketchier. Although there seems to be no doubt that this play was performed, there does not appear to be direct reference to those performances. There is some conjecture that *All's Well* may be the actual identity of a play by Shakespeare that Francis Meres recorded in his diary in 1598 as *Love's Labor's Won*, but that theory has fallen into disfavor. Whatever the case, *All's Well* was sufficiently regarded to be included in the First Folio of 1623. See Sylvan Barnet, introduction in *All's Well That Ends Well* (1965; repr., New York: Signet Classic, 1988), xxiii, xxvii–vii and Anne Barton, introduction, *All's Well That Ends Well*, in The Riverside Shakespeare (Boston: Houghton Mifflin, 1974), 502.

2. Hackett, 30–32

3. Bakhtin, *Rabelais*, 11, 81–82, 88–89.

4. Anthony Dawson, *Indirections: Shakespeare and the Art of Illusion* (Toronto: University of Toronto Press, 1978), 87.

5. Philip Sidney, "Disprayse of Courtly Life," in Kermode, 141–43.

6. William Shakespeare, *All's Well That Ends Well, The Riverside Shakespeare*, ed. G. Blakemore Evans (Boston: Houghton Mifflin, 1974). All future references from the play will be from this text.

7. Anthony Brennan, "Helena Versus Time's Winged Chariot in *All's Well That Ends Well, The Midwest Quarterly,* no. 4 (1980): 398.

8. That the King is not merely missing "the good old days" but speaking the truth is born out by the behavior of the young lords of the kingdom. One of the Lords admits that the young "gentry" "are sick / For breathing and exploit" (1.2.16–17). The actions of the representative courtiers of the play in this court and in Florence prove this point. Most obviously, Parolles has proven himself "a snipt-taffata fellow" (4.5.1–2) rather than a true courtly ideal. However, even some of the more reputable of the young Lords also fall short of being "copy" (1.2.46) to the earlier Count Rosillion. None of the Lords lets his obligation to honor the King's directives get in the way of a desire for adventure. They join Parolles to applaud and encourage Bertram to run away to the wars and reject his duty to the King's service by ignoring the order to attend his sovereign at court (2.1.1–47). The Lords may criticize Bertram behind his back (4.3.14–34) but never directly advise him against his abandoning Helena or trying to "pervert . . ." Diana, instead encouraging him at one point (4.3.14–15). They may claim they want to expose Parolles to enlighten Bertram about his bad companion (3.6.1–33), but their main goals seem to be entertainment (34) and delight in gossiping about and humiliating one another (4.3.329). This use of wit to trick Parolles into exposing his true nature shows the "contempt" and "bitterness" that the original Count of Rosillion eschewed.

9. David McCandless, "Helena's Bed-trick: Gender and Performance in *All's Well That Ends Well. Shakespeare Quarterly* 45, no. 4 (Winter 1994): 449.

10. McCandless, 449–51 and Regina Buccola, 185–86, 187–90, 193–96. Jay Halio describes Helena's words as "peculiar incantatory verse" in *"All's Well That Ends Well," Shakespeare Quarterly* 15, no. 1 (1964): 37. G. Wilson Knight, quoted in Leggatt (26), even more specifically alludes to Helena's language magically giving her control over the King: "Observe the gnomic, formal, incantatory quality of the rhymes, functioning, as in Helena's first recognition of her own magical powers . . . as the language of inspiration: she seems to be mesmerizing the King." Alexander Leggatt believes that by enchanting the King to trust her powers to heal, Helena directs the power of the King's mind and spirit to heal his body, the returned health of which reciprocally strengthens the spirit with joy: "What will cure him is not so much the power of the medicine as his own willingness to believe in it. . . . The King's cure is not so much a medical achievement as an act of faith and grace," *"All's Well That Ends Well* The Testing of Romance," *Modern Language Quarterly* 32 (1971): 27. Anthony Brennan, 397–99 and Ian Donaldson, *"All's Well That Ends Well*: Shakespeare's Play of Endings," *Essays in Criticism* 27 (1971): 42, have also noted Helena's empowerment by God, but neither has delved deeply into how the depiction of this relationship reflects concerns about female challenges to patriarchal hegemony. For more observations on the folk motifs in *All's Well,* including their sexual and reproductive connotations, see Leggatt, 25–28, 31, 39–40; Anthony Brennan, 394–98, 408–41; Jay Halio, 34–35, 42; and Lisa Jardine, "Cultural Confusion and Shakespeare's Learned Heroines: 'These are Old Paradoxes' ". *Shakespeare Quarterly* 38, no. 1 (Spring 1987): 7, 12.

11. Mikhail Bakhtin, "Discourse in the Novel," in *The Dialogic Imagination*, trans. Caryl Emerson and Michael Holquist, ed. Michael Holquist (Austin: University of Texas Press, 1981), 262–63. See also 271–79.

12. Jardine, "Cultural Confusion," 18.

13. Pico della Mirandola, *Dignity*, 26–31; Paracelsus, *Defensiones*, 20–29.

14. Robert Codrington, from *The Second Part of Youth's Behavior; or, Decency in Conversation Amongst Women* (London, 1664), in Goreau, 40.

15. Many contemporary preachers, philosophers, and educators denied women the justification of rebelling against a husband's abuse for one or a combination of the following reasons: she had no right to subvert the natural hierarchy, she deserved punishment for other sins for which she was never caught, she might teach morality by her stoic example, or she would earn a place in heaven for her virtuous endurance of suffering on earth. For examples, see Gouge, from *Third Treatise*, section 5, part 2 and section 8; Vives, 99, 101, 105; and Francis Meres, *God's Arithmetic*, in Aughterson, 447–48.

16. McCandless, 459. See also 462, 467.

17. Ibid., 451.

18. Jardine, "Cultural Confusion," 18.

19. McCandless, 453–55; Jardine, "Cultural Confusion," 10–12.

20. Leggatt, 31–32.

21. McCandless, 467.

22. For the quotation, see Bakhtin, *Rabelais*, 12. See also 11–12.

23. Ibid., 242–43.

24. Ibid., 123.

25. Ibid.

26. McCandless, 449. See also 459–67.

27. Bakhtin, *Rabelais*, 239–44.

28. Ibid., 242.

29. Garber, *Coming of Age in Shakespeare* (London: Routledge, 1981), 178–79.

30. Ibid., 175–78.

31. Ibid, 178.

32. Bakhtin, *Rabelais*, 123.

33. Veach Sadler, 166.

34. Bahktin, Rabelais, 122–23.

35. Gouge, *Domestical Duties*, Treatise 1, section 10.

36. Castiglione, *The Courtier*, trans. by Hob, Book 4, p. 7.

37 Donaldson, 53 and Gerald Gross, "The Conclusion to *All's Well That Ends Well*," *Studies in English Literature 1500–1900* 23 no. 2, 270–71. See also Halio, 42–43.

38. Paracelsus, *Diseases*, 146, 152–56, 160–65, 176–78.

39. Ibid., 178–81.

40. *Homily on the State of Matrimony*, 2:18.1.91–94.

41. Halio, 34–37; McCandless, 465.

42. Donaldson, 48.

Chapter 7. "Curing by Counsel"

1. Barber, 30. C. L. Barber explores how *As You Like It*, among other comedies, transfers to the stage Elizabethan holiday's release from social pressures by moving characters from the court or workaday world into a green world where harsh authoritarian figures are subjected to ritual abuse much in the mode of Bakhtin's carnival. Victimizers may be reformed or disempowered while victims gain temporary agency and can work off their frustrations in the green world. See 6–15, 24–35, 139–62, 224–39.

2. Bakhtin, *Rabelais*, 303–4.

3. Thomas Lodge, *Rosalynd*, ed. Brian Nellist and Simône Batin (Staffordshire, England: Keele University Press, 1995), 125–26.

4. Bakhtin, *Rabelais*, 122–23.

5. Bakhtin, *Dialogic Imagination*, 263.

6. This depiction of Hymen first presented itself to me at a production of *As You Like It* at the Long Wharf Theatre in New Haven, Connecticut in the 1990s.

7. Peter B. Erickson, Excerpt from *Sexual Politics and Social Structure in* As You Like It, in *As You Like It* by William Shakespeare, ed. Albert Gilman (New York: Signet, 1998), 180–81.

8. Bakhtin, *Rabelais*, 12.

9. Vives, 23–24.

10. Bakhtin, *Rabelais*, 123.

11. Quotation from Carol Thomas Neely, *Broken Nuptials in Shakespeare's Plays* (Urbana: University of Illinois Press, 1993), 200; Marjorie Garber, quoted in Clare Kinney, "Feigning Female Faining: Spenser, Lodge, Shakespeare, and Rosalind," *Modern Philology* 95 (February 1998): 308.

12. For Paracelsus on treatment by drugs, natural elements, or involving God, see *Diseases*, 18, 179, 181–82, 188, 167, 17 and on matching treatment to behavior, see *Diseases*, 167, 182–83, 174.

13. Ibid., 195, 167, 178.

14. Quotation from ibid., 193. See also *Seven Defensiones*, 16 and 29–33.

15. Ibid., 188, 195.

16. Clara Claiborne Park, "As We Like It: How a Girl Can Be Smart and Still Popular," in *The Woman's Part: Feminist Criticism of Shakespeare*, ed. Carolyn Ruth Swift Lenz, Gayle Greene, and Carol Thomas Neely (Urbana: University of Illinois Press, 1983), 107, dismisses Orlando as "a nice young man" who is far from being in Rosalind's league when it comes to wit. However, this assessment of Orlando is not accurate. With his generous care for Adam as a "doe" to her "fawn" in the forest of Arden (2.7.95–135, 167–73); sharp wit countering his brother's chidings and Jaques' cynicism, as well as in ultimately holding his own with Rosalind; and the tremendous forgiveness he shows in saving his sleeping brother from the lion and snake, Orlando proves himself a young man whose strong potential develops into intelligence, compassion, and strength.

17. Brathwaite, in Goreau, 38.

18. Bakhtin, *Rabelais*, 122–23. See also 101–3, 109, 119–20.

19. Ibid., 121.

20. Allestree, in Goreau, 55.

21. Barber, 228–29.

22. Ibid., 230.

23. Lodge, 69.

24. Ibid., 71–72.

25. Barber, 7, 6–10, 37, 236.

26. Vives, 16.

27. Peter Erickson, 181–82 also does not see Rosalind's badinage here as a sample of woman as inherently lustful and unfaithful. However, his interpretation differs in that he proposes Rosalind's humor about infidelity affirms the role of woman as subservient: "we are reassured that, once married, she will in fact be faithful. Her humor has the effect of exorcising and renouncing her potential weapon . . . Her previous wit notwithstanding, for Rosalind the scene is less a demonstration of power than an exercise in vulnerability. She is once again consigned to anxious waiting for her tardy man." The underlying problem with this argument is its basis on a faulty syllogism that fidelity equals subservience and independence equals adultery. Erickson's argument ignores the middle ground that one could

be faithful without being completely subservient or "vulnerable." Though this syllogism might have been a truism for many in the early modern era, to ignore any expression of such a middle ground in early-modern thought flies in the face of the writings of Montemayor/ Yonge, Lanyer, Wroth, the many defenders against Swetnam, Torshell, not to mention other of Shakespeare's plays. It certainly flies in the face of the philosophy of not being limited by extremist perspectives, which powerfully informs *As You Like It* itself.

28. Erickson (187) would have it that Orlando develops a deeper understanding and compassion enabling him to forgive his brother because Duke Senior had been kind to him when he stumbled upon the royal exiles when the young man was in need of food. There are three problems with this theory. First, Orlando shows a great deal of emotional callowness when he cannot even make his first appointment with Ganymede/Rosalind on time and in his initial spouting of courtly love clichés directly after his interchange with the Duke. Second, the deepening of his emotional insight finally starts to show in his beginning to laugh at faux romantic visions with Rosalind in their meeting. Third, his momentous forgiveness comes almost immediately after his interchange with Ganymede/Rosalind not the Duke.

29. Alpers, 128–30.

30. Bakhtin, *Rabelais*, 95, 142, 297. See also 242–43.

31. Ibid., 70.

32. Park, in Swift Lenz, Greene, and Neely, 107–8; Erickson, 181–88, 191.

33. Quotation from Neely, 56; Alpers, 134; Erickson, 182–83, 187–88, 190; Montrose, quoted in Alpers, 134.

34. Park, in Swift Lenz, Greene, and Neely, 107–8; Erickson, 181–88, 191.

35. See especially Peter Erickson, 192. For a useful run down of critics making this claim, see Michael Shapiro, *Gender in Play on the Shakespearean Stage: Boy Heroines and Female Pages* (Ann Arbor: University of Michigan Press, 1996), 132–33.

36. Park, in Swift Lenz, Greene, and Neely, 107–8.

37. Alpers, 134, Park, 108, 107.

38. Rackin, 19–21.

39. Erickson, 182.

40. Kinney, 314.

41. Shapiro, 133; Dusinberre, quoted in Shapiro, 133. The passage Shapiro cites in Dusinberre reads differently in her revised edition of 1996, the same year as the publication of Shapiro's book. The quotation from the revised edition asserts Rosalind's freedom or "escape" from the repression of patriarchal control even more strongly than Shapiro's quotation: "Shakespeare himself wanted his heroine to escape [masculine containment by marriage] and brought her back as insouciant and elusive as ever to tell the audience she was still Jove's own page." Natalie Zemon Davis also agrees with Dusinberre (165). Clare Kinney provides an informative summary of conflicting views up to 1998 (307–8, 314). Also see Rackin, 75–77 and Hackett, 146–47.

42. Shapiro, 132.

43. Erickson, 192.

44. Kinney, 314.

45. Richard Levin, 168.

46. Kinney, 314–15.

Chapter 8. "And Afterwards"

1. Leo Marx, *The Machine in the Garden: Technology and the Pastoral Ideal in America* (Oxford: Oxford University Press, 1964), 36–55.

2. Patterson, 135, 138, 142–46.

3. Patterson, 147–48; Dusinberre, 48–49.

4. Quotation from Greg, 420. See also 379–421.

5. For *The Faithful Shepherdess*'s stage history, cf. Chapter 5, n1. The quotation on *As You Like It*'s stage history is from Jean Marsden, *The Reimagined Text: Shakespeare, Adaptation, & Eighteenth-Century Literary Theory* (Lexington: University of Kentucky Press: 1995), 30. See also, Marsden, 30, 163 n. 31; Agnes Latham, introduction in *As You Like It*, lxxxvi; and Edith Holding, "'As You Like It' Adapted: Charles Johnson's 'Love in the Forest,'" *Shakespeare Survey* 32 (1979): 37.

6. Marsden, 80.

7. Pope, 3–7; Johnson, 335, 336.

8. Carol Barash, *English Women's Poetry, 1649–1714: Politics, Community, and Linguistic Authority*, (Oxford: Oxford, University Press, 1999), 40.

9. Ibid., 41.

10. Dusinberre, 269.

11. Barash, 41.

12. Dusinberre, 270.

13. Ibid., 269.

14. Barash, 41; Dusinberre, 269.

15. Holding, 37, 46–47; Latham, lxxxvi ii; Charles Wingate, *Shakespeare's Heroines on the Stage* (New York: Thomas Y. Crowell & Co., 1895), 132–33.

16. Marsden, 30.

17. Barash, 33–37, 106, 138, 190–91.

18. Ibid., 190.

19. Jane Stevenson and Peter Davidson, "Jane Barker," in *Early Modern Women Poets, An Anthology* (Oxford: Oxford University Press, 2001), 426.

20. Quotation from Barash, 27–29. See also Barash, 27–29, 61–63.

21. Ibid., 30.

22. Ezell, 37–46; Otten, 353–61.

23. Quotation from Barash, 32. See also Barash, 65–67, 77.

24. Ibid., 175–76, 185–88, 201–2.

25. Stevenson and Davidson, "Margaret Cavendish," 302, in *Early Modern Women Poets*, in "Katherine Philips," 326; Barash, 32–35.

26. Quotation from Barash, 149–50. See also Barash 149–76; Stevenson and Davidson, "Aphra Behn," 365; "Jane Barker," 426; "Anne Killigrew," 453, in *Early Modern Women Poets*.

27. Quotation from Barash, 35; See also Stevenson and Davidson, "Margaret Cavendish," 302; "Katherine Philips," 326; "Aphra Behn," 365, in *Early Modern Women Poets*.

28. Barash, 283, 174.

29. Ibid., 6–7.

30. Ibid., 70–74.

31. Quotation from Barash, 279. See also 169–74, 279–82.

32. Ibid., 129.

33. Ibid., quotation 191. See also 179–82, 188–91.

34. Ibid., 189. See also Goreau, 225.

Bibliography

Alighieri, Danté. *The Paradiso.* Translated by John Ciardi. New York: Signet Mentor Books, 1970.

Allestree, Richard. Excerpt from *The Ladies Calling.* 1673. In Goreau, 43–44, 55.

Alpers, Paul. *What Is Pastoral?* Chicago: University of Chicago Press, 1997.

Anderson, Micheal H., on "The Nicene Creed, The." 381 C.E. Ancient Creeds. 12/11/2008. http://www.creeds.net/ancient/nicene.htm.

Ankarloo, Bengt, and Stuart Clark. *Witchcraft and Magic in Europe: The Period of the Witch Trials.* Philadelphia: University of Pennsylvania Press, 2002.

Apuleius. *The Golden Ass.* Translated by Jack Lindsey. Bloomington, IN: Midland, 1965.

Aughterson, Kate, ed. *The English Renaissance: An Anthology of Sources and Documents.* London: Routledge, 1998.

Bakhtin, Mikhail. "Discourse in the Novel." In *The Dialogic Imagination: Four Essays.* 1975. Translated by Caryl Emerson and Michael Holquist. Edited by Michael Holquist. Austin: University of Texas Press, 1981.

———. *Rabelais and His World.* 1965. Translated by Helene Iswolsky. Bloomington: Indiana University of Press, 1984.

Barash, Carol. *English Women's Poetry, 1649–1714: Politics, Community, and Linguistic Authority.* Oxford: Oxford, University Press, 1999.

Barber, C. L. *Shakespeare's Festive Comedy: A Study of Dramatic Form and Its Relation to Social Convention.* Princeton, NJ: Princeton University Press, 1959.

Baring, Anne, and Jules Cashford. *The Myth of the Goddess: Evolution of an Image.* London: Penguin/Arkana, 1991.

Barnet, Sylvan. Introduction to *All's Well That Ends Well,* by William Shakespeare. 1965. Reprint, New York: Signet, 1988.

Barroll, Leeds. *Anna of Denmark, Queen of England: A Cultural Biography.* Philadelphia: University of Pennsylvania Press, 2001.

Barry, Jonathan, Marianne Hester, and Gareth Roberts, eds. *Witchcraft in Early Modern Europe.* Cambridge, England: Cambridge University Press, 1998.

Barton, Anne. Introduction to *All's Well That Ends Well.* In *The Riverside Shakespeare,* edited by G. Blakemore Evans. Boston: Houghton Mifflin, 1974.

Beauchamp, Virginia Walcott, Elizabeth H. Hageman, and Margaret Mikesell, eds. Introduction. *The Instruction of a Christen Woman,* by Juan Luis Vives. Urbana: University of Illinois Press, 2002.

Becon, Thomas. Excerpt from *A New Catechism.* 1564. In Paster and Skiles, *A Midsummer Night's Dream: Texts and Contexts,* 251–53.

Beilin, Elaine. *Redeeming Eve, Women Writers of the English Renaissance.* Princeton, NJ: Princeton University Press, 1987.

Benson, Pamela. *The Invention of the Renaissance Woman.* University Park, PA: University of Pennsylvania Press, 1992.

Bettelheim, Bruno. *The Uses of Enchantment: The Meaning and Importance of Fairy Tales*. New York: Vintage, 1989.

Bevington, David. Introduction to *Endymion*, by John Lyly, 1–72. Manchester, England: University of Manchester Press, 1996.

Bleeth, Kenneth. "Joseph's Doubting of Mary and the Conclusion of *Merchant's Tale*." *Chaucer Review* 21 (1986): 58–66.

Boccaccio, Giovanni. *L'Ameto*. 1341. Translated by Judith Serafini-Sauli. Garland Library of Medieval Literature. New York: Garland, 1985.

———. *Diana's Hunt*. 1333/4. Edited and translated by Anthony K. Cassell and Victoria Kirkham. Philadelphia: University of Pennsylvania Press, 1991.

Bond, R. Warwick, ed. *The Complete Works of John Lyly*. 3 vols 1902. Oxford: Clarendon Press, 1967.

———. Introduction to *Endimion*. In *The Complete Works of John Lyly*. Vol. 3.

———. Introduction to *Loves Metamorphosis*. In *The Complete Works of John Lyly*. Vol. 3.

Bonnefoy, Yves. *Greek and Egyptian Mythologies*. Translated by Wendy Doniger. Chicago: University of Chicago Press, 1991.

———. *Roman and European Mythologies*. Translated by Wendy Doniger. Chicago: University of Chicago Press, 1992.

Boose, Lynda. "Scolding Brides and Bridling Scolds: Taming the Woman's Unruly Member." *Shakespeare Quarterly* 42, no.2 (Summer 1991): 179–213.

Brant, Clara, and Diane Purkiss, eds. *Women, Texts, and Histories: 1575–1760*. Cambridge: Routledge, 1992.

Brathwaite, Richard. Excerpt from *The English Gentleman*. 1630. In Aughterson, 465–66.

———. Excerpt from *The English Gentlewoman*. 1631 (repr. 1641). In Goreau, 36–39.

Brennan, Anthony. "Helena versus Time's Winged Chariot in *All's Well That Ends Well*. *The Midwest Quarterly* 21, no. 4 (Summer 1980): 391–411.

Briggs, Robin. "'Many Reasons Why': Witchcraft and the Problem of Multiple Explanation." In Barry, Hester, and Roberts, 49–63.

———. *Witches and Neighbors: The Social and Cultural Context of European Witchcraft*. London: Penguin, 1996.

Bullinger, Henry (Heinrich). Excerpt from *The Christian State of Matrimony: Wherein Husbands and Wives May Learn to Keep House Together with Love*. 1541. In Paster and Skiles, *A Midsummer Night's Dream: Texts and Contexts*, 253–56.

Calabresi, Bianca F. C. "'you sow, Ile read': Letters and Literacies in Early Modern Samplers." In Hackel and Kelly, 79–104.

Campbell, Joseph. *Occidental Mythology*. 1964. Reprint, New York: Penguin, 1988.

Cassell, Anthony K., and Victoria Kirkham. Introduction to *Diana's Hunt*, by Giovanni Boccaccio.

Cassirer, Ernst. *The Individual and the Cosmos in Renaissance Philosophy*. Translated by Mario Domandi. Philadelphia: University of Pennsylvania Press, 1983.

Castiglione, Baldessar. *The Courtier*. 1528. Translated by Thomas Hoby. 1561. Renascence Editions. 1992–2009. University of Oregon. Edited by Risa Stephanie Bear. University of Oregon. https://scholarsbank.uoregon.edu. pdf.

Cellier, Elizabeth. Excerpt from "To Dr.———An Answer to His Queries Concerning the College of Midwives." In Otten, 206–11.

Cerasano, S. P., and Marion Wynne-Davies. Introduction to *Love's Victory.* In *Renaissance Drama by Women, Texts and Documents,* edited by Cerasano and Davies. London: Routledge, 1996.

Chambers, Edmund K. Introduction to *English Pastorals.* London: Blackie and Son, nd.

"Chelmsford Witches Again." In Rosen, 92–99.

Clemen, Wolfgang. Introduction to *A Midsummer's Night's Dream,* by William Shakespeare. New York: Signet, 1998.

Cobb, Noel. *Propero's Island: The Secret Alchemy at the Heart of the Tempest.* London: Coventure, 1984.

Codrington, Robert. *The Second Part of Youth's Behaviour; or, Decency in Conversation Amongst Women.* 1664. In Goreau, 40–41.

Cody, Richard. *The Landscape of the Mind: Pastoralism and the Platonic Theory in Tasso's Aminta and Shakespeare's Early Comedies.* Oxford: Clarendon, 1969.

Cooper, Helen. *Pastoral: Medieval into Renaissance.* Ipswich, England: D. S. Brewer, 1977.

Cooper, Kate. *The Virgin and the Bride: Idealized Womanhood in Late Antiquity.* Cambridge, MA: Harvard University Press, 1996.

Daniel, Samuel. *Hymen's Triumph.* 1615. The Malone Society Reprints, 1994. Oxford: Oxford University Press, 1994.

———. *The Queen's Arcadia.* 1606. Vol. 4 of *The Complete Works in Verse and Prose of Samuel Daniel.* 1885. Reprint. Edited by Alexander B. Grosart. New York: Russell and Russell, 1963.

Dawson, Anthony. *Indirections: Shakespeare and the Art of Illusion.* Toronto: University of Toronto Press, 1978.

"Death of a Queen." In Rosen, 310–12.

"Death of an Earl." In Rosen, 305–309.

D'Elia, Anthony F. "Marriage, Sexual Pleasure, and Learned Brides in the Wedding Orations of Fifteenth-Century Italy." *Renaissance Quarterly* 55, no.2 (2002): 379–433.

Demers, Patricia. *Women's Writings in English: Early Modern England.* Toronto: University of Toronto Press, 2005.

"Devil in the Nursery, The." In Rosen, 227–97.

Dod and Cleaver. Excerpt from *A Godly Form of Household Government.* 1598. In Aughterson, 448–50.

Donaldson, Ian. *"All's Well That Ends Well*: Shakespeare's Play of Endings." *Essays in Criticism* 27 (1971): 34–55.

Doody, Margaret Anne. *The True Story of the Novel.* New Brusnwick, NJ: Rutgers University Press, 1996.

Drayton, Michael. *The Muses Elizium.* Vol. 1 of *The Poems of Michael Drayton.* Edited by John Buxton. Cambridge, MA: Harvard University Press, 1967, 203–305.

Du Bosc, Jacques, trans., *The Complete Woman.* 1639. In Aughterson, 469–72.

Duncan-Jones, Katherine. *Sir Philip Sidney: Courtier Poet.* New Haven, CT: Yale University Press, 1991.

Dunn, Jane. *Elizabeth & Mary: Cousins, Rivals, Queens.* New York: Vintage, 2005.

Dusinberre, Juliet. *Shakespeare and the Nature of Women.* 2nd ed. London: Macmillan, 1996.

Eagleton, Terry. *Literary Theory, an Introduction.* Minneapolis: University of Minnesota Press, 1983.

262 BIBLIOGRAPHY

Eaton, Sara. "Defacing the Feminine in Renaissance Tragedy." In Wayne, 181–98.

Eliot, George. "The Natural History of German Life." In *Selected Essays, Poems and Other Writings*. London: Penguin, 1990, 107–39.

Elizabeth I. "The Doubt of Future Foes." 1589. In Gilbert and Gubar. *Norton Anthology: Literature by Women*, 28.

———. "Speech to the House of Commons, January 28, 1563." In *Norton Anthology of English Literature*. Vol. b. Edited by Steven Greenblatt, et al. 691–92. New York: W. W. Norton, 2006.

Ellis, Sarah Stickney. *The Women of England*. 1839. Victorian Women Writers Project. Edited by Perry Willett. February 5, 1999. Indiana University. http://www.indiana.edu/~letrs/vwwp/ellis/womeneng.html#p9.

Elmer, Peter. "'Saints and Sorcerers': Quakerism, Demonology and the Decline of Witchcraft in Seventeenth-Century England." In Barry, Hester, and Roberts, 145–79.

Elyot, Sir Thomas. Excerpt from *The Book Named the Governor*. In Paster and Skiles, 168–74.

Empson, William. *Some Versions of Pastoral*. New York: New Directions, 1974.

English Pastoral Poetry: From Beginnings to Marvell. Edited by Frank Kermode. London: Harrap, 1952.

Erickson, Peter B. Excerpt from *Sexual Politics and Social Structure in* As You Like It. In *As You Like It* by William Shakespeare. Edited by Albert Gilman, 180–95. New York: Signet, 1998.

Ezell, Margaret J. M. *Writing Women's Literary History*. Baltimore: Johns Hopkins University Press, 1996.

"The Fairy Queen in Hampshire." In Rosen, 213–18.

Ficino, Marsilio. *Platonic Theory* (Books 1–8). 2 vols. Translated by Michael J. B. Allen with John Warden. Cambridge, MA: Harvard University Press, 2001.

Fletcher, John. *The Faithful Shepherdess*. 1609. In *Typical Elizabethan Plays*. Edited by Felix E. Schelling and Matthew W. Black. Harper and Bros., n.d.

———. "To the Reader." In Schelling and Black, 609.

Freccero, John. Introduction to *The Paradiso* by Dante Alighieri.

Frye, Northrop. *Anatomy of Criticism*. Princeton, NJ: Princeton University Press, 1973.

Garber, Marjorie. *Coming of Age in Shakespeare*. New York: Routledge, 1981.

Gaskill, Malcolm. "Witchcraft in Early Modern Kent: Stereotypes and the Background to Accusations." In Barry, Hester, and Roberts, 257–87.

Giamatti. A. Bartlett. *The Earthly Paradise and the Renaissance Poets*. New York: W.W. Norton, 1989.

———. *Play of the Double Senses: Spenser's Faerie Queene*. New York: W. W. Norton, 1975.

Gibson, Jonathan, and Gillian Wright. "Editing Perdita: Texts, Theories, Readers. In Hurley and Goodblatt, 155–73.

Gilbert, Sandra M. and Susan Gubar. *The Madwoman in the Attic. The Woman Writer and the Nineteenth-Century Literary Imagination*. New Haven, CT: Yale University Press, 1984.

———. eds. *The Norton Anthology: Literature by Women*. 2nd ed. New York: W. W. Norton, 1996.

Gilgamesh, The Epic of. Translated by N. K. Sanders. 1960. Reprint, Harmondsworth, Middlesex: Penguin, 1985.

Ginzburg, Carlo. *The Night Battles: Witchcraft and Agrarian Cults in the Sixteenth and Seventeenth Centuries.* Translated by Henry John and Anne Tedeschi. Baltimore: Johns Hopkins University Press, 1992.

Goreau, Angeline, ed. *The Whole Duty of a Woman: Female Writers in Seventeenth-Century England.* Garden City, NY: Doubleday, 1985.

Gottlieb, Beatrice. *The Family in the Western World: From the Black Death to the Industrial Age.* New York: Oxford University Press, 1993.

Gouge, William. *Of Domestical Duties.* 1622. Fire and Ice: Puritan Reformed Writings. n.d. http://www.mountzion.org/text/gouge-duties.rtf

Grant, Michael. *Myths of the Greeks and the Romans.* New York: Meridian, 1995.

Graves, Robert. *The White Goddess.* New York: Noonday, 1948.

Greenblatt, Stephen. *Renaissance Self-Fashioning: From More to Shakespeare.* Chicago: University of Chicago Press, 1980.

Greene, Thomas. "Labyrinth Dances in the French and English Renaissance. *Renaissance Quarterly* 54, no. 4.2 (Winter 2001): 1403–1466.

Gregg, W. W. *Pastoral Poetry and Pastoral Drama: A Literary Inquiry, with Special Reference to the Pre-Restoration Stage in England.* London: A. H. Bullens, 1906.

Griffin, Patsy. "Lady Egerton Herbert As Sabrina in *A Maske Presented at Ludlow Castle.*" *English Language Notes* (June 1999): 27–44.

Gross, Gerald J. "The Conclusion to *All's Well That Ends Well,*" *Studies in English Literature 1500–1900* 23, no. 2, (1983): 257–76

Guarini, Battista. *Il Pastor Fido.* 1590. Translated by Thomas Sheridan. 1647. Edited by Robert Hogan and Edward Nickerson. Newark: University of Delaware Press, 1989.

Hackel, Heidi Brayman, and Catherine E. Kelly, eds. *Reading Women: Literacy, Authorship, and Culture in the Atlantic World, 1500–1800.* Philadelphia: University of Pennsylvanian Press, 2008.

Hackett, Helen. *Women and Romance Fiction in the English Renaissance.* Cambridge, England: Cambridge University Press, 2000.

Hageman, Elizabeth H., and Sara Jayne Steen. From the Editors. *Shakespeare Quarterly* 47, no. 4 (1996): v–viii.

Halio, Jay. "*All's Well That Ends Well.*" *Shakespeare Quarterly* 15, no. 1 (1964): 33–43.

Harbage, Alfred. *Shakespeare's Audience.* New York: Columbia University Press, 1941.

Hart, F. Elizabeth. "Cerimon's 'Rough' Music in Pericles, 3.2." *Shakespeare Quarterly* 51, no. 3 (2000): 313–31.

Harvey, Elizabeth. *Ventriloquized Voices: Feminist Theory and English Renaissance Texts.* London: Routlege, 1992.

Hayward, John. Excerpt from "An Answer to the First Part of a Certain Conference." 1599. In *Macbeth,* by William Shakespeare. Edited by William C. Carroll. 203–4. Boston: Bedford/St. Martin, 1999.

Herford, C. H., Percy Simpson, and Evelyn Simpson, eds. Introduction to *The Sad Shepherd* in Vol. 7 of *Ben Jonson.* Oxford: Oxford University Press, 1941.

Hermann, Peter. "Authorship and the Royal 'I': King James VI/I and the Politics of Monarch Verse." *Renaissance Quarterly* 54, no. 4.2 (Winter 2001): 1495–1530.

Hesiod. *Theogony.* In *Theogony, Works and Days, Shield.* Translated by Apostolos N. Athanassakis. Baltimore: Johns Hopkins University Press, 1983.

Hester, Marianne. "Patriarchal Reconstruction and Witch Hunting." In Barry, Hester, and Roberts, 288–306.

Hoffman, Nancy Jo. *Spenser's Pastorals:* The Shepheardes Calender *and "Colin Clout."* Baltimore: Johns Hopkins University Press, 1977.

Holding, Edith, "'As You Like It' Adapted: Charles Johnson's 'Love in the Forest.'" *Shakespeare Survey* 32 (1979): 37–48.

Holy Bible (King James). Longmeadow, 1984.

Holy Bible (Catholic Family Edition: Confraternity of Christian Doctrine and Challoner/ Douay Text). New York: John J. Crawly, 1953.

Homily on the State of Matrimony. Ed. Ian Lancashire. 1997. Short-Title Catalogue 13675. Renaissance Electronic Texts 1.2. University of Toronto UTEL Home Page. http:// www.library.utoronto.ca/utel/ret/homilies/bk2hom18.html.

Horne, R. H. "William and Mary Howitt." Vol. 1 of *A New Spirit of the Age.* 1844. 179– 98. New York: Garland, 1986.

Howard, Jean. "Script and/versus Playhouses: Ideological Public Production and the Renaissance Stage." In Wayne, 221–36.

Hurley, Ann Hollinshead, and Chanita Goodblatt, eds. *Women Editing/Editing Women: Early Modern Women Writers and the New Textualism.* Newcastle on Tyne: Cambridge Scholars Publishing, 2009.

Hutson, Lorna, ed., *Feminism and Renaissance Studies: Oxford Readings in Feminism.* Oxford: Oxford University Press, 1999.

Jardine, Lisa. "Cultural Confusion and Shakespeare's Learned Heroines: 'These are old paradoxes.'" *Shakespeare Quarterly* 38, no. 1 (Spring 1987): 1–18.

———. *Still Harping on Daughters: Women and Drama in the Age of Shakespeare.* 2nd ed. New York: Columbia University Press, 1989.

Johnson, Samuel. Excerpt from *Milton.* In *Rasselas, Poems, and Selected Prose.* 3rd ed. Edited by Bertrand H. Bronson. 331–52. New York: Rinehart, 1971.

Jonson, Ben. *Ben Jonson: The Sad Shepherd, The Fall of Mortimer, Masques and Entertainments.* In. Herford and Percy Simpson and Evelyn Simpson, 3–49.

———. *The Sad Shepherd.* In *Ben Jonson's Masques and Plays,* edited by Robert M. Adams, 275–310. New York: W. W. Norton, 1979.

Kathman, David. "Grocers, Goldsmiths, and Drapers: Freemen and Apprentices in the Elizabethan Theater." *Shakespeare Quarterly* 55, no. 1 (2004): 1–49.

Katritzky, M. A. *Women, Medicine, and Theatre, 1500–1750: Literary Mountebanks and Performing Quacks.* Aldershot, Hampshire: Ashgate, 2007.

Kelly, Joan Gondal. "Did Women Have a Renaissance?" In Hutson, 21–47.

Kelsall, Malcolm. *The Great Good Place: The Country House and English Literature.* New York: Columbia University Press, 1993.

Kennedy, Judith M. Introduction to *Diana of George of Montemayor,* by Bartholomew Yonge. London: Oxford University Press.

Kermode, Frank, ed. *English Pastoral Poetry: From Beginnings to Marvell.* Toronto: George G. Harrap, 1952.

———. Introduction to *English Pastoral Poetry: From Beginnings to Marvell.*

Kinney, Clare. "Feigning Female Faining: Spenser, Lodge, Shakespeare, and Rosalind." *Modern Philology* 95 (February 1998): 291–315.

Knevet, Ralph. *Rhodon and Iris, a pastorall, as it was presented at the florists feast in Norwich, May 3. 1631.* London : Printed [by J. Beale] for Michael Sparke, at the Blew Bible in Greene-Arbour, 1631. Early English Books Microfilm. Homer Babbidge Library. University of Connecticut, n.d.

Knox, John. Excerpt from *The First Blast of the Trumpet against the Monstrous Regiment of Women.* 1558. In Trill, Chedgzoy, and Osborne, 32–38.

Kors, Alan Charles, and Edward Peters, eds. *Witchcraft in Europe 400–1700.* Philadelphia: University of Pennsylvania Press, 2001.

Kramer, Heinrich, and James Sprenger. *Malleus Maleficarum: The Classic Study of Witchcraft.* Translated by Montague Summers. 1928. London: Bracken Books, 1996.

Krontiris, Tina. *Oppositional Voices: Women as Writers and Translators of Literature in the English Renaissance.* London: Routledge, 1992.

Lacan, Jacques. "The Function of Speech in Psychoanalysis" In *Écrits a Selection,* trans. Bruce Fink. New York: W. W. Norton, 2002, 31–106.

———. "The Instance of the Letter in the Unconscious," In *Écrits a Selection,* 138–68.

Excerpt from *Ladies Dictionary, The.* 1694. In Goreau, 50–51, 56–59.

"Lancashire Witches." In Rosen, 357–368.

Lamb, Mary Ellen. "Inventing the Early Modern Woman Reader through the World of Goods: Lyly's Gentlewoman Reader and Katherine Stubbes." In Hackel and Kelly, 15–35.

———. "Taken by Fairies: Fairy Practices and the Production of Popular Culture in *A Misummer Night's Dream. Shakespeare Quarterly* 51, no.3 (2000): 277–312.

Lanyer, Amelia. "The Description of Cooke-ham." In *Early Modern Women Poets, An Anthology.* Edited by Jane Stevenson and Peter Davidson. 104–08. Oxford: Oxford University Press, 2001.

———. "Eve's Apology in Defense of Women" in *Salve Desu Rex Judaeorum.* In *The Norton Anthology of English Literature.* 8th ed. Vol. B. Edited by George M. Logan, Stephen Greenblatt, Barbara K. Lwealski, and Katherine Eisamen Maus. New York: W. W. Norton, 2006.

Laroque, François. *Shakespeare's Festive World: Elizabethan Seasonal Entertainment and the Professional Stage.* Translated by Janet Lloyd. Cambridge, England: Cambridge University Press, 1993.

Latham, Agnes. Introduction to *As You Like It,* by William Shakespeare. London: Arden, 2000.

Leeming, David, and Jake Page. *Goddess: Myths of the Female Divine.* New York: Oxford University Press, 1994.

———. *The World of Mythology: An Anthology.* New York: Oxford University Press, 1990.

Leggatt, Alexander. "*All's Well That Ends Well* The Testing of Romance." *Modern Language Quarterly* 32, no. 1 (1971): 21–57.

Leslie, Michael. "Something Nasty in the Wilderness: Entertaining Queen Elizabeth on her Progresses" In *Medieval and Renaissance Drama in England* Vol. 10 Edited by John Pitcher (Madison, NJ: Farleigh Dickinson University Press, 1998), 47–72.

Levaek, Brian. "State-building and Witch Hunting in Early Modern Europe." In Berry, Hester, and Briggs, 96–115.

———. *The Witchcraft Sourcebook.* Edited by Brian Levack. New York: Routledge, 2004.

Leventen, Carol. "Patrimony and Patriarchy in *The Merchant of Venice.*" In Wayne, 59–79.

Levin, Carole. *The Heart and Stomach of a King: Elizabeth I and the Politics of Sex and Power.* Philadelphia: University of Pennsylvania Press, 1994.

Levin, Harry. *The Myth of the Golden Age in the Renaissance.* New York: Oxford University Press. 1969.

Levin, Richard, "Women in the Renaissance Theatre Audience." *Shakespeare Quarterly* 40, no. 2 (1989): 165–174.

Lodge, Thomas. *Rosalynd*. Edited by Brian Nellist and Simône Batin. Staffordshire: Keele University Press, 1995.

Longus. *Daphnis and Chloe*. Translated by Paul Turner. London: Penguin, 1989.

Lyly, John. *Endymion*. 1588. Edited by David Bevington. Manchester, England: Manchester University Press, 1996.

———. *Gallathea*. 1592. Edited by R. Warwick Bond. In Vol. 3 of *The Complete Works of John Lyly* (1902). 419–72. Oxford: Clarendon, 1967.

———. *Loves Metamorphosis*. 1601. In R. Warwick Bond. 290–332.

Maclean, Ian. "The Notion of Woman in Medicine, Anatomy, and Physiology." In Hutson, 127–55.

Maidment, James, and W. H. Logan. Introductory Notice to *Love Crowns the End*. In *The Dramatic Works of John Tatham*, 3–6. Edinburgh: William Paterson, 1879.

———. Introductory Notice. to *The Dramatic Works of John Tatham*, x–xii.

Makin, Bathsua. Excerpt from *An Essay to Revive the Antient Education of Gentlewomen in Religion, Manners, Arts and Tongues*. 1673. In Trill, Chedgzoy, and Osborne, 239–45.

Marsden, Jean. *The Reimagined Text: Shakespeare, Adaptation, & Eighteenth-Century Literary Theory*. Lexington: University of Kentucky Press: 1995.

Marx, Leo. *The Machine in the Garden: Technology and the Pastoral Ideal in America*. Oxford: Oxford University Press, 1964.

Marvell, Andrew. "Upon Appleton House." In *The Complete Poems*. Edited by Elizabeth Story Donno. 75–99. London: Penguin, 1985.

McCabe, Richard, ed. *Edmund Spenser: The Shorter Poems*. London: Penguin, 1999.

———. Notes to *Colin Clouts Come Home Againe*, 649–61.

———. Notes to *The Shepheardes Calender*, 514–74.

McCandless, David. "Helena's Bed-trick: Gender and Performance in *All's Well That Ends Well*. *Shakespeare Quarterly* 45, no 4 (Winter 1994): 449–68.

Meador, Betty De Shong. *Inanna, Lady of Largest Heart. Poems of the Sumerian High Priestess Enheduanna*. Austin: University of Texas Press, 2000.

Mebane, John S. *Renaissance Magic & the Return of the Golden Age: The Occult Tradition and Marlowe, Johnson, and Shakespeare*. Lincoln: University of Nebraska Press, 1989.

Meres, Francis. Excerpt from *God's Arithmetic*. 1597. In Aughterson, 447–48.

Miller, Paul J. W. Introduction to *On the Dignity of Man*, by Pico della Mirandola.

Milton, John. *Comus: A Mask*. 1637. In *John Milton, Selected Poems*. ed. Stanley Appelbaum. 28–51 New York: Dover, 1993.

———. *Comus*. In *The Complete Poetical Works*. Ed. W. V. M. 40–53. New York: Leon Amiel, n.d.

Montagu, Walter. *The Shepherds' Paradise*. 1658. Vol. 159 of The Malone Society Reprints. Oxford: Oxford University Press, 1997.

Montemayor, Jorge de. *The Diana*. 1559. Translated by RoseAnna M. Mueller. Lewiston, NY: Edwin Mellen, 1988.

Montrose, Louis. "'Eliza, Queene of Shepherdes,' and the Pastoral Power." *English Literary Renaissance*. 10 (1980): 153–82.

———. "Of Gentlemen and Shepherds: The Politics of Elizabethan Pastoral Form." *English Literary History* 50 (1983): 415–59.

————. *The Purpose of Playing: Shakespeare and the Cultural Politics of the Elizabethan Stage*. Chicago: University of Chicago Press, 1996.

"More Executions at Chelmsford." In Rosen, 182–189.

Motz, Lotte. *The Faces of the Goddess*. Oxford: Oxford University Press, 1997.

Mueller, RoseAnna M. Introduction to *The Diana*, by Jose de Montemayor. New York: Edwin Mellen.

Mullaney, Steven. "Mourning and Misogyny: The Final Progress of Elizabeth, 1600–7." *Shakespeare Quarterly* 45, no. 2 (Summer 1994): 139–162.

Nash, Ralph. Introduction to *Arcadia and Piscatorial Eclogues,* by Jacopo Sannazaro. Detroit, MI: Wayne State University Press.

Neely, Carol Thomas. *Broken Nuptials in Shakespeare's Plays*. Urbana: University Illinois Press, 1993.

Neumann, Erich. *The Great Mother*. 1963. Translated by Ralph Manheim. Princeton, NJ: Princeton University Press, 1991.

"Nicene Creed, The." 381 C.E. [Ancient Creeds. Editor Michael Anderson, 12/11/2008], http://www.creeds.net/ancient/nicene.

"Northamptonshire Witches." In Rosen, 344–356.

Norwood, Vera. *Made from This Earth: American Women and Nature*. Chapel Hill: University of North Carolina Press, 1993.

Odell, George C. D. *Shakespeare from Betterton to Irving*. 2 vols. 1920. New York: Dover, 1966.

Otten, Charlotte F. *English Women's Voices, 1540–1700*. Miami: Florida International University Press, 1991.

Ovid. *Metamorphoses*. Translated by Rolfe Humphries. Bloomington: Indiana University Press, 1955.

Pabel, Hilmer M. "Reading Jerome in the Renaissance: Erasmus' Reception of the Adversus Jovinianum." *Renaissance Quarterly* 55, no. 2 (2002): 470–97.

Paracelsus. *A Book on Nymphs, Sylphs, Pygmies, and Salamanders, and on the Other Spirits*. 1566. Translated and edited by Henry E. Sigerist. In Sigerist, 213–253.

————. *The Diseases That Deprive Man of His Reason, Such as St. Vitus' Dance, Falling Sickness, Melancholy, and Insanity, and Their Correct Treatment*. 1567. Translated and edited by Gregory Zilboorg. In Sigerist, 127–212.

————. *Seven Defensiones, the Reply to Certain Calumniations of His Enemies*. 1564. Translated and edited by C. Lilian Temkin. In Sigerist, 1–41.

Park, Clara Claiborne. "As We Like It: How a Girl Can Be Smart and Still Popular." In *The Woman's Part: Feminist Criticism of Shakespeare*, edited by Carolyn Ruth Swift Lenz, Gayle Greene, and Carol Thomas Neely. 100–16. Urbana: University Illinois Press, 1983.

Parker, Patricia. *Shakespeare from the Margins: Language, Culture, Context*. Chicago: University of Chicago Press, 1996.

Paster, Gail Kern, and Howard Skiles. Introduction to *A Midsummer Night's Dream: Texts and Contexts*, by William Shakespeare. In Pastor and Skiles.

————. "The Making of Men." In Paster and Skiles, 149–191.

————. eds. *A Midsummer Night's Dream: Texts and Contexts*, by William Shakespeare. New York: St. Martin's, 1999.

Pater, Walter. "The Child in the House." 1878. In *Victorian Literature 1830–1900*, edited by Dorothy Mermin and Herbert Tucker. 960–67. Fort Worth, TX: Harcourt College Publishing, 2002.

Patmore, Coventry. "The Angel in the House." 1854. In *The Poems of Coventry Patmore*. London: Oxford University Press, 1949.

Patterson, Annabel. *Pastoral and Ideology*. Berkeley: University of California Press, 1987.

Payne, Robert O. "Canterbury Tales." In *Geoffrey Chaucer, Second Edition*. Boston: Twayne, 1986.

Pelikan, Jaroslav. *Mary through the Centuries: Her Place in the History of Culture*. New Haven, CT: Yale University Press, 1996.

Percy, William. *The Faery Pastorall or Forrest of Elves*. 1603. Early English Books on Microfilm. Homer Babbidge Library. University of Connecticut.

Pico della Mirandola, Giovanni. *Heptaplus*. 1489. In Wallis, Miller, and Carmichael, 63–174.

———. *On Being and the One*. 1492. In Wallis, Miller, and Carmichael, 35–62.

———. *On the Dignity of Man*. 1486. In Wallis, Miller, and Carmichael, 1–34.

Pinch, Geraldine. *Magic in Ancient Egypt*. Austin: University of Texas Press, 1994.

Pincombe, Michael. *The Plays of John Lyly*. Manchester, England: University of Manchester Press, 1996.

Pope, Alexander. "A Discourse on Pastoral Poetry." In *Poetry and Prose of Alexander Pope*, edited by Aubrey Williams. Riverside Edition. Boston: Houghton Mifflin, 1969. 3–7.

Purkiss, Diane. "Material Girls: The Seventeenth-Century Woman Debate." In Brant and Purkiss, 69–101.

———. *The Witch in History: Early Modern and Twentieth-Century Representations*. London: Routledge, 1996.

Rackin, Phyllis. *Shakespeare and Women*. Oxford: Oxford University Press, 2005.

Reiss, Timothy J. "Corneille and Cornelia: Reason, Violence, and the Cultural Status of the Feminine: Or, How Dominant Discourse Recuperated and Subverted the Advance of Women. 1987. In Rose, 171–209.

Roberts, Gareth. "The Descendants of Circe: Witches and Renaissance Fictions." In Barry, Hester, and Roberts, 183– 206.

Roberts, Jean Addison. "Shades of Triple Hecate in Shakespeare." *Proceedings of the PMR Conference* 12/123 (1987–88): 47–66.

———. "Shakespeare's Maimed Birth Rites." In Woodbridge and Berry, 123–44.

Roberts, Josephine. Critical Introduction to *Urania*, by Lady Mary Wroth In Roberts.

———. "Editing the Women Writers of Early Modern England." In Hurley and Goodblatt, 17–23.

Roberts, Sasha. "Engendering the Female Reader: Women's Recreational Reading of Shakespeare in Early Modern England." In Hackel and Kelly, 36–54.

Roper, Lyndal. "Witchcraft and Fantasy in Early Modern Germany." In Barry, Hester, and Roberts, 207–36.

Rose, Mary Beth, ed. *Renaissance Drama as Cultural History: Essays from Renaissance Drama 1977–1987*. Evanston, IL: Northwestern University Press, 1990.

Rosen, Barbara, ed. *Witchcraft in England 1558–1618*. Amherst: University of Massachusetts Press, 1969.

Ruskin, John. "Of Queens' Gardens." In *Sesame and Lillies*. New York: John W. Lovell, n.d. 72–101.

Russo, Mary. "Female Grotesques: Carnival and Theory." In *Feminist Studies/Critical Studies*, edited by Teresa de Lauretis. Bloomington: Indiana University Press, 1986.

Sadler, Lynn Veach. "Eye Imagery in *All's Well That Ends Well*: A Neglected Problem." *Literatur in Wissenschafft und Unterricht* 10 (1977): 156–68.

Sannazaro, Jacopo. *Arcadia and the Piscatorial Eclogues*. Edited and Translated by Ralph Nash. Detroit: Wayne State University Press, 1966.

Savile, George. Excerpt from *The Lady's New-Year's-Gift: or, Advice to a Daughter*. 1688. In Goreau, 45–46.

Schelling, Felix E., and Matthew W. Black, eds. *Typical Elizabethan Plays*. Harper Brothers, n.d.

Schleiner, Louise. *Tudor and Stuart Women Writers*. Bloomington: Indiana University Press, 1994.

Schwarz, Kathryn. "Chastity, Militant and Married: Cavendish's Romance, Milton's Masque." *PMLA* 118, no. 2 (March 2003): 270–85.

Scot, Reginald. *The Discoverie of Witchcraft*. 1584. New York: Dover, 1972.

Serafini-Sauli, Judith. Introduction to *L'Ameto*, by Giovanni Boccaccio. New York: Garland, 1985.

Shakespeare, William. *All's Well That Ends Well*. In *The Riverside Shakespeare*. G. Blakemore Evans, ed. Boston: Houghton Mifflin, 1974.

———. *As You Like It*. The Arden Shakespeare, edited by Agnes Latham London: Arden, 2000.

———. *A Midsummer Night's Dream*, edited by Gail Kern Paster and Howard Skiles. New York: St. Martin's, 1999.

Shapiro, Michael. *Gender in Play on the Shakespearean Stage: Boy Heroines and Female Pages*. Ann Arbor: University of Michigan Press, 1996.

Sharp, Jane. Excerpt from *The Midwives Book*. In Otten, 197–205.

Sharpe, Jim. "The Devil in East Anglia: The Matthew Hopkins Trials Reconsidered." In Barry, Hester, and Roberts, 237–54.

Sherman, Sarah Way. *Sarah Orne Jewett, an American Persephone*. Hanover, NH: University Press of New England, 1989.

Sidney, Philip. *An Apology for Poetry*. 1595. Edited by Forrest G. Robinson. Indianapolis: Bobbs-Merrill, 1970.

———. "Disprayse of Courtly Life." 1611. In Kermode, 141–43.

———. *Old Arcadia (The Countess of Pembroke's Arcadia)*. 1586. Edited by Katherine Duncan-Jones. Oxford: Oxford University Press, 1999.

Sigerist, Henry E., ed. Introduction to *A Book on Nymphs, Sylphs, Pygmies, and Salamanders, and on the Other Spirits*. In *Paracelsus: Four Treatises*. 1941. Baltimore, MD: Johns Hopkins University Press, 1996.

———. Preface to *Paracelsus: Four Treatises*.

Singh, Jyotsna. "The Interventions of History, Narratives of Sexuality." In *The Weyward Sisters: Shakespeare and Feminist Politics*, edited by Dymphna Callaghan, Lorraine Helms, and Jyotsna Singh. 7–58. Cambridge, MA: Blackwell, 1994.

Smith, Hallett. *Elizabethan Poetry, a Study in Conventions, Meaning, Expression*. Cambridge, MA: Harvard University Press, 1952.

Somerset, Anne. *Elizabeth I*. New York: St. Martin's Press, 1991.

Sowernam, Ester. *Ester Hath Hanged Haman: or, An Answere to a Lewd Pamphlet, Entituled The Arraignment of Lewd, Idel, Froward, and Unconstant Women; or the Vanity of Them, Choose You Whether With a Commendation of Wise, Virtuous, and*

Honest Women. London 1617. Renascence Editions. 1998. http://darkwing.uoregon.edu/%7Erbear/ester.htm .

Spaeth, Barbette Stanley. *The Roman Goddess Ceres*. Austin: University of Texas Press, 1996.

Spence, Lewis. *Ancient Egyptian Myths and Legends*. 1915. New York: Dover, 1990.

Spenser, Edmund. "Colin Clouts Come Home Againe." In *Edmund Spenser: The Shorter Poems*, edited by Richard A. McCabe. 343–71. New York: Penguin, 1999.

———. *The Faerie Queene*. Edited by Thomas P. Roche, Jr. New York: Penguin, 1987.

———. *Shepheardes Calendar. Edmund Spenser: The Shorter Poems*. In McCabe, 23–156.

Stallybrass, Peter. "The World Turned Upside Down: Inversion, Gender and State." In Wayne, 201–20.

Stevenson, Jane and Peter Davidson. "Anne Finch." In *Early Modern Women Poets, An Anthology*. 456–58. Oxford: Oxford University Press, 2001.

———. "Anne Killigrew." In *Early Modern Women Poets*, 452–53.

———. "Aphra Behn." In *Early Modern Women Poets*, 364–65.

———. "Aemilia Lanyer." In *Early Modern Women Poets*, 100–01.

———. "Jane Barker." In *Early Modern Women Poets*, 425–26.

———. "Katherine Philips." In *Early Modern Women Poets*, 325–27.

———. "Margaret Cavendish." In *Early Modern Women Poets*, 301–03.

Stubbes, Philip. Excerpt from *A Christal Glass for Christian Women, Wherein They May See Most Wonderful and Rare Examples of a Right Virtuous Life and Christian Death, as in the Discourse Following May Appear*. 1591. In Trill, Chedgzoy, and Osborne, 57–62.

Swetnam, Joseph. Excerpt from *The Arraignment of Lewd, Idel, Froward, and Unconstant Women; or the Vanity of Them, Choose You Whether With a Commendation of Wise, Virtuous, and Honest Women*. 1615. In Goreau, 69–74.

"Swimming Test, The." In Rosen, 331–43.

Tasso, Torquato. *Aminta*. 1573. Edited and Translated by Charles Jernigan and Irene Merchegiani Jones. New York: Italica, 2000.

Tatham, John. *Love Crowns the End*. 1640. In *The Dramatic Works of John Tatham.*, edited by James Maidment and W. H. Logan. 1–31. Edinburgh: Willaim Paterson, 1879.

Tattle-Well, Mary, and Joan Hit-Him-Home. Excerpt from *The Women's Sharp Revenge*. 1640. In Aughterson, 472–75.

Teague, Frances. "Judith Shakespeare Reading." *Shakespeare Quarterly*. 47, no. 4 (Winter 1994): 361–73.

Temkin, C. Lilian. Introduction to *Seven Defensiones, the Reply to Certain Caluminations of His Enemies*, by Paracelsus. In Sigerist, 1–9.

Theocritus. *The Idylls*, edited and translated by Robert Wells. Penguin: London, 1989.

Thomas, Keith. *Religion and the Decline of Magic*. (1971) Oxford: Oxford University Press, 1997.

Tilney, Edmund. Excerpt from *The Flower of Friendship*. 1568. In Aughterson, 443–47.

Torshell, Samuel. *The Woman's Glorie; A Treatise Asserting the Due Honour of That Sex and Directing Women Wherein That Honour Consists*. 1645. In Goreau, 42.

Traub, Valerie. "Desire and the Difference It Makes. In Wayne, 81–114.

Travitsky, Betty. *The Paradise of Women: Writing by Englishwomen of the Renaissance.* New York: Columbia University Press, 1989.

————. and Anne Lake Prescott. "Studying and Editing Early Modern Englishwomen: Then and Now." In Hurley and Goodblatt, 1–15.

Trill, Suzanne, Kate Chedgzoy, and Melanie Osborne, eds. *Lay by Your Needles Ladies, Take the Pen.* London: Arnold, 1997.

Turner, James Grantham. *One Flesh: Paradisal Marriage and Sexual Relations in the Age of Milton.* Oxford: Clarendon, 1999.

————. *The Politics of Landscape.* Cambridge, MA: Harvard University Press, 1979.

Turner, Paul. Introduction to *Daphnis and Chloe* by Longus.

Tuvil, Daniel. Excerpt from *Asylum Veneris, or a Sanctuary for Ladies.* 1616. In Goreau, 35.

Virgil. *Eclogues.* In *Eclogues, Georgics, Aeneid 1–6,* Translated by H. Rushton Fairclough. 2–77. Cambridge, MA: Harvard University Press, 1978.

Vives, Juan Luis. *The Instruction of a Christen Woman.* 1529. Translated by Richard Hyrde. Coordinating Editors, Virginia Walcott Beauchamp, Elizabeth H. Hageman, and Margaret Mikesell. Urbana: University of Illinois Press, 2002.

Wall, Wendy. *The Imprint of Gender: Authorship and Publication in the English Renaissance.* Ithaca, NY: Cornell University Press, 1993.

————. "To be 'A Man in Print.'" In Hurley and Goodblatt, 131–54.

Wallis, Charles Glen, Paul J. W. Miller, and Douglas Carmichael, translators and editors of *Pico Della Mirandola: On the Dignity of Man.* Hackett, 1998.

Warner, Marina. *Alone of All Her Sex: The Myth and the Cult of the Virgin Mary.* New York: Alfred Knopf, 1976.

Wayne, Valerie. "Historical Differences: Misogyny and *Othello.*" In Wayne, 153–79.

————. Introduction to *The Matter of Difference: Materialist Feminist Criticism of Shakespeare.* In Wayne.

————. ed. *The Matter of Difference: Materialist Feminist Criticism of Shakespeare.* Ithaca, NY: Cornell University Press, 1991.

Wells, Robert. Introduction to *The Idylls,* by Theocritus.

Welsh, Alexander. "The Loss of Men and the Getting of Children: *All's Well That Ends Well* and *Measure for Measure.*" *Modern Language Review* 73 (January 1978): 17–28.

Excerpt from *Whole Duty of a Woman, The.* 1696. In Goreau, 52–54.

Wingate, Charles. *Shakespeare's Heroines on the Stage.* New York: Thomas Y. Crowell & Company, 1895.

"Witches Abroad." In Rosen, 316–22.

"Witches and Fairies." In Rosen, 64–71.

"Witches at Chelmsford." In Rosen, 72–82.

"Witches at St. Osyth." In Rosen, 103–157.

"Witches at Windsor." In Rosen, 83–91.

"Witches' Sabbath." In Rosen, 190–203.

Witt, R. E. *Isis in the Ancient World.* Baltimore, MD: Johns Hopkins University Press, 1971.

Woodbridge, Linda. *The Scythe of Saturn: Shakespeare and Magical Thinking.* Urbana: University of Illinois Press, 1994.

———. and Edward Berry, eds. *True and Maimed Rites: Ritual and Anti-Ritual in Shakespeare and His Age.* Urbana: University of Illinois Press, 1992.

Woolley, Hannah. Excerpt from *The Gentlewoman's Companion; or A Guide to the Female Sex.* London 1675. In Trill, Chedgzoy, and Osborne, 261–65.

Wordsworth, William. Preface to the Second Edition of the Lyrical Ballads (1800). In *English Romantic Writers*, edited by David Perkins. 423–36. Forth Worth, TX: Harcourt College Press, 1995.

———. *The Prelude* (1850). In *The Prelude 1799, 1805, 1850. Norton Critical Edition.* 29–483. W. W. Norton: New York, 1979.

Wroth, Lady Mary. *The First Part of the Countess of Montgomery's Urania.* 1621. Edited by Josephine Roberts. Binghamton, NY: Medieval and Renaissance Texts and Studies, 1995.

———. *Love's Victory.* In *Renaissance Drama by Women: Texts and Documents.* Edited by S. P. Cerasano and Marion Wynne-Davies. 97–126. London: Routledge, 1996.

Wynne-Davies, Marian. Introduction to *Love's Victory*, by Lady Mary Wroth. 91–95. London: Routledge, 1996.

———. "'The Swallowing Womb': Consumed and Consuming Women in *Titus Andronicus.* In Wayne, 129–51.

Yates, Frances A. *Astraea: The Imperial Theme in the Sixteenth Century.* London: Pimlico, 1975.

———. *The Occult Philosophy in the Elizabethan Age.* 1979. London: Routledge, 1999.

Yonge, Bartholomew, trans. *Diana of George of Montemayor.* 1598. Edited by Judith M. Kennedy. London: Oxford University Press, 1968.

Zemon Davis, Natalie. "Women on Top." In Hutson, 156–85.

Zilboorg, Gregory. Introduction to *The Diseases That Deprive Man of His Reason, Such as St. Vitus' Dance, Falling Sickness, Melancholy, and Insanity, and Their Correct Treatment.* In Sigerist, 129–34.

Index